MW00332174

929 Fecha: 30/9/96

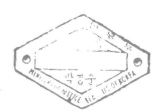

RTMENT OF IMMIGRATION
ERMITTED TO ENTER
AUSTRALIA

24 APR 1986

For stay of 12 Month

SYDNEY AIRPORT 54

IMMIGRATION DIVISION BANGKOK THAILAND
A 72 DEPARTED
- 9 FEB 1987
SIGNED

IMMIGRATION & ETHNIC AFFAIRS
.......Person
30 OCT 1989
DEPARTED
AUSTRALIA
SYDNEY 32

T R A V E L E R ' S

CUBA

C O M P A N I O N

上陸許可
ADMITTED
15. FEB. 1986
Status: 4-1-4
Duration: 90 days
NARITA(N)
Immigration Inspector
日本国

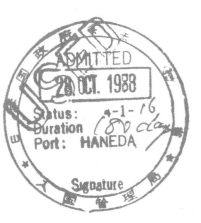

ADMITTED
20 OCT. 1988
Status: 4-1-16
Duration 180 days
Port: HANEDA
Signature

№ 011278

THE UNITED STATES
OF AMERICA
NONIMMIGRANT VISA
ISSUED AT

SED
Air Port

U.S. IMMIGRATION
170 HHW 1710

JUL 2 0 1983

HONG KONG
(1038)
- 7 JUN 1987
IMMIGRATION
OFFICER

The 1999–2000 Traveler's Companions

ARGENTINA • AUSTRALIA • BALI • CALIFORNIA • CANADA • CHILI • CHINA • COSTA RICA • CUBA •
EASTERN CANADA • ECUADOR • FLORIDA • HAWAII • HONG KONG • INDIA • INDONESIA • JAPAN •
KENYA • MALAYSIA & SINGAPORE • MEDITERRANEAN FRANCE • MEXICO • NEPAL • NEW ENGLAND •
NEW ZEALAND • PERU • PHILIPPINES • PORTUGAL • RUSSIA • SOUTHERN ENGLAND • SOUTH AFRICA •
SPAIN • THAILAND • TURKEY • VENEZUELA • VIETNAM, LAOS AND CAMBODIA • WESTERN CANADA

Traveler's Cuba Companion
First Published 1999
The Globe Pequot Press
6 Business Park Road, P.O. Box 833
Old Saybrook, CT 06475-0833
www.globe.pequot.com

ISBN: 0-7627-0250-8

By arrangement with Kümmerly+Frey AG, Switzerland
© 1999 Kümmerly+Frey AG, Switzerland

Created, edited and produced by
Allan Amsel Publishing, 53, rue Beaudouin
27700 Les Andelys, France
E-mail: Allan.Amsel@wanadoo.fr
Editor in Chief: Allan Amsel
Editor: Anne Trager
Original design concept: Hon Bing-wah
Picture editor and designer: Chita-Geneviève Lévy

ACKNOWLEDGMENTS
The Publishers wish to express their gratitude to the Cuban authorities, particularly to
Manuel Garcia Crespo and Elisa Dimitrov Lorenzo of Publicitur, Rene Ceballo Prats of the
International Press Center, and Perkunas Liutkus at the Paris Havanatour Office for advice,
permissions and for facilitation of travel in Cuba for our writer and photographer. We also
acknowledge the generous assistance given by the airline AOM and the hotel chains Cubanacan,
Gaviota, Gran Caribe, Horozontes, Islazul and Sol Melia Fina. On behalf of the photographer
we extend a special thank you to their friend and driver in Trinidad, Renan Turino.

Printed by Samwha Printing Co. Ltd., Seoul, South Korea

TRAVELER'S CUBA COMPANION

by Kirsten Ellis

Photographed by Mireille Vautier

Kümmerly+Frey

The Globe Pequot Press

OLD SAYBROOK

Contents

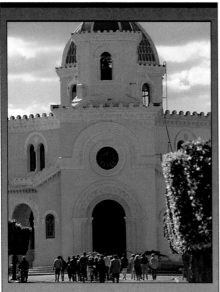

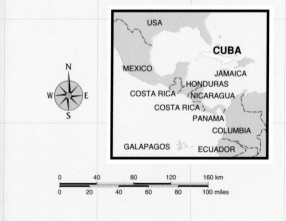

LEGEND

Populations

SAN JOSE — Capital
○ ATENAS — Large Towns
○ Lagarto — Small Towns

Transportation

Secondary Roads
Major roads
⎯21⎯ Expressways/Highways
Railways

Physical Features

Bordering Countries
National and State Boundaries
Forests, Reserves, and National Parks
Lakes and Rivers
Aquatic Parks
▲ Cerro 3030 — Mountains and Volcanoes

ATLANTIC OCEAN

Cayo Guillermo
A CLARA
Cayo Coco
Punta Alegre
Meneses Chambas San Rafael
án
Faguasco
Jatibonico
CAMAGÜEY
CIEGO DE ÁVILA
Morón
Cayo Romano
Playa Jigüey
Ciego de Avila
Gaspar Brasil
Cayo Guajaba
Baraguá
Cubitas Sola
Cayo Sabinal
Júcaro
Piedrecitas
Lugareño
SIRITUS
DE ÁVILA
HAVANA
MARÍA
GULF
Florida
Mínas
Nuevitas
CAMAGÜEY / LAS TUNAS
Camagüey
Guimaguayú
Sibanicú Camalote Manatí
LAS TUNAS / HOLGUÍN
Siboney Cascorro
CIEGO DE ÁVILA / CAMAGÜEY
Concordia
Martí Bartle San Manuel
Gibara Guardalavaca
Colombia Guaimaro
Velasco
los Jardines (Jardinillos) de la Reina
Cándido
González
Igbabo Las Tunas
Rafael Freye
Holguín
Amancio
Mir
Cacocum
Bahía de Nipe
HOLGUÍN / GUANTÁNAMO
Santa Cruz del Sur
Haiti
Sábalo
Cuelo
Cayo Mambí Moa
CAMAGÜEY
Guamo
Vado del Yeso
Mayarí
Punta Gorda
Río Cauto Cauto Cristo
Sagua de Tánamo
Manzanillo
Bayamo
Mayari Arriba
Baracoa
Palma Soriano
Media Luna La Herradura
San Luis
Mesa Abajo
Aguacate Sierra Maestra
Guantánamo
La Marea
El Cobre Santiago de Cuba
San Antonio del Sur
Cabo Cruz
Pilón
Uvero Chivirico
Caimanera Playa Uvero
GRANMA / SANTIAGO DE CUBA
SANTIAGO DE CUBA / GUANTÁNAMO

TOP SPOTS

Explore Old Havana

THAT AGING BEAUTY, LA HABANA VIEJA, WITH ITS EXOTIC MIXTURE OF HISTORIC BUILDINGS, RETAINS ITS ENIGMATIC CHARMS AND INVITES THE URGE TO SIMPLY WANDER. Whether you have several days or only a few hours available, the time you spend exploring the historic and evocative quarter of La Habana Vieja — the colonial heart of the city near the waterfront — may well prove to be the highlight of your visit to Cuba. Old Havana's stone fortresses and monuments, not to mention its labyrinth of magnificent houses, imposing columns, grand stone steps and tinted glass windows, offer an extraordinary, if desuetudinous, glimpse of the Spanish colonial era. At almost every step, the old city is literally four centuries deep. More

than 900 of La Habana Vieja's 3,157 listed buildings have been deemed of historical importance, and only a fraction of these were built this century.

For many, Old Havana's streets exert a kind of siren call, and exploring them becomes a compulsion. For me, nothing quite compares to watching dawn break across the slate-colored stones of the ancient buildings on the Plaza de Armas, hours before the booksellers clatter across the cobbles to set up their stalls; hearing the first early footsteps echo in the stillness of the vaulted archways of stone loggias in the magnificently restored Plaza de la Catedral. Over the years I have seen the old city's main boulevard of Obispo change dramatically: beleaguered historic façades and empty stores have been replaced by a flotilla of gaily painted, re-faced buildings bustling with commerce that in some cases look, to my eyes, perplexingly brand-new. Yet the enduring fascination remains: I remain captivated by the old city's many hidden corners and secrets; its quiet sun-filled courtyards and balcony hideaways. The narrow streets hum with people gossiping between balconies, lugging sacks of provisions or buckets of water, and the "tring-tring" of bicycle bells. There is so much life here, so many layers of the past mingling with the quotidian, that every visit, each different street taken — and

---

Remnants of the past in Havana: the neo-baroque Gran Teatro OPPOSITE and a mosaic ABOVE.

every change of the day's light — reveals some new vista.

Recent restoration has transformed old Havana's most historic squares — Plaza de Armas, Plaza de la Catedral, Plaza Vieja and Plaza de San Francisco de Asís — which are a must on any visit. Equally, you should see the interiors of such grandiose palaces and mansions as the Palacio de los Capitanes-Generales and the Casa de los Condes de Jaruco, among others, which allow you to admire the unique tropical *Mudéjar* style that flourished in Cuba during the seventeenth and eighteenth centuries, a decorative synthesis of Spanish and Moorish styles. From the same era, you cannot miss seeing Havana's formidable fortresses — the Castillo de Real Fuerza, the Castillo El Morro and the Fortaleza de San Carlos de la Cabaña.

Certainly, those faint of heart and trusting of nature take heed: the gentle lull of the early morning offers one face, allowing quiet contemplation of the old city's beauty; while the velvety Havana night shows another, where overt hustling by women in skimpy Lycra outfits (even directed at men with their hand held firmly by their wives) and tugs at your sleeve to buy fake cigars or bootleg rum are hard to ignore.

Take a Trip to Trinidad

WHERE SUGAR ONCE WAS KING: THE COLONIAL CITY OF TRINIDAD AND ITS NEARBY VALLE DE LOS INGENIOS OFFER A TRANQUIL GLIMPSE INTO THE ISLAND'S LONG-DISAPPEARED HISTORY. If Havana is Cuba's wild heart, then Trinidad is its calm soul. The perfectly preserved city of Trinidad radiates quiet colonial charm, lying in a beautifully scenic spot between the sea and the nearby Escambray mountains close to the coast in Sancti Spíritus Province in central Cuba. With its intimate scale, winding cobbled streets and restored mansions, you can easily imagine how life might have been for Cuba's early sugar barons and their families in the seventeenth and eighteenth centuries, when this was the

¡ZAFRA SIN SANGRE!

island's affluent sugar capital. Trinidad remains uncannily frozen in time: during the nineteenth century it was all but abandoned, and nothing new was added to the city's colonial core, although repairs were carried out. After Havana, Trinidad's pace is sleepy and traditional, and you can wander about with ease, with no traffic and none of the hustling associated with the capital. Trinidad is rich in stylish Creole *palacios*, many of which have been turned into museums, some with preserved living quarters decorated throughout with murals, Italian marble tiles, and period furniture, good examples are the Palacio Brunet (now the Museo Romántico) and the Palacio Cantero (the Museo Histórico Municipal).

Make sure you visit at least part of the nearby Valle de los Ingenios (Valley of the Sugar Mills) which casts Trinidad's history as a bastion of provincial luxury into another light; for here, thousands of African slaves toiled in the valley's many sugar mills, under harsh conditions and the unforgiving sun. Although this lush

OPPOSITE: The Iglesia San Francisco de Asís dominates Trinidad's skyline. ABOVE: A 1959 issue of the weekly *Bohemia*, harvest "not tainted with blood."

valley looks peaceful now, it once whirred and hummed with dozens of large sugar mills. This valley has now been officially converted into a vast outdoor Museum of Slavery. A very scenic way of getting there is by riding through the neck-high sugarcane fields aboard a restored vintage steam train, making stops at El Guarisco — a stockpile center at Magua where the seasonal sugarcane harvesting still takes place today; at the Guachinango estate (which has beautiful frescoes); and at the charming Manacas-Iznaga plantation and tower, where you can have a delicious lunch on a balcony overlooking the entire valley before the return trip. Of course, you can also make your own way by road, especially if tagging along with large tour groups is not your idea of a good time.

Explore Tobacco Country

FAMOUS FOR CENTURIES FOR THE QUALITY OF ITS TOBACCO, THE WESTERN PROVINCE OF PINAR DEL RÍO IS ONE OF THE ISLAND'S MOST SCENICALLY BEAUTIFUL AREAS TO EXPLORE, AND IS ALSO WITHIN EASY DRIVING DISTANCE OF HAVANA. If you are a cigar connoisseur, there is little doubt that you will enjoy a visit to the province of Pinar del Río. This is a region renowned for producing the raw material for such cigars as Cohibas, Coronas, H. Upmanns, Romeo y Julietas — and now Trinidad, Cuba's

latest brand. Here, the province's key tobacco-growing areas of Vuelta Abajo and the Partido may look modest: ploughed by oxen and dotted with traditional thatched *bohíos* (rustic huts) and archaic-looking drying sheds like a Hispanic version of a Monet haystack landscape. But it's quite something to see the entire process from the fields to the processing plant (where expert rollers make it look deceptively easy), and the humidored results are heaven for cigar aficionados.

You can combine your cigar safari with a foray into the province, whose landscapes range from the fertile plantation flats of the Vuelta Abajo to the lush, forested mountain heights of the Sierra de los Órganos and Sierra del Rosario and the gloriously green Valle de Viñales where, where Jurassic-era limestone mountain cliffs and unusual *mogotes* (flat-top hills) tower with eerie beauty like soldiers in the valley's vast open-air grotto. The mountains contain huge cave and underground river networks, only a few dozen of which have been officially mapped; including the largest cave system in Cuba, Cueva Santo Tomás, part of which (Cueva del Indio) can be explored by boat on an underground river.

The two hotels in the area, the Los Jazmines and La Ermita, vie for the perfection of their equally splendid views across the entire valley. You can also stay at Hotel Moka, Cuba's first so-called ecological resort, within the Sierra Rosario's beautiful settlement of Las Terrazas, a well-tended wilderness of many mountain trails, the ruins of former French coffee plantations, and natural waterfalls and pools, and you can visit Cuba's largest orchidarium at Soroa. Try to make sure that you take the scenic northern coastal road one way of your journey, leaving time to make stops at any of the seaside villages that catch your eye, such as Puerto Esperanza.

Cuba's famous cigars LEFT are made by hand, from the harvest OPPOSITE ABOVE to rolling BELOW.

Revel in Cuba's Musical Heritage

THE MUSIC CREATED BY CUBA'S SEASONED MUSICIANS — AND BY MANY OF ITS YOUNG, UP-AND-COMING PERFORMERS — IS VERY OFTEN PURE MAGIC. When you are in Cuba, music seems to be everywhere, most of it happening right in front of you, with live bands, musicians and singers serenading almost literally at every street corner, in every restaurant and café, and even when you least expect it, such as on a remote beach, as I discovered on Playa Daiquirí near Santiago de Cuba when a quartet of formally dressed musicians (complete with a double bass) materialized across the sands and proceeded to stage an incredible performance. Even seemingly sleepy towns conjure up dynamic musical performances after the siesta hours.

Especially in Havana, Matanzas, Trinidad, Camagüey, and Santiago de Cuba, you will have a difficult time not hearing many wonderful impromptu performances, often for the price of a cocktail or a coffee. Equally, even remarkably talented musicians and singers can barely get by on what they earn, making their dedication to their music even more impressive.

A local Casa de la Trova can be found in many Cuban cities or towns, named for *trovas*, pre-Revolutionary poetic ballads — often about love — that originated during the island's colonial period, and, more recently, *nuevas trovas*, or contemporary ballads. At Casas de la Trova, *trovadores*, or exponents of the *trova*, often play for free, keeping the tradition alive. Of all these establishments, it has to be said that Santiago de Cuba's Casa de la Trova is a breed apart, with a history intertwined with that of Cuban music itself: generations of Cuba's music legends have played here, many from the eastern province of Oriente, the birthplace of improvisational son and *trova* music. Portraits of famous musicians who performed here in times gone by line the walls, and include the Trio Matamoros, Beny Moré, and Sindo Garay, the father of *trova* music.

Some of Cuba's most celebrated musicians now include those who had gone into retirement, and who are now in their 70s, 80s and 90s, yet have recently come back into the spotlight through their success in reviving this nostalgic, pre-Revolutionary music that had almost been forgotten. One of the featured musicians, Ibrahím Ferrer, who once sang alongside Beny Moré, had been shining shoes for a living. With the widely celebrated albums, the *Buena Vista Social Club* and the *Afro-Cuban All Stars*, a new wave of appreciation for the nation's musical heritage has begun.

Try to hear as many different types of Cuban music as you can during your stay. Havana is widely regarded as Cuba's musical capital (although this title is hotly disputed by Santiago de Cuba and Matanzas) with many venues at which to hear an array of musical styles. You should definitely visit the Casa de la Trova and the Casa de la Música — and if you enjoy bold, big band salsa, the Palacio de la Salsa. Aside from the nightly program offered by

ABOVE: The Museo de la Musica offers a fine display of musical instruments. OPPOSITE: A singer relaxes after rehearsal in Havana's Casa de la Obrapa.

these establishments, La Habana Vieja's Casa de la Cultura has regular performances of popular music, dance, and Afro-Cuban rumba. Other venues to seek out include La Divina Pastora restaurant, and La Habana Vieja's Casa de la Amistad, Casa de las Infusiones and Bar Nostalgia.

Throughout the country, also look for touring performances by famous salsa bands Los Van Van and Irakere; Conjunto Folklórico Nacional (National Folklore Dance Group); Los Muñequitos de Matanzas (known as the "kings of rumba"); pianists Chucho Valdés and Gonzalo Rubalcava; the jazz fusion group Cuatro Espacio; and the jazz singer Xiamara.

Relax on Cuba's Best Beaches

PEOPLE TEND NOT TO COME TO CUBA JUST FOR ITS BEACHES, which doesn't mean that the island doesn't have its share of shores worth visiting. Cuba's premier beach resort is Varadero, just over two hours' drive from Havana, with an 18-km (11-mile)-long strip that is increasingly built-up with modern hotels, with all the water sports and nightlife you could want, but little in the way of real Cuban atmosphere. Varadero's beach is beautiful, but you may be disappointed if this is all you have come to see.

The tourist-only beaches of Cayo Coco and Cayo Guillermo in Ciego de Ávila, as well as Cayo Largo, which lies off the mainland's southeast coast, have been earmarked as Cuba's next hot sites for beach development. Both these isolated resort islands (Cayo Coco and the smaller, nearby Cayo Guillermo are reached by a causeway from the mainland, while Cayo Largo is reached by plane, increasingly by direct international charter flights) already have a significant hotel infrastructure. Of these two regions, Cayo Largo is closest to everybody's vision of an idyllic tropical island, with its soft snow-white sands at the aptly named Playa Sirena, Playa Blanca and Cayo Rico, all of which are bordered by blue-green sea. However, once again, as with Varadero, the only Cubans you are likely to meet will be waiters and housemaids.

For beautiful beaches as well as a relaxed beach scene and some of the island's better resorts, head for Playa Esmeralda (also known as Playa Estero Ciego) in the Bahía de Naranjo, near the beach resort of Guardalavaca in Holguín Province. Here you can find a series of calm, beautiful, sandy bays amidst lush vegetation and some very good hotels. Within this region, the lovely, sheltered beach of Cayo Saetía can reached by

helicopter, and is a popular day excursion. Playa Santa Lucía in Camagüey Province can also be recommended for both its beach (and nearby beaches) and resorts, with the exceptionally pretty, soft-sanded shores and clear seas of Cayo Sabinal within easy reach.

Elsewhere in Cuba, other notable beaches (most of which have adjacent tourist resorts and facilities) include Matanzas's Playa Girón and possibly Cuba's most perfect snorkeling spot at Caleta Buena; Pinar del Río's Cayo Levisa; Sancti Spíritus's Playa Ancón, a pleasant locale from which to make forays to the nearby colonial town of Trinidad; Santiago de Cuba's Playas Siboney, Bucanero, Daiquirí and Sigua, which have a great atmosphere with seaside restaurants and local Cubans as well as tourists; and Guantánamo's Playa Maguaná, a pleasant place to stay as well as to swim.

Although close to Havana, the beaches of Habana del Este are not especially recommended, with an unrestful atmosphere of soliciting *jineteras* (figuratively speaking, "female jockeys," or "women who go along for the ride") as well as littered sands and loud music.

María La Gorda beach, at the extreme western end of the island, is one of Cuba's finest and an excellent base for scuba diving.

See Havana's Museo de la Revolución

YOU SHOULD NOT MISS THIS ICON OF FIDEL CASTRO'S REIGN — an essential showcase of just about all the memorabilia of the *Revolución* you might ever care to see. Overlooking Havana's Malecón stands the capital's former Presidential Palace, an imposing white Spanish Revival pile with glittering interiors designed by Tiffany's of New York. Cuba's former dictator Fulgencio Batista was once king of this castle — until, by hiding in a elevator shaft, he barely escaped being lynched by students who stormed this citadel in March 1957.

Now this building is a virtual walk-through of the Revolution's history, with many exhibits offering detailed, even forensic, insights. Detailed maps chart the day-by-day progress of Castro's ultimate victory, as he and his gang of revolutionary rebels withstood attack in the tangled undergrowth of the Sierra Maestra mountains. Photographs, yellowed communiqués, blood-stained clothing, and personal items of fallen revolutionaries are displayed alongside hundreds of rifles and pistols. One room is dedicated to Che Guevara, where you can gaze at objects that once belonged to the larger-than-life dead hero.

Outside, in the former Presidential Palace gardens, stands the *Granma*, the large cabin cruiser that bore Fidel and his followers from Mexico to Cuba in 1956. It is now enshrined in a glass case in the garden of the museum, an object of patriotic veneration. You can also see the bullet-ridden "Fast Delivery" truck used in the student's assault on the Presidential Palace; the Land Rover that a victorious Fidel rode into Havana (it has *Commandancia General Sierra Maestra* painted onto it); a remnant of a U-2 reconnaissance plane shot down by the Cuban military during the missile crisis in 1962; and the tank used by Fidel himself during the Bay of Pigs confrontation.

Visit Hemingway's Home

GONE BUT NOT FORGOTTEN, HAILED AS A DEMI-GOD IN CUBA, HEMINGWAY'S LEGEND LIVES ON IN HIS HOME FOR MANY YEARS, LA FINCA VIGÍA. "Ernesto," as the Cubans called him, lived in Cuba between 1939 and 1960, the longest period of time the ever-restless writer was to spend anywhere. About a 40-minute drive from Havana, on a hillside atop the sleepy village of San Francisco de Paula, is La Finca Vigía, Hemingway's former house, where he wrote some of his finest work (including *For Whom The Bell Tolls*), weathered two marriages and entertained a stream of famous visitors.

It is now a museum, preserved to a fascinatingly evocative degree, with many personal possessions, clothes, books and furnishings left just as they were when the Hemingways left Cuba. The writer's boat, the *Pilar*, is displayed in the garden, "like the *Granma*" commented Hemingway's third wife, Martha Gellhorn, as she inspected the museum many years after having once lived there herself.

Not far away is the fishing village of Cojímar — the setting for *The Old Man and the Sea*.

OPPOSITE: Museo de la Revolución ABOVE and a former presidential mansion BELOW.
ABOVE: Hemingway's former home, La Finca Vigía.

Birdwatch in the Swamps

YOU DON'T HAVE TO BE A SERIOUS BIRDER TO APPRECIATE THE MAGNIFICENCE OF THE SWAMPY ZAPATA PENINSULA — which is one of the best bird-watching arenas in Cuba. Several hours' drive from Havana, you can be deep in the heart of one of Cuba's most lushly impressive, ecologically intact, bird sanctuaries. This is the Zapata Peninsula, which lies on the southern coast of Matanzas Province, a realm of pristine wetlands, isolated beaches, crystal-clear water, underground *cenotes*, or sunken tectonic caves, and mangrove forests. It is also home to the island's most complete array of bird species.

You may get to see Cuba's tiny hummingbird, the *zunzuncito*, considered to be the world's smallest bird; you can certainly see flocks of many other birds, including flamingos, black-necked stilts, herons, white ibises, parrots, and endemic species of exotic birds.

While you are in the Zapata Peninsula, make sure you take time to see the region's other attractions. You could visit La Boca Crocodile Farm and take a boat ride through the Laguna del Tesoro to the resort village of Guamá, where a life-size replica of a Taíno Indian village has been built. Also, you cannot miss going to nearby Playa Girón, where you can visit the Museo Girón. Further on, and even more pleasurable, is the lovely bay of Caleta Buena, one of Cuba's idyllic beach spots.

Thousands of birds migrate to the protected area of Las Salinas between November and May.

YOUR CHOICE

The Great Outdoors

Cuba, clad in fields of sugarcane and tropical vegetation, with high mountain ranges and lush valleys, certainly has plenty of wilderness; and like many Caribbean islands, Cuba's geological diversity shelters a wide variety of plants and animals, including some unique endemic species. In many ways the drive through the countryside, passing by small rustic towns, to reach Cuba's nature reserves in the more remote parts of the island can be just as interesting as the destination itself. So can the conversations you could strike up with local guides who lead you through unmarked forest trails, pointing out medicinal plants or hidden caves that

may have been variously occupied by *cimarrones* (runaway slaves), *mambisas* (independence fighters), and revolutionaries or counter-revolutionaries over the years.

While Cuba is not exactly on the map as a destination for **ecotourism**, its large regions of wilderness have some potential for this sort of development. If you make time to appreciate it in this light, don't expect for a moment to be unimpressed by Cuba's natural beauty. So far, Cuba has only one "eco-lodge": the Hotel Moka in Pinar del Río Province, and you may want to consider an overnight stay at this delightful place to see where ecotourism is "at" in Cuba.

So far, Cuba's **national parks** — a relatively new concept whose definition remains somewhat loose — are not yet extensively developed to welcome visitors. Don't expect the sort of facilities you might associate with national parks and reserves elsewhere: Cuba is just catching up when it comes to promoting itself as a nature destination. Visitor centers, interpretive trails, park maps, and camping facilities are few, meaning that the island is not exactly an ecotourist's paradise. **Hiking** is not really big in Cuba (at least, not since the days when Fidel Castro and his revolutionaries camped out in the hills), and Cubans tend to consider walking less macho than

OPPOSITE: Dense Baracoa vegetation. ABOVE: The coconut is one of the island's many palm varieties.

horseback riding — but the island's infrastructure for the lay-hiker is pretty good, especially if you are happy just to spend a few hours walking (in some cases climbing fairly steep trails) within the island's scenic forest reserves, although marked walking trails are rare.

It is possible that some enterprising and experienced hikers may see this situation as an advantage: with some perseverance and a yen for self-sufficiency, they will be able to explore much of the island's scenic wilderness almost entirely by themselves. Whether for security reasons or not, it is impossible to get decent, detailed maps of Cuba's terrain for use as a navigational aid. Suffice to say that getting lost could be problematic.

The lack of infrastructure for exploring reserves and parklands on your own means that, often, you will feel pressured to have a guide along with you. In my own experience, this can be helpful. When exploring the Sierra del Escambray mountains, we were informed by the Kurhotel management that a walk to a secondary waterfall in the area was an easy hour's hike, but that we should have a guide along with us. As New Zealanders, to whom rugged wilderness hikes are part of the national psyche, we assumed this would be a stroll in the park. Four hours later, having reached the (admittedly beautiful) falls, torrential rain struck, after which we labored uphill along a slippery muddy trail that would have been near impossible to follow correctly on our own. Our guide, a local from the Topes de Collantes region, revealed that his expert skills had been further honed with army survivalist training by the Vietnamese (who, it appears, instructed squads of Cubans to walk backwards through these mountains, among other things). Suffice to say he proved invaluable.

Generally, hotels close to parks and reserves can assist with hiring a guide, although in some areas guides are a rare commodity. Throughout my stay in Cuba, I was always grateful for the presence of the experienced guide I was assigned in

this way. However, finding (or, in the case of Cuba, being assigned) a trained naturalist guide can be an unpredictable business: some individual travelers reported that they were not impressed with this set-up, which could just as easily send tourists off on their nature excursions with any available Cuban, be it the hotel receptionist or the local party delegate. Also, if you are traveling through Cuba as part of a tour group, you will no doubt be trotted along some limited sections of a few mountain trails en masse, or stop off at a tourist restaurant strategically located at some beauty spot, and neither of these are an ideal way to experience the stillness and the beauty of a the country's wilderness, let alone see any wildlife.

You may not be keen to explore areas of wilderness on your own by rental car (or jeep in some parts of the island, where roads can be very rough, such as the Parque Nacional Sierra Maestra) and may prefer to join one of the many available **tours**. If so, contact the newly formed Cubamar ((53-7) 33-8317, located on the Fifth Floor, Hotel Plaza, Calles Zulueta and Neptuno, La Habana Vieja (or ((53-7) 66-2523 or 30-5536 FAX (53-7) 33-3111, 752 Calle 15, Vedado), a Cuban entity set up to develop the camping and ecotourism

OPPOSITE: Resplendent foliage on desolate Cayo Guillermo. ABOVE: A resident of Las Salinas in the Ciénaga de Zapata.

infrastructure; or Alcona SA ((53-7) 22-2526 FAX (53-7) 24-1531, Calle 42 N°. 514, at the corner of Avenida 7, Miramar, Havana, which runs week-long "eco-tour" package trips to nature reserves in Sierra del Rosario in Pinar del Río and Isla de la Juventud, as well as in the Parque Nacional Desembarco del Granma and the Parque Nacional Pico Turquino.

Many of the island's mainstream organizations also offer nature excursions or will be able to make suggestions for tours you could take. You will find listings for Cubatur, Cubanacán, Havanatur, Gaviota, Rumbos or San Cristóbal, in the TAKING A TOUR, page 59. Oddly enough, Gaviota, which is backed by Cuba's Ministry of Defense, has developed a good reputation for arranged excursions of all kinds — on foot, on horseback, by helicopter, and by boat — into Cuba's protected natural regions, many of which are no-go areas taken over by the military.

For lush scenery, mangrove swamps, rivers, clear lagoons, and crocodile watching — and especially for **bird watching** — don't miss a visit to the Parque Nacional Ciénaga de Zapata on the Zapata Peninsula in the province of Matanzas, several hours' driving distance from Havana. You should aim to spend at least two or three days exploring the park, and visit, among other sites, the breeding grounds of birds and other wild fauna within the protected area of Las Salinas and the crocodile breeding grounds at La Boca. Ideally, go in February, March or early April and make your base in either Playa Larga (which has a bird watching center) or Playa Girón. Like many parts of Cuba, mosquitoes are a part of the landscape: bring strong repellant.

The Zapata Peninsula is also wonderful for **snorkeling**: you are likely to see *manatees* as well as many species of tropical fish, and the submarine caves or *cenotes*, provide dramatic opportunities for **underwater spelunking**. For the latter, contact the International Scuba Diving Center ((53-59) 4118 or 4110 FAX (53-59) 4117, at Villa Playa Girón, Peninsula de Zapata, Matanzas.

From Havana, it is also an easy drive to Pinar del Río's spectacular **Parque Nacional Viñales**. There is something sublime about watching the sun rise and set here from the stillness of your own hotel balcony: watching the landscape — with its huge forested *mogotes*, or limestone humps, which conceal hidden caves and subterranean rivers — is like watching the shifting canvas of an ancient Chinese master. Just as beautiful can be exploring forested pathways and discovering the park's many butterfly species , or catching sight of the Cuban *trogon* (also called the *tocororo*) along with nightingales and woodpeckers, all of which lay their eggs in the crevices of the region's limestone cliffs.

If you plan to visit Trinidad, it is worthwhile making an overnight side trip to the **Parque Nacional Topes de Collantes**. You can inquire about hiring a "nature guide" from either the Kurhotel or the Los Helechos hotels, who can point out endemic species, including ferns, orchids, birds and butterflies, along trails that can vary from an hour's easy stroll to a very demanding six-hour round-trip hike to waterfalls along the Caburní and Vega Grande rivers (only recommended for people in good physical shape). You should make your preferences clear to the guide at the outset.

Renting a boat ABOVE is the only way through the mangroves to Laguna del Tesoro OPPOSITE.

You can travel further east to visit the **Gran Parque Nacional Sierra Maestra** in Granma Province, the island's largest natural reserve It is an obvious attraction for serious hikers and trekkers and encompasses both the Parque Nacional Pico Turquino, which has as its centerpiece the highest mountain in Cuba: Pico Turquino (1,973 m or 6,470 ft), and the Parque Nacional Desembarco del Granma (Granma Landing National Park). Diehards can aim to complete the island's premier mountain hike: a strenuous three-day trek over the Sierra Maestra from Alto de Naranjo, south of Bartolomé Masó in Granma Province, to Las Cuevas on the southern coast, crossing Cuba's highest peak, Pico Turquino. The Desembarco del Granma reserve has two excellently laid out trails, the Morlote-Fustete and El Guafe; the first of which requires some heavy-duty mountaineering, while the second is easier and much the better choice to start with. It winds through dense native forest to reach limestone caves, where you can see pre-Columbian cave paintings and stone idols. It is worth mentioning that the Desembarco del Granma reserve is relatively easy to

access by road from the provincial town of Bayamo. However, sections of the Pico Turquino reserve have been taken over by the Cuban military, making certain trails impossible unless you have authorized permission. It is worth bearing this in mind as you plan your trip, and always check the current situation with the Cuban authorities.

The Parque Nacional Desembarco del Granma is also notable for its marine reserve, especially at **Cabo Cruz**, where closer inspection by scuba diving reveals a spectacular underwater terrace of coral: the so-called "Stairway of Giants." Cabo Cruz can be reached by boat excursions from the Commonwealth resorts at Marea del Portillo.

Cuba has four UNESCO-designated Biosphere Reserves, although these zones may not necessarily correspond to what you might expect. In fact, this UNESCO designation corresponds to a model designed to promote sustainable development based on several zones, each with a different emphasis on human activities. Generally, a central zone is designated for conservation and the outer zones have different levels of sustainable use of resources involving

local communities. The recently reforested **Reserva Sierra del Rosario**, worth visiting to see Las Terrazas and the Hotel Moka, and the **Reserva Península de Guanahacabibes**, more notable for its offshore diving sites than its onshore wilderness, are both in Pinar del Río Province. **Parque Baconao** in Santiago de Cuba Province contains the lovely reforested area surrounding the stone-outcrop of La Gran Piedra, and several beautiful beaches. The **Cuchillas del Toa Biosphere Reserve**, in Guantánamo Province, is home to the Parque Nacional Alejandro de Humboldt, which contains the island's largest expanse of rainforest in Cuba, and is one of the most isolated, pristine parts of the island, home to many endangered species including the magnificent ivory-billed woodpecker. The Toa River, which flows through this region, is just about the only part of the island where it may be possible to make short river-rafting trips. If you get this far east and have the chance to visit this area, take it: only sections of it can be accessed by visitors, and only if accompanied by a guide. Indeed, few Cubans ever see this part of the country. At present, walking and rafting trips can be organized from the Hotel El Castillo or Hotel Porto Santo in Baracoa. Although large parts of these reserves are off-limits, there are sufficient trails to allow at least several (guided) half-day walks through glorious landscapes. Of the four, Sierra del Rosario and the Parque Baconao have nearby lodges and the best infrastructures for exploring. The hotels recommended for each location (see relevant chapters) can arrange guided tours and can suggest trails if you go on your own.

While you are planning your trip you might also want to contact certain travel agencies in Canada and the United States, that can tailor nature tours for you. The Toronto-based Cuba Cycling/Hiking Connection ((416) 922-2232 US TOLL-FREE (800) 268-7229 FAX (416) 922-8410, 21 St. Clair Avenue East, Suite 1003, Toronto, Ontario M4T IL9, have

recently begun operating all-inclusive seven-day hiking trips, with accommodations provided at four-star hotels and mountain lodges (see also SPORTING SPREE, below). In the United States, contact Wings of the World US TOLL-FREE (800) 465-8687, 1200 William Street, Suite 706, Buffalo, New York 14240, which offers tailored eco-tours of Cuba, including the 11-day "From Mountain to Forest" all-inclusive US$2,695-tour that visits the Zapata Peninsula in Matanzas, the Valle de Viñales and Las Terrazas in Pinar del Río, the Sierra de Nipe mountains and Pinares de Mayarí in Holguín, and Parque Baconao in Santiago de Cuba (see also TAKING A TOUR, page 59). This company also offers all-inclusive eight-day birdwatching tours in January, February, and March for US$2,295, visiting the Zapata Peninsula, the Long Point Observatory and La Güira reserve in Pinar del Río.

Sporting Spree

SCUBA DIVING

As an international scuba-diving destination, Cuba is still fairly off the map, yet its attractions are comparable to the Bahamas, Cozumel and the Grand Cayman Islands — perhaps, in many ways, more impressive. Increasing numbers of enthusiasts have been discovering how magnificent and unspoiled the archipelago's underwater world is. Add to this the fact that facilities for diving in Cuba are, in some resorts, at an international level of professionalism, and Cuba's obscure status in this respect may be about to change.

There is certainly no lack of potential diving locations to explore: offshore, more than 4,000 small (in some cases, tiny) islets and keys make up the Cuban archipelago, facing the Atlantic Ocean on the north coast, and the Caribbean on the south (which tends to have warmer waters). You can expect to see entire forests of multi-colored coral formations, dramatic drop-offs, gulf walls, caverns and wrecks alive with many species of fish and other marine life. The creatures that abound in Cuba's waters include rays, sharks, tarpon, turtles, barracuda, angelfish, grouper, bigeyes, butterflies, grunts, parrotfish, snapper, triggerfish, and wrasses, as well as *manatees,* found off near mangrove swamps. Sunken galleons and even the odd submarine can be seen off the island's southern coast.

Cuba's most important diving sites coincide with the four archipelagos which encircle the mainland: Canarreos, which lies to the southwest between Isla de la Juventud and Cayo Largo; Jardines de la Reina, located to the south, off Ciego de Ávila and Camagüey provinces; Sabana, reached from Cayo Coco and Cayo Guillermo in Ciego de Ávila Province; and Los Colorades, off Cayo Levisa in Pinar del Río. Many sites are being explored off Cayo Largo, Cayo Coco, Cayo Guillermo, Playa Santa Lucía and off the tip of Cabo de Corrientes at the westernmost point of Cuba.

As elsewhere in the Caribbean, water temperatures — which range from 27°C to 29°C (80°F to 85°F) — are perfectly suited to diving, and because so much of Cuba's marine environment has been left untouched, and has not yet been affected by cruiseliners, the visibility is noticeably better. Outside of hurricane season (August to October), you can dive all year round in Cuba, but the period from October to March is the most agreeable, as the southern and western coasts are free of the *nortes;* the cold north winds that bring with them cold rains. The northern coast is generally calmer from May to September.

If you plan to combine a sightseeing visit with a few days (or weeks) scuba diving, you can take your pick from a number of international diving centers across the island, which offer organized dives, courses, and equipment for rent.

Cuba's premier diving destination is the **Isla de la Juventud**. The Puertosol Hotel Colony International Diving Center

La Gran Piedra offers views filled with gigantic ferns and exuberant vegetation.

here is among the best-equipped in Cuba (with one of the country's few decompression chambers), and there are 56 marked dive sites offshore, which apparently offer an incredible array of underwater landscape vistas. Divers and tour-operators on the Isla de la Juventud are also good places for beginners to complete certification courses. You can contact Marinas Puertosol, who operate the Hotel Colony center, directly in Havana ((53-7) 24-4705 or 24-4708 FAX (53-7) 24-4703, at Calles M and L, Edificio FOCSA, Vedado, Havana. This company specializes in organizing scuba diving, yachting, underwater photography, deep-sea fishing, freshwater fishing, and boat rentals. However, beware: word has it their staff seeks clever schemes to have you pay more than is necessary.

In addition to the Isla de la Juventud center, they also operate the Marina Tarara outside Havana, the Marina Dársena in Varadero; the María La Gorda International Diving Center in Pinar del Río Province; the Marina Cayo Guillermo, the Jucaro Nautical Base in Ciego de Ávila Province (from which you can explore one of Cuba's most spectacular diving destinations, the **Jardines de la Reina** archipelago), and the Marina Cayo Largo del Sur on the tourist-only island of Cayo Largo.

Several other companies are equally reputable. The company Marlin Marinas y Nauticas operates another string of marinas and diving centers: La Aguja Diving Center at Marina Hemingway outside Havana; Barracuda Diving Center in Varadero; Faro Luna Diving Center in Cienfuegos; Marina Cayo Coco and Coco Diving Center at the Hotel Tryp Cayo Coco in Ciego de Ávila Province; Santa Lucía Nautical Point and Diver Den and Shark Friends Diving Center at Santa Lucía in Camagüey; Eagle Ray Diving Center at Playa Guardalavaca in Holguín; Albacora Diving Center, Playa Marea del Portillo, Pilón, Granma; and finally, in Santiago de Cuba Province, Marina Punta Gorda, Sigua Diving Center both in Parque

Baconao and Marlin Diving Center at Los Galeones, Chivirico. Contact them at ((53-7) 24-6675 FAX (53-7) 24-1629, Calle 184 N°. 123, Miramar Playa, Havana; or Marina Hemingway ((53-7) 21-5277 or 24-1155 FAX (53-7) 24-6848 or 24-1831, at Avenida 5 and Calle 248, Santa Fé, Playa, Havana.

Gaviota, the tourism wing of the Cuban Ministry of Defense, operates the Marina Varadero; Bahía Naranjo Diving Center and Playa Esmeralda Diving Center, near Playa Guardalavaca, as well as Cayo Saetía Nautical Point in Holguín Province. Contact them at ((53-7) 23-6977 or 22-7670 FAX (53-7) 24-2780, Calle 16 N°. 504 between Avenida 5 and Calle 7, Miramar Playa, Havana.

In general, the diving centers cited above are professionally run, with modern, imported Mares and Cressisub equipment and CMAS and PADI-trained instructors. By international standards, charges are not expensive: expect to pay around US$40 per dive, with extra charges if you need to rent equipment. It's still a good idea to bring your own equipment, although you can rent tanks and weight belts on site. Diving lessons and packages of one or two weeks can be arranged on request, including study or photography tours specializing in underwater flora and fauna, accompanied by researchers or university professors.

Less elaborate facilities for diving can be found throughout the island at many beach resorts. You should contact Villa Cayo Levisa at Cayo Levisa in Pinar del Río; Hotel Horizontes Costasur at Playa Ancón near Trinidad in Sancti Spíritus; and Villa Playa Girón for diving (and spelunking) in and around the Zapata Peninsula, notably near Playa Girón in Matanzas. It should be said that diving in the Zapata Peninsula's submerged caves is only for experts.

In the future, Cuba will probably start drawing attention to its considerable interest as a destination for **underwater archaeology**. Official estimates put the number of sunken ships over the centuries at over a thousand, only a few of which have been charted and

Vacationers scuba dive at Playa Esmeralda.

WATER SPORTS

Generally speaking, most major beach resorts (especially those run as a joint-venture with a foreign company) offer a smorgasbord of Club Med-style water sports: para-sailing, water skiing, snorkeling, jet skis, banana boats, catamarans, water bicycles, and kayaks. Charges for these activities can be quite pricey. By its own definition, Varadero is Cuba's capital of water sports, so this is probably the best place to come if a constant round of water sports is your idea of vacation heaven. Varadero holds various water sports festivals and events, including the Water-bike Cuban Cup in March, the Caribbean Open Water-skiing Contest in June and the Rowing Regatta in July. Otherwise, other resorts which are exceptionally well-equipped for water sports enthusiasts are the two Tryp hotels in Cayo Coco, Ciego de Ávila Province; the two Golden Tulip hotels in Playa Santa Lucía in Camagüey Province; and the Sierra Mar Club Resort in Chivirico, Santiago de Cuba Province.

If you enjoy snorkeling and wish to head off on your own as much as possible, bring your snorkeling equipment with you.

Although not especially *de rigueur* in Cuba, **surfing** may well become more popular in years to come. The north-easterly trade winds bring good swells between December and April, but surfers will have to bring their own boards as none are available locally for rent. This being said, you are not likely to see a single surfer during your stay.

For further information, contact the Cuban Water Sports Federation ((53-7) 24-0945 or 24-0948 FAX (53-7) 24-1914.

SAILING

If you are interested in sailing around Cuba, or perhaps even sailing your own yacht into Cuba, your first points of reference should be the Marina Hemingway, in Santa Fé, about twenty minutes drive from central Havana, which is a one-stop facility for all nautical activities. It is the seat of Cuba's International Yacht Club and the Club Náutico Internacional

explored. One of the best examples that can be easily explored is the *Nuestra Señora del Rosario*, a cargo galleon which was gunned down by an English pirate off the coast of Pinar del Río, laden with all its treasures. Expeditions to the sunken galleon can be made from the diving center at Cayo Levisa.

There are several companies you can contact to arrange dive-related trips to Cuba. In the United Kingdom, contact Aquatours ((44-181) 339-0040 FAX (44-181) 339-0080, Milboa Lodge, Portsmouth Road, Thames Ditton, Surrey KTZ OES1; in Canada, Fuji Incentive Group ((416) 777-0098 FAX (416) 777-0099, 463 Adelade, Toronto, Ontario M5V 1S7; and in the United States, Wings of the World US TOLL-FREE (800) 465-8687, 1200 William Street, Suite 706, Buffalo, NY 14240, which offers week-long diving packages to Isla de la Juventud.

If you are planning to do any serious diving, look out for *The Diving and Snorkeling Guide to Cuba* by Diana Williams (Houston: Pisces Books, 1996) which is a detailed account of the island's diving spots. Also see the relevant sections in the book for more information on their diving opportunities.

Hemingway de la Habana, which between them organize a formidable annual program of international **yachting regattas** and **fishing tournaments**, including the Havana Cup Regatta from Tampa, Florida to Havana in May, the Key West-Varadero Regatta in November, the Christmas Regatta, and the recently launched Caribbean Conch Regatta held in April, all of which attract many participants from the United States. (Cubans can participate in these regattas, but are barred from entering United States waters.) Cuba is keen to increase its profile internationally in this field and is forging good-will alliances with yacht clubs and organizations around the world. International yachties are warmly welcomed at the Marina Hemingway, and you'll usually see a large contingent of North American flags amongst the boats moored here as well.

Generally speaking, Cuba has good conditions for sailing throughout the year, although the months between December to April and June to November can bring unpredictable weather, affecting the northern and southern coasts at different times. The northern Atlantic coast tends to get the full brunt of storms and squalls, and is often rainier than the south coast. August to October are notable as months when hurricanes are likely to hit the region, although freak hurricanes can descend in other months too.

You can apply for temporary or so-called transient membership at the International Yacht Club if you are docked at the Marina Hemingway. Rates vary from US$25 to US$60 per boat per week, depending on the size of your boat. Membership entitles you to discounts on berthing, accommodations throughout Cuba, car rental, and any nautical activities, as well as free use of the gymnasium and the swimming pool of the Hotel Viejo y El Mar, also within the Marina Hemingway complex, which is run by Cubanacán. Contact the International Yacht Club ((53-7) 24-1150 or 24-1156 FAX (53-7) 24-1149, Marina Hemingway, Avenida 5 and Calle 248, Santa Fé, Playa, Havana.

The Marina Hemingway has four berthing channels — each a kilometer (half-mile) long and capable of holding a hundred vessels — and can cater to

A dolphin laughs OPPOSITE at Bahía de Naranjo. ABOVE: A typical coastline near Santiago de Cuba.

cruisers of all sizes. All the necessary amenities are provided: power outlets, water connections, telephone, guard service, supplies and land facilities, and the complex includes several restaurants, supermarkets, shops, tennis courts, and bicycle and car rental.

If you are thinking of sailing to or around Cuba, look for the excellent *A Cruising Guide to Cuba* by Simon Charles (Cruising Guide Publications, 1994). It has all the information you will need, as well as directives for entering Cuba by sea. In Cuba, get a copy of the detailed *Yachtsman's Guide Cuba*, published jointly by Marina Puertosol, Marina Gaviota and Marina Marlin. It is available at the International Yacht Club and the Club Náutico Internacional de la Habana.

You may want to charter a yacht for a day or several days, or perhaps just go for a yacht cruise with others at the helm. If so, the company Marlin Marinas y Nauticas, also at the Marina Hemingway, can supply you a choice of fully equipped boats and crew. Contact them at Marina Hemingway ((53-7) 21-5277 or 24-1155 FAX (53-7) 24-6848 or 24-1831, Avenida 5 and Calle 248, Santa Fé, Playa, Havana.

The four marinas in Varadero: the Marina Gaviota ((53-5) 66-292, Carretera Sur, Punta Hicacos, Varadero; the Marina Chapelín ((53-5) 66-7550 FAX (53-5) 60-7093, Carretera Las Morlas, Varadero; the Marina Dársena ((53-5) 66-8060 FAX (53-5) 66-7456, Via Blanca, Dársena, Varadero; and the Marina Acua ((53-5) 61-2818 FAX (53-5) 66-8804, 201 Avenida Kawama between Calles 2 and 3, Varadero, can also offer yachts for hire or for crew-manned cruises. Prices range from US$20 for a two-hour cruise to US$150 for a day charter.

FISHING

When you contemplate the fact that Cuba was the setting for Ernest Hemingway's famous fishing tale, *The Old Man and the Sea*, it comes as no surprise to learn that there are thought to be few better places than the Gulf Stream off Cuba's northern coast to catch blue marlin, sail fish, white marlin, dolphin fish, wahoo, barracuda, tuna, bonito, bonefish, and tarpon.

From its headquarters at the Marina Hemingway, Marlin Marinas y Nauticas offer daily boat rental for fishing in the Gulf Stream for around US$250 to US$350 per day, depending on the size of the boat and the number of passengers, including tackle and baits, snacks and lunch, which is cheap compared with other Caribbean destinations. For contact details see SAILING, above.

You can expect similar rates at Varadero's marinas. Several other principal resorts also have boats equipped for off-shore and deep-sea fishing, notably at Isla de la Juventud, Cayo Coco in Ciego de Ávila Province, Guardalavaca in Holguín Province, Marea del Portillo in Granma Province, and in particular, the Sierra Mar Club Resort, Chivirico, Santiago de Cuba Province.

The Marina Hemingway stages a number of international events for visiting fishing enthusiasts (many of whom come from North America), notably the Ernest Hemingway International Marlin Tournament, founded by the writer himself and usually held each May or June, and the Blue Marlin International Fishing Tournament held each August or September, both governed by the International Game Fishing Association. In an effort to conserve the marine environment, they have recently adopted the "tackle-release procedure" and urge visiting participants to do the same.

Fly-fishing is becoming increasingly popular in Cuba, and the Zapata Peninsula in Matanzas Province especially is becoming a top destination. Other ideal places for this type of fishing are Varadero, Santa Lucía in Camagüey Province, Marea del Portillo in Granma Province, Punta del Este in Isla de la Juventud, and Cayo Largo.

Inland, Cuba's most popular freshwater fish is the largemouth bass, which was introduced in 1928 from Texas and New Orleans. Good fishing spots

Sailing on turquoise waters is a favorite activity of sea-loving visitors to Cuba.

include Lake Hanabanilla in the Escambray Mountains, Laguna del Tesoro (also known as Treasure Lagoon) at Guamá in the Zapata Peninsula in Matanzas Province, Largo Redonda lagoon in Ciego de Ávila Province and Lake Zaza in Sancti Spíritus, which is the largest reservoir in Cuba. The chain Horizontes Hoteles ((53-7) 24-4042 FAX (53-7) 24-3722, Calle 23 No. 1567 between Calles N and O, Vedado, Havana, specializes in excursions and has fishing lodges in these locations. You can also contact Cubamar ((53-7) 33-8317, Fifth Floor, Hotel Plaza, Calles Zulueta and Neptuno, La Habana Vieja, who can help arrange fishing trips and accommodation at on-site lodges.

You can also contact the tourist organization Cubanacán ((53-7) 21-9457, 20-0569 or 24-6006, Calle 68 and Avenida 5, Miramar, Postal 16046, Zona 16, Havana, for information on their special fishing vacation program, as well as their lodge, the Viramas Hunting and Fishing Lodge in Granma Province.

In the United States, Wings of the World US TOLL-FREE (800) 465-8687, 100 William Street, Suite 706, Buffalo, NY 14240, arranges deep-sea and bass fishing trips within Cuba; and Pan-Angling Travel ((312) 263-0328 FAX (312) 263-5246, 180 Michigan Avenue, Chicago, Illinois 60601, publishes a newsletter with regular information about fishing in Cuba, and arranges fishing trips to the Zapata Peninsula.

SPELUNKING

Cuba has one of the most elaborate limestone cave systems in the Americas: its mountains conceal vast networks of subterranean caverns, galleries and rivers. Potentially, Cuba may develop into a popular destination for spelunkers. The most interesting and accessible caves are in Pinar del Río, where the galleries of the Cueva Santo Tomás stretch for more than 45 km (30 miles); the Cueva del Bellamar, outside of Matanzas, and the underwater caves along the Zapata Peninsula, the Cueva Jibara within the Gran Parque Nacional Sierra Maestra, which drops some 248 m (814 ft); and the Punta del Este caves on the Isla de la Juventud, which contain ancient cave paintings.

Contact the Hotel Horizontes Los Jazmines or the Hotel Horizontes La Ermita in Viñales, the Villa Horizontes Playa Girón near the Zapata Peninsula, or the Hotel Horizontes Villa Santo Domingo in the Gran Parque Nacional de Sierra Maestra.

Cuba has great potential for spelunking activities, but experienced guides are few. Given that this activity requires that you feel secure in your guide's expertise, you may want to be careful about who you choose to accompany you.

CYCLING

Although they will be regarded as something of an oddity by ordinary Cubans, cycling enthusiasts will find it fairly easy to arrange short itineraries or even to circumnavigate the island. It is certainly a unique way to see the country up close, as it were, along with vistas of its many changing landscapes; and you are likely to encounter much curiosity and warmth, and perhaps even hospitality from the people you meet along the way. It is a good way to get around if you savor the sensation of being off on your own, especially in a country where interaction between foreigners and Cubans often feels somewhat monitored. You will certainly find the roads relatively free of traffic, due to the transportation crisis of Cuba's Special Period, and you won't see too many other tourists either, except those that are whisked by in air-conditioned buses, at the mercy of their tour schedule.

It is preferable to bring your own multi-speed bicycle — you'll need to check with your airline for details — otherwise face renting Cuba's ubiquitous Chinese-made Flying Pigeon bicycles (although these days modern mountain bikes can be purchased in Havana's dollar-shops). The supply of rental bikes can be quite unreliable, and is generally limited to Havana and the beach-resort hotels. Some visiting cyclists report that, having finally managed to rent a bicycle, the next consideration is to prevent it from being stolen, however, the system of neighborhood CDR's ("Committees for the Defense of the Revolution") and the high penalties associated with theft in

Cuba do not make this a particularly high risk. (Given the fact that during the Special Period a pair of wheels is worth its weight in gold, it is rather easy to understand the temptation a bicycle can pose.)

The Toronto-based Cuba Cycling/Hiking Connection ((416) 922-2232 US TOLL-FREE (800) 268-7229 FAX (416) 922-8410, 21 St. Clair Avenue East, Suite 1003, Toronto, Ontario M4T IL9, which runs **bicycle tours** in Cuba, says that their practice is to bring in quality mountain bikes for the trip, then sell them before leaving Cuba, usually to hotels and tour agencies keen to swell their limited supply. This company offers seven-day inclusive cycling package tours in rural parts of Cuba, such as Pinar del Río Province, combining cycling with various cultural activities such as visiting tobacco and coffee plantations, a Cuban school, or even a Havana ball game, all for under US$1,000. In the United Kingdom, Hazel Pennington Bike Tours ((44-122) 548-0130 FAX (44-122) 548-0132, PO Box 75, Bath, Avon BA1 1BX, offers 14-day bicycle tours every March, November, and December (£1,070 including round-trip fare from Stansted) that include Havana, Pinar del Río, Trinidad and the Sierra del Escambray. In the United States, call Wings of the World US TOLL-FREE (800) 465-8687, 1200 William Street, Suite 706, Buffalo, New York 14240, who offer eight-day guided bicycle tours to Cuba every month. Their US$1,895 all-inclusive tour begins in Havana, then concentrates on the eastern part of Cuba, notably Santiago de Cuba, Parque Baconao and Guantánamo Province.

Within Cuba, contact the Federación de Ciclismo ((53-7) 66-3776 or 68-3661.

HORSEBACK RIDING

Horseback riding is not a commonplace activity in Cuba. Generally speaking, horses are taken up with other activities such as assisting in meeting the nation's agricultural quota. Don't expect great equipment for your horse-riding

An infant crocodile in the Ciénaga de Zapata reserve.

excursions: you will be lucky if you have a saddle, let alone a helmet. Very often farmers lend out the meager equipment they possess along with the horse. However, some beach resorts and hotels can arrange horseback riding excursions such as Varadero, Playa Santa Lucía, Guardalavaca, Marea del Portillo and — the most secluded of these beaches — Cayo Largo, and this can make for an entirely pleasant way to enjoy the Cuban countryside.

Of all these suggestions, Playa Santa Lucía, which is located within Camagüey Province, renowned in Cuba for its ranches and *vaqueros*, or cattle-ranchers, has the best facilities: your hotel can arrange rides at the nearby King Ranch, a working cattle farm. In addition, special horse ranches have been set up for tourists at the Finca Guajira Rodeo at El Oasis (El Crucero) in Parque Baconao and the Finca María Dolores outside Trinidad. See the relevant destinations for more details.

GOLF

Havana and Varadero have the island's only golf courses. The Havana course is in the Diploclub complex in Boyeros, about 15 minutes' drive from central Havana. The brand-new 18-hole Varadero Golf Club is between the Melía and Tuxpan hotels, and incorporates the Du Pont mansion, now the Las Americas restaurant.

The newly opened, private Club de Golf Habana (Havana Golf Club) ((53-7) 44-4836 or 44-8227, Carretera de Vento, near Boyeros, 20 km (slightly over 12 miles) from central Havana, is housed in the former Havana Biltmore Yacht and Country Club on Avenida 5, and is Havana's top-level sports center. Originally founded in 1943, it has nine holes and beautifully landscaped lawns. There are also tennis courts, a bowling alley, billiard tables, a swimming pool, two restaurants and the 19th Hole Bar. Contact your hotel concierge to help you arrange temporary membership, or contact the club directly.

Another course is the Campo de Golf Las Américas (Varadero Golf Club) ((53-5) 66-7750, Carretera Las Américas, Reparto La Torre, Varadero. You can also make inquiries about staying within the complex at Rumbos ((53-7) 66-2113 or (53-7) 66-2115, Calles Línea and M, Vedado, Havana.

BASEBALL AND BOXING

Two reigning passions of this island nation, baseball and boxing have produced a handful of world-class Cuban players, a number of whom have famously defected, like Livian Hernandez, probably the most famous Cuban pitcher since Fidel Castro himself, who is now with the Florida Marlins.

Beisbol, as it is called, has early origins in Cuba. The first recorded game of baseball was played in 1874, at what is now the world's oldest baseball stadium. The island's national team traditionally wins out over the United States team at the Olympic Games, and it is little surprise that many of Cuba's star players are eyed with considerable interest by the United States professional leagues. Although they earn about 400 pesos a month (about the same salary as a bricklayer), Cuba's top players play more than a hundred games during the annual season, which lasts from December to June. It is well worth attending one of these games — or even a local game — at one of the huge stadiums built by the state throughout the island. Entrance to spectator sports in Cuba is generally free or nominal.

If you are interested in having a more in-depth look at Cuba's amateur sports, you might consider joining an eight-day tour offered by Wings of the World US TOLL-FREE (800) 465-8687, 1200 William Street, Suite 706, Buffalo, New York 14240, which includes visits to training sessions and games of baseball, boxing, and volleyball, as well as to the national baseball training center in Cienfuegos and the Sports Medicine center.

The Open Road

You need at least a month to explore the island properly by car. But even if you plan to spend less than two weeks in Cuba, you can still manage to see a great deal, especially if you opt to rent a car or jeep for at least part of your stay. Just bear in mind that Cuba can be a surprisingly expensive place to rent a car or jeep, with inflated rental and fuel costs.

From either Havana or Varadero, try to make a side-trip westwards of at least two days, either by rental car or by joining a tour, to the beautiful province of **Pinar del Río**, to enjoy its stunning scenery, limestone caves, and rustic atmosphere, and perhaps to sample the products of its famous cigar factories. Try to take the picturesque coastal route at least one way.

Another very rewarding side trip, also either from Havana or Varadero, is to the **Zapata Peninsula** and **Playa Girón** (otherwise known as the Bay of Pigs) in Matanzas Province, which deserves at least two nights stay.

If you are on a two-week visit, you will only have time to visit one other part of Cuba on this trip. A good second choice is **Trinidad**, in the island's central region. If you are driving or have joined a bus tour, you will probably overnight en route to Trinidad in the port city of Cienfuegos.

From Havana, you may prefer to fly to Santiago de Cuba, rather than make the long road journey across the entire

OPPOSITE: The modern-day Mural de la Prehistoria. ABOVE: Bicycles are one answer to fuel shortages.

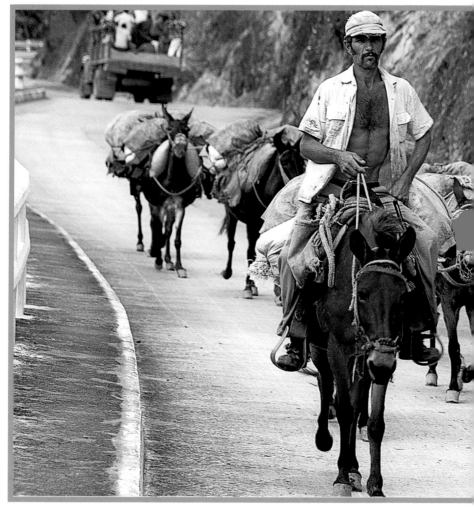

stretch of the island, which ideally needs to be broken up over at least two or three days for comfort. It's best to book your return flight well in advance to be sure of availability, perhaps through your travel agent before you get to Cuba. The road journey, on the other hand, allows you a window on rural Cuba, with its changing landscapes and many interesting small towns along the way.

You can rent a car from Santiago de Cuba and make a day excursion to nearby **Parque Baconao** or, if you crave a couple of days of beach relaxation, drive west along the coast to stay at the Superclub beach resort at Chivirico. Further west is the peaceful resort of Marea del Portillo, reached from

Santiago de Cuba by the newly completed coastal road that passes through some of the island's most wild and stunning scenery.

Further east, Guantánamo Province offers a spectacular drive along its **La Farola highway** across high mountain passes to the colonial outpost of **Baracoa**, Cuba's oldest Spanish settlement. This route is beautiful and varied enough to go there and back without ever getting bored, within the space of an hour you can pass from arid desert flatlands indented by pretty inlets to exuberant mountain vegetation, then, beyond Baracoa, to tropical groves of coconut palms. To many, this is the most beautiful road on the island.

When planning your driving itinerary in Cuba, don't forsake a handful of Cuba's other, often neglected, colonial towns: Remedios and Santa Clara, Sancti Spíritus, Camagüey, and Bayamo. Of these, only Camagüey is recommended as an overnight stop.

You may wish to investigate the Hotel Horizontes chain's Flexi Fly and Drive Program, a package including car rental, accommodations and domestic flights, which should be booked from outside Cuba (see GETTING AROUND, page 309 in TRAVELERS' TIPS).

A horseman travels from Guant·namo to Baracoa in Cuba's most remote region.

Short Breaks

There are many alternatives for places that you can escape to for just a few days. Some are mentioned above, in THE OPEN ROAD — such as the rewarding side-trips from Havana to Pinar del Río, the Zapata Peninsula and Playa Girón; as well as toTrinidad and Santiago de Cuba, for example.

Some regions are enjoyable to visit because of their diversity: from **Trinidad**, you can base yourself at the nearby beach of Playa Ancón, visit the Valle de los Ingenios and make an overnight stop in the Sierra del Escambray, all within two or three days.

In **central Cuba**, three main beach resorts along the northern coast — Cayo Coco, Santa Lucía, and Guardalavaca — each have their individual charms.

If you really want to experience a short break, perhaps you should consider a trip to either **Isla de la Juventud** or **Cayo Largo**, both of which offer a taste of Cuba's version of getting away from it all.

Living It Up

STAYING IN STYLE

Cuba has some wonderfully character-full and decadent hotels. In Havana, the luxurious five-star **Melía Cohiba** has all the facilities you might want. But the louche grandeur of such retro classics as the **Hotel Nacional** (officially five-star, but not in terms of food, service or facilities) or the elegantly restored **Hotel Santa Isabel** have far more character and style. The newly restored nineteenth-century hotels, the **Sevilla**, the **Plaza** and the **Inglaterra** provide atmosphere and history in that order of comfort and with a certain amount of noise, while the 1930s-style **Hotel Ambus Mundos** is charming. One of the best bargains in La Habana Vieja is the quirky and stylish 12-room **Hostal Valencia**, which is frequently booked-out. If you want to stay in a restful environment outside the capital, **Hotel El Viejo y el Mar** in the Marina Hemingway complex is a good choice.

In Varadero, the five-star **Melía Varadero** and the **Melía Las Americas** are outstanding, while the **Hotel Internacional** has retro chic and the best stretch of beach. In Pinar del Río, **Los Jazmines** in the Valle de Viñales is charming and has sublime views, and **Hotel Moka** in Las Terrazas, Sierra del Rosario is the island's first ecological resort, and is stylishly designed and rather luxurious to boot.

Of the many beach resorts throughout the country, the **Hotel Tryp Cayo Coco** and the **Hotel Tryp Club Cayo Coco** in Cayo Coco, Ciego de Ávila; the **Club Caracol** in Playa Santa Lucía, and Superclub's **Sierra Mar Club Resort** in Santiago de Cuba Province are all impressive tourist complexes. In remote Granma Province, the **Farallón del Caribe** in Marea del Portillo deserves praise for its attractive landscaping and special relaxing atmosphere.

In Santiago de Cuba, the newly restored **Hotel Casa Granda**, first opened in 1914, has elegant charm — and plans for modernization — and outshines — in style if not range of facilities — the city's longtime standby, the **Hotel Santiago de Cuba**. Meanwhile, towards the island's eastern tip, in Baracoa, the **Hotel El Castillo** has a commanding position and occupies what used to be a Spanish fortress.

WINING AND DINING

Cuba has many enjoyable and special restaurants, some of which are notable as much for their splendid settings as for their food.

In Havana, one of the most scenic restaurants is **La Divina Pastora**, set within the Morro-Cabaña fortress which overlooks the bay and the Malecón. Others, such as Hemingway's favorites, **El Floridita** and **La Bodeguita del Medio**, are classics from the pre-Revolutionary era, although not to be visited with high expectations. For the best of Cuban Creole cuisine amid stylish settings in Miramar mansions, **La Ferminia** and **Tocororo** are both popular with Havana's cognoscenti. Near Havana, in the fishing village of Cojímar, (famous as the setting for Hemingway's *The Old Man and the Sea*), **La Terraza** serves the best seafood paella on the island.

In Varadero, aside from ubiquitous hotel buffets, the most sophisticated dining is undoubtedly at the Basque restaurant **Fuerteventura** at the Hotel Melía Varadero and the **Las Américas**, set in the 1930s Du Pont mansion. In Pinar del Río, both the **Casa de Don Tomás** in the rustic town of Viñales, and the fresh prawns served at **La Casa del Marisco** in the Valle de Viñales should not be missed.

In Cienfuegos, for its grandiose setting alone, a meal at the **Palacio Valle** is a highlight of visiting the city; a description which applies equally to Santiago de Cuba's **1900** restaurant, which occupies a former *palacio* and glitters with antique chandeliers and musty rococo elegance.

In Trinidad, you must try a *canchánchara* cocktail at **La Canchánchara**, while elegant dining is best at the **Trinidad Colonial**. In the nearby Valle de los Ingenios, lunches are served in historic **Manacas-Iznaga** plantation mansion. In Camagüey, for colonial

ambiance and excellent local food, **La Campaña de Toledo** and the **Parador de los Tres Reyes** both have beautiful settings in the historic Plaza de San Juan de Dios.

In some cases, glorious surroundings appear to be everything, but the meals served also seem to rise to the occasion, assisted by the melting glow of the afternoon sun and the *Mayabe* beer. A special mention must be made of **La Taberna del Morro**, the restaurant at the harbor entrance to Santiago de Cuba, which has magnificent views across the sea and fortress of the same name; the **beachside tavern** at Playa Daiquirí in Parque Baconao in Santiago de Cuba Province; and the sea-facing restaurant **La Punta**, housed in the former fortress lookout in Baracoa.

Generally speaking, restaurants at hotels run by foreign chains, particularly the Spanish **Sol Melía** chain, offer fresh and varied food at reasonable prices, and the best food safety guarantees.

OUT ON THE TOWN

Cubans are a famously musical people, and it is no exaggeration to say that music is an integral part of life here.

Almost every night in Havana, it is possible to find some of Cuba's best salsa and jazz bands playing live in various nightclubs. One of the best places to start an evening out is with cocktails at the Hotel Habana Libre's **Turquino Bar**, and to go on to the Hotel Riviera's **Palacio de la Salsa**, or the **Casa de la Música**, depending on who is performing. The Hotel Melía Cohiba's **Aché** is the most exclusive discotheque in town. Elsewhere, almost all the capital's bars and nightclubs, notably at La Bodeguita del Medio and El Floridita, have live musicians and singers who, even in more modest and less touristy surroundings, are shockingly professional. And of course, one must not forget the **Tropicana** cabaret — the original version in Havana, that is.

As you travel throughout Cuba, you can enter almost any of the island's many music halls, known as *Casas de la Trova* — from nondescript rooms in the countryside with peeling paint and a bar which has nothing to serve, to the more famous establishments in Trinidad and Santiago de Cuba — and hear the

A young woman poses near Santiago de Cuba.

true soul of Cuban music. The Casa de la Trova in Santiago de Cuba is the best of its kind, with memorable performances every night, and regular appearances by its house band, Vieja Trova Santiguera.

Backpacking

The Cuban government is not exactly trying to encourage backpacking or budget travel as a trend, preferring tourists to stay in designated hotels and put as many dollars into the Cuban economy as possible. Although Cubans themselves seem to exist on next to nothing, you will soon realize that tourism is the bootstrap that the government hopes to use to lift the nation out of its economic crisis. There are no youth hostels or student travel discounts in Cuba. The former standby for budget travelers used to be Cuban peso hotels and vacation camps (usually run through Cubamar or operated by the Islazul chain) but now that these facilities are obliged to finance themselves in dollars they have modernized many of their accommodations for foreigners;

which remain modestly priced, just not as ridiculously cheap as before.

However, if you are resourceful there are a number of ways to make traveling in Cuba both rewarding and less expensive.

You may find it both more interesting and economical to stay — at least some of the time — in private homes, or *casas particulares*. Price is always a matter of personal negotiation, and they are not available as an option through the official tourism organizations. By law, Cubans are allowed to rent up to two rooms in their own homes, and this practice is becoming widespread. The price for a room usually ranges from around US$10 to US$20 per day, and no two homestays will be the same. You will usually have to share the bathroom, and your hosts are usually happy to prepare meals for you for an additional cost. On that subject, it's not advisable to accept solicitations to stay in a private home from street *jineteros*, or hustlers, who may not have your best interests at heart, and who you will have to pay commission. You may soon make Cuban friends, and can raise the issue word of mouth.

While attempting to get around the country by bus is likely to try the patience of most visitors, regardless how keen to economize, you may well find that riding the island's railway network suits you better, for it is a reasonably reliable and inexpensive way to travel long distances (see GETTING AROUND, page 309 in TRAVELERS' TIPS).

One of the best ways to ensure that you keep your travel costs low in Cuba is to arrive on an all-inclusive package tour booked through a travel agency overseas. If you are an individualist, this can chafe. But if you shop around, you may be able to find a tour package that allows you a maximum amount of freedom for a minimum cost.

Family Fun

Cubans love children and treat them with genuine kindness and interest, a welcome attitude that you will encounter where ever you go. Many of the hotels — especially the beach resorts — offer special children's entertainment programs, and some hotels offer babysitting upon request. Particularly

good hotels to choose if you are traveling with your children are the **Delta Las Brisas Club Resort** in Guardalavaca; the **Golden Tulip** hotels at Playa Santa Lucía, and the **Hotel Melía Varadero**, all of which are geared towards families with play areas for children, game rooms, and activity programs. The two Tryp hotels in Cayo Coco, Ciego de Ávila Province, are currently improving and expanding their children's clubs.

Depending on their age, children will probably enjoy the sights in and around the historic cities of Havana, Trinidad and Santiago de Cuba, although fortresses, museums and hotels will probably begin to pall. Some of the best side trips from Havana for children would be to visit the **replica Indian village** at Guamá, the **crocodile breeding farm** at La Boca, or to admire the birdlife in the **Parque Nacional Ciénaga de Zapata**, in Matanzas Province.

Generally, children under the age of 12 traveling with their parents in Cuba are often granted discounted accommodation. Check with your hotel beforehand.

Full comfort resort hotels ABOVE grace the peaceful beach of Playa Esmeralda OPPOSITE near Guardalavaca.

Galloping Gourmet

Unless you are invited to a Cuban home, you are probably best off sticking to the dollar restaurants or *paladares* (private home-restaurants). It is something of an understatement to observe that Cubans themselves frequently spend the better part of their days trying to obtain many of the provisions which appear freely on hotel buffet tables. As you may find, the Revolution has not been kind to the nation's cuisine, being more intent on creating an agricultural industry that puts food on the table rather than a culture of fine dining. Although the situation has improved over the last couple of years, as has the cuisine, we are still a far cry from the rich, inventive and savory cuisine of yesteryear.

For tourists, who are generally able to remain almost oblivious to the shortages, Cuban restaurant food is frequently stodgy and bland, although if you are invited to private homes, you may be amazed at the way delicious meals can be magically prepared: Cubans often pride themselves on being

excellent and ingenious cooks, and will go to huge lengths to make sure their guests are well-fed.

You should definitely visit a *paladar* during your stay. During the worst years of the Special Period, a popular Brazilian television series captured the heart of Cubans through the misadventures of a woman who ended up triumphing over her daily difficulties (reflecting the quotidian trials of many Cubans) by opening a small restaurant called Le Paladar. Today, all the small home-restaurants are called *paladares*, and although they began as more or less legal establishments, they are now officially allowed. There are now many of them in Havana, as well throughout the country. Like family *tavernas* in Greece, *paladares* are full of character and authentic atmosphere.

The food could be good or mediocre, the decor sumptuous or touchingly sordid, the service clumsy or already professional. They can range from very rustic establishments with simple Creole dishes to rather professionally run family mansions serving elaborate French cooking. Although you may not make any gastronomic discoveries, in

potato-like cassava root covered in garlic-laced oil) or *maduros* (fried plantain bananas).

You will probably find it hard to avoid indulging in a *"sandwich Cubano"* at some stage during your visit: these calorific door-stoppers are served as all-day snacks (as they are in Little Havana, Miami), with a combination of *jamon* and *queso* tucked into lard-smeared thick bread which is then grilled. Cubans regard this as a national dish, as Cuban as *cafecitos*, dominoes and cigars.

Dessert is often fresh fruit, Cuban-made ice-cream, cake or *dulce de leche*, a sweet milky *blanc manger*.

After a meal, a bottle of rum or *marasquino*, a sweet local liqueur, is often passed around.

Coffee is generally best when taken the Cuban way: as a tiny cup of *cafecito*, an expresso with lots of sugar. *Cafecitos* are sold everywhere. Other variations include the short, strong *cortaditos* and *café con leche*, half milk, half coffee (and the nickname second-and third-generation Miami Cubans give themselves). If you order the mockingly named *Americano* coffee, you will get what usually tastes like mediocre dishwater. Good cappuccino and expresso made the European way is starting to make its appearance in several of the restored coffee shops and bars in La Habana Vieja.

It doesn't take long to discover that **rum** is the national drink. A dozen distilleries across the island produce a variety of brands, the best known of which are the dry Havana Club and the sweeter Caribbean Club preferred by locals. You can choose from the transparent "Silver Dry" or the amber-hued three-year-old Havana Club brands, as well as the smoother five- and seven-year-old varieties. The masterpiece of Cuban distilleries is the 15-year-old Havana Club Gran Reserve: proudly exhibited at the Sevilla 1992 World's Fair, it has an international following. Both

any case, it's an experience that allows you to get that much closer to the Cuban reality: it's difficult to run a restaurant when it was not your original vocation, in a country where officially you have been condemned to the fires of hell for a shadow of a personal "profit," where blackouts and water cuts are frequent, and where what is permitted today may be forbidden again tomorrow. Word-of-mouth recommendations for *paladares* are best, since their longevity can never be taken for granted. Avoid fish and seafood as a general rule.

Cubans like to start their meals with fresh fruits or a coleslaw salad to clear the palate (although the supply of fresh fruits and vegetables can be sporadic), followed by a fairly heavy main course of grilled or Creole-style fried or fricasseed seafood, chicken or pork. (With the prevalence of meat dishes, vegetarians may find their choice very limited.) Suckling pig roasted on a spit, known as *lechón asado*, is Cuba's special national dish, and *chicharrónes*, or pork cracklings are a popular bar dish.

Other staples include *congri* (rice with beans) or *moros y cristianos* (rice with black beans), *yucca con mojo* (the

OPPOSITE: Santa Lucía's beachside fish restaurant.
ABOVE: Havana's neoclassical Hotel Inglaterra.

Cuban-produced **wine** is now a budding industry, the result of an Italian-Cuban joint venture, and you may soon see red, white and sparkling brands in Cuban shops.

Cuba's national **beers**, Hatuey and Cristal are very popular, but Polar, Bucanero as well as many other regional brands are worth trying. If you don't want to drink alcohol, the malt-based drink, *Mayabe*, with its beer-like foam, is a good alternative. Another of Cuba's nonalcoholic specialties is *guarapo* — pure sugarcane juice made fresh by juicing a cane stalk through a grinder.

the Ron Matusalen and Pati Cruzada rums made in Santiago de Cuba, are interesting variations. Bucanero, Caney and Varadero are other brands. You may hear about a rough, home-distilled version of rum, nicknamed *chispa del tren* ("train spark"), which you would be wise to avoid.

The best rum is generally consumed straight, however Cuba has many refreshing and delicious **rum cocktails**, notably the two Hemingway favorites, the *mojito* (light dry rum, lemon, crushed mint, sugar, soda and ice) and the *daiquirí*, the *cuba libre* (dry light rum, cola, lime and ice), the *cubanito* (a rum-based Bloody Mary), the *piña colada*, and the *isla de pinos* (light dry rum, grapefruit juice and red vermouth).

Cultural Kicks

Some of Cuba's most remarkable museums are colonial mansions or *palacios* that have been turned into museums and are furnished in the traditional style — offering the most evocative look at Cuba's past. Some are steeped in history, such as the **Museo de la Ciudad de la Habana**, which is housed in the magnificent Palacio de los Capitanes-Generales, seat of the colonial Spanish government, with private living quarters that saw many of the island's former masters come and go, or the city's first fortress, the **Castillo de la Real Fuerza**. You can also explore museums housed inside the islands impressive colonial fortresses, and wander their battlements afterwards, notably at the **Castillo de los Tres Santos Reyes Magos del Morro** and **San Carlos de la Cabaña** in Havana; and the **Castillo del Morro** fortress in Santiago de Cuba.

Others are restored to an approximation of their original grandeur, like the **Museo Romántico** in Trinidad, which gives a very accurate sense of how the colonial sugar-rich aristocracy lived during colonial times; while the **Museo de Arte Colonial** and the **Museo de Artes Decorativas** in Havana, and the **Museo de Ambiente Historico Cubano** (also known as the Casa Velásquez) in Santiago, house the country's most

exceptional furniture and antiquity collections within notable historic former homes.

More contemporary museums on a slightly different theme are the **Casa-Museo de Hemingway**, La Finca Vigía (Hemingway Museum) at La Finca Vigía, outside Havana, which displays the writer's home and possessions much the way they were left, and the **Museo Napoleónico**, in Havana, a quirky repository of one man's tribute to the great Corsican.

To become acquainted with Cuba's archaeological and natural history, the **Museo Antropológico Montané** and the **Museo de Ciencias Naturales Felipe Poey** are worth a look, as are the **Museo Indocubano** in Banes, in Holguín Province and the **Museo Matachín** in Baracoa, Guantánamo Province. The newly discovered site at **Punta Alegre**, in Ciego de Ávila, where the largest extant Taíno settlement was uncovered in mid-July, may well eventually become an important museum.

The most important art museum in Cuba is Havana's **Museo Nacional de Bellas Artes**, while you should not miss the **Museo de las Parrandas Remedianas** if you visit the town of Remedios in Villa C lara Province. To learn more about Cuba's Afro-Caribbean traditions, visit the **Casa de Africa**, the **Museo de Regla** and **Museo Historico de Guanabacoa** in Havana.

You may become quite a connoisseur of Cuba's unique revolutionary museums, such as the **Museo de la Revolución** (formerly the Presidential Palace of dictator Fulgencio Batista) with prize exhibits like the *Granma* boat and the **Museo del Minsterio del Interior** in Havana; the **Museo Girón** at Playa Girón, Matanzas Province; the **Tren Blindado** in Santa Clara, Villa Clara Province; the **Museo de Lucha contra Bandidos** in Trinidad, and the **Moncada Barracks** in Santiago.

Museum hours can be very erratic in Cuba. Generally, all the documentation about exhibits is in Spanish, but most museums allow language students training as guides to walk around with you. Although museums are free for Cubans, the entrance fee for tourists is usually around US$1 or US$2.

During your visit to Havana, you may wish to visit the venerable Gran Teatro to see a performance of the **Ballet Nacional de Cuba**. There is an almost surreal ambiance to the moment when the lights dim, the orchestra begins to play and the faded red curtains part — created by the creaking majesty of the theatre itself, a glorious Miss Havisham out to trot. Here again, should you need any reminding, is another example of the outstanding talent shown by Cuban performers, especially musicians and dancers (not to mention baseball players). The **Ballet Nacional de Cuba** follows a strong classical tradition, and its founding director, Alicia Alonso (Cuba's answer to Margot Fonteyn), runs a tight ship. It has produced some internationally famous stars, most notably, Carlos Acosta, who now dances with the Houston Ballet in the United States and is being heralded as a young Nureyev or Baryshnikov.

Shop till You Drop

When it comes to shopping, Cuba is best known for its pre-eminently popular export — its famous cigars.

You could always start your exploration by a visit to the **Hotel Melía Cohiba's cigar bar**, a veritable temple to cigar smoking in which you can familiarize yourself with Cuba's many brands.

Cherished by tobacco lovers, the **Cohiba** is a symbol of the Revolution to many Cubans, because they were first made for Fidel Castro by a fellow soldier, (a cigar-maker turned revolutionary) and it remained his favorite cigar until he gave up smoking. Equally famous is the **Montecristo**, which uses the specially graded Ligeuro leaf, followed by the

Lining up for the bus ABOVE is a common sight in Havana. BELOW: Children play in Old Havana.

cigars is the **Casa del Tabaco** at Avenida 5 and Calle 16 in Miramar, where the staff is knowledgeable and helpful and the prices are about right. The shop at the **Partagas Factory**, behind the Capitolio, is also good, as is the **Casa del Tabaco** on Calle Mercaderes, near the Hotel Ambus Mundos.

Cuban **Havana Club rum** is something of a cult for some. A good place to buy rum or Cuba's **Cubita coffee** is the large supermercado at Avenida 3 and Calle 70 in Miramar, although you may find the **Casa del Ron**, at the corner of Calles Obispo and Bernaza, next to El Floridita, is more conveniently located in La Habana Vieja.

It is an ironic fact that you may find a better selection of superior quality recordings by Cuban musicians in New York, London and almost any other major city than in Cuba itself. However, many high-quality recordings of Cuban music produced in Canada and Mexico are available at competitive prices in Cuba. It is hard to go wrong if you buy any of the Cuban greats, ranging from classic recordings of Ernesto Lecuona, Beny Moré (the so-called El Bárbaro del Ritmo), Trio Matamoros, Machito, Issac Oviedo, Celia Cruz, Elena Burke and El Guayabero (master of the *guaracha*) to contemporary balladists Silvio Rodriquez and Pablo Milanes; salsa masters Los Van Van, Issac Delgado, NG La Banda, El Medico de la Salsa and Toto Gomez, or African jazz musicians such as Chucho Valdez and his band Irakere, and newcomers such as Geraldo Alfonso.

The best place to buy music is at the main outlet of **ARTEX**, the Cuban Art Export enterprise, which also has a better choice of CDs and cassettes than most government-run shops in Cuba. It is located at Calles L and 23 in Vedado. The **Casa de la Música** at Calle 20 between Calles 33 and 35, has a good shop, but can run low on its stocks.

The **Palacio de Artesania** on Calle Cuba between Calles Tacón and Cuarteles, in La Habana Vieja is worth a look: its several floors of shops have a

Romeo y Julieta brand, famed for its consistency. **H. Upmann** and **Ramon Allones** are also fine examples, light-flavored and full-flavored respectively. Each brand — but most notably Cohiba, Montecristo and Romeo y Julieta — has a range which varies in size and quality. In 1998, Cuba launched a new brand, **Trinidad**, made at El Laguito — the same factory that makes Cohibas — and the Trinidad Fundador is currently the darling of the cigar-smoking world. Another new brand is named after Cuba's most famous tobacco-producer Alejandro **Robaino**.

The streets of Havana (and Santiago de Cuba) are full of hucksters trying to sell what they claim are boxes of fine cigars smuggled by employees from factories at a tenth of the usual price. Most of what they sell turns out to be a low-grade imitation, but some are not, as workers will sometimes admit. It is not advisable to buy cigars on the street, especially if you expect them to be the real thing. There's a good chance that the Cuban customs authorities will take them away from you at the airport anyway, since they are trying to crack down on fake cigars, which they fear will ruin the reputation of their real ones.

If you shop for cigars at your hotel you can expect to pay inflated prices, although the quality and selection will be good. One of the best non-hotel government-run shops in Havana for wide variety of Cuban-made arts and crafts, but is probably best as a place to buy Cuban music.

Cuba can be a good place to find old and rare books and maps, many of which turn up in street markets, but are most notably to be found at the **Feria de Libros** set up every day in the Plaza de Armas. You can find all sorts of books here, including nineteenth-century architectural surveys of Havana, reproductions of works by Cuban artists, accounts by early travelers, works by the ethnologist Fernando Ortiz and by Natalie Bolivar, the Cuban expert on Santería, as well as political treatises written by Fidel Castro and Che Guevara at the beginning of the Revolution. Some of the street markets sell what are certainly collector's items: comic books printed during the 1960s for schoolchildren to teach them about the Revolution. You can also find old movie posters and other pre-Revolutionary memorabilia at these street markets.

Havana's best bookshops include the **Libraría La Bella Habana** in the Palacio de Segundo Cabo in Plaza de Armas and the **La Moderna Poesía** on Calle Obispo. The **Cuban Writers and Artists Union** (UNEAC) at the corner of Calles 17 and H in Vedado, sells the Union's small edition folios of poetry and other books.

If you are interested in buying contemporary art, start your inquires at the **Fondo de Bienes Culturales**, the government-run artists agency, which runs several galleries around the country. The Fondo's main office is in the Galleria Diago on Plaza Vieja, in La Habana Vieja. The many art galleries along Calle Obispo and in Plaza Catedral may be able to help with introductions to local artists, so that you can visit their studios. It is important to know that if you leave Cuba having purchased original art, you need official authorization to export it. If you have purchased the art in a gallery or hotel, your receipt will include that authorization, but not if you have struck an independent deal with an

OPPOSITE: A woman cooks traditional black bean and rice dish for a family celebration. BELOW: Café scene on Isla de la Juventud.

individual artist. In that case, you'll have to take the art to the Ministry of Culture on the corner of Calles 17 and 12 in Vedado to get the necessary stamped piece of paper, which usually takes several days.

The **Museo de Bellas Artes** and the **Centro Wilfredo Lam** sell art books, catalogues, posters and artistic T-shirts.

Considering what they might be, Cuban T-shirts are quite lack-luster. However, postcards and revolutionary photographs are good purchases. You'll find postcards in hotels and bookshops. Look out for photographic posters and books, particularly those by Alberto Korda, Raúl Corrales and Osvaldo Salas. You'll find a particularly good selection at the La Terraza restaurant in Cojímar, due to the fact that Raul Corrales is a local (reclusive) resident. If all else fails, the airport shop is pretty good.

Dollar-shops and *supermercados* are appearing all over Havana, called "*shopees*" by locals, run by the Panamericanas and the Caracol chains, which accept only dollars and convertible pesos. They are useful for buying food supplies and bottled water.

Festive Flings

Should you need any reminding that you are in Cuba, New Year's Day is celebrated as the **Anniversary of the Triumph of the Revolution**, which is often marked with a speech by Fidel Castro in the Plaza de la Revolución.

It is well worth coinciding your visit to Havana with the capital's annual week-long **International Jazz Festival**, held in mid-February. This is a heady time of year, with many of Cuba's great musicians such as Chucho Valdés and Irakere, Juan Formell and Los Van Van and Silvio Rodríquez performing in venues across the city, notably the Hotel Riviera's Palacio de la Salsa, the Casa de la Cultura in the Plaza de la Revolución area, and the José Echeverria Stadium. You should check with your hotel about how to go about buying tickets at the Casa de Cultura. If you want to be certain of seats for performances, you may be interested in the **pre-arranged tours** offered by the Caribbean Music

OPPOSITE: The striking marble staircase of Havana's venerable Gran Teatro. ABOVE: Trinidad's El Museo Romántico dates from the early 1880s.

CASA DEL TABACO

and Dance Programs ℂ (510) 444-7173
E-MAIL caribmusic@igc.apc.org, 1611
Telegraph Avenue, Suite 808, Oakland,
California 94612, whose all-inclusive
tours cost from US$1,275 to US$1,475.
Alternatively, Wings of the World US
TOLL-FREE (800) 465-8687, 1200 William
Street, Suite 706, Buffalo, New York
14240, offers a week-long all-inclusive
festival tour for US$2,195. Both of these
tours include reserved seating and visits
to jazz workshops, and include round-
trip airfare.

Also in mid-February, Havana gears
up for its annual **Carnival**, which takes
place in La Habana Vieja and along the
Malecón, where a street party
atmosphere takes over, along with
skimpily clad revelers, and outdoor
performances of salsa, folkloric and jazz
groups. The week-long festival
culminates in a parade of floats, with
conga-dancing part of the scene.
Although the Carnival is great fun, it can
get a bit chaotic and claustrophobically
crowded in La Habana Vieja, so take it at
your own pace.

Later in February, the **Havana Book
Fair** takes place, which can be an
interesting cultural event, with

opportunities to meet Cuban writers. For
more information, contact the Cámara
Cubano del Libro, Feria Internacional del
Libro Habana ℂ (53-7) 32-9526 FAX (53-7)
33-8212, Calle 15 No. 604, Vedado,
Havana. Or contact the Center for Cuban
Studies ℂ (212) 242-0559 FAX (212) 242-
1937, 124 West 23rd Street, New York,
New York 10011.

In May, Havana stages its always-
impressive **May Day Parade** on May 1 in
the Plaza de la Revolución, where
thousands of Cubans throng to wave
flags and banners at the annual parade of
the island's military might, along with
school children in their Young Pioneer
uniforms. Fidel Castro traditionally
makes an appearance and a long speech,
along with other Cuban leaders. If you
happen to be in Havana, the event is not
to be missed.

During May, the biannual
International Guitar Festival in Havana
attracts many devotees.

In June, Trinidad's **Fiestas
Sanjuaneras**, held at the end of the
month, is a fun celebration of musical
styles which centers on the Casa de la
Trova, if you happen to visit during this
hot month.

In July, the **Carnival**, now relaunched
as the **Festival del Caribe** runs from
July 22 to 28. Despite the heat, this is
probably the island's most exuberant
and exciting music festival, held in the
birthplace of son music, which features
musicians from Cuba and many other
Caribbean island nations. It is
impossible not to enjoy the street
festivities, or not be swept up in a
rumba or conga line. The center of
action is La Trocha, near the harbor at
the southern end of Jesús Menéndez and
the Avenida 24 de Febrero. Santiago's
Carnival is centuries-old, and was
traditionally timed with the end of the
zafra harvest; however, it is no
coincidence that today it is timed to
culminate on the July 26 public holiday
marking the day when Fidel Castro
stormed the Moncada Barracks under
the cover of Carnival in 1953, honored
throughout the nation as the

Remembrance of the National Rebellion. It was cancelled for several years, but is now part of Cuba's festival scene once more, and includes dance, music and theater performances, as well as art exhibitions. Contact the Caribbean Music and Dance Programs and the Center for Cuban Studies (see above) for more details if you plan to attend.

August has two interesting music festivals: the **Boleros de Oro** in Santiago de Cuba and the **Beny Moré International Festival of Popular Music** in Cienfuegos, notable if you happen to be in either of these cities.

Late August sees the biannual **Havana International Theater Festival**.

Held during the month of September every two years, the **Biennial de la Habana** (Visual Arts Biennial) celebrates work by artists from Cuba and abroad, providing a showcase for local artistic expression since it began in 1984. The most recent biennial included artists from some 50 countries, and also featured 30 North American artists. Exhibitions are staged throughout the capital, including the Centro Wilfredo Lam and the El Morro. The next biennial is the seventh to be held and is set for 1999. Contact the

Centro Wilfredo Lam ((53-7) 61-7008, Calles Oficios and Acosta, La Habana Vieja.

October is a particularly active month: the 10-day **Havana Festival of Contemporary Music,** and the **International Ballet Festival** are held in Havana, and the **Festival de Bailador Rumbero** takes place in Matanzas.

In November, Trinidad stages its **Semana de la Cultura Trinitaria**, which takes place in the town's main cultural centers.

In mid-December, Havana's **International Festival of New Latin American Cinema**, puts the capital on the map, with a flurry of international celebrities often parachuting in to glamorize the event. If you happen to have connections, this is a great time for parties, and if you can stand the lines, this is an excellent chance to see the latest Cuban and Latin American films.

Also in December, if you will be traveling to Remedios in central Villa Clara Province, you might want to ask

La Casa del Tabaco OPPOSITE sells famed cigars, while collectors prize vintage cigar box labels ABOVE.

about a unique festival that takes place here: **Las Parrandas de Remedios**. Apparently, this Carnival-type event which features colorful floats and festivities, was cooked up by the Catholic priests trying to stir up more enthusiasm for Christmas Mass during the town's early colonial era. It has been cancelled for several years during the Special Period, but may well be revived. It is traditionally held on the Saturday before December 26th.

Taking a Tour

Although not for everyone, joining a tour can be one of the best ways to get a first-hand look at as much of the country as possible in a limited time. They can offer extremely good value and may mean the most effective use of your time in Cuba, with one other notable advantage being that you will not have to trouble-shoot any potential travel hitches or problems that might crop up if you are traveling independently. Indeed, there may be minimal obligation to stay with the group once you arrive in Cuba.

Prices for all-inclusive tours, which include your return flights and accommodations, will vary depending on whether you will be arriving during peak season or not, the hotels you choose (or have chosen for you, as can be the case in some package tours) and the range of destinations you wish to visit. It is wise to compare prices and phone around until you are satisfied with what you are being offered, and also to query any hidden or add-on costs. Touring tourists generally enjoy a good level of comfort, and are ferried around in modern, air-conditioned minibuses and coaches.

You will find listed recommendations for conventional tour companies outside Cuba under GETTING THERE, page 298 in TRAVELERS' TIPS. Also look within this section for listed contacts for local tour agencies in Cuba that can arrange guided city day tours, or specific destination tours within the island.

However, if you are keen to depart from the usual sightseeing tours and interested in pursuing more in-depth acquaintance with things Cuban, you may wish to know about the existence of various cultural institutions and agencies that offer specialized tours and courses for foreigners. Bird watching, bicycling, hiking, scuba diving tours are offered, as well as cigar appreciation excursions, study tours, language courses and musical seminars are all possible.

Here is a list of recommended tour companies and organizations outside Cuba you may wish to contact about their wide range of special-interest tours.

IN THE UNITED STATES
The Center for Cuban Studies
((212) 242-0559 FAX (212) 242-1937 E-MAIL cubanctr@igc.apc.org, 124 West 23rd Street, New York, New York 10011, organizes custom-planned trips to Cuba for both groups and individuals that fall within legal exemptions to the United States ban on travel to Cuba, for example professional research, news-gathering and educational study, as well as cultural activities. It is worth checking with them to find out which of their tours might suit you best. They also offer fact-finding tours each month for members of their center, which, including airfares, costs US$800. This is an excellent and well-grounded organization to be in touch with, and they have great contacts in Cuba.

Wings of the World US TOLL-FREE (800) 465-8687, 1200 William Street, Suite 706, Buffalo, New York 14240, has 27 years of experience organizing tours to Cuba from the United States, all of which abide by the United States State Department's legal requirements because the company's tours are "fully hosted and totally prepaid" and technically speaking, participants "neither exchange nor spend money while in Cuba." Well-planned tours include those with a bicycling, hiking, bird-watching, fishing, cigar appreciation, scuba diving, golfing and "cultural adventure" theme.

Arrangements for attending festivals and cultural events can also be made. Prices and length of stay vary, with round-trip flights frequently made from Toronto. This company, which is a corporate member of the New York Explorer's Club and the Chicago Union League Club, often tailors its trips to specific notable events, such as the annual Hemingway International Marlin Tournament, or the recent launch of the new Trinidad brand cigar. If you want to leave on a Friday for a long weekend bass-fishing in Cuba sure of arriving back in your office first thing on Tuesday morning, with all arrangements taken care of, this is the company to call.

Global Exchange ((415) 255-7296 FAX (415) 255-7498 E-MAIL globalexch @ipc.org, 2017 Mission Street, Suite 303, San Francisco, California 94110, offers educational and study tours focusing on Afro-Cuban culture, the arts, as well as the Cuban health care system and environmental issues. It also arranges for individual trips on this basis. Most trips are ten days long and cost US$1,300, including round-trip airfare from Mexico or the Bahamas. This organization started the so-called "Freedom to Travel" campaign, which seeks to bring an end to the restrictions on travel to Cuba by United States citizens.

Cloth dolls OPPOSITE and artwork ABOVE sold at the market in La Habana Vieja.

IN CANADA

The Toronto-based **Cuba Cycling/Hiking Connection** ((416) 922-2232 US TOLL-FREE (800) 268-7229 FAX (416) 922-8410, 21 St. Clair Avenue East, Suite 1003, Toronto, Ontario M4T IL9, runs various tours, ranging in price, destination and length of stay. All-inclusive tours usually start in Havana or Varadero and visit rural parts of Cuba, such as Pinar del Río Province, combining cycling with various cultural activities.

Contact **Quest Nature Tours** ((416) 221-3000 FAX (416) 221-5730, 36 Finch Avenue West, Toronto, Ontario M2N 2G9, for the latest information about their eco-tour trips to Cuba.

IN THE UNITED KINGDOM

Hazel Pennington Bike Tours ((44-122) 548-0130 FAX (44-122) 548-0132, PO Box 75, Bath, Avon BA1 1BX, offers 14-day bicycle tours every March, November and December, (£1,070 including round-trip fare from Stansted airport) and includes Havana, Pinar del Río, Trinidad and the Sierra del Escambray.

Special Places ((44-189) 266-1157 FAX (44-189) 266-5670 E-MAIL specialplaces @cricketer.com, Brock Travel Ltd., 4 The White House, Beacon Road, Crowborough, East Sussex TN6 1AB, offers a one-week cigar tour, among its other tour packages to Cuba. The aim of this tour is to give participants detailed knowledge of how cigars are produced from the seed to the factory, combined with a scenic sightseeing tour of Havana and the mountain region of Pinar del Río, where Cuba's finest cigars are produced. The Cuban tobacco season is from mid-September to the end of March and the tours run from January to March, which is the best period to see all the main processes of cigar production.

Progressive Tours ((44-171) 262-1676 FAX (44-171) 724-6941, 12 Porchester Place, Marble Arch, London W2 2BS, offers intensive 14-day study tours designed to meet Cuban people and learn about their unique society with factory, hospital, farm, university and school visits; and language courses in Santiago de Cuba and Baracoa.

IN CUBA

Mercadu SA ((53-7) 33-3893 FAX (53-7) 333028, Calle 13 N°. 951 at the corner of Avenida 8, Vedado, Havana, can arrange for study or work experience at Cuba's main universities and research institutes in the fields of agriculture, languages, science, education, technology and sports. Probably the most popular courses organized by Mercadu are intensive Spanish courses at the University of Havana, which can last from two weeks to four months, with various levels of participation and costs.

The **Centro Nacional de Conservación, Restauración y Museología** ((53-7) 61-5043, Calle Cuba No. 610, Havana, is a specialized government organization run under the auspices of Havana's city historian, Eusebio Leal, which offers courses in the architectural restoration, with the possibility of on-site work experience in La Habana Vieja.

The **Promotor Cultural at the Casa del Caribe** ((53-226) 4-2285 FAX (53-226) 4-2387, Calle 13 N°. 154, Vista Alegre, Santiago de Cuba, This organization organizes the Caribbean Culture Festival, and during the rest of the year runs courses and workshops on Cuban music and dance which last from two weeks to two months.

A dancer in traditional costume pauses during a performance on Isla de la Juventud.

Welcome
to
Cuba

EVOCATIVE AND LUSH, Cuba is a subtle country that nonetheless likes to live up to its larger-than-life reputation. It still has the white-sanded beaches and palm-trees of Caribbean postcards; exotic hotels and bars where film-stars, along with the Mafiosi, swanned around in the 1950s; and the magnificent colonial fortresses and timeworn architecture left over from the time when it was gateway to the Spanish Main. It remains the legendary place where a people's revolution was buoyed up by rum, cigars and salsa. But Cuba is much more.

Lying off the coast of Florida, wedged between the Atlantic, the Gulf of Mexico and the Caribbean, the so-called "Pearl of the Antilles" has played host to many cultures: the indigenous Siboney and Taíno Indians, Spanish colonists and African slaves. Christopher Columbus described it as "the most beautiful land that human eyes have ever seen." Things have changed somewhat since then of course, and aficionados of paradisiacal islands may not immediately think of Cuba. Yet, although you may not decide to visit Cuba for its exotic, tropical landscapes alone, expect some pleasant, if not spectacular, surprises. In fact, because it has been slow to develop tourism, Cuba is a rare find for delightful off-the-beaten-track places and experiences, even for the jaded or adventurous.

Don't expect many similarities to other Caribbean islands aside from the balmy climate and tropical flora: no Jimmy Buffet, legions of Spring Breakers, or packaged margaritas here. It does not have a series of look-alike hotels, restaurants and shops dispensing practiced, efficient service. While it is often less polished, it is never as dull, with a quirky kind of charm.

Often, the rule is simple: get out of your hotel, rent a car and explore; if you can, meet Cubans and enter their world. You know you've arrived if you find yourself addressed as "*Chino*" or "Chinese," an affectionate term between friends.

Cubans themselves are your best guide to their own vibrant and passionate culture. Who else, for example, would you choose to teach you how to dance? For Cuba pulses to the music of salsa, son, rumba, mambo, chachachá, all of which originated here, and is, as Gabriel García Márquez, one of Cuba's most famous part-time expatriates puts it, "the most dance-oriented society on earth."

When the revolution of Fidel Castro and Che Guevara became superimposed on the sultry glamorous style of 1950s Havana, it was going to be a strange and compelling mixture. This was the canvas for the novels of Ernest Hemingway and Graham Greene; then, after decades of the United States embargo, it became known to cinema-goers as the backdrop for such successful cinematic exports as *Fresa y Chocolate* (Strawberry and Chocolate) and *Guantánamera* by the late Cuban director Tomás Gutiérrez Alea, both bittersweet comedies which exactly convey love, tenderness and acid humor — Cuban style. Indeed, at times you might feel you have to pinch yourself to make sure that you are not an extra in a giant open-air film set, with the last adjustments being made to the script after some four decades of directions by that well-known first-time author-director, Fidel Castro.

You are bound to encounter something of the strange mixture of ideologies and circumstances that have shaped the island. As one visitor joked, half-in-jest: "Cuba is like a 1950s Cadillac — held together by American design, Russian bits and pieces, and Cuban imagination."

As you may be about to find during your travels, the term "magic realism" seems to have been coined just for this fascinating country, where as an outsider, trying to understand the real Cuba can feel like an excursion into the unexpected and improbable, a Spanish-speaking version of *Alice in Wonderland*.

Connoisseurs of the ironic, Cubans love bantering jokes, ripostes and a version of anecdotal word-play they call "double-morals." In the world of double-morals, nothing is quite as it seems, and every statement or remark can conceal at least one other meaning. Once you have taken this in your stride, you can enjoy the way Cubans have made flirting with contradictions and ambiguities part of their national character, along with a uniquely spirited humor that so often triumphs over adversity, and a

knowing attitude to sex, which many Cubans joke is the national pastime. After all, in a country where the national slogan is "*Socialismo o Muerte*" ("Socialism or Death"), it could be argued that survival would be impossible without a sense of the absurd, or at the very least, a talent for living in the moment. Like the music and the dancing, these semi-secret jokes make the daily weight of life much easier to bear.

Arrive expecting appointments to be met, especially business meetings, but be prepared for the unexpected. After all, this is

where although "*ahorita*" means "any minute," in practice it can mean five minutes or five hours. Equally, as you may find, there is always something faintly unpredictable about even the most carefully laid plans in Cuba. Sometimes what can follow is better than what you planned. Perhaps it's all about a certain outlook, expressed in the quintessential Cuban expression "*No hay mal que por bien no venga*," which roughly translates as "good can come from even the worst experiences." Cuban people are remarkable for their incredible exuberance for life, and their gusto for life is catching.

All in all, like trying to get around in Havana in one of its aged, but lovingly preserved chariots of chrome from Detroit, Cuba is unique, fun and worth any minor inconveniences.

PREVIOUS PAGES: Musicians play at El Morro, Santiago de Cuba LEFT and costumed women in Old Havana RIGHT. OPPOSITE: Colorful naïve painting. ABOVE: Musician from the Orquesta Siglo XX performing at La Casa de la Obrapía.

The Country and Its People

SINCE THE EARLY 1990S, Cubans have liked to joke that they live in the "Land of Miracles," a sarcastic popular term to describe the paradox of living in a communist country at a time when the rest of world had all but decided that Marxism was outdated. Since then, Cuba has existed in what is officially termed the "Special Period in the Time of Peace," a continuing regimen of economic hardship and cut-backs that followed the collapse of the Soviet Union. Still suffering from the United States embargo, the sudden deprivation of Moscow's subsidies

created desperate shortages of everything: medicine, food, water, housing, transportation and electricity. Endless jokes ensued about the "miracles" that ordinary Cubans have had to perform in order, say, to arrive at work on time during the transportation crisis ("the authorities are testing to see how many Cubans can fit on a bus," quip the people of Havana) or to put a decent meal on the table during the cut-back in rations.

When Pope John Paul II visited the island in January 1998, Cubans joked that the pontiff's motivation was, first, to visit hell; second, to see a people making a living out of miracles; and third, to meet with the very devil.

These days, Cubans remain a resolutely entrepreneurial people, although not in ways you might expect. *Resolver* (which roughly translates as "to fix a problem by any means available") is the probably the most commonly used verb in Cuba, where for many, the difficulties of merely getting by involve all manner of daily struggles.

A girl's disco finery might be discarded for her usual costume of ragged shorts and T-shirt the next day; car engines revived with the help of a shoelace; cigarette lighters filled with fly spray; house paint concocted from quicklime mixed with kerosene; black-market beef bartered for rusty spare parts and matches swapped for cigarettes because of the frequent *apagones* or power outages.

Throughout the island, shops and cafés with empty shelves are a common sight, especially in the provincial towns; yet the assistants keep working, explaining in answer to each request how they don't have this, and they don't have that, until finally the customer might ask, in exasperation, "Well, what do you have?"

"*Nada, ahora,*" ("Nothing today") is often the answer.

When asked how they are, most Cubans no matter what their profession, shrug and smile, and say, in what has become a catchphrase: "Inventing and struggling, so what's new?"

Yet no matter where you go, you are bound to encounter those qualities that are also so distinctly Cuban: an outgoing, welcoming attitude to foreigners and a sense of solidarity and community that has all but been lost in other societies, which some see as a touching by-product of the economic situation. In the words of Pico Iyer, author of the novel *Cuba and the Night*: "It's everyone against the system. It's: I'll give you a chicken and your brother can fix my TV. An ironist can have a field day in Cuba."

As a visitor, perhaps on your first trip, much of this might not even be especially apparent. It is possible to see Cuba through a well-protected bubble if you are staying

PREVIOUS PAGES: Passengers prepare for departure LEFT in Santiago Province. RIGHT: A rest in the shade in Trinidad. ABOVE: Magnificent but decaying houses dot Old Havana. OPPOSITE: Portraits of Che are everywhere, from T-shirts to mosaics.

in one of the more luxurious hotels and are whisked by tour bus from one sightseeing jag to another. Increasingly, the Cuba that many visitors see is another emerging Cuba, one that is flush with new joint-venture businesses and foreign investments from Canada, Europe and Latin America. This new Cuba has a raft of gleaming new hotels, expensive-looking restaurants and country clubs which cater to influential Cubans and the foreign business community alike. Is this a preparation for the political change that would put an end to the United States embargo, which so many in Cuba blame for all their problems? Perhaps. Or it may be possible to regard this new Cuba as experimental one which is trying to keep alive the most important values of the socialist system using the capitalist system.

Under the helm of Fidel Castro, Cuba is proving a canny self-marketer. After all, this is the country which exported radical chic to a generation of urban youth around the world. Its cigars are international symbols of costly fat-cat glamour, and it sells its tourists vast quantities of Che Guevara memorabilia. However, it did not approve when a United Kingdom company marketed its beer with Che's image and the slogan: "Banned In The USA. It Must Be Good." In a telling twist, the product *was* banned soon after it went on sale, not by the United States, but by Cuba, which had received complaints from Guevara's widow, Aleida.

Along the familiar tourist routes, with Cuban bands playing irresistible salsa music, amid some of the most glorious and historic settings in the Caribbean, it is easy to sink into a blissful appreciation of the moment. And why shouldn't you?

Yet it is always interesting to probe beneath the façade a little, and to contemplate how this Cuba has come to be the way it is today.

EARLY CUBA

The human story in Cuba begins almost two thousand years ago, when tribes from Central or South America began arriving on the island. The Siboney settled first, sheltering in caves and subsisting on fishing. They were followed by the Taíno, (pronounced TIE-no) a tribe of Arawak Indians, who soon dominated the less aggressive Siboney, and whose agrarian lifestyle, which included making pots and figurines from clay, represented the peak of pre-Columbian culture in Cuba.

Christopher Columbus landed near what is now Baracoa at the eastern tip of Cuba, on October 27, 1492, on his first voyage to the New World. Convinced he had reached a great Asian continent, he sent his men off into the mountains in search of a great cities and a king, but instead they came back with reports of communities of near-naked Indians living in thatched huts. Spain did not immediately jump at the opportunity to colonize Cuba. However, Spanish occupation began in earnest in 1511, with the arrival of conquistador Diego Velásquez and 300 men near Guantánamo Bay in southeast Cuba. Subjugation of the native Indian population was a fairly swift and brutal affair. Only one Taíno chief was able to briefly inspire any resistance amongst his people: Hatuey, who had come to Cuba after fleeing the Spanish in his homeland of Hispaniola, (now Haiti and the Dominican Republic). When Hatuey (after whom the nation's premier brand of beer is named) was finally captured, he preferred to be burnt at the stake than to be forced to convert to the Christianity of his captors. Within little more than a generation, the Taíno appear to have disappeared, leaving behind no written language or monumental structures. Today, only fleeting shadows of past ancestors live on the features of some Cubans, mostly from the Baracoa region.

In July 1998, Canadian archaeologist Dr. David M. Prendergast and a team of Cuban specialists discovered the first nearly complete piece of Taíno architecture — a community building of wood and thatch, as well as what may be as many as 25 preserved houses, which stood on Cuba's northern coast, in Punta Alegre, Ciego de Ávila Province, some 500 to 700 years ago. Archaeologists are now sifting through evidence that small communities of Taíno may have been able to survive along this isolated coast unnoticed long after the Spaniards arrived, perhaps until the early seventeenth century.

SPANISH COLONIZATION

As patriarch of colonial Cuba, Velázquez set about founding seven *villas*, or fortified settlements, in Baracoa, Santiago, Bayamo, Puerto Príncipe (now Camagüey), Trinidad, Sancti Spíritus, and Villa de San Cristóbal de La Habana, later known simply as La Habana. Cuba's value to the Spanish was its position at the mouth of the Gulf of Mexico and its formidable network of fortresses which enabled crucial protection for

system, in which each Spanish landowner was allotted between 40 to 200 indigenous Indians as forced laborers, who became *peones* or serfs. This unforgiving regime of feudal slavery ultimately destroyed the indigenous Indians, either through overwork, starvation, disease, or suicide. The Spanish *conquistadores* were soon on the look-out for a new workforce for their tobacco and sugar plantations, and began importing thousands of African slaves. Slavery in Cuba was as brutal as anywhere, and most slaves were worked as much as

Spanish ships from the constant threat of attack by pirates and foreign fleets, as they ferried riches from Central and South America back to Spain. Havana grew steadily in importance and soon became the jewel in the Cuban crown, becoming the capital in 1589. Along with Mexico City and Lima, Havana became one of the most extravagantly imposing cities outside Europe, its militaristic fortresses beautified by elaborate stone pediments and cornices, with the wealthiest of the merchant and ruling classes living in magnificent town palaces or *palacios* that still captivate the visitor today. Yet outside Havana, development elsewhere in Cuba was sporadic. The early colonizers had adopted the *encomienda*

19 hours a day, each day of the week, with as many as 10 percent dying each year, literally like flies. Those who managed to escape, known as *cimarrones*, formed surreptitious communities called *palenques* deep in the island's mountainous forests.

Yet Cuba's fortunes remained relatively modest until the mid-eighteenth century, when the British attacked and won Havana, marking a turning point in the island's history. The British occupation began in 1762 and lasted for almost a year, ending when they consented to return the city to Spain in exchange for Florida. By opening up trade restrictions which had banned the

An unusual food stand in Santiago de Cuba's central Market.

island from trading with any other country other than Spain, the British had effectively launched Cuba's export trade, an achievement which was soon to prove enormously important for Cuba, albeit effected during such a relatively short stay. When the Spanish took Cuba back, they immediately set about making sure that their fortresses would be impregnable for any future attacks, (which would remain the case until the Spanish-American conflict took the history of Cuba into an entirely new era). Another unexpected boost to the island's econ-

omy occurred with the slave revolution in the French-ruled half of Hispaniola (now Haiti), and Cuba soon took its place as the largest and most profitable sugar producer in the Caribbean, vying with British-occupied Jamaica for the profitable sugar market in the newly independent United States.

The sugar boom soon swallowed up almost all the island's hardwood forests, and Cuba prospered, exporting almost all of its sugar to the United States. Shackled slaves, on the other hand, were worked harder than ever. By the mid-nineteenth century, slaves made up almost half the population. Despite the abolition of slavery in most other Caribbean islands by 1848, slavery continued unabated in the Spanish colo-

nies, largely due to an almost obsessive fear by the Spanish elite that history — in the form of the slave revolt in Haiti — would repeat itself in Cuba. Meanwhile, social unease was growing. Despite a shared fear of the oppressed and mutinous African slaves, the island's *criolles* (Creoles) — Cubans of Spanish descent — were increasingly resenting playing second fiddle to the so-called *peninsulares* — the island's designated aristocratic elite, who were born in Spain. Long after the independence of Spain's former South American republics and Mexico, anti-colonial unrest in Cuba finally crystallized into action. Calling for independence from Spain and the abolition of slavery, the *criolles* rebelled in 1868, led by Carlos Manuel de Céspedes, who launched the first war of independence by freeing his own slaves. The so-called Ten Year's War took the lives of more than 250,000 Cubans, including Céspedes, and saw the rise of two other early revolutionary heroes, Antonio Maceo, a rebellious mulatto known as the "Titan of Bronze," and Máximo Gómez, a defector from the Spanish army, whose forces were made up of disenchanted peasants and former slaves.

INDEPENDENCE: AT A PRICE

Although brutally crushed by the Spanish, the resistance by the rebel army contributed to the abolition of slavery in Cuba in 1886. It took the unlikely figure of José Martí, a short, soulful man with a droopy moustache, to galvanize the next insurrection. Martí, a revolutionary and poet who lived an exile's existence in Spain and New York before dying a martyr's death in Cuba, is regarded as the George Washington of Cuba, and his statue can be seen in every town square and school. He passionately defended Cuba's right to self-rule, democracy, social justice and, importantly for Cuba, racial equality. Enlisting Maceo and Gómez, Martí unified the island under the banner of his Partido Revolucionario Cubano (PRC), and by 1897, forced the Spanish authorities to concede autonomy.

With the Cubans on the brink of victory, the United States intervened. The island, although governed by an increasingly weakened Spain, was by now tied economically to the United States, which was reluctant to forfeit such an advantageous relationship for the sake of an independent Cuba. Relations between the United States and Spain become increasingly strained, and the United States declared war after the USS *Maine* was blown up in Havana harbor in February 1898, although no evidence was ever found linking the Spanish to the downed battleship. Within months, the colonial army surrendered to the American occupying force, preceded by Theodore Roosevelt's famous charge against Spanish troops at San Juan Hill in Santiago, which eventually propelled him into the White House. Washington contemplated annexation but finally decided to concede Cubans the right to elect their own government. On May 20, 1902, Cuba was declared a republic, and American troops withdrew. However it was freedom with a yoke: the United States had exacted acceptance of the Platt Amendment to the Cuban constitution, which gave Washington the right to intervene at any time "for the preservation of Cuban independence." It also provided for the establishment of an American naval base at Guantánamo Bay.

Cubans found, to their dismay, that one colonial master now replaced the other. Cuban history books frequently refer to the five decades that followed the island's independence as the "pseudo-Republic." American monopolies swiftly took control over almost every economic activity on the island, turned Cuba into a giant tobacco, sugar, and citrus fruit factory, and forced islanders to import almost everything (apart from sugar and cigars) from the United States. Amid public outrage at the widely known corruption within the Cuban government, General Gerardo Machado won the elections in 1924 with the slogan "Honesty in Government." Soon, however, Machado was giving Cubans their first taste of a military dictatorship. In 1933, a rebellion by Havana University students and army sergeants led to General Fulgencio Batista taking power. Meanwhile, the United States, although they distrusted the student rebellion, saw Batista as a military man on whom it could depend. He stepped down in 1944,

but seized power again in 1952, holding onto it with a grip that was to prove both ruthless and brutal. He abolished the Constitution, dissolved Congress and crushed his opponents, unleashing an orgy of police violence that killed estimated thousands.

During the 1950s, Havana was the belle of the Caribbean ball, (presenting a beautiful face while still concealing dark secrets), and attracted legions of America's rich and famous, along with Hollywood celebrities like Marilyn Monroe and Frank Sinatra, not to mention its infamous Mafia. Between

them, Batista and the mob (led by the Jewish mob chief, Meyer Lanksy) controlled tourism, and they built many of the city's high-rise hotels, including the Hilton (now the Habana Libre), the Riviera, and the Capri, and the city thrilled to casinos, extravagant cabarets, salsa bands and glamorous showgirls. In the meantime many Cubans prospered: Havana's affluent suburbs of Vedado and Miramar glittered with grand mansions, where the elegant, cultured, and largely contented bourgeoisie threw soirées, wore the latest European fashions, and enjoyed the city's lively in-

OPPOSITE: Castro has delivered many speeches under the statue of Martí on the Plaza de la Revolución.
ABOVE: A crumbling rampart in Havana.

tellectual and cultural life, which attracted glamorous and worldly-wise expatriates, many of them American, and refugees from Franco's Spain; a pattern echoed in many of the island's provincial towns. Yet underneath it all, rural poverty was widespread, unemployment was around 50 percent, many Cubans were illiterate and malnourished, and prostitution was rife.

This was the Havana that piqued the fancy of Graham Greene and Ernest Hemingway, captivated the visiting Anais Nin, and for many now-aging exiled Cubans, is the beloved island they struggle to recall, splintered into fragments of memory. For Cubans was soon to become divided into two camps, and not only by the Florida straits — into *los gusanos* (the "worms") who would leave the island, and *los comunistas*, who would stay behind.

REBELS IN THE MOUNTAINS

A clean-shaven, 26-year-old lawyer named Fidel Castro began the road to Cuba's Revolution when, on July 26, 1953, he and 125 other militants attacked the Moncada barracks in Santiago de Cuba. Although the assault was a disastrous failure, resulting in the death of most involved, its daring captured the imagination of the island, as did Castro's speech during trial proceedings against him. That speech, known as the "History Will Absolve Me" speech, formed the basis for Cuba's new revolutionary movement, the *Movimiento 26 de Julio*, named for a series of coincidences involving the number 26, and devoted to the ousting of Batista. By another series of coincidences, Castro was released from prison after just 20 months (instead of the 15 years he had been sentenced). Castro left for Mexico City, where he gathered around him a group of idealistic revolutionaries, one of whom was the Argentinean doctor, Ernesto "Che" Guevara.

In October 1956, Fidel, Che and 80 other rebels (including Fidel's brother Raúl) crossed from Mexico to Cuba in the leaking six-berth cabin cruiser, *Granma*, only just managing to avoid disaster. "It wasn't a disembarkation, it was a shipwreck," recounted Guevara of the landing, which took place in the eastern province now named Granma. Having lost all their equipment, the rebels soon lost many of their men: within a month they were ambushed by Batista's men, and only about 15 of the rebels (including Fidel, Raúl and Che) managed to hide out near Pico Turquino in the Sierra Maestra mountains, west of Santiago. Here the men adopted guerilla tactics, picking off soldiers at military outposts and broadcasting exhortations for a general strike from their makeshift radio station, *Radio Rebelde*. Within months, Castro's promises of agrarian reform had won over the landless farmers and laborers whose collaboration would be vital to his cause, and the insurgency began in earnest, supported by agitation in the cities by the underground M-26 movement. When Batista sent 10,000 soldiers into the Sierra Maestra to defeat the rebel army in 1958, many soldiers defected to the guerilla movement and, as Castro's army moved westwards, refused to fight. On January 1, 1959, as Castro's rebel army approached Havana, Batista fled to the Dominican Republic. Within a week, the 31-year-old leader, by now sporting his trademark beard and smoking Cohiba cigars, was greeted by thousands of jubilant Cubans as he traveled across the island from Santiago to a triumphant reception in the capital.

Around the world, but of course, especially in Cuba, the bearded, fatigue-wearing revolutionaries became folk icons overnight. However, despite the euphoria, many Cubans were apprehensive about what changes Fidel Castro had in store. Many of the island's wealthy bourgeoisie had misgivings about the rather militant zealousness of this as-yet untested revolutionary movement. Large numbers left the island, especially those who had profited from the Batista regime, while revolutionary tribunals were set up to track down and punish (and frequently execute) those whose collaboration was alleged to have resulted in the persecution of Batista's victims.

Under Castro, the so-called Integrated Revolutionary Organization (re-named the Cuban Communist Party in 1965) assumed control of the country, and instituted

Travel is slow on this remote dirt road between Baracoa and Moa.

widespread political, educational and agricultural reforms. A huge literacy campaign was organized, and eager revolutionary volunteers left the cities to live and work in the country. Within a year, the government had acquired more than 40 percent of Cuba's formerly foreign-owned farmland, dividing most of it up into state farms, and soon further nationalized foreign banks and other businesses.

INTERNATIONAL CONFLICT

For the United States, who had been increasingly alarmed at developments in Cuba, the wholesale nationalization of all American enterprises on the island — whose in-terests amounted to around US$1 billion — was an invitation to a showdown. In April 1961, anti-Castro Cuban exiles backed by the United States government attempted an invasion of Cuba at Playa Girón — forever after known as the Bay of Pigs — and were promptly routed by Castro's forces, led by *El Jefe Máximo* (the "Maximum Leader") himself. The United States, who had already imposed a partial embargo on trade with Cuba since 1960, retaliated by extending the embargo in March 1962 to include all goods. Thus began the United States trade embargo, which has remained in place ever since.

In what became another turning point in Cuba's history, Castro declared the socialist nature of the Revolution in mid-1961, just at the time of the Bay of Pigs invasion. He was to proclaim "I am a Marxist-Leninist, and I shall be to the day I die." Given that Cuba was by now facing complete isolation from the United States, the question of whether Castro was merely pragmatically paving the way for closer economic ties with Moscow has long been a matter of speculation.

In February 1960, the Soviet Union agreed to an oil-for-sugar arrangement

that helped to bolster the Cuban economy through to the late 1980s. Trade with other socialist countries also became a priority. In October 1962, the Soviet Union had begun to move nuclear missiles to the island, shifting the balance of power between the two super-powers. President Kennedy sent a United States naval fleet out towards Cuba, and threatened war unless they were removed. In what was one of the most harrowing moments of the Cold War, six days of stalemate during the so-called Cuban Missile Crisis brought the two nations to the brink of nuclear war. Without consulting Castro, President Kennedy and Premier Krushchev came to an agreement: the missiles would be withdrawn if the United States pledged not to invade Cuba. Declaring, "We will build a wall around Cuba," President Kennedy further tightened the trade embargo. This prompted another wave of some half a million Cubans into the United States; mostly urban, white and middle class, and many of whom settled in Miami.

BUILDING THE REVOLUTION

The 1960s were a decade of major social and political restructuring in Cuba. Che Guevara was put in charge of the centralization of the country's economy, becoming Minister of Industry. *Comités de Defensa de la Revolución* ("Committees for the Defense of the Revolution") or CDR's, were deployed in every neighborhood, to monitor every aspect of Cuban life, and those who were not obviously enthusiastic about the Revolution often faced harassment or imprisonment, as did homosexuals, dissident intellectuals, and Catholics. The regime mobilized hundreds of thousands of Cubans, so-called "volunteer workers," to increase its agricultural production, while "microbrigades" were set up to provide housing for the rapidly growing population.

In Cuba, the oft-heard phrase, "Triumph of the Revolution" is generally used to reference three things: education, medical care, and relatively equal distribution of wealth. It is indeed one of Cuba's sources of pride that sufficient food, health care, and education was made available to all, particularly when compared to pre-Castro days or to the rest of Latin America. However, "moral incentives" for collective advancement were not enough to keep the Cuban economy from suffering a series of economic woes. Rationing was introduced in 1962, while Guevara resigned in 1965, going off to fight a series of guerilla wars before he was assassinated in Bolivia two years later.

By 1975, Castro's regime staged the country's First Communist Party Congress, launching a new centralized system of national and local government, called *Poder Popular*, or People's Power. The new constitution espoused Marxism-Leninism as the state's ideology, and recognized the Communist Party as the only legitimate political organization in Cuba. The early 1970s are remembered as tough and repressive years, with restrictions on personal freedoms such as choice of work and travel. Many so-called "social deviants" were jailed. By the end of the decade, the economy had begun to improve. However, 1980 marked the most significant period of widespread dissatisfaction with Castro's government since 1959, an exodus in which 125,000 Cubans left for Miami with the Mariel boatlift. (Unbeknownst to United States immigration officials, with a timely opening of his country's prisons and asylums Castro ensured that large numbers of these new immigrants were criminals and lunatics.)

In an effort to rapidly improve living conditions and morale in Cuba, Castro initiated a series of changes, allowing private agricultural markets, so-called "farmer's markets," at which farmers could sell any surplus produce beyond the quota allotted to the state. However these reforms were so successful, prompting many Cubans to abandon their state jobs to prospect in this new, albeit-limited free market, that Castro dissolved this reform, announcing a "Rectification of Errors" program that reverted back to strict centralization under Party supervision.

During the 1980s, with President Reagan in the White House, American foreign policy within the region took a more hawkish stance against burgeoning socialist liberation movements in Grenada and Nicaragua, and stepped up its covert activities, many of them now notorious. Castro himself was the target of many assassination attempts, as he wryly commented, "It's not my fault that I haven't died yet; it's not my fault that the CIA has failed to kill me!" Meanwhile, the island was sending its soldiers into the conflict in Angola — an involvement some refer to as "Cuba's Vietnam" — where Castro supported the Marxist government against rebels backed by the United States and South Africa. Some 370,000 soldiers went into action, and during the 15-year-long war, which ultimately ended with an negotiated accord in 1988, the number of those who died is debated as being anything from Cuba's official figure of 2,077 to at least five times that number. Meanwhile, since the mid-1980s, President Gorbachev in the Soviet Union had been spearheading widespread reform, a reform that Castro pronounced himself as firmly against. *Perestroika*, he said, would never be allowed to bring down Cuban socialism.

However, the status quo in Cuba was shattered by the collapse of the Soviet Union. Over the years, Cuba had received over US$1 billion in aid, and it had largely survived, if not thrived, on its long-standing deal with Moscow in which sugar was bartered for oil. Confronted with its most serious economic crisis ever, the Castro government implemented the "Special Period" in 1990, a severe austerity package that has drastically affected the lives of most Cubans. The already-depleted ration system was cut back, while queues multiplied; *apagones*, or power cuts, became ever-more frequent; the lack of fuel has meant that public transportation has become virtually impossible,

with many rural Cubans reverting to medieval methods of transportation and farming, replacing their machines with horses and oxen. Although education and medical care is free, even basic supplies are lacking.

In 1992, the United States tightened its embargo with the introduction of the Torricelli Bill, which extended the embargo to foreign subsidiaries of American companies, including those shipping food and medicine to Cuba. In August 1994, widespread discontent and despair drove an estimated 30,000 Cubans to attempt to leave the island

OPPOSITE: Castro's famous slogan "Socialism or Death" neighbors an ad for a fast-food restaurant. ABOVE: Fidel Castro in the Sierra Maestra, 1959.

illegally, flinging themselves into the Gulf Stream off Cuba's northern coast on inner tubes and makeshift rafts, the largest exodus of refugees since the Mariel boatlift in 1980. Many who attempted this desperate measure did not make it to Florida's shores alive, and just as many were moved back to Cuba to be held in camps at the Guantánamo naval base while their request for asylum was processed.

CUBA TODAY

By now, the Cuban leadership had begun to realize that restricted liberalization of its policies was probably inevitable. "To return to capitalism would be a step backward in history," Castro had warned his people in 1991. However, saying later that the move was "unavoidable to save the Revolution," he has since taken a couple of tentative steps in that direction. In August 1993, to quash rampant black marketeering, Castro decriminalized the possession of foreign currency and accepted the United States dollar as a de facto national currency, circulated alongside the Cuban peso (referred to as "dollarization"); legalized small private enterprises, such as *paladares* or private restaurants; and reinstated farmer's markets, thus allowing work independent of the state and creating a small class of self-employed Cubans.

Another major reform was the promotion of tourism, which as an industry is barely a decade old in Cuba. Now, with an estimate of more than a million tourists visiting Cuba a year, tourism has sparked a parallel economy, where Cubans with access to dollars can buy supplies and consumer goods at hard-currency shops. Many trained professionals, including doctors and university professors, have opted to work in tourist hotels and restaurants where they can earn considerably more with dollar tips than they would on their monthly peso wage, which ranges between 200 and 700 pesos (US$9 and US$32). The average wage has fallen to about US$13 a month. Most Cubans immediately convert their salary to American dollars because it is impossible to buy anything in pesos: the scanty food rations provided by the government usually run out

about mid-month.

One depressing result of the economic situation is that young prostitutes are now pervasive in Havana streets and bars, and bag-snatching has become more common.

Yet while Havana suffered, the gap between the capital and rural provinces grew ever wider, sparking a wave of migrants from the countryside (referred to in Cuban slang as "*palestinos*" or "Palestinians," alluding to their homelessness).

Cuba continues to protest the decades-long United States embargo, which on the

island tends to be regarded as the source of all woes. In 1997, despite wide opposition by United States trading partners in both Europe and the Western Hemisphere, the United States Congress passed the Helms-Burton Act, which discourages foreign investment in Cuba and allows Americans to sue foreign companies using property in Cuba that had been confiscated from Americans after 1959. The Act was passed after Cuban jets shot down two planes operated by a Miami-based Cuban exile group, killing four people. America's allies claim the Helms-Burton Act is merely about putting the squeeze on Castro, and have objected to its extra-territorial nature at the United Nations and the European Court. Despite this, and despite the fact that the continued hardship being faced by the Cuban people is hard to ignore, some observers have been cautiously commenting that the dollar-powered influx of foreign companies and tourism is bringing about a new optimism in Cuba.

With the historic visit by Pope John Paul II in January 1998, Cuba — or rather the Castro regime — was seen by the world as taking a more conciliatory stance towards the need for change. In this instance, Castro lifted restrictions on the Catholic Church and allowed Christmas to be celebrated in 1997

have a profound impact on the standard of living of many Cubans, although at the moment the demand for help is much greater than the supply.

Certainly, there is avid speculation about what the future holds for Cuba's estimated 11 million people. After four decades in power, Castro formally selected his brother Raúl as his eventual successor. Raúl Castro has been playing a more prominent role in the running of the Cuban government and the Communist Party. Another strong figure in Cuban politics is Ricardo Alarcón, Pres-

for the first time since 1969. While in Cuba, the Pope called upon Cuba to open up to the world, and reiterated the international opposition to the United States embargo.

In the wake of the Pope's 1998 visit the Clinton administration moved to ease the embargo, announcing humanitarian initiatives to help Cuba become less dependent on the communist government, and to ease Havana's isolation. These measures included resuming direct charter fights to the island, which had been cancelled in 1996; allowing Cuban-Americans to send US$1,200 a year to relatives in Cuba, which had been banned in 1994; and relaxing restrictions on the sale of medicine and medical supplies to the island. These measures are likely to

ident of the Cuban National Assembly of People's Power, whose articulate and moderating influence may offer Cuba its very own bridge to the twenty-first century.

As far as the Helms-Burton Act is concerned, its precise wording specifically states that the United States embargo will only be rescinded when "a transition government in Cuba is in power," one that "does not include Fidel or Raúl Castro." That may be so. However, although the economic embargo remains in place, on January 5, 1999, the United States government announced its plans to relax certain restrictions for humani-

OPPOSITE: "Committee for The Defense of The Revolution." ABOVE: Approved reading in Old Havana.

tarian reasons, namely to expand direct charter flights to Cuba to help facilitate family reunions; to re-establish a direct mail service with Cuba and to increase educational, cultural, journalistic, athletic, and religious exchanges between the two countries. These days, Castro is a gaunt and graying figure, yet he still commands respect and fascination on the world stage, despite his faults. Meanwhile, it appears that whatever Cuba's next big gamble with its future might be, it is waiting in the wings.

PASSIONS OF A PASSIONATE ISLAND

Cuba has a culture like no other. The mixture of Spanish and African religious and artistic traditions — Roman Catholicism and Yoruba religious ritual — has created an exotic people whose genes reflect history's conspiracy to blend together Spanish, African, French and even Chinese cultures — Spanish and Indian *mestizos*, Spanish and African *mulattos* and African *zambos* — producing a culture that is passionate, mystical, literate, sensual, and often self-ironic.

CUBA'S REAL RELIGION

Although Cuba has millions of baptized Catholics, the island's most popular religion originated from Africa. Known outside Cuba as Santería, this religious tradition is a mixture of practices brought to Cuba by African slaves and the Catholicism they

The Country and Its People

were forced to adopt under the Spanish. To a large extent, Santería evolved from the cult of Yoruba or Lucumi people of Nigeria. Many practitioners regard the term Santería as a misnomer, and call the so-called syncretistic religion by another name, "Ifaism." (In Haiti, a variant of the same belief is known across the world as "voodoo"). Experts estimate that 70 percent of Cubans practice Santería, whether through daily ritual or merely an occasional offering. Even many of those who call themselves practicing Catholics also believe in Santería, which in Cuba, a deeply superstitious nation, could be regarded as keeping on the safe side, just in case. Tucked away in certain neighborhoods, you will always find a local *bótanica*, which sells special incense, herbs and amulets for Santería rituals, as well as the distinctive beaded necklaces and bracelets denoting a person's patron *orisha*.

Santería recognizes a single supreme being, of no known gender. As a practicing *babalao* or priest put it: "How can you describe the gender of electricity? For us, God is the energy that is created and it is the energy behind creation." This supreme being presides over *orishas*, which can be described as anthropomorphic spirits, who watch over the human world. Because worshipping *orishas* was heresy to Catholics, the slaves concealed the worship of their African deities behind the names and images of Catholic saints. During this process, aspects of Catholicism

The Cuban armed forces are numerous and well equipped under the leadership of Raul Castro.

became mingled with their own religion.

In the Yoruba celestial world, Olofí is regarded as the supreme *orisha*. He communicates through Orula, the *orisha* of wisdom, whose corresponding saint is San Francisco. By means of divination, Orula allows believers to communicate with their patron *orisha*, although he is always consulted himself by Cubans before they make an important decision. For Cubans, the Virgen de la Caridad del Cobre, (Virgin of Charity of Cobre) is identified with Ochún, the powerful goddess of rivers, lakes, beau-

a pilgrimage site in Cuba. Altogether, there are many hundreds of *orishas*, but these are the most dominant.

Santería *babalaos* (the priesthood is male-only) perform the divination ceremony in their own homes, which according to belief, should only ever take place during daylight hours.

Just as a doctor has a stethoscope, each *babalao* has an *okpele*, a chain with eight pieces of coconut shell which when swung onto the floor can produce one of a possible 256 combinations, each one with a spe-

ty, love, money, and maternity. Like Aphrodite, she is known for her dalliances with lovers, yet manages to somehow be ever-virtuous. Other central *orishas* include Yemayá, worshipped as the Virgen de Regla, Havana's patron saint, goddess of the sea and protector of loved ones; Elegguá, the warrior god, identified with San Antonio and the messenger of prayers between the human and the spirit world; Changó, god of thunder and lightning, music and virility, whose inseparable companion is Oyá, the *orisha* of winds, storms, night lightening and cemeteries; Obatalá, goddess of light, worshipped through the Virgen de las Mercedes; and Babulu-Ayé, the *orisha* of healing, who is recognized in San Lázaro,

cific interpretation that has been passed down and refined over the centuries, which the *babalao* relates to his client. Various devices are used in "cleansing" ceremonies, including certain herbs, smoke blown through a cigar, and spurts of *aguardiente* expelled from the mouth. No one who ever witnesses or is involved with a Santería ceremony will ever forget the experience.

In what is sometimes regarded as a controversial aspect of the religion, certain rituals and initiation ceremonies involve the sacrifice of animals, usually black chickens or roosters, but sometimes goats or larger animals. Its practitioners shrug their shoulders and say that all religions have been blood-related at one time, while the animal

The Country and Its People

that is killed is always eaten. Another contentious aspect is the fact that *babalaos* are known to demand quite hefty financial payments for their services. Santería apparently demands that those who practice it must be made to take it seriously: free dispensing of the *orisha*'s advice is not agreeable to the religion.

Initiates are known as *santeros* or *santeras*, and are recognizable by the immaculate white clothes and the colorful necklaces they must wear for an entire year; you will probably see one or two during your stay.

Cuba has two other important Afro-Cuban cults, Palo Monte and Abakuá, both of which have a limited and more secretive following. Palo Monte, also known as Regla Mayombé, is practiced mostly in eastern Cuba. It was brought to Cuba by Bantu slaves, and combines animal sacrifice with a fetish for skulls and spells, and in this respect, has much in common with Haitian voodoo. Abakuá, practiced only by white Cuban males, is a very secretive society, feared by many in Cuba. Initiates are known as *abakuás*.

MUSIC — A CUBAN PASSION

Another aspect of the island's culture indisputably linked to its Afro-Cuban heritage is the rich mix of African rhythms and European instrumentation that form Cuban music. There is no question that Cuba has evolved one of the world's richest and most exuberant musical traditions. Music, song and dance are an inseparable part of the national identity. Equally, over the past century, the island's music has profoundly influenced the development of such international musical styles as jazz, blues, swing, and the contemporary ballad structure.

Juan Formell, bassist and founder of Los Van Van, one of Cuba's leading music ensembles, has this to say about his country's music heritage: "Cuba is the historical source of Latin music, more so than any other Latin American or Caribbean country. The main elements of today's Latin music are directly descended from music of the 1920s and the 1930s, beginning with Miguel Matamoros, Ignacio Piñeiro, Orquestra Aragon and Beny Moré. Even today, popular salsa

is still much more Cuban than anything else. In general, we utilize the same musical elements and forms our predecessors used. When you say the "introducción," the "montuno," the "estribillo" and the "mambo," for example, much younger musicians from other countries and from newer styles all recognize, respect and use these elements, and identify them as Cuban."

In the words of musician Ry Cooder, (who produced the Grammy-winning album, *Buena Vista Social Club*, a compilation of son): "Music is alive in Cuba, not some

remnant of a museum. In Cuba the music flows like a river. It takes care of you and rebuilds you from the inside out."

Fernando Ortíz, the late Cuban ethnologist, famously wrote that the island's music stemmed from "the love affair of African drums and Spanish guitar."

Certainly, the Cuban music we know today only took off after the abolition of slavery allowed cultural barriers to collapse somewhat between the white *criolle* bourgeoisie and the newly enfranchised blacks. The power of African rhythm soon created a musical transformation of the more sedate European contradanse, incorporating the rhythms, chants and dances used ceremonially to summon *orishas*; today, dance bands openly make Santería references.

Of all Cuban music forms, rumba — which originated by the docks and in the poorest barrios of Matanzas and Havana as fiesta music, cathartic and intoxicating — expresses this fusion most openly. The most fa-

With dramatic shortages, stores are nearly empty OPPOSITE and the reality of rationing daily ABOVE.

mous rumba dance is the columbia, a rapid, almost gymnastic solo man's dance which conveys the contortions of the devils, a feature of certain ceremonies of the Afro-Cuban cult Abakuá. Rumba has three main styles: the sensual and exciting guaguanacó; the columbia, and the yambú and conga. The latter styles are often a feature of the carnival festivities in Havana and Santiago de Cuba.

Over the past century other musical styles have evolved. Some are inseparable from the voices of singers: like the romantic bolero and the more flirtatious guaracha, both of which began in nineteenth-century Havana as forms of serenading by suitors — the object of their affections was required by the social dictates of the day to remain coyly unseen behind colonial latticework screens. Others, such as the habenera, the danza and, lastly, danzón, are known more as dance genres.

Son, which dates from the first decade of this century, has proved one of the most enduring and inspirational forms of Cuban music. It began in Oriente Province and involved an ensemble of a double bass, trumpets, bongos and other percussion instruments, as well as a three-stringed guitar called a *tres*. Cuba's most famous son artist was Beny Moré, the so-called "Barbarian of Rhythm." It was largely his influence that inspired a generation of musicians to experiment with son during the 1950s, especially in New York where Machito, Chano Pozo, Xaiver Cugat, Mario Bauza, and Tito Puente and his Mambo Boys each had their moment of fame. Dizzy Gillespie and Charlie Parker listened, created their own fusion; and thus Cu-bop, Jazz Mambo or Cubano Jazz came into its own. Another offshoot of son was salsa — which, with its brass, syncopated percussion and choruses, became an international sensation.

While salsa, along with chachachá, swept the world, Cuba was busily concocting septets and charangas and other dance rhythms, and meanwhile, Joseito Fernandez's *Guantánamera* became internationally synonymous with Cuba. Contemporary Cuban bands, such as Los Van Van, NG La Banda, Issac Delgado, El Medico de la Salsa and Grupo Sierra Maestra have kept alive these rhythm phenomena while adding

their own modern twists.

There are many other aspects and styles to modern Cuban music, as any musicologist will tell you. Even if you regard yourself as an absolute beginner when it comes to Cuban music, if you are acquainted with the mainstream sounds of Desi Arnaz (for the older generation) and Gloria Estefan, then you already recognize something of the Cuban sensibility. Overall, it is accurate to say that Cuban music often fuses African sources and aspects of Santería rhythms with traditional folk dance music, along with jazz, rock and classical elements. Indeed, this description exactly sums up the sound of Irakere, one of Cuba's most popular jazz fusion bands, led by Chuco Valdéz, as well as the fusion group,

Sintésis.

Since the Revolution, the most significant development in Cuban music has been the so-called *Nueva Trova*, typified by the ballads of Silvio Rodríquez and Pablo Milanés; while more recently, singers such as Gerardo Alfonso, whose lyrics speak of the pain of exile and the realities of modern-day Havana, represent the new wave, termed *Novísima Trova*. Outside Cuba, you may want to follow the career of the platinum-haired Albita, who was once one of the island's darlings, dubbed Cuba's Lili Marlene, but who defected to a new life in Miami in 1993.

If you want to familiarize yourself with the best of Cuban music, as well as those musicians mentioned above, you would do

well to start with various compilation records, such as *Buena Vista Social Club*, *Afro Cuban All Stars*, and *I Am Cuba*. For detailed listings see SHOP TILL YOU DROP, page 52. Some of the featured musicians in the *Buena Vista Social Club* album, such as Ibrahim Ferrer and Compay Segundo, were side men for the great Cuban innovators of the 1940s and 1950s: Ferrer, who worked as a shoe-shiner in Cuba for decades before making this album, yet had recorded with Beny Moré; Rubén Gonsález, who had retired in 1991, has played with Arsenio Rodríguez and Enrique Jorrin, Cuban greats both. Also, don't overlook the sweetly nostalgic compositions of Cuba's famous classical pianist,

Goats are sacrificed during a Santería ceremony.

Ernesto Lecuona, who was born last century, or the voice of Celina Gonsález, born in 1920 and Cuba's diva of *guajira*, traditional country music.

CUBAN ART

Prior to the Revolution, Cuba produced one major internationally renowned artist: Wilfredo Lam (1902–1982), of Chinese descent, who was both a friend and student of Picasso. Despite the fact that Lam lived most of his life as an expatriate, his influence on Cuban graphics and dashes of hot, earthy color, weaving themes from Afro-Cuban mythology and folklore. Another contemporary artist is Flora Fong, a Chinese Cuban, like Lam, who paints vivid, tropical landscapes.

A visit to Havana's Museo Nacional de Bellas Artes is a must for familiarizing yourself with the island's art.

The Biennial de la Habana (Visual Arts Biennial) celebrates work by artists from Cuba and abroad, providing a showcase for local artistic expression since it began in 1984. Increasingly, young Cuban artists often

art remains profound. Today in Havana, the Centro Wilfredo Lam is one of the city's most vibrant cultural centers.

René Portocarrero (1912–1985) is also one of the island's best-loved artists, known for his ethereal paintings and stained-glass windows of women and churches, with their Marc Chagallesque quality. Two other artists, Amelia Peláez (1897–1968) and Mariano Rodríguez (1912–1990) are known for their ceramics and murals, respectively. In the 1960s, Raúl Martínez created some of the Revolution's most memorable images, such as his poster paintings of Fidel Castro, Che Guevara and José Martí.

Today, Manual Mendive is Cuba's leading living artist, whose work features bold address sensitive topics like emigration and economic hardship. An article in the *New York Times* noted: "Havana's still-young festival makes up in high spirits and unpredictable freshness what it sorely lacks in money or manpower." The biennial is held in several locations in the Cuban capital, including El Morro Fortress and the Centro Wilfredo Lam. The next biennial is scheduled for September 1999.

As with all cultural institutions in Cuba, all art galleries are state-run.

CUBAN FILM

Following the Revolution, Castro's government made the island's film industry a national priority. It created the Instituto Cubano del Arte y la Industria Cinematográficos (ICAIC), the Cuban Institute of Film Art and Industry, which has had a virtual monopoly on Cuban filmmaking ever since, producing everything from animated cartoons, to features, documentaries, and newsreels.

Cuba's best known film director is the late Tomás Gutiérrez Alea (1928–1996), who worked with Juan Carlos Tabio on the critically acclaimed films *Fresa y Chocolate* and *Guantánamera*, both starring his wife, the luminous Mirtha Ibarra, and both reflecting ironically on the faults of the Cuban system while conveying the wit and passion of the Cuban soul. Earlier films by Alea include *La Muerte de un Burórata*, *Memorias del Subdesarrollo* and *Cartas del Parque*.

Another leading director is Humberto Solás (born 1941) whose 1968 film, *Lucía*, is one of the classics of Cuban cinema.

Recently, two notable Cuban films, Daniel Diaz Torres's *Kleines Tropicana* and Arturo Sotto's *Amor Vertical* can be said to carry on Alea's tradition of lovingly mocking the system.

ICAIC also runs the annual International Festival of New Latin American Cinema, founded in 1979 and usually held in the first two weeks of December. Bringing a whiff of business and glamour to the capital, the festival usually centers at the Hotel Nacional, with screenings at some dozen cinemas. The two-week run generally plays to packed audiences with at least half a million tickets sold.

Novelist Gabriel García Márquez (a part-time Cuba resident) is regarded as the founding godfather of the event. Many of the world's most talented filmmakers from other hemispheres come to take part too, including Robert Redford, who has visited several times, and who is instrumental through his Sundance Institute in bringing independent American films to Cuba and in screening the work of talented Cuban and Latin-American filmmakers at his Sundance Festival. (In doing so, frequently they come up against the United States embargo on Cuba. Given the political situation between the two countries, Cubans have a peculiar interaction with American movies, which are often seen on borrowed satellite in a contraband kind of way.)

Previous years have featured a jumble of such visiting celebrities as Robert De Niro, Francis Ford Coppola, Peter Greenaway, Stephen Frears, Arnold Schwarzenegger, Gerard Depardieu, Sydney Poitier, Harry Belafonte, Helen Mirren, Taylor Hackford, Hanna Schygulla, Julian Schnabel, Matt Dillon, and Treat Williams. And of course, there is always the nation's famous *deus ex machina*, Fidel Castro himself, who often chooses the festival to make one of his surprise entrances.

CUBAN LITERATURE

Although Cuba *prides* itself on being a fiercely literary nation, many Cubans today have very restricted access to books beyond those deemed politically and ideologically correct. Indeed, as the Argentinean writer, Jacob Timerman, commented: "If it is true that every Cuban knows how to read and write, it is likewise true that every Cuban has nothing to read and must be very careful about what he writes."

Although it has certainly proved to be an almost irrepressible topic one way or another, Cuba's communist revolution has not always been kindest to the writers who have grown up in its shadow. Some went into exile, such as

OPPOSITE: Drummers play in a Santería ceremony in Havana.
ABOVE: One sees few sculptures in Cuba, this one is in Santiago de Cuba.

Guillermo Cabrera Infante, whose work was at the forefront of the 1960s renaissance in Latin American writing, and who was hailed by *The New York Review of Books* as Cuba's most important living writer. His books cannot be found in Cuba.

However, in Havana bookshops, along with the writings of Fidel Castro, Che Guevara, Marx and Lenin, (as well as agricultural handbooks and anti-CIA literature), you will find books by the revolutionary leader, José Martí, as well as the two authors the island claims as its greatest: the avant-garde sur-

Paradiso, which explores homosexuality (a pet hate of Fidel Castro), and Miguel Barnet's *Biografía de un Cimarron* ("The Autobiography of a Runaway Slave") was published in 1967; both are regarded as seminal works.

In Cuba, younger writers such as Senel Paz and Reinaldo Gonsález have tackled subjects viewed as somewhat contentious, such as disillusionment, AIDS, and poverty. This younger generation includes Zoé Valdés, an exile living in Paris, whose works have been banned in her native Cuba. Her book *La Nada Cotodiana* (which translates as

realist writer Alejo Carpentier (1904–1980) and the mulatto poet Nicholas Guillén (1902–1989), both of whom came of age well before the Revolution's triumph. Guillén is regarded as the father of Cuban letters: he helped found the Unión Nacional de Escritores y Artistas Cubanos (National Union of Writers and Artists). You can also look for works by Cuba's greatest nineteenth-century novelist, Cirilo Villaverde y la Paz, a revolutionary who foreshadowed José Martí. His best-loved work is *Cecilia Valdés*, about a tragic affair between a slave trader's son and a beautiful *mulatta*, who, it transpires, is his illegitimate half-sister.

More recently, José Lezama Lima (1910–1976) caused ripples with his 1966 novel

"The Nothingness of Everyday Life"), recently published as *Yocandra in the Paradise of Nada*, paints a devastating portrait of Cuba during the Special Period.

In the United States, the novels of Havana-born Cristina García, *Dreaming in Cuban* and *The Agüero Sisters*, lift the troubled relationship between the two countries, as well as the emotional fallout created between those who left and those who stayed behind, into the realm of remarkable literature.

THE ISLAND'S NATURAL HERITAGE

Lying like a crocodile caught between the fishing nets of its neighbors, the United States and Mexico, Cuba is the largest of Greater

Antilles — and by far the largest island in the Caribbean — stretching some 1,250 km (about 775 miles) in length and 191 km (about 120 miles) across at its widest, 31 km (about 19 miles) at its narrowest. This enchantingly beautiful island has three main mountain regions — the Cordillera Guaniguanico in Pinar del Río Province to the west, the Sierra del Escambray above Trinidad in Sancti Spíritus Province in the center, and the Sierra Maestra in the southeast Oriente Province — each with isolated pockets of tropical rainforest. The Pico Turquino in the Sierra Maestra is Cuba's highest point at 1,973 m (6,473 ft).

The island's scenery varies from snow-white sandy beaches, protected by coral reefs and shaded by sea grape and palm trees, to high mountains smothered with native forest and coffee plantations, and vast plains where fertile ochre-colored soil grows abundant swathes of sugarcane and tobacco for which Cuba is so famous — not to mention mangrove swamps, offshore islands, limestone caves, subterranean rivers, and waterfalls. The island has more than 200 rivers, the longest of which is the 343-km (213-mile)-long Río Cauto in Oriente Province. Offshore, including the Cuba's second largest island, Isla de la Juventud, are some 4,000 keys and islets, many of which are untouched.

Almost half of the 6,000 plant types found in Cuba are endemic, as are many thousands of animal species. Although Cuban forests once teemed with mahogany, teak, ebony and cedar, Spanish colonials systematically deforested the nation and it is rare to find these trees in any great number. Also, about 200 species of Cuba's plants and animals are on the United Nation's list of endangered species. Cuba does however have among the highest concentrations of palm trees in the world. Of the 60 species of palms, the royal palm is the most impressive, with its towering height and smooth silvery trunk, and is the national tree. Other palms include the barrigona or big belly palm, (rudely called *puta palma* because it looks pregnant) and the rare, stunted prehistoric cork palm which dates from the dinosaur age, seen in the hilltops of the Valle de Viñales, in Pinar del Río Province.

Other notable plants include the *jagüey*, a fig tree with aerial roots; the *ceiba*, the sacred silk cotton tree; and the fragrant white butterfly *mariposa*, the national flower. You will see many flowering trees, which burst into blossom during summer, such as the flame-red *flamboyán* and the African tulip tree. If you drive through central Cuba, you will also see endless orchards of oranges, lemons and limes, as well as more exotic fruits like mangos, soursops and guavas.

It is a curious fact that both the smallest bird in the world and the smallest frog in

the world are found in Cuba. You are unlikely to see the frog, nicknamed *el sapito*, but you may possibly see the beautiful *zunzuncito* or bee hummingbird, which is just bigger than a grasshopper, weighs only two grams, and flaps its wings at an astonishing speed, producing a unique sound. The fingernail-sized frog lives under ferns within the dense forest of Cuba's eastern tip, in the Cuchillas del Toa region. Other unusual species include the polymite, a land snail with a colorful swirled shell, found in abundance in the forested mountains near Baracoa; and two rat-like mammals: the *almiqué*,

OPPOSITE: Paintings by local artists are sold at street markets for dollars to access new food stores. ABOVE: Browsing on the Plaza de Armas.

with a long snout and large padded claws, and the *jutia*, the size of small beaver, which is sought out as a delicacy and eaten in rural Cuba, in the Sierra del Escambray for instance.

Cuba has over 300 bird species, of which 23 are endemic and found nowhere else in the world. South of Havana, the Zapata Peninsula is the Caribbean's most important stopover for migratory birds such as flamingos, and is a year-round home for many endemic species. You can't avoid seeing Cuba's ubiquitous white egrets (and their constant companions, the crows), but

Cuba is rich in reptilian life, including crocodiles, iguanas, lizards, salamanders, and turtles, and has 15 species of non-poisonous snakes. Cuban Crocodiles — potentially the island's most dangerous creatures — are found in only one part of the island, the swampy Zapata Peninsula, where they are now protected under a breeding program after being an endangered species for many years. You may also see the alligator gar, an endemic species considered to be a living fossil, a breed between a reptile and a fish and lives in rivers.

serious birders will love seeing rare species, such as the *zunzuncito*, and the national bird, the *trogon*, also known as the *tocororo* — a member of the quetzal family, which has red, white and blue plumage, the colors of the Cuban flag.

You may be lucky enough to see one of the world's loveliest moths, the Cuban *Urania*, a strange and beautiful tailed and gilded moth whose habits are those of a butterfly, which is found in the forests of the Sierra del Escambray and the Sierra Maestra. The profusion of exotic butterflies — among them the exquisite *Greta Cubana* — along with the rare native orchids that line mountain trails offers one of Cuba's more ephemeral and unexpected pleasures in the wild.

Wild boar, deer, and horses can be found in some parts of the island, including the Guanahacabibes Peninsula in Pinar del Río, and monkeys live in some isolated areas, including a key off Cayo Largo.

Don't be too taken aback if you encounter Cuba's fist-size tarantulas in rural areas — although avoid them as best you can and, without being obsessive about it, check your hotel bed sheets, bathroom and terrace. It's most unlikely you'll find any there.

ABOVE: Returning from the fields in Santiago de Cuba Province. OPPOSITE: A coconut plantation near Baracoa in Guantánamo Province.

Havana

HAVANA

SOMETHING ABOUT THE HAUNTING BEAUTY of Havana seems to affect the heart as deeply as a love affair, the memory of which brings a twinge of melancholy and has a compulsive pull on the emotions; triggered by an old song or the smell of a certain flower. It is impossible to forget the exotic decadence of Havana's crumbling mansions; the mesmerizing slap of waves against the Malecón; the summer air with its wistful traces of salt and frangipani. It is easy to romanticize Havana, but as visitors soon observe, perhaps harder to live like a *habanero* in matrimony with some of its imperfections.

For more than two decades, this most sensual of cities existed in a state of socialist purdah. Even now, almost a decade after Fidel Castro opened the doors to foreign tourists, those visiting the island nation can't help but feel a shiver of unreality as they contemplate the sight of one of the most remarkable cities in the world.

Havana has a beguiling flavor all of its own, a strangeness that is at first baffling. Its source is partly rooted in the paradox that Havana is a grandly extravagant city built with fortunes created by slavery and capitalism, but which has became more famous as the crucible of Fidel Castro's radical Revolution. Certainly, the city is better known for having the world's most famously obdurate communist government than as the first in the Americas to have had a Spanish fortress. (Indeed, it has both the oldest and the largest; the Castillo de la Real Fuerza and the Fortaleza de San Carlos de la Cabaña.)

BACKGROUND

Havana was one of the seven cities founded by the Spanish expeditionary Diego Velásquez, who established the colonial *villa* or settlement of what was then called San Cristóbal de La Habana in 1514. Although it was the de facto capital of Cuba from 1553, Havana was officially declared the capital in 1607, and was always the island's most affluent and cosmopolitan city.

By 1750, about one half of the island's entire population (some 170,000) lived in the city; today that figure is just over two million, making it the largest city in the Caribbean.

A look at the map of the Caribbean quickly reveals why Havana's strategic location and its superb natural harbor made it Spain's most important New World port: it was the perfect staging post for all Gulf Stream traffic between Spain and its other colonial outposts. From the sixteenth century onwards, so much wealth flowed through the city that

by the eighteenth century, Havana had seven fortresses, a network of sentry towers and a massive stone wall, making it the most well-defended city in the Americas. While sugar, tobacco, coffee and rum were being transported out of Havana, galleons bringing back riches from Mexico and Peru passed through its ports, as did those from Seville, and even from as far away as Manila.

More recently, in the 1950s, Havana was considered to be the Las Vegas of the Caribbean, a playground for rich tourists run by the American mob, a palm-lined port

PREVIOUS PAGES: LEFT: Havana's Plaza de la Catedral. RIGHT: An elegant staircase in Vedado. ABOVE: Diego Velasquez, founder of Havana.

city filled with casino wheels, rum cocktails and dancing under an open sky. It was sexy, decadent and corrupt to the core, underlaced with prostitution and smuggling. It was becoming one of Latin America's major financial centers when Castro took over in 1959.

As Cuba's principal city, Havana is the point of entry for most visitors, and unquestionably its main attraction for visitors. Over the centuries, Havana has developed into a beautiful but chaotic architectural jumble, with a constant juxtaposi-

coffee wafting from portable heating coils. Very often, these narrow streets contain hidden marvels behind otherwise unremarkable walls notable only for their large iron-studded wooden doors. You may catch glimpses of carved stone and marble interiors, perhaps awaiting restoration. Distinctive features of Havana's colonial buildings include high, multi-colored stained-glass windows of *mediopuntos* (fan-shaped windows divided with wooden struts) and *vitrales* (divided with metal instead of wood), elaborate carved window bars (*rejas*), lou-

tion of eras. In the capital's colonial core, La Habana Vieja, it is possible to walk along streets lined with grand baroque buildings that look little changed since the seventeenth and eighteenth centuries, with churches, plazas and imposing colonial mansions that were once places of elegant residence for the Creole aristocracy, in a style named after Havana's *Mudéjar*, the skilled Spanish-Moorish craftsmen responsible for decorating so much of the city's colonial construction in the early days.

As you wander the streets, many as-yet-unrestored mansions are propped up by scaffolding and tangled with electrical wires, with brightly colored washing suspended across peeling stucco, and the smell of sweet

vered blinds (*persianas*) to keep out the sun, intricate latticework window screens (*celosias*), double-hinged half-doors (*mamparas*), upper balconies, inner *portales* or arcades, and intricately carved *alfarje* wooden ceilings.

As well the profusion of colonial buildings in the La Habana Vieja, other sections of the city, such as the formerly wealthy neighborhoods of Vedado, Miramar and El Cerro, have a varied mixture of twentieth-century architecture: Art Nouveau palaces, Art Deco houses, Spanish Colonial mansions, and modernist architecture from the 1950s. Many of these buildings — some once occupied by sugar barons and industrialists who fled after the Revolution —

are in a notoriously shocking state of disrepair; some have become *cuidadelas* — or "little cities" — home to more than a dozen families.

However, an ambitious drive for architectural restoration and renovation of Havana — most notably of La Habana Vieja — is underway, largely under the energetic direction of the city's historian, Eusebio Leal. Although La Habana Vieja is protected as a UNESCO World Heritage Site, many are somewhat taken aback at the cracking pace at which the government is turning it into a quaint tourist attraction. While the city's aristocratic colonial buildings and monuments have received careful treatment and are nothing less than dazzling, many secondary buildings have lost their charming authenticity under solid coats of salmon pink and canary blue, creating a slightly surreal, too-quaint effect.

Certainly, the rash of newly constructed flashy hotels, shops, cafés and fast food outlets in the old city give the impression that Cuba's new romance with capitalism is in full swing. Meanwhile, the architectural wonders in Vedado, Miramar and El Cerro, less likely to attract tourists, have been allowed to crumble into almost derelict state. On the outskirts of the capital, rundown military installations and crumbling Soviet-style apartment buildings (built by the so-called micro-brigades, teams of volunteers who build their own homes with government-supplied cement and equipment) offer a harsher reality. It is true that the pervasive hardship experienced by most of the city's citizens during the on-going Special Period gives a stranger's enjoyment of Havana a certain sting. It is hard not to be moved by their optimism and the warmth. Yet, in a profound way, Havana — the aging beauty — radiates real lusty life, and is not easily forgotten.

GENERAL INFORMATION

Most hotels, especially the four- or five-star ones, have information desks which are equipped to deal with most queries. They can also arrange prompt medical assistance should it be necessary.

Asistur ((53-7) 62-5519 or 63-8284 FAX (53-7) 33-8087, Paseo de Martí (Prado) No. 45, La Habana Vieja is a Cuban company specializing in assistance to international visitors. The staff are friendly and speak English. This 24-hour service is available if you if you require any of the following: emergency medical aid or dental treatment, repatriation, legal aid, help with tracing lost baggage, or new travel documents.

For reservations for hotels, tours and other travel arrangements, as well as general inquiries, you can contact the Havana

headquarters of **Cubanacán** ((53-7) 21-9457 or 20-0569 or (53-7) 24-6006, Calle 68 next to Avenida 5, Miramar, Cuba's largest tourist organization.

Other than these two organizations, tourist offices supplying general information do not exist: you will find plenty of agencies whose primary aim is to sell you tour packages and excursions.

The Hotel Nacional and the Hotel Habana Libre have banking outlets where you can get cash advances on credit cards, or

OPPOSITE: The tower of the Castillo de la Fuerza and El Palacio del Segundo Cabo at sunset.
ABOVE: Stylish balconies in La Habana Vieja.

you can cash traveler's checks even if you are not staying at the hotel; you will need to show your passport. Otherwise, try the privately run **Banco Financiero Internacional** ((53-7) 33-3423 or 33-3424, Calle Línea No. 1, Vedado. It is open Monday to Friday from 8:30 AM to 3 PM, but lines tend to be lengthier than at the above mentioned hotel outlets, which are also open on the weekend. You can exchange dollars for Cuban pesos at any of the capital's **Casas de Cambio** (Cadesa). The most conveniently located one is near the Lonja del Comercio building in the Plaza de San Francisco de Asís in La Habana Vieja.

For visitors, unless you are staying at one of Havana's top hotels, the most convenient post office, which also offers international telephone services, is located at the Hotel Habana Libre.

Should you require medical attention, you can contact the **Hospital Nacional Hermanos Almeijeiras** ((53-7) 70-7721, Calle San Lázaro No. 701, off the Malecón in Centro Habana. Another option is **Servimed** ((53-7) 24-2658 or 24-2023, Calle 18 No. 4304, between Calles 43 and 47, Miramar, Playa. You can also contact the **Clínica Cira García International Clinic and Pharmacy** ((53-7) 33-2811. If it's urgent, call your hotel doctor and proceed from there.

In emergencies, the telephone contact for Havana's **Tourist Police** is ((53-7) 30-1621 or 30-3119; for an **Ambulance** ((53-7) 44-5551 to 44-5553.

WHAT TO SEE AND DO

The first two tours suggested here can be made on foot, and together they cover the most important places to visit in La Habana Vieja, which is easily the most interesting area to explore for visitors. The remaining tours are best made with a rental car or taxi, and cover Havana's main neighborhoods and places of interest, including the historic fortresses built to protect the bay. Be sure to check EXCURSIONS FROM HAVANA, below, for several highly rewarding trips that can be made within an afternoon, including a trip to Hemingway's house-museum, La Finca Vigía and the nearby fishing village of Cojímar.

La Habana Vieja — A Walking Tour of the Old City

If time is short, you can conceivably manage this walking tour, which covers the main sights in La Habana Vieja, in one day. Equally, if time permits, you can choose to follow parts of this suggested tour at your leisure, perhaps over repeated wanderings in the old city.

The place to begin is **Plaza de Armas**, in many ways the crucible of Havana's colonial history. Facing the mouth of Havana Bay, it is ringed with baroque stone buildings, walls, and columns that are astounding to behold at any time of day, but especially at dawn and sunset or beneath a full moon. To the right is the four-sided **Castillo de la Real Fuerza** (Castle of the Royal Forces), considered to be the oldest stone fort in the Americas, and certainly Spain's first fort in Cuba. What you see now is an elaboration of the original fort, first begun by Governor Hernando de Soto in 1538, which proved to be vulnerable to an attack in 1555 by an infamous French pirate by the name of Jacques de Sores, whose men took Havana within half an hour and pillaged and torched the entire city, terrorizing and slaughtering its citizens and taking to the seas again laden with treasures. This event, and the constant threat of roaming pirates, prompted the Spanish King Philip II in 1558 to commission military engineer Bartolomé Sánchez to construct the new Castillo de la Real Fuerza, which took until 1582 to be fully completed.

Surrounded by a deep, greenish-watered moat spanned by a drawbridge, and with its formidable, six-meter (20-ft)-thick walls, the fort was both the seat of Cuba's colonial government and the residence of the Commander-in-Chief until 1762. These days, its vault-like interiors house a permanent collection of works by Cuba's top artists and ceramists, including Wilfredo Lam, Amelia Peláez and Mariano Rodríguez.

Passing through the entrance, embellished with a crest of the royal arms, you can wander up to the fort's battlements

for a panoramic view across the harbor to
the horizon beyond. A bronze weather-
vane, known as **La Giraldilla**, stands in a
narrow tower, and is regarded as a symbol
of Havana (also appropriated on the Havana Club rum label) and has a sad history. After Hernando de Soto had ordered the
construction of this fort, he sailed away
from Havana in 1539 to try and conquer
Florida, leaving his wife, Doña Isabel de
Bobadilla, behind as governor in his place,
who thus became the first, and only, woman
governor in Cuba's history. By all reports,
Doña Isabel was much-loved by the people, as much for her good judgement as for
her lovely appearance. But after four years
of waiting, she was to learn that her husband had died days after discovering a
great river, the Mississippi. She herself
soon died, heartbroken. Cast in 1632, La Giraldilla is said to portray the sad woman
scanning the horizon for some sign of her
husband's return. There is a pleasant terrace coffee shop with tranquil views of the
harbor.

From here, a few steps bring you back into
Plaza de Armas, the oldest and perhaps
the most beautiful civic square in Havana,
at the sea-facing end of Calles O'Reilly and
Obispo. During the sixteenth century, this
square was known as Plaza de la Iglesia, after
what was then Havana's main church (de-
molished two centuries later); it was later
named after the Real Fuerza's troops who
paraded here every day. To commemorate
this, every day at 4 PM, a troop dressed in
eighteenth-century garb parades ceremonially through nearby streets in La Habana
Vieja and around the square. (Although a
quaint sight, this parade is not worth going
out of your way to see.)

After 1750, the city's colonial masters
built a series of grand military and administrative buildings around the square,
planting its center with royal palms, laurel
trees, fragrant plants, fountains and pathways. By the nineteenth-century, it was
considered Havana's most fashionable meeting place, around which elegant, elongat-
ed horse-drawn carriages with huge wheels
known as *volantes* clattered, and the city's

Colonnades on the Plaza de Armas in Old Havana.

elite strutted jauntily on their dusk promenades. These days, book-sellers tirelessly unpack cardboard crates for another day of commerce at **La Feria de Libros** (Book Fair) in this leafy square, hoping to interest tourists in ethnological tomes by studies by Fernando Ortíz, battered texts by Marx, Lenin, Castro or Guevara, as well as exposés of the CIA and the KGB. You are equally likely to find that certain book-sellers are nationally recognized poets, so do not be so hasty or dismissive of them as mere hustlers. The centerpiece of the square

15 years to be completed. Outside, to the left, is the statue of Spanish king Fernando VII that originally stood in the center of Plaza de Armas.

As you pass through the exterior arcade and huge arched entrance with its mahogany doorway, you enter a stately inner courtyard encircled by cavernous chambers that once served as government departments. Side annexes led to sections that were formerly coach houses, stables, guardrooms and an underground dungeon. Above, luxurious upper quarters crammed with

is a statue of rebel leader, Carlos Manual de Céspedes.

On the west side of the Plaza de Armas facing the square, stands the formidable Palacio de los Capitanes-Generales (Palace of the Commanders-in-Chief), from which some 65 successive Spanish colonial governors enforced their rule over the entire island. Later it became the presidential palace and then the town hall. It is now the **Museo de la Ciudad de la Habana** (City Museum), Calle Tacón No. 1, La Habana Vieja. This magnificent example of Cuban-baroque architecture was commissioned in 1776 by then-governor and captain-general Marqués de la Torre. It took 100,000 bricks from Malaga, quantities of marble from Genoa, wrought iron from Bilbao and

rich furnishings, treasures and works of art were reserved for the governor and his family. Apparently, the unusual wooden paving on the street outside was devised to muffle passing carriage wheels so as not to disturb the governor's sleep.

Open to the elements, the courtyard is filled with a fragrant tropical garden, draped with flowered creepers, and planted with varieties of the royal palm, the national tree. A statue of Christopher Columbus stands in the center, some discarded cannonballs at his feet. This beautiful setting is frequently as a background for photographic portraits of *quinceañeras*, girls of fifteen on their coming-of-age celebration day, who pose in full-makeup, frilly white dresses, stockings, hats, ribbons and high heels as their first day as a young lady is captured for posterity.

As museums go, this is one of the best to visit in Cuba, as much for the building itself, as for its rich historical collection, with paintings, furniture, ornate ceramics, decorations, colonial military uniforms and all manner of weaponry (including an unusual cannon made completely from leather), important documents, utensils and relics displayed in their original context. Upstairs, aside from the plum-red

throne room (intended for the King of Spain and never used), don't miss seeing the two enormous marble baths shaped like nautilus shell chariots and the glittering shards of light cast onto gilded mirrors by enormous chandeliers.

On the ground floor, a nineteenth-century model train waits to be sent spinning around its tracks; a room is dedicated to the fight against colonial imperialism (displaying both a fragment of the stone "Eagle of Imperialism" from the USS *Maine* monument and various Batista-era relics); and you can see a small bronze replica of La Giraldilla. Some speculate that the palace ought to have ghosts: not only was it built over the ruins of a church graveyard, many

slaves died in its construction. A plaque commemorates the death of a young beauty, Doña María de Cepero, who was accidentally killed in the courtyard in 1557 during a ritual firing round of harquebuses at a feast held in her honor. In addition, an open-air shaft reveals an mysterious metal casket adorned with a sword. Open Tuesday to Saturday from 11:30 AM to 5 PM, Sunday from 9 AM to noon, and closed on Monday, entrance costs US$3 (and US$2 extra for cameras). A guided tour is US$1, and a small tip is often expected. You may want to buy the US$9 museum pass which can be used for admittance for all museums in Havana.

As you leave, to your left is the darker-hued Moorish-style baroque masterpiece **Palacio de Segundo Cabo** (Palace of the Second Lieutenant). Completed in 1772, it was originally used as the city's *casa de correos* (post office), then later used successively as the office of the royal estate and the court of justice, then finally as the residence of the second lieutenant, who was, in effect, the vice-governor. It now houses the offices of a government publishing institute, the Instituto Cubano del Libro, as well as the Bella Habana bookshop at street level. This beautiful building, with its row of neoclassical columns and two-story Andalusian-style courtyard is worth a look, and visitors can enter and go up to the first floor to wander around its gallery and look down into the courtyard, with a US$1 charge if you want to take photographs.

From here, cross the square (passing the Castillo de Real Fuerza on your right) to **El Templete**, a small neoclassical temple built in 1828 on what is regarded as the site where Havana, then San Cristóbal de la Habana, was founded, next to a *ceiba* (silk-cotton) tree, marking the spot where the city's first mass and town council meetings were held in 1519. It is said that the *ceiba* tree (one of a long line planted here, this one in 1959) has sacred powers; and that the spirit of the tree will grant your wish if you walk three times around the tree in silence. The Templete contains three large

A lighthouse looms over the entrance to Havana's old harbor.

paintings by the French artist Jean-Baptiste Vermay, worth seeing for their portrayal of contemporary personalities and events in Havana. Vermay, who was a student of Jacques-Louis David, had studied in Florence and Rome and founded Havana's first art school. Both the artist and his wife died in Havana's 1833 cholera epidemic; their ashes are interred in an urn in front of the paintings.

Completing this side of the square is the Palacio del Conde de Santoveni, now transformed into the elegant **Hotel Santa Isabel**. It was the residence of the Count of Santovenia, whose nineteenth-century parties were the talk of Havana, including one in which a hot-air balloon carrying revelers set off from the roof. In 1867, it was converted into the city's most exclusive hotel, and in many ways, this can also be said of its current incarnation, which has been beautifully restored and preserves a period ambiance throughout; and indeed is perhaps the loveliest hotel in Havana. Aside from the stone structure, which has been gleamingly scrubbed down, you can see the original grand interior columns and stone staircases, as well as the restored crescents of tinted-glass known as *mediopuntos*.

From here, follow the cobblestones back along the Plaza de Armas to **Calle Obispo**, La Habana Vieja's main street, lined with grand old *palacios* and shops, painted up in candy-spiced stucco and festooned with delicate iron balconies as part of the old city's restoration project. Obispo has changed almost beyond recognition several times, from being the city's most fashionable shopping district to showcasing nothing but empty shelves, with only the most pathetic array of consumer items at its worst moment, while today, there is a proliferation of dollar-shops as well as new galleries and shops selling Cuban art. You will pass the restaurant **La Mina**, housed in a former girl's convent and the **Amistad** café, where, side-by-side, bands of musicians seem to be in full swing at almost every time of day; then **La Tinaja**, which during colonial times would dispense stone-filtered water from its

underground source (originally discovered in 1544) and now sells glasses of mineral water. Next door is the nineteenth-century **Dulceria Doña Teresa** bakery, where you can buy fresh cakes and breadsticks. It is flanked by the **Oficina del Historidades de la Ciudad** (Office of the City Historian) at Calle Obispo No. 117, marked by a miniature copper galleon hanging above its doorway, with a bookshop at street level. This is notable as Havana's first residence, dating to 1570; you can peer inside a grilled gateway to see various artifacts in the courtyard, including a two-wheeled *volante*, the common means of transport in early colonial days. Next door, is the **Boutica Francesa de Santa Catalina**, an historic pharmacy with a beautiful wooden interior with rows of antique bottles.

At the corner of Calle Mercaderes, you will come to the **Hotel Ambus Mundos**. Ernest Hemingway spent long sabbaticals here before moving into La Finca Vigía. While staying in Room 511, he wrote *For Whom The Bell Tolls*, and the room is now a Hemingway shrine, displaying his typewriter, his shoes, books, fish-hooks and other memorabilia. You can ask to visit for a $1 fee, and have the windows thrown open to see his majestic harbor view.

Opposite, you can see the stunning new **Hotel Florida**, renovated from the historic former Palacio de Joaquín Gómez.

If you are in need of a rest, try **La Casa de las Infusiones**, just around the corner on Calle Mercaderes, which serves excellent cappuccinos, and all types of teas. On the same side, the **Casa de Asie**, a small museum dedicated to the arts and crafts of Asia housed in an old mansion, with what must be Cuba's only bonsai shop. Across the street is the **Casa de Puerto Rico**, which also houses the small but interesting **Museo del Tabaco** with its exhibition of Cuban cigar wrappers and humidors, which is open Tuesday to Saturday 10:30 AM to 1 PM and Sunday 10:30 AM to 5 PM. At street level is the **Casa del Tabaco**, which is as good a place to buy cigars as any in La Habana Vieja. Both are located at Calle Mercaderes No. 120. One block south is the **Casa Simón Bolívar**, which houses the Venezuelan Embassy and the **Museo de**

OPPOSITE: The *Mudéjar*-style Palacio des Ursulinas ABOVE and the Museo de la Ciudad BELOW.

Simón Bolívar, which has a collection of paintings and artifacts from Venezuela, but is most impressive for its nineteenth-century interiors.

At the corner of Calle Obrapía are three cultural institutes. **Casa de Benito Juárez** is a museum of Mexican art and culture funded by the Mexican government, which stages shifting exhibitions and musical performances. **Casa de la Obrapía**, at No. 158, is a beautifully restored two-story seventeenth-century mansion, built on a grand scale by a wealthy philanthropist who gave the street its name (*obra pía* means "pious act"), and now preserved as one of Havana's finest house museums, with fine painted frescoes, period furniture and wall-hangings. It is open Monday to Saturday 10:30 AM to 4:30 PM. Last but not least, **Casa de Africa** ((53-7) 61-2472, at No. 157, also housed in a former colonial *palacio*, is a museum, gallery and study-center dedicated to Afro-Cuban history as well as the works of ethnologist Fernando Ortíz. Music and dance performances take place on important Santería festival days. You can call ahead to check whether your visit coincides with any interesting events. There is a fantastic collection of paraphernalia used in various Santería and other African religions. Statues of the leading *orisha* divinities — Eleggúa, Changó, Yemayá and Ochún — are surrounded by objects associated with them. Fidel himself made a triumphant tour through Africa in 1977, and many of the zebra skins, chief's chairs and other ceremonial gifts he brought back with him are displayed here, as are many contributions from the some 17 African embassies represented in Havana. It is open Monday to Saturday from 10:30 AM to 4 PM and Sunday from 9 AM to noon.

From here, continue back along Calle Obrapía, and you will find **Casa Guayasamin** to your left, between Calle Mercaderes and Calle Oficios. This beautiful colonial mansion with its open interior courtyard is both an art gallery and home to Ecuadorian artist Oswaldo Guayasamin. If he is out-of-town, you can be guided through his living quarters upstairs, seeing original eighteenth-century wall frescoes as well as Guayasamin's portrait of Castro,

given to *El Jefe* for his 70th birthday. Havana's historian, Eusebio Leal, initiated a project wherein local children take painting lessons from the city's well-known artists here.

Turn left into Calle Oficios, one of the oldest streets in Havana, named for the *oficios de escribanos* or scribe's offices where early settlers could commission documents to be drawn up. On the left is the exotic **Casa de Arabe**, which in the late seventeenth century was purchased by the then-bishop Diego de Compostela to open as Havana's first school. It has a lovely interior courtyard and exhibits on Cuba's Arab immigrants. To your right is the **Museo de Autos Antiguos** (Vintage Car Museum), which displays a small, but diverse, array of cars, with past owners ranging from Beny Moré to Che Guevara. However, you are likely to see equally remarkable old cars parked on Havana's streets. At this corner, turn into Calle Justiz, which has several places of interest: the **Casa de la Comedia**, one of the city's oldest buildings; the **Salon Ensayo**, founded in 1990, which showcases Cuban dramatic talent; and the characterful **Caserón de Tango**, where gray-haired aficionados celebrate the dance with agile enthusiasm. From here, a left-hand turn along Calle Baratillo brings you back to Plaza de Armas and Calle Obispo.

From Calle Obispo, continue west one block, turn right on Calle San Ignacio and walk two blocks, crossing Calle O'Reilly (named after the Irish General who gave the key to Havana back to the Spanish in 1763) until you reach the other great square in Havana, the **Plaza de la Catedral**. It is adorned with some of the prettiest and most sophisticated examples of colonial baroque *palacios* to be seen, with sternly solid stone exteriors belied by enormous loggias, coquettish stained-glass windows, brightly painted shutters and tiny romantic balconies. Despite the crowds of stalls, hawkers and tourists, it is still easy to imagine that these mansions were once places of splendid retreat for the Creole aristocracy.

During Havana's early colonial period, this spot was so flood-prone that it was referred to as the Plazuela de la Ciénaga, or "the Little Square of the Swamp." But all that changed when this became the site of the first Spanish aqueduct in the New World. When you enter the square, look to your left to see where the Zanja Real (Royal Aqueduct), an irrigation channel which carried water from the Almendares River, 11 km (about seven miles) away, was situated, from which the people of Havana collected their drinking water, commemorated by a late sixteenth-century plaque. Today, the small side street is lined with artist's galleries, including a government collective.

Carpentier, adding that the baroque façade was "huge, but not fine, old yet not ancient, dilapidated and, as it were, worm-eaten." It was almost entirely built by the Jesuits, whose work on this site began in 1748, but after the order was expelled in 1767, the Spanish crown took over its completion. Its weathered, six-column façade is flanked by two unmatched bell towers, and seems to change its mood with the light. For over a century a casket containing what were believed to be the mortal remains of Christopher Columbus were

To your left as you approach the cathedral is the site of Havana's first public baths, it now houses the **Victor Manuel Gallery**, a well-stocked arts and crafts gallery. Next door is the sixteenth-century **Palacio de los Marquesas de Aguas Claras**, lived in by a series of well-born, or well-connected Spanish colonists. Now it is the restaurant **El Patio**, which has the best vistas across the square.

Havana's cathedral, **La Catedral de la Virgen María de la Concepción Inmaculada**, to give it its full name, dominates the north end of the square. Its eccentric, almost whimsical asymmetry somehow only enhances its majesty. "Music turned to stone," breathed Cuban novelist Alejo

kept in the cathedral, having been transferred from Santo Domingo after Hispaniola (now Haiti and the Dominican Republic) passed to France in 1795 (the casket was removed to Seville in 1898). The cathedral is open Monday to Friday, 9 AM to 11 AM, then 2:30 PM to 6 PM, and for mass on Sunday, 9 AM to 11 AM.

As you stand at the cathedral door looking back onto the square, the first building to your left is the grand, arcaded **Casa de Lombillo**, lived in by various colonial aristocrats, including a somewhat notorious slave-trader after whom the building is named. Notable for its exterior decorative

Straw hats for sale at the market in Old Havana.

paintings, it now houses the **Museo de la Educación** (Museum of Literacy) at Calle Empredaro No. 151, which proudly documents Castro's *campagna de alfabetizacion* (literacy campaign) during the 1960s.

The palace facing the cathedral is the **Casa de Chacón**, an eighteenth-century building that was built for the island's then-governor, Don Luis Chacón. Its unembellished simplicity makes it look more ancient than other buildings in the square. It has been used variously as offices, first for notaries, and later a newspaper and a rum manufacturer. Now it houses the **Museo de Arte Colonial** (Museum of Colonial Art) at Calle San Ignacio No. 61. It is crammed with a fascinating profusion of architectural details and household ware: stained-glass *vitrales* and *mediopuntos*, carved furniture, elaborate door-knockers, wrought-iron lamps, silver, porcelain, marble baths; varieties of the quirky carriages known as *volantes*, and an entire set of *caoba*-wood bedroom furniture. It is open daily except Tuesday from 9 AM to 5 PM, closing at 1 PM on Sunday.

A block away from the square, on Calle Empedrado, you will see the sign for the **Bodeguita del Medio**. Although everything else has changed since Hemingway's time, his favorite drink here, the famous *mojito* (a mix of rum, lemon juice, crushed mint leaves, soda water and sugar) remains excellent, although for some reason, the bar upstairs seems to produce a superior version. Errol Flynn's remark that this was "the best place to get drunk" seems to remain an apt one. Despite an abortive bomb attempt in 1997, which caused non-fatal injuries and considerable damage to the interiors that have since been revamped, La Bodeguita is perennially popular, with visitors eager to add their signature scrawl to walls already crammed with graffiti. Although it is a tourist trap, it is nonetheless fun, especially when the crowds thin out later in the evening.

Leaving La Bodeguita, retrace your steps towards the cathedral, and turn left into Calle San Ignacio. Continue to walk along the side of the cathedral, and beside it, you

Milling crowds and craft wares at the street market on the Plaza de la Catedral.

Havana

will see the **Semanario de San Carlos y San Ambrosio**, with its huge façade facing the bay, which, like the cathedral, was also built by the Jesuits. It has an exceptionally beautiful and peaceful inner garden, lined with columns and full of trees and vines: frangipani, ginger-lilies, and many varieties of palms, bounded by ancient stairwells.

Continue along, and near the intersection of Calle Cuba and Calle Tacón, opposite the ruins of Havana's colonial armory, is the **Palacio de la Artesanía** (Place of the Arti-

square is enclosed by various historic buildings. To the left is the Italian Renaissance-inspired **Lonja de Comercio**, built early this century and now renovated into a swanky office complex, with **Café Mercurio** on the ground floor. Opposite are several symbols of creeping consumerism: a Benetton franchise and the "Novio Wedding Shop" specializing in wedding finery that looks straight out of a Fellini film. You may want to stop for a cappuccino at the nineteenth-century style **Café del Oriente**.

sans). This charming colonial mansion has been converted into a shopping complex, with several floors in which you can browse for recordings of Cuban musicians, coral jewelry, beaded necklaces, Che Guevara T-shirts, rum and embroidered tablecloths under less pressure to buy than in the Plaza de la Catedral.

A Second Walking Tour of Old Havana
From Plaza de Armas, a two-minute stroll along Calle Oficios brings you to **Plaza de San Francisco de Asís**, a graceful wide-open square facing the city's main port and dock warehouses, with a central stone fountain adorned with lion statues. Gleaming from a spate of recent restoration, the

Although the order of San Francisco de Asís was founded in 1563, the majestic **Iglesia de San Francisco de Asís** was constructed much later, during the 1730s, above an earlier, modest hermitage. Its 40-m (130-ft)-high, three-tiered bell tower was added as an afterthought. During the English occupation of Havana this church was commandeered by the Earl of Ablemarle as a place of Protestant worship, and afterwards it was largely shunned by the devout Catholics of Havana, who even let it be used it as a military warehouse. Today however, classical concerts are frequently held within its immense barrel-vaulted interior, and you can often hear singers practicing. A passage leads to the portico cloisters of the adjacent convent, which in 1915 was converted into a telephone exchange. Part of the cloisters displays gilt-accented statues, bejeweled crosses and delicate ceramics; the convent itself is being renovated ir.to a children's dance and theatre school. It is, simply, a lovely place to linger in the quiet of the afternoon. If a choral performance in the church coincides with your stay, try to attend: a notice of upcoming performances (usually held at 6 PM on Saturdays) is posted at the church's main entrance. Entrance costs US$2.

Across the way, looking towards the port, you'll see the **Terminal Sierra Maestra**, the city's main cruise terminal.

On the corner of Calles Oficios and Brasil (Teniente Rey) you will reach the **Convento de Santa Clara de Asís**, a renovated seventeenth-century convent, encircled by an imposing wall, between Calles Sol and Luz. It was founded as a haven for young dowry-less women who had no other prospects, and built to house hundreds of nuns and slaves. It is now the headquarters of Cuba's **Centro Nacional de Conservación, Restauración, y Museología** (CENCREM), the institute responsible for the country's conservation research, training and architectural preservation, which was founded in 1982, the same year UNESCO recognized the international historical and archaeological value of La Habana Vieja by declaring it a World Heritage Site. It is open Monday to Friday from 9 AM to 3 PM. Next door, a small seventeenth-century house that is part of the convent, **Casa del Marino**, has been renovated for visiting scholars.

From here, follow Calle Brasil (Teniente Rey) until you reach **Plaza Vieja** (Old Square), which after Plaza de Armas and Plaza de Catedral, is one of the city's three great squares. Unlike the other squares, it is not dominated by churches or government buildings, but is purely residential. Begun in the late sixteenth century, it became home to many wealthy families, although many of the existing Creole *palacios*, with their arched *portales*, curved stained-glass windows and filigree balconies, were built a century later. Markets used to be held in its grand square, in which meats, vegetables and fruits were sold by peasants and freed slaves. Plaza Vieja has undergone dramatic renovation, involving the removal of a subterranean parking lot (added in 1952), renovation of former *palacios* into cultural centers and apartments, and the addition of a new hotel, Aparthotel Santo Angel, as well as a cinema and shops.

One of restored mansions that now has the appearance of emerging unblemished from the eighteenth century is the **Casa de los Condes de Jaruco** at Calle Muralla No. 107-111 between Calles Inquisidor and San

Ignacio. It was built in the late seventeenth century by the Count of San Juan de Jaruco, whose taste in interior and exterior decoration was clearly exuberantly whimsical: lyres, fruit, flowers and scrolls embellish the mansion's walls, offset by a giant entrance hall and carved *rejas* or fretted windows bar the upper gallery, but allow a gentle breeze. Look out for the macabre lock fashioned in the form of a female slave. The building now houses the **Cuban Foundation for the Fine Arts**, and the ground-floor gallery is a good place to start looking if you

OPPOSITE: Ernest Hemingway drank his *mojitos* at the Bodeguita del Medio. ABOVE: Detail of Havana's cathedral, built by the Jesuits in the eighteenth century, prior to their expulsion from Cuba in 1767.

are interested in buying works by Cuban artists. On the other side of the square, is the **Casa de Esteban José Portier**, which is now a photographic gallery. Art nouveau admirers should look out for the **Hotel Palacio Vienna** at the corner of Calles Muralla and Inquisidor, recently unveiled from scaffolding and soon to be divided up into apartments.

From here Calle Muralla, heading west, will lead you to Calle Cuba. By continuing south several blocks, passing the Convento de Santa Clara, you will come to the gothic **Iglesia Parroquial del Espíritu Santo**, Havana's oldest church and one of the most moving to visit, full of architectural quirks and surprises. It was originally a hermitage built in 1638, and was dedicated to "the devotions of free Negroes." Inside is a statue of Santa Barbara, the Catholic saint associated with Changó, the god of fire, thunder, passion and dance in the Santería religion. On each side of the church nave is a small catacomb; the more recent one dates from 1783 and is decorated by macabre fresco paintings featuring skulls adorned with tiaras and miters. The name of the church derives from its popularity amongst sailors and travelers, who used to pray for a safe voyage here.

If you turn right on Calle Acosta you will pass the monumental **Convento de Nuestra Señora de Belén**, which occupies the entire block. Part of its cloisters are scheduled to be renovated as a new hotel. Look for the **Arco de Belén** (Belén Archway), and head for Calle Leonor Pérez (Paula), where you will find the tiny, yellow-painted **Casa Natal de José Martí**, where the nation's great independence hero was born in 1853: it is now a house museum which details his life and times. It is open Tuesday to Saturday from 10 AM to 6 PM, Sunday from 9 AM to 12:45 PM, and is closed Monday.

Opposite the neo-Moorish **Estación Centrale de Ferrocarriles** (Central Railway Station), exhibits *La Junta*, a European-style 1843-model steam engine, Cuba's first.

From here, you can take a look at Havana's **Mercado Central** (Central Market), located opposite the Railway Station. This is the city's largest and most well-patronized

market, but the image of plenty is somewhat misleading: what people can't afford to purchase, either with their ration books, pesos or dollars, they come to look at.

It's a chaotic scene, with live roosters and chickens (some destined to have their throats cut in a Santería ritual), goats and tortoises; piles of vegetables such as *yucca* and potatoes; tins of sweetened condensed milk, flowers and medicinal herbs. Outside, rows of *habaneros* sit on hemp sacks, some trying to sell just a single item, such as an old rusty lock, or barter possessions for food. Outside, young boys sell re-filled plastic lighters that most often contain flyspray or solvents.

From here, you can either take Calle Leonor Pérez as a shortcut or meander

along the seafront Désamparados. Look out for the former **Iglesia Antigua de San Francisco de Paula**, now used as a small exhibition space; and further along, near the seafront Avenida Paula, at the corner of Calles Acosta and Oficios, the **Wilfredo Lam Center**, an important cultural and arts center and the sponsor of the Havana Biennial. It is open Monday to Friday, and every other Sunday from 8:30 AM to 4:30 PM.

From here, take Calle Oficios back into the heart of La Habana Vieja, or perhaps make a detour along Avenida San Pedro (Avenida del Puerto) to stop for a drink at the **Bar Dos Hermanos**, an atmospheric place where locals like to unwind. It is named for the two American brothers who were former proprietors during the Batista years.

Parque Central and the Prado
This walking tour begins at Parque Central, where the edges of the old city blur with the new. Suddenly the architecture is from a different era: streets widen into boulevards; hulking makeshift buses lumber to a halt for yet more passengers; people stand in line outside government department stores. Formerly called the Parque de Isabela, the leafy, dilapidated Parque Central has a statue of José Martí as its centerpiece. Although lovely, it's hard to ignore the park's somewhat desperate

The newly restored sixteenth-century Plaza Vieja.

ambiance: it is popular with *jineteros* (hustlers) and the *portales* of the Spanish-Renaissance Centro Asturiano are used as a nocturnal pissoir. This being said, unlike many of Havana's other main squares, it is also a gathering place for Cubans rather than tourists, and consequently you'll often see groups of men of all ages playing chess or discussing baseball results, and office workers having a break. Hawkers sell twists of salted peanuts along the dank, tree-lined boulevard. All this may change: the park is being renovated, as well as the Centro Asturiano, and the huge five-star, 282-room joint-venture Hotel Parque Central is being constructed to occupy a full block facing it.

A few steps away, at the beginning of Calle Obispo is **El Floridita**. El Floridita is one of Havana's fixtures. More than 70 years ago, the frozen *daiquirí* was created here by barman Constante Ribailagua. But it was Hemingway who made *daiquirís* famous, and this is where he drank them: you can see the Napoleonic-style barstool where he sat. In Havana's giddy pre-Revolution days, El Floridita was all the rage, and its enthusiasts also included Gary Cooper, Ingrid Bergman, Tennessee Williams, Jean Paul Sartre, Marlene Dietrich, Spencer Tracy and Ava Gardner. Like the Bodeguita del Medio, it is a tourist trap, but worth at least one visit, and sampling its truly delicious *daiquirí* is a must. Above El Floridita, you can sample and buy most brands of Cuban rum at the **Casa del Ron**.

Across the street is the **Manzana de Gómez**, a turn-of-the-century department store occupying the entire block, once filled with the latest Paris fashions but now rather desolate and empty. From here, a few steps take you into the lobby of the charming nineteenth-century **Hotel Plaza**, where you can take an elevator up to its top floor terrace and perhaps have a cold drink while admiring the view, which looks back into parts of La Habana Vieja and across Centro Habana. As you walk around the terrace, you'll have an excellent view of the **Edificio Bacardí**, built in 1929 for the rum and sugar tycoon, Emilio Bacardí, and the most impressive art deco building in Cuba,

decorated with beautiful ceramic tiles and stylized nymphs. It has been restored as an office building and is leased out to foreign companies.

Back on the street, at the corner of Calle Animas, look out for the mosaic in the pavement and for **Sloppy Joe's**; as legendary in its own time as El Floridita, fictionalized by Hemingway as Freddy's Bar in his *To Have and To Have Not*, and now awaiting restoration before re-opening to quench the thirst of new admirers.

Heading back to the Parque Central, you'll see the extravagant, neo-baroque façade of the **Hotel Inglaterra**, opposite. This is Havana's oldest hotel, first opened in 1884. It has been restored, and its dining room and patio are cool havens of patterned tiles, potted palms and stained glass. At its side, across a small alley, is the **Gran Teatro**, formerly known as the **Centro Gallego**, built as a private club for descendents of Galician immigrants. This extraordinary architectural confection is a wonderful, slightly surreal sight; full of Neo-baroque ornamentation, with its statues depicting illustrious muses and winged angels atop each of its four towers. The Gran Teatro was an ambitious renovation of Havana's former nineteenth-century **Tacón Theatre**, which has was absorbed into the new design by its Austrian architect, Paul Belau. Inside, grand staircases and elaborate marble detailing were once the backdrop for the club's libraries, smoking, billiard and dining rooms. A performance of Aida marked the inauguration of the club in 1915. Today, this is where you see the National Ballet de Cuba and the National Opera de Cuba perform.

It is impossible to miss the nearby Capitolio. Built in 1928, it is the spitting image of the United States Capitol, although it was styled by Cuban architects. It was intended to be the sparkling centerpiece of that democracy-averse dictator, Geraldo Machado, and he spent a quarter of his US$50 million annual budget on it. Like the original, it is magisterially lined with marble, and has two long lateral galleries leading from a central vestibule. A compass set into an inlaid rose on the floor beneath the 91-m (300-ft)-high dome marks the point from which distances from Havana are measured. Looming beneath the high, vaulted ceiling is a massive bronze statue representing the Cuban Republic. Guided tours (for US$3) run through its grandiose interior, now a technical library, into the former presidential offices and halls of the pre-Revolution Cuban congress. The Capitolio houses the Museo de Ciencias Naturales (Museum of Natural Sciences) and the Museo de Ciencias y Técnicas (Museum of Science and Technology) which has a planetarium. It's open Tuesday to Saturday from 10:15 AM to 5:45 PM and Sunday from 9:15 AM to 12:45 PM.

To the left of the Capitolio is the **Parque de la Fraternidad**, which is chiefly known these days as a gathering place for freelance *taxi particulares* or private taxis. But these are no ordinary taxis, as their proud owners will attest. On an average day there is an extraordinary line-up of antique American cars, with Chevrolets, Buicks, Plymouths, Packards and Studebakers in various states of polish and still-operable decay. For car buffs, this is a good place to meet your fellow Cuban enthusiasts. Opposite the square is the **Palacio de Aldama**, possibly Havana's most splendidly decorative example of an aristocratic nineteenth-century residence, with ornate neo-classical frescoes, intricate carvings and a beautiful cloistered patio. It is now the Instituto de Historia del Movimiento Obrero de Cuba (Cuba's Worker's Movement) which, unfortunately, is not generally open to the public.

Tucked behind the Capitolio and the Parque de la Fraternidad, on Calle Industria, is the **Partagas Cigar Factory**, one of the oldest and largest in Cuba. You can take a guided tour through the building's several floors, where cigars are hand-made from the sorting of leaves to the packaging, or simply browse from the extensive and well-stocked array of cigars, and sample their delicious expresso coffee in the shop. It is open for tours Monday to Friday, from 9 AM to 3 PM. Guided tours are at 10:30 AM and 1:30 PM, for US$5. The shop is also open on Saturday.

From here, retrace your steps, past the Hotel Inglaterra and you will find yourself

facing the **Paseo del Martí** (also known as Paseo del Prado), a raised boulevard lined with laurel trees, statues, wrought-iron lamp posts and coral rock benches laid out in the late seventeenth century. For two centuries, this promenade was frequently a crush of horses and carriages; as the favored meeting place for an hour or two of decorous dalliance by Havana's high society, while military musicians in bright uniforms marched up and down playing overtures, polkas and marches. Often referred to as the "Prado," this boulevard remains

a popular place to stroll, and there's always something interesting to see. About half-way down, there is a sort-of open-air housing bureau which specializes in "*Se Permuta*" ("For Swap"), where people animatedly discuss swapping their house or apartment for another property, either in Havana or in another part of Cuba: the only legal way Cubans are allowed to move, with no cash changing hands. You might see a wedding party file out of the **Palacio de Matrimonia**, the grand mansion that conducts civil weddings at the corner of Calle Animas, where shining Chevrolets

Grandmother and grandchild in the Callejón de Hamel, Central Havana.

festooned with bouquets and streamers are the day's chariot of choice. Teachers gossip while their charges play; or urchins compete with their home-made skateboards. On either side, the Prado is also architecturally interesting, full of once-aristocratic mansions and quirky residential façades, many of them *cuidadelas*, or home to a dozen or so families.

As you walk towards the Malecón, to the right you will see the back of the **Hotel Sevilla**, the former Sevilla-Biltmore, another of the city's classic and beautifully restored nineteenth-century hotels, which is where Graham Greene had his character Wormold stay in Room 507 while on his beleaguered undercover mission, in *Our Man in Havana*. Between Calle Zulueta (Agramonte) and Avenida de las Misiones (Monserrate) are two of Havana's important museums. First up, in an unprepossessing modernistic building is the **Museo Nacional de Bellas Artes** (National Art Museum) ℂ (53-7) 61-1864 at Calle Animas. Despite its contradictory exterior, it is the most important art museum in Cuba. A permanent exhibition displays antiquities from Egypt, Greece and Rome; Spanish and Italian Renaissance paintings and even works by Rubens, Velásquez, Gainsborough and Degas. Among the notable works by Cuban artists are those by Wilfredo Lam, René Portocarrero and Amelia Peláez. Open Wednesday to Sunday, 9 AM to 5 PM, it is closed on Monday and Tuesday.

Walking away from the Prado towards the seafront on Calle Refugio No. 1 is the former **Palacio Presidencial**, notable as the place where Batista only just escaped being lynched by an attack by 40 students in March 1957 — he was lucky to escape detection by hiding in an elevator shaft. Built in 1920, this Spanish Revival former presidential palace is now the **Museo de la Revolución**, with three floors devoted to what it describes on its pamphlet as "the natural rebellion of the Cuban people." At the entrance is a tank used by Fidel Castro in Playa Girón during the Bay of Pigs invasion. The museum has an exhaustive display that covers Cuba's history from Spanish colonization to the wars of independence and the subsequent Republican era — then, having set the scene for the Cuban Revolution, proceeds to detail almost everything you ever wanted to know about Fidel, his modus operandi in the Moncada Barracks and the Sierra Maestra and his triumph as "*El Jefe*" over the Bay of Pigs debacle. The profusion of charts, maps and 3-D models of battle sites are fascinating but they start to make you feel battle-weary yourself, but the photographs are evocative: an American marine drunkenly urinating on a statue of José Martí, Celia Sánchez gravely loving look towards her comrade-lover Fidel in the depths of the jungle, the many faces of Che Guevara. Touching remnants are preserved: the blood-stained uniforms of unlucky revolutionaries, Che's black beret and his asthma inhaler, Fidel's trousers, Celia's shirt. A bizarre touch is added by the mock *mise en scène* capturing the moment when Che and Camilo Cienfuegos emerged from the mountains, leading their horses — their *actual* horses, which were stuffed for posterity.

Outside, in an open-air glass-walled pavilion, sits the **Granma**, the famous leaky cabin cruiser in which Fidel and 81 other revolutionaries, including his brother Raúl and Che, returned to Cuba from their exile in Mexico. Trying to visualize how all these men actually managed to fit themselves aboard this modestly sized boat is something of a mental challenge. Other icons of the Revolution include the delivery van used by the students in their raid against Batista; pieces of an American B-26 shot down over the Bay of Pigs and a U-2 reconnaissance plane downed by Russian missiles during the Cuban Missile Crisis. It is open Tuesday to Sunday, 10 AM to 5 PM.

From here you can stroll out towards the Malecón. As you leave the museum, to your left you'll see the white **Iglesia de Santo Angel Custodia** (Church of the Holy Angel Savior), largely destroyed by a hurricane in 1844; gothic spires were added as part of its nineteenth-century restoration; and the extravagant Art Nouveau architectural confection that is now used as the **Spanish Embassy**. At the northern end of Avenida de las Misiones at Calle

Capdevila No. 1 is the **Museo Nacional de la Música** (Music Museum) which has an extensive collection of Cuban instruments as well as a shop selling CDs and cassettes. It's open Tuesday to Saturday, 10 AM to 6 PM, Sunday 9 AM to noon, and is closed Monday.

The avenue continues down to the seafront, and beyond the mounted statue of the Cuban independence hero, General Máximo Gómez, is the small fortress of Castillo de San Salvador de la Punta, known by all as "La Punta."

Centro Habana

Central Havana, often referred to by *habaneros* as "Centro," stretches between its boundary with the Malecón, the Paseo del Prado, which connects it to La Habana Vieja, and the Calzada de Infanta, which marks its border with the district of Vedado. While there are few obvious attractions for tourists, sections of Centro Habana are interesting, for this was Havana's former commercial district. Today, plenty of street life spills out from its run-down turn-of-the-century apartments and depressed-

OPPOSITE: Paseo del Martí was once an elegant place to see and be seen. ABOVE: Edificio Bacardí is Havana's finest example of art deco.

looking shops. Most of it is not considered dangerous to walk around in, although it is disreputable in parts, which you should be alert to. You should avoid this area at night however, when it is almost completely blacked-out, with no streetlights. If you are driving, the main streets — Calles San Rafael, Zanja, Neptuno and San Lázaro — provide a fast route through the district.

Centro's main shopping district is along **Calle San Rafael**, which begins behind the Hotel Inglaterra, and is a somewhat miserable medley of 1950s-era department stores; the furtive spirit of free enterprise is more in evidence on the streets, with people offering things for sale, such as newspaper twists of peanuts, shots of *guarapo* (sugarcane juice), or Santería amulets.

At the intersection of Calles San Rafael and Galiano, continue until you reach Calle Dragones, then turn on Calle Zanja. This will bring you to Havana's own Barrio Chino or **Chinatown**, centered on **Calle Cuchillo**, a block-long street that runs between Calles Zanja and San Nicolás, a few blocks west of the Capitolio. This unexpected part of Havana is all that is left of a once-thriving district that was traditionally home to many thousands of Chinese immigrants during the nineteenth century. Many of these immigrants came from Guangdong Province and were imported — albeit voluntarily — as workers on Cuba's sugar plantations, but faced tremendous hardships once they arrived and discovered they had become virtual slaves. Many moved either to Havana or Santiago de Cuba to establish themselves as traders. Many Chinese *habaneros* chose to leave Cuba after the Revolution, and now only around 700 remain.

Although this is not one of Havana's obvious attractions, it is interesting to explore this tiny section which used to be a thriving tourist attraction in the 1950s — and see its remaining shops, restaurants and pharmacies. Look out for the ornate, dragon-festooned **Restaurant Pacifico** (on Calles San Nicolas and Cuchillo); the **Casino Chino**, the headquarters of the **Mi Chang Society** (a brotherhood founded

400 years ago, which has 300 active members) and the office of the **Partido Democrata Chino**.

It's too far to walk from here, but you must include a visit to **Callejón Hamel**, which lies between Calles Hospital and Aramburo, best reached from the nearby Malecón. It is known for one of its residents, the painter **Salvador**, an easily recognizable figure with his white beard, light skin and head of gray curls. He has a small gallery here, but it's his work outside that's better known: Salvador is Havana's best-

known muralist and has used the city's dilapidated walls as his canvases for many years. His bright, bold murals have a folkloric quality, charged with painted words and phrases and the best place to admire them is this narrow road, also called by some, Callejón de Filin ("Street of Feeling"). Come to see the neighborhood transformed by Santería dances accompanied by musicians playing rumba each Sunday.

The Malecón

The sweeping **Malecón** is Havana's much-loved and most recognizable feature, a constant symbol of its enduring attachment to the sea. Tightly packed around a splendid bay, its famously decayed mansions and apartments resemble a curving stage set on the sea rim, open to the immense emptiness of the horizon. It stretches seven kilometers (just over four miles) between the La Punta fortress and the mouth of the Almendares River, and is the fastest route from La Habana Vieja to Vedado as well as to Miramar. You might want to walk part of the way, and explore the rest by taxi.

Laid out in 1901, the Malecón's sea wall is fronted by an arcaded row of sea-pocked mini-mansions, each house spiritedly different from the next: Moorish-domed windows, mosaics, calligraphic iron balconies, crumbling stone caryatids, and heavy carved doors. Seen from a distance, the paint on the stone buildings fades into a nostalgic patchwork of soft pastels; up close, their former brilliance (pink trimmed with purple, green with cobalt, blue with yellow) has been worn away by salt, heat, and high humidity, not to mention periodic hurricanes.

At times, the Malecón has a festive air, an almost giddy mood of camaraderie: when, on hot days, children (and adults) flirt with the salty sea spray, shrieking with glee when they are drenched, and daredevils launch themselves off the rocks and then clamber back to shore; when a popular salsa song on a crackly sound system gets its listeners on their feet for an impromptu dance; when Lycra-clad girls drape themselves on the sun-warmed wall, chatting amongst themselves, keeping an eye out for admirers. At other times, it can seem almost desolately sad: when, as your late-night taxi speeds back to the hotel, you see a small army of disturbingly young *jineteras* in microskirts and spandex.

The promenade has many guises, changing with the light and the color of the sea and sky. When the tropical storms rage, the waves can knock pedestrians off their feet, and sometimes sweeps cars skidding across the pavement. On still, clear days, you can see sun-scorched men casting themselves into the sea in inflated tires (the same used by the *balseros* or rafters) in their attempts to catch a meal for their families. The Malecón itself is changing quickly, for as part of Havana's restoration program, 14 square blocks of the Malecón are scheduled to be rehabilitated and work has already begun, as evidenced by the transformation of the Catyrid's House, close to La Punta, now

School children cluster on Paseo del Martí.

the Spanish government's office for cultural affairs. The project is estimated to eventually cost US$50 million, of which more than a half has been pledged by the Spanish government.

As you continue along the seafront promenade, you'll see the **USS *Maine* monument**, just west of the Hotel Nacional, constructed in memory of the 267 sailors who died when the American warship exploded in Havana Bay in 1898. Shortly after the Revolution, jubilant anti-American crowds knocked off the stone eagle that used to adorn this monument; its broken wings can now be seen in the Museo de la Ciudad de la Habana. The *Maine* has a different meaning in Cuba than in the United States. "To the victims of the *Maine* who were sacrificed to imperialist greed in its fervor to seize control of the island of Cuba," reads the inscription at the base of the monument. The head of the stone eagle is now mounted on the wall of the snack bar at the American Interests Section, Washington's quasi-embassy in Havana.

As the Malecón curves still further on, it is impossible to miss the seven-story mirror-plated, hermetically sealed **United States Special Interests Section**. In the sort of quirk to be expected given the political stand-off between Cuba and the United States, the building is in fact sub-leased to the American government by the Swiss Embassy, and a similar arrangement characterizes Cuba's Special Interest's Section in Washington.

Onwards, various places of interest loom into view: the **Calixto García monument**; the Art Deco **Casa de las Americas**, founded in 1959 as a forum to showcase cultural exchanges between Cuba and Latin America; and the open-air **Mercado Feria Malecón**, where you can browse among old political comic books, 1950s movie posters, curios and many second-hand goods. It has a very Cuban atmosphere and is open daily except Monday.

You can turn off the Malecón momentarily to see the **Museo de Artes Decorativas** (Museum of Decorative Arts) at Calles 17 and E, housed in the former mansion of the Countess Revilla de Camargo, a famous

lady-about-town. It has a charming and in many ways exceptional display of important European and Oriental decorative arts from the eighteenth century through to the twentieth century. You can admire the rococo gilt Neoclassical Hall that was once the Countess's bedroom, with the *secrétaire* that once belonged to Marie Antoinette. The museum is open Tuesday to Saturday from 11 AM to 6:30 PM, and Sunday from 9 AM to 1 PM.

Two hotels come next, both symbols in their own way of their own era, representing the Cuban tourism industry, past and present. First is the **Hotel Melía Cohiba**, considered the most up-to-date and luxurious hotel in Cuba. Further along is the 20-story **Hotel Habana Riviera**, which

had major backing from the Mafia when it opened as a hotel-casino in 1957, just before the Revolution took over and dashed their expectations that Havana was about to become the next Las Vegas. Jewish mob boss Meyer Lanksy lived in the top-floor suite, which is now the hotel's business center with staggering views across the sea.

About eight blocks away, when the Malecón dips down into the underground tunnel, lies the district of Miramar. Just before you enter the tunnel, to your right you can see the small **Torreón de Santa Dorotea de Luna de la Chorrera**, a seventeenth-century fort that was part of the city's protective phalanx. Near the fort's parapet is **1830**, a restaurant housed in an elegant white colonial mansion, and you can stop at its open-air terrace to enjoy a much-deserved drink and the view.

Vedado and La Rampa

Along the Malecón, mid-way between La Habana Vieja and the tunnel to Miramar, lies the district known as Vedado, which is now Havana's business district with many commercial offices, including agencies for airlines and tour companies. During the early colonial era this area was deliberately left densely forested as an additional deterrent to pirates, to protect the city from attack by land as well as by sea. It was not until early this century that the forests were

---

The Museo de la Revolución was completed in 1920.

razed, to make way for larger and more modernized homes for Havana's elite who had began to desert La Habana Vieja, a phenomenon which accelerated during the 1930s. Many elaborate stone mansions — some small palaces — date from the Art Deco and Art Nouveau period, mostly one or two stories high, with eclectic stucco façades often bearing French, Italian and even Mayan designs and decorative patios. During the 1950s, when reinforced concrete was all the rage, the Hilton, Riviera and Capri hotels as well as the FOCSA

sight of their grand-children. For many exiled Cubans who fled their homes after the fall of Batista, Vedado *is* Cuba, or at least the Cuba they remember as children: fluttering laundry suggests that these once-stylish private houses that belonged to their parents are now multiple dwellings. During the early days of the Revolution, the Castro government ordered enforced squatting in Vedado's abandoned houses, in order to ensure that their former owners would find it all but impossible to reclaim their possessions.

building rose on Vedado's skyline, along with New York-inspired high-rise apartment blocks and prefabricated-looking government offices.

Laid out like a chessboard in grid-like squares with streets identified by numbers or letters, this immense neighborhood is easy to wander around in and offers compelling glimpses of its former glory amid its ugly tower blocks. Off its main avenues, tranquil streets reveal many lived-in scenes of Havana life: falling-down mansions where frangipani trees blossom in the hot shadows and bedraggled, tail-down dogs find respite from insults; while old ladies in frayed dresses keep vigil on their verandahs, their world-weary eyes softening at the

If you are exploring Vedado on foot, begin at the **Hotel Nacional**, perhaps Cuba's only truly legendary hotel, modeled on the Breakers Hotel in Palm Beach, Florida. Since it opened in 1930, this has been the hotel of the rich and famous, including Winston Churchill, the Prince of Wales Edward VIII, Charles de Gaulle, Buster Keaton, Frank Sinatra, Nat King Cole Ava Gardner, and Marlon Brando among others. It also featured as the site of a lengthy (and bloody) siege during a coup-attempt against dictator President Machado during the 1930s. In 1955, part of the hotel was converted into a Mafia-owned casino, managed by the Jewish-American mobster Meyer Lansky. Like a stately old ship ebbing with the tide of visitors, the Nacional is an essential part of experiencing Havana, so a drink on its verandah and a stroll through its gardens is called for.

After walking through the entrance gates of the Nacional, the **Hotel Capri** is a glance away; shabby these days, it is a far cry from its incarnation as the libidinous playground of the Mafia, built by the notorious American Mafioso, Santo Traficante Jr. Just northwest of the Hotel Capri looms the massive concrete **Edificio**

Up the hill, on Calle L, is the ugly, albeit recently modernized and much-patronized **Hotel Habana Libre**, the former Havana Hilton which in the heady early days of the Revolution served as Fidel's headquarters. A few days after Fidel claimed Havana, a memorable interview was filmed here, with the seasoned American broadcaster Edward R. Murrow laconically questioning Cuba's new leader, who, with his small son, Fidelito on his lap, answered in his halting English and was clearly more than a little overwhelmed at

FOCSA, Cuba's largest building, a 1950s apartment block that used to house visiting Russian delegates, officials and technicians during the Cold War period. These days, it is chiefly known for its rooftop **La Torre** restaurant and its dollar *supermercado*.

Walk downhill and turn right and you will find yourself at the corner of Avenida 23, the main thoroughfare of the city center, which, on its uphill rise, is known by all as **La Rampa**, lined with offices, shops, cinemas and fast-food parlors. You can browse for publications and pick up an English-language copy of *Granma* at the **Centro de la Prensa** (Press Center) directly on your right.

his sudden transformation of history. Later, Fidel, Che and other revolutionary leaders were prone to sweep in unannounced for ice-cream milkshakes at the poolside bar here, leading to an famously bungled CIA assassination attempt by an operative posing as a bartender. Then, as now, the top floors offer fantastic aerial views across the entire city.

Opposite the Habana Libre is the spaceship-like **Heladería Coppelia**, one of the fixtures of the Revolution, a cafeteria that used to specialize in many varieties of

OPPOSITE LEFT: The Hotel Nacional, a Havana icon, was inaugurated in 1930. OPPOSITE RIGHT AND ABOVE: Nineteenth-century Hotel Sevilla played a role in Graham Green's *Our Man in Havana*.

Cuban-made ice-cream, including guava, mango and papaya, but unfortunately now limited due to the shortages of the Special Period. Tomás Gutiérrez Alea's film *Fresa y Chocolate* (Strawberry and Chocolate) sets its memorable opening scene here. Most *habaneros* have to wait in long queues to be served, but tourists or those with dollars can bypass the lines and head straight for the first floor to be served promptly.

Several blocks away from the Habana Libre, continuing up Calle L, is the **University of Havana**, an acropolis-like complex begun early this century intended by its planners to be the epitome of classical monumentality. Its impressive Corinthian columns and 88-step entrance were the scene of many political demonstrations during the Republican era of Machado and Batista. Aside from wandering through its leafy campus, one of the main reasons to visit the university is to visit two museums here, both housed in the Felipe Poey building, which is named for the Cuba's eminent nineteenth-century naturalist. The **Museo de Ciencas Naturales Felipe Poey** is crammed with stuffed and pickled exhibits of Cuban wildlife, including some rare endemic species; while the **Museo Anthropológico Montané** displays the island's most important archaeological artifacts, and there is no better place to discover the history of Cuba's earliest inhabitants, although the sketchy labeling of the exhibits can be frustrating. There are many fascinating artifacts, including carved turtle shells and shark-teeth necklaces; reconstructions of pre-Columbian burial rituals, and two stylized carved idols, one thought to be a god of tobacco, dating from AD 1500.

Across the road from the university entrance, at the corner of Calles San Miguel and Ronda, is the **Museo Napoleónico** (Napoleonic Museum) at Calle San Miguel No. 1159. Set in a beautiful Italianate mansion that is perhaps Havana's most unexpected museum, the legacy of the building's former owner, Orestes Ferrara, who had a magnificent obsession for all things Napoleonic. Imperial-era furniture adorns every room, and there are some fine paintings and weapons in the Hall of the First Empire; while among the personal effects on display that belonged to Napoleonic are a lock of his hair, a toothbrush and the hat he is said to have worn on St. Helena, as well as the pistols he used at the battle of Borodino, his spy-glass, and a unique piece, his death mask, brought to Cuba by Dr. Francesco Antommarchi, the doctor who attended him until the end. It's open from Monday to Friday, 9 AM to noon, 1 PM to 4 PM, and alternate Saturdays; it is closed Sundays.

In the vicinity, you may wish to explore a little-visited gem. Tucked away in the extensive and tranquil gardens of Havana's **Botanical Gardens**, with its entrance on Avenida Salvador Allende, south of the university, is the graceful house-museum, **Quinta de los Molinos**. It was built for as a summer residence for Governor Tacón in 1837, and named after the royal snuff mills, which used to be located on the site. Just beyond the Quinta is the eighteenth-century **Castillo del Principe**, an inland fortress that has been converted into Havana's main prison.

Plaza De La Revolución and Necrópolis Cristóbal Colón

Due the distances that have to be covered to explore this area, you will need a rental car or taxi. South of Vedado lies the **Plaza de la Revolución**, the political nerve-center of the Cuban nation, around which is the district known as "Plaza." The square's wide paved expanse dominated by the towering **José Martí monument** — a huge white marble statue of the nation's hero that stands in front of a giant four-sided obelisk. The observation platform (reached after climbing 567 steps or by taking the elevator) is not always open. The stand in front of the monument has often been used by Fidel for his marathon speeches, and by other leaders to address the mass rallies that take place here: it was here that Pope John Paul II addressed the Cuban people during his landmark visit in January 1998, and here that the body of Che Guevara — for a long time, the equivalent of Cuba's patron saint — lay in state in 1997, after its return from being unearthed in a mass grave in Bolivia.

Surrounding the square are the most important government buildings in Cuba: the former Justice Ministry, now the **Central Committee of the Communist Party** (where Fidel's office is rumored to be); the Ministry of Communications, the Ministry of Defense, and the Ministry of Industry, which has an enormous metal sculptural portrait of Che. None of these monolithic edifices are open to the public — except for the **Biblioteca Nacional** and the **Teatro Nacional** (which presents mainly symphonic music and operas) and all have a rather foreboding, slightly Orwellian-look about them, and show the influence of Le Corbusier. All of these civic buildings, as well as the José Martí monument, were completed before the Revolution. An eccentric postal museum, the **José Luis Guerra Aguiar Museo Postal**, is housed in the Ministry of Communications.

Head back to Vedado, taking the roundabout route looping back via Avenida 23. At its intersection with Avenida Zapata and Calle 12 stands the grand Romanesque entrance to the nineteenth-century **Necrópolis Cristóbal Colón**. Unusual as it may seem, this historic cemetery is one of Havana's hidden marvels, with its many mausoleum equivalents of architectural follies, decorated with cherubs, angels, griffins and life-size statuary, set along tree-lined avenues where you can wander at whim, or rest on strategically-placed benches. Since 1871, this has been Havana's city for the dead. At 56 hectares (138 acres), it is the largest cemetery in Latin America, with mausoleums, tombs and vaults laid out in grid-like blocks, with a yellow-hued Greek Orthodox church at its core, the **Capillo Central**. Traditionally, plots were segregated by social status; professional and mutual societies also built tombs for their members. Just across Avenida 26, at the cemetery's southwest corner, lies the cemetery for Havana's Chinese community. Many of Cuba's greats are buried here, including Máximo Gómez, Alejo Carpentier, Celia Sánchez and Haydee Santamaría. Just left of the main entrance gate is the **Buro de Turismo**, which sells entrance tickets for US$1 and offers free guided tours of the main tombs, although tips are welcome. The cemetery is open from 6 AM to 6 PM daily.

The much-adorned roof of the Gran Teatro.

Follow Avenida 23 back to central Vedado. At the intersection of Avenida 23 and Calle 12, look for a bronze plaque on the corner which commemorates the spot where, on April 16, 1961, Fidel first proclaimed the "Socialist Nature of the Revolution" to listening masses, exhorting them to offer armed resistance to the Bay of Pigs invasion.

Miramar and West Havana
From Vedado, the Malecón continues west, through an underground tunnel, to reach the residential suburb of **Miramar**, which in

many ways is a respite from the rest of Havana, with its leafy parks and spacious boulevards lined with flame and jacaranda trees. This is where many of the wealthiest *habaneros* lived before the Revolution: perhaps it is no mistake that its main boulevard is called **Quinta Avenida** (Fifth Avenue), a continuation of the Malecón. Miramar is a constantly fascinating place if you are interested in seeing the evolution of Havana's residential architecture, which ranges from formal turn-of-the-century decorative buildings set in elaborate gardens to more whimsical eclectic designs with stucco embellishments in stucco and concrete built during the 1940s and 1950s. Miramar still has an air of privilege, and is largely occupied by embassies, diplomatic residences, private schools, exclusive dollar boutiques, supermercados, and ritzy restaurants.

The **Museo del Minsterio del Interior** (Museum of the Interior Ministry) at the corner of Avenida 5 and Calle 14 is strangely overlooked by visitors but it is a not-to-be-missed glimpse into the paranoiac mechanics of the

Cold War spying game between Cuba and the United States. All sorts of tools of the trade are displayed, ranging from exploding soap dishes to plastic rocks hiding radios, and there is a comprehensive description of the many attempts over the decades on Castro's life by his opponents. By the end of the exhibition, you will be comprehensively briefed about the activities of the Ministry of the Interior up to the present day.

Further west, at the corner of Avenida 5 and Calle 16, the **Casa del Tabaco** is one of the best cigar shops in Cuba, with knowledgeable staff and a wonderfully aromatic environment. A block south, at the corner of Avenida 7 and Calle 16, is **La Maison**, a colonial mansion with the soul of Imelda Marcos which has become the playing ground for Cuba's nouveau-riche. At night there are fashion shows; by day, you can come here to browse in its dollar-boutiques, cosmetic and jewelry shops or indulge in the beauty parlor or shiatsu clinic. Fidel's daughter Alina once worked as a model here, before she defected in 1993. During the day, La Maison's café restaurant is also open.

Further along Avenida 5, at the intersection of Calle 60, you will see to your left the imposing **Iglesia de San Antonio de Padua**, perhaps Cuba's only air-conditioned church, built after the Second World War. As you continue on, next in view is **Cubanacán**, also known as the "Country Club," a more secluded, greener neighborhood where gated walls offer glimpses of palatial mansions and estates, some of which are now home to Havana's foreign ambassadors and senior Cuban government officials, while others have remained locked and empty, their original occupants long since fled. The **Palacio de las Convenciones** is located here, where international conferences are held in its numerous meeting rooms and halls.

Marina Hemingway
On the western outskirts of the city, just off Avenida 5 in the suburb of Santa Fé is the **Marina Hemingway**. An increasing number of yachting enthusiasts — roughly half of whom are Americans — have been sailing to Cuba in recent years, and this is where they berth their yachts. The marina compound includes various dollar supermarkets, bars,

and restaurants, like **Papa's**. You can stay here at the **Hotel El Viejo y el Mar**, or in pleasant condominium-style apartments run by the marina. Every year, the marina hosts several international fishing events and regattas: the **Ernest Hemingway International Marlin Tournament** in May or June, and the **Blue Marlin International Fishing Tournament** in August or September.

If you continue beyond Santa Fé, the road passes the Granma Naval Academy and an industrial zone, then Playa Salado, you would arrive in **Mariel**, the industrial port that was

the fortress megaliths that now stand as Havana's architectural emblems look downright formidable. Like scimitars of stone, these impressive military forts straddle the strategic harbor entrance, one on each side of the narrow channel, towering over passing freighters and tankers. When it was finally completed, this became the best-defended harbor in the Americas, unchallenged for almost two centuries.

Construction began in 1590, under the command of Giovanni Baptista Antonelli, an Italian military engineer selected to con-

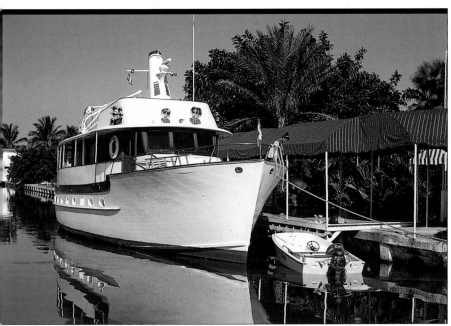

the embarkation point for the 1980 boatlift, which resulted in the emigration of 125,000 Cubans. If you plan to take the coastal route to Pinar del Río, on an excursion out of Havana, this is where the route begins.

Havana's Fortresses

To explore the fortresses in the route suggested here, you need a rented car, or to hire a taxi for a few hours, or perhaps to join a tour group. You may want to combine your excursion with a drink or meal at **La Divina Pastora** or **Los Doce Apóstoles**, perfect for watching the sunset glow across the Malecón.

Devised to keep warring armies and aggressive pirates at bay, it is no mistake that

struct Havana's defensive fortresses by the Spanish crown. Taking the city's traumatic earlier experience of pirates into account, he cast his eye on the ridge buttressing the entrance to the city's harbor and pronounced: "Whoever is master of this hill will be master of Havana."

Antonelli designed two forts — the **Castillo de los Tres Santos Reyes Magos del Morro** ("El Morro") and the **Castillo de San Salvador de la Punta** ("La Punta") — which together were intended to form a staunch defensive triangle with the already-built Castillo de la Real Fuerza. Although both were begun at the same time, El Morro

OPPOSITE: In Havana, you can see the making of Partagas cigars. ABOVE: The Marina Hemingway.

took some 40 years to reach final completion, with requests for more money and new consignments of slaves a constant refrain from the then-governor.

Begin at **La Punta**, located at the seafront tip where the Malecón begins. Facing El Morro across the harbor mouth, La Punta seems rather undramatic as a defense installment, with its low walls shaped in a rough quadrilateral and small bastions or watchtowers. Bear in mind that much of it has already been eroded by battering waves over the centuries. It was devised to work in tandem with El Morro, and if any danger was sighted on the horizon, a vast chain of metal and wooden logs could be launched into the channel between the two forts, creating an effective seal to the harbor entrance. These days, La Punta is where scores of *habaneros* congregate, hoping to hitch a ride home through the tunnel to La Habana del Este (East Havana). This is also your cue to take the tunnel and follow the road signs to **El Morro**.

From any angle, El Morro is impressive indeed, and as you look down from its battlements to see the huge green waves thrashing against its base far below, the difficulty faced by any potential aggressors trying to take it by force becomes apparent. El Morro looms over the harbor entrance, has a tall nineteenth-century lighthouse tower in its northwest corner and is connected to the shore 150 m (490 ft) below by a series of ramps. A very deep dry moat protects its inner citadel, which comprises officer quarters, a chapel, cisterns, a wine cellar, stables, dungeons, and vaults.

For decades, El Morro held out against attacks by French, Dutch and English pirates. But in 1762 an English fleet with over 11,000 troops and a formidable lineup of ships took the fort after a 44-day siege. It was hardly a bloodless battle: the English burst through the breach into the fort with mines, and both sides hacked at each other in hand-to-hand fighting; some 400 Spanish soldiers died, as many were taken prisoner, and many drowned trying to escape. For nearly a year, the English occupied Havana, and it was only due to the Treaty of Versailles that Spain was able to recover Cuba in return for Florida and Louisiana.

An extraordinary museum-piece in itself, El Morro will soon open a new maritime museum detailing the history of navigation in and around Cuba, with some actual historic ships on display, as well as replicas, and salvaged relics from galleon wrecks. You can climb to the top of the lighthouse, perhaps meet its keeper, who continues to operate its strong beam across the harbor entrance.

As soon as Spain regained possession of Havana, Carlos III set out to ensure that they never again would they face such a humiliating defeat. He immediately ordered the construction of a new fortress, **Fortaleza de San Carlos de la Cabaña**, on the ridge close to El Morro. This was by far the largest and most ambitious fortress to ever be com-

pleted by the Spanish in the Americas. This fortress, together with El Morro make up the Morro-Cabaña Historical Military Park and is operated by Gaviota, Cuba's Ministry of Defense and is open daily from 9 AM to 8 PM.

You can wander through the restored San Carlos de la Cabaña fortress, seeing where at one time some 3,000 soldiers were housed in barracks, the cannon-dotted battlements, magazines and moats. You may want to hire a horse-drawn *calesa* to explore this large military settlement, which is almost a small city in itself. From 1926, the fortress was used as a military prison; after the Revolution, Che Guevara himself was commander here, and he married Aleida in the fortress chapel in 1959. It is worth looking at the museum's collection, which de-

tails the history of fortress design, and displays many medieval weapons, from catapults made with animal skins to fearsome antique muskets and daggers.

Come here for the **Ceremonia del Cañonazo**. Each evening at 9 PM, soldiers dressed as eighteenth-century guards march through the fortress accompanied by the beat of drums, and light a cannon flare, a ritual that announced the closing of the city's gates and the raising of the chain to seal the harbor mouth during Spanish colonial times. Not only is the cannon salute enjoyable to witness, the atmosphere of the fortress at night, its cobbled streets lit by burning staffs, creates the almost eerie impression that you

The Castillo de San Salvador de la Punta, completed in 1600, marks the start of the Malecón.

really have stepped back two centuries in time. You should arrive at the fortress by 8:45 PM at the latest to be in time for the ceremony, and may wish to repair to the nearby **El Bodegón de los Vinos** tavern, located in the old fortress, which serves a good selection of wine and Spanish snacks.

WHERE TO STAY

Deciding where to stay hinges on which part of Havana you prefer to wake up in and the nature of your trip: whether you want to be surrounded by the historic colonial center of La Habana Vieja or the newer district of Vedado, with its concentration of government and business offices, as well as hotels, restaurants, bars and nightclubs. Some luxurious hotels, such as the unquestionably magnificent Hotel Nacional and the exceptionally elegant Hotel Santa Isabel, as well as the inexpensive but stylish Hostal Valencia, are destinations within themselves. In La Habana Vieja, a string of classic hotels dating from the turn of the century — the Sevilla, the Inglaterra, the Plaza and the Ambus Mundos — have been restored to their former colonial-era glory, offering modern comfort as well as quirky charm, although rooms themselves don't quite match up to the wonderful exteriors.

Over the past few years, the number and quality of Havana's hotels have improved dramatically, and a slew of new hotels are in the process of being constructed, and in some cases restored, most notably, in La Habana Vieja. Most hotels — especially the (Cuban-designated) four- and five-star hotels — have security safes, satellite television and minibars in their rooms. Miramar district also offers a choice of hotels — the Copacabana, the Comodoro and the Chateau Miramar — with beaches and natural swimming pools on the coast, but unless you prefer to be at a distance from central Havana, you may find that you are spending a lot of time and money taking taxis.

For information about Havana's *Casas Particulares*, or privately rented accommodation, see the end of this section. For details on price categories, see ACCOMMODATION, page 314 in TRAVELERS' TIPS.

Expensive

The beautifully restored **Hotel Santa Isabel******* ((53-7) 33-8201 FAX (53-7) 33-8391, Calle Baratillo No. 9, between Calles O'Reilly and Narciso López, Plaza de Armas, La Habana Vieja is decidedly the most charming and benignly staffed place to stay. Originally, this was a palace built for the Count de Santovenia in the nineteenth century, and its historic exterior is notable for half-moon shaped stained-glass windows, while the inner courtyard is open to the sky. Each of its 27 rooms has a period feel, with attractive colonial-style wooden furniture, iron beds, and swish bathrooms. Third-floor rooms have a semi-private terrace from which to survey the Plaza de Armas below, while the so-called Junior Suites contain a living room area and have a jacuzzi. Even if you are not staying here, breakfasts here are the best in town. There is a restaurant specializing in Cuban and international dishes, a lobby bar and coffee shop, and a small shop. You climb to the rooftop for stunning views across the old city. Future plans for this hotel include an adjacent swimming pool and hotel-style apartments.

Hotel Melía Cohiba***** ((53-7) 33-3636 FAX (53-7) 33-4555, Paseo between Avenidas 1 and 3, Vedado, considered to be the most slickly modern of Havana's five-star hotels, designed to be comfortable and efficient, is much like any other international hotel, except of course, it has a specialist bar devoted to the appreciation of fine cigars. Each of the 342 rooms and 120 suites is equipped with minibar, satellite television and a direct-dial telephone. The hotel facilities include a Havana's nicest swimming pool, a gymnasium and sauna, squash courts, beauty salon, conference room, and banquet rooms that can accommodate up to 900 people. It also has an Executive Floor for business travelers, a choice of restaurants, shops, a nightclub and 24-hour room service. The Italian restaurant serves a decent rendition of pasta and pizza.

There's nothing quite like raiding the minibar and watching the Caribbean sea wash across the Malecón at dusk from one of the upper stories of the **Hotel Nacional******* ((53-7) 33-3564 to 33-3567 FAX (53-7) 33-5054, Calle 0 and Avenida 21,

Vedado. Set on a promontory that has unrivalled views across the sea and the Malecón, El Morro and the Vedado district, it is Havana's most majestic and elegant hotel and gives a powerful impression of the decadent splendor of Havana during the 1940s and 1950s. It was recently renovated, but with its colonnades, old Cuban tiles and wrought-iron lifts, the period ambiance remains. The sixth floor caters for business travelers, and is smart and comfortable with special work and meeting rooms, and separate check-in. Its many restaurants and bars are good, and its swimming pool, steam room, beauticians and barber add a pampering touch. The wide verandah bar is perfect for sociable lolling, at any time of day or night.

Hotel Habana Libre***** ((53-7) 33-4011 FAX (53-7) 33-3141, Calle L and Avenida 23, Vedado, is located on La Rampa, Havana's main thoroughfare. With its 534 rooms the Habana Libre is the city's largest hotel. It attracts a steady clientele of business and package travelers, as well as journalists. Despite its convenient location and the fact that its arcades contain many useful tourist offices, agencies and shops, is has the feeling of a large impersonal mall, reflected most dismally in its breakfast room. However rooms have fantastic views, and the Turquino Bar on the top floor is a must for dusk cocktails.

When it opened in 1957, **Hotel Habana Riviera******* ((53-7) 33-4051 to 33-4055 FAX (53-7) 33-3154 or 33-3738, Paseo and Malecón, Vedado, was one of Havana's most popular hotels, with Hollywood stars making a regular appearance. Although it has been recently renovated, it still feels steeped in the 1950s, and it is almost possible to imagine the time when notorious gangster lawyer Meyer Lansky ran his operation from the twentieth floor. With its superb location on the Malecón, its sea-facing rooms offer outstanding views. As well as its regular rooms, there are two executive floors at the top of the hotel and a presidential suite. Its seawater swimming pool is often used as a venue for afternoon salsa concerts. But the real draw is the hotel's Palacio de la Salsa, which showcases the best of Cuba's salsa bands. Otherwise, this hotel appears to be popular with group tours and Cuban functionaries.

Like Hotel El Viejo y el Mar, the condominium-style complex of **Cubanacán Residencial Hemingway****** ((53-7) 33-1150 to 33-1155 FAX (53-7) 33-1149, Calle 248 and Avenida 5, Santa Fé, is landscaped alongside the Marina Hemingway. There are 186 rooms — many with their own kitchens — 42 villas and 36 bungalows. Facilities include two swimming pools, tennis courts, fishing and scuba diving equipment for excursions. Longer-stay guests can ask about

staying on the exclusive nearby **Isla Paradiso**, which has a number of vacation villas and mansions available for rent.

Moderate

Beautifully restored, and re-opened in 1993, **Hotel Sevilla****** ((53-7) 33-8560 FAX (53-7) 33-8582, Calle Trocadero 55 at Prado, La Habana Vieja, has plenty of colonial-era charm, with its splendid, Moorish tiled marble lobby and fountains. It remains one of the loveliest of Havana's traditional turn-of-the-century hotels, and has a swimming pool, sauna and gymnasium. Readers of Graham Greene's *Our Man In Havana* may

The Cuban flag flies above the Hotel Plaza.

recall the scene that takes place here in Room 501, with the fictional protagonist, Wormold. Opera legend Enrico Caruso stayed here, and so did Josephine Baker and Gloria Swanson. Even if you are not staying here, the Roof Garden Restaurant is worth bearing in mind for dinner, with its city views and excellent trio of classical musicians. It is within easy walking distance of the old city.

Havana's oldest hotel, **Hotel Inglaterra****** ((53-7) 24-8593 to 24-8597 FAX (53-7) 33-8254, Prado. No. 416 next to Calle San

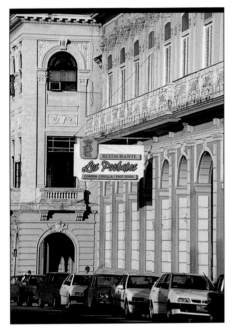

Rafael, La Habana Vieja, first opened in 1875, and still retains a nineteenth-century feel, with its high ceilings, over-head fans, mosaic tiles, stained-glass windows and idiosyncratic elevators. Past guests include Sarah Bernhardt and Cuba's independence movement hero, Antonio Maceo. Although not the best buy for your money, some of the 83 rooms have balconies that overlook Parque Central and across to La Habana Vieja. The Sevillan-style patio bar on the ground floor is a popular meeting point. Talk of modernization is in the air.

Hotel Plaza**** ((53-7) 33-8583 to 33-8590 FAX (53-7) 33-8591, Calles Zulueta and Neptuno, La Habana Vieja, is another Havana classic with a recently modernized

colonial ambiance and an ideal location for exploring the old city, just a few steps from Hemingway's famous haunt, El Floridita. One of its best features is its roof terrace, with its daily breakfast buffet, from which there are panoramic views across all of the old city as well the harbor. There is no swimming pool. Anna Pavlova and Isadora Duncan stayed here during the hotel's heyday.

Located close to the seafront, the large 527-room **Hotel Neptuno-Tritón****** ((53-7) 33-1606 FAX (53-7) 33-0044, Avenida 3 and Calle 74, Miramar, is one of Miramar's most important hotel complexes. It has a good swimming pool, as well as an aqua-bar, a barbecue and a car rental service. Some visitors report successfully negotiating discounts.

Inexpensive to Moderate

Gleamingly modernized, the salmon-pink **Hotel Ambus Mundos** (Both Worlds)*** ((53-7) 66-9530 FAX (53-7) 66-9532, Calle Obispo No. 153, at the corner of Calle Mercaderes, La Habana Vieja, is chiefly known as the place where Ernest Hemingway sporadically based himself while writing *For Whom The Bell Tolls*. You can ask to see Room 511, which has been turned into a museum of Hemingway memorabilia. The hotel has a *faux*-1930s atmosphere, with the antique elevator and original marble staircase restored, and an art gallery exhibiting work by Cuban ceramists. Ask for a room overlooking the old city — the views are best on the top floors. The rooftop bar is one of the best places to while away a cocktail or two, with wraparound views across the city. There is no swimming pool.

Hotel Victoria**** ((53-7) 33-3510 or 32-6531 FAX (53-7) 33-3109, Calles 19 and M, Vedado, is considered a good choice for business travelers. This small 30-room hotel has high marks for efficient service and is in the heart of Vedado's commercial center. Good business facilities and a pool.

Located almost at the end of the Miramar district, the best thing about **Hotel Comodoro*** ((53-7) 33-5551 or 33-0700, Calle 84 and Mar, Miramar, is its conscientious service — it is attached to Havana's tourism and hotel school. It has a swimming pool and overlooks a man-made beach.

Located right on the seafront, the small **Chateau Miramar***** ((53-7) 24-1951 to 24-1957 FAX (53-7) 24-0224, Calle 1, between Calles 44 and 46, Miramar Playa, is popular with business travelers. Suites have jacuzzis. Ask for a room facing the sea.

With its dramatic location right on the seafront, the **Hotel Copacabana****** ((53-7) 24-1037 FAX (53-7) 24-2846, Calle 1, between Calles 44 and 46, Miramar, is both a city hotel and a beach resort. During the 1950s, this was a hugely popular playground, and it has recently undergone extensive reno-

a pleasant swimming pool area. Alternatively, there are 40 poolside rooms, slightly larger with a kitchen and dining area. An executive floor caters for business travelers. Tennis courts, boat rentals, surface fishing and sea cruises can be arranged from the adjacent Marina. The buffet meals served here are excellent.

Inexpensive

The two-story colonial-era **Hostal Valencia***** ((53-7) 62-3801 FAX (53-7) 33-8697, Calle Oficios No. 53 between Calles Obrapía and

vations, with a Brazilian theme throughout. Rooms are average, but the sea views, and the wonderful natural swimming pool at the rim of the Caribbean, are the compelling features here. Amenities include a discotheque, tennis and squash courts, and a shopping center, and there is a marina from which you can go on fishing or diving excursions.

Located in the Marina Hemingway complex, right on the seafront, a very pleasant place to stay, two kilometers (a little over one mile) from central Havana is the **Hotel El Viejo y el Mar****** ((53-7) 24-6336 FAX (537) 24-6823, Calle 248 and Avenida 5, Santa Fé. It has a tranquil, seaside atmosphere with comfortable rooms overlooking the sea and

Lamparilla, La Havana Vieja, located just off the Plaza de Armas, is a charming find. It has a total of 12 rooms — including three suites — around its upper story (each named after a province of Spain) all lofty, with ceiling fans and decorated in a simple, authentic old-style with tiled floors and shutters. The upper verandah overlooks the cobbled, bougainvillea-festooned open-air courtyard, where breakfast and drinks. Its staff — as well as its band — are very friendly and courteous. All rooms have television, private bathrooms and minibars. The restaurant, La Paella, serves good renditions of the

OPPOSITE: Los Portales attracts many tourists, while Hotel Inglaterra ABOVE boasts nineteenth-century charm.

Valencian dish, and the Bar Nostalgia showcases local musical talent and is quite a soulful place. It also has a good Casa del Tabaco. Reserve well in advance.

Notorious as the place where the Mafia bosses went to unwind before the Revolution, **Hotel Capri****** ((53-7) 33-0511 FAX (53-7) 32-0525, Calles 21 and N, Vedado, is even mentioned in Mario Puzo's *The Godfather*. The Salon Rojo cabaret is no longer quite so outrageous, but still attracts swarms of young *habaneros* for its nightly musical performances. (This is not the place to stay if

to experience its historic terribleness: it could be viewed as a symbol of Cuba's Special Period. It used to be a favorite with foreign journalists, and is described with affection by the writer Martha Gellhorn, who was also Hemingway's third wife. Its main attraction is its location and its views across to the fortress of Los Tres Treyes del Morro.

Hotel Lincoln* ((53-7) 62-8061 to 62-8064, Calle Galiano between Calles Virtudes and Animas, Centro Habana, is one of the better inexpensive hotels — it does have

you like early nights.) Badly in need of renovation, the best thing about the Capri is its central location, very close to the Hotel Nacional, the Hotel Habana Libre and La Rampa.

Located on La Rampa, the small **Hotel St. Johns*** ((53-7) 32-9531 to 32-9536, Calle O between Avenidas 23 and 25, Vedado, is a popular budget choice, with its main advantage being its location to the Vedado business district. Its rooftop bar, El Rincon del Feeling, specializes in romantic ballads from the 1940s.

Hotel Deauville* ((53-7) 33-8812 or 33-8813, Calle Galiano and Malecón, Centro Habana is right on the Malecón and has seen better days; in fact it is worth staying in only

television and air-conditioning — as long as you can put up with the uninspiring decor.

The somewhat tacky 20-room **Hotel Morro Horizontes*** ((53-7) 32-7584 or 30-9943 FAX (53-7) 33-3907, Calle 3 between C and D, Vedado, located between the Riviera and Presidente hotels, is a budget standby.

Casas Particulares

Casas Particulares, or "private houses," are a definite option for visitors who would prefer to have more interaction with Cubans, as well as cheaper accommodation, during their stay. Prices per night are usually in the US$20 to US$25 range.

Vedado and Miramar have the largest number and variety of *casas particulares*;

many families rent out rooms in their houses, or in some cases will rent you their entire house. Prices can usually be negotiated, as can requests for types of meals. Facilities and comfort can vary, and in general, your experience will be colored by your rapport with your hosts, so don't commit yourself until you have met them and seen the premises. Unfortunately, there is no tourist agency specializing in recommendations and the business of finding a good *casa particular* is very much by way of word of mouth. Once you start asking around, offers will start multiplying, but bear in mind that touts receive a commission.

Hotels Scheduled to Open Soon

The state-owned company Habaguanex, which develops and runs many of Havana's prominent hotels, restaurants, shops and offices, is currently restoring a slew of new hotels, so-called *apartelles* and new restaurants scheduled to open soon in La Habana Vieja, under the direction of city historian Eusebio Leal. They range from expensive boutique hotels to inexpensive versions of the popular Hostal Valencia. In La Habana Vieja, expect to see the following hotels open soon:

Hotel Saratoga*****, Calle O'Reilly, will be an 80-room historic boutique hotel.

Gran Hotel****, Calle Teniente Rey, near Capitolio is planned as a boutique hotel renovated from one of Havana's popular turn-of-the-century's hotels.

Hotel Florida****, Calle Obispo, is being built in one of La Habana Vieja's eighteenth-century administrative buildings and is sure to be stylishly renovated.

Hostal Condes de Villanueva****, on Calle Mercaderes at the corner of Calle Lamparilla, might already be a small boutique hotel of only nine rooms with a specialist gallery catering to cigar aficionados.

Hostal Humboldt***, Calles Lamparilla and Mercaderes. Modeled on the Hostal Valencia, will have some rooms reserved for visiting academics and students.

In addition, **Hotel Parque Central*******, Calle Neptuno between the Prado and Calle Zulueta, operated by the Dutch Golden Tulip joint-venture company that already has hotels in Santa Lucía, will be a large luxury hotel. Facilities will include a swimming pool and fitness center as well as conference and meeting facilities.

WHERE TO EAT

Havana has some excellent restaurants and *paladares* at which to enjoy Cuban cooking; and generally visitors bask in that wonderful trademark knack possessed by Cubans to make you feel both indulged and relaxed at the same time, whatever the surroundings.

Despite the fact that the Cuban capital has become increasingly cosmopolitan, don't expect *haute cuisine* in Havana. You can, however, expect to pay quite high prices, especially if you order imported wine, which can be up to five times its usual price despite being of indifferent quality, so it can be a good idea to check the wine list. Most restaurants offer a mixture of Caribbean seafood, red meat and Creole dishes, as well as memorable Cuban cocktails which are usually variations on the theme of rum.

Most hotels in Havana offer at least one daily buffet meal, if not three, which is an option if you want to dine quickly on what is generally dreary food in a cafeteria-style atmosphere.

See TRAVELERS' TIPS, page 315, for descriptions of price categories.

Expensive

El Tocororo ((53-7) 24-2209 or 22-4530, Calle 18 between Avenida 3 and 5, Miramar, Playa, named after Cuba's national bird, is considered to be the most sophisticated restaurant in Havana (*the* place to see and be seen), and is popular with executives working for joint-venture companies. You may not enjoy the seemingly complicated arrangement involved when ordering your meal, however. Guests decide how much they wish to pay per head — which can be anything from US$15 to $35 — and the chef will whip you up a meal of several courses accordingly, taking your preferences into account. You can always just order an array of the house *tapas*, especially *pechitos de ca-*

President Gomez's former mansion is now a hotel.

marones. Excellent live music features Cuba's famous white-haired jazz pianist, Bola de Nieve ("Snow Ball").

Despite the tour buses that pull up outside and the constant photo flashes and video cameras at **El Floridita** ((53-7) 63-1060, Calle Monserrate 557 at Calle Obipso, La Habana Vieja, the *daiquirís* themselves are consistently good, as are the seafood specialties served in the adjacent salon. Aside from entering the computer era, El Floridita still seems steeped in the 1930s, its low-lit rococo interior dominated by a mahogany saloon-style bar nearly chest high to its bartenders, backed by an antique mural depicting eighteenth-century Havana. A bust of Hemingway looms over his favorite seat, while the resident band, Trio Brindis, entertain.

Thursday to Tuesday is formal dining at its most elegant in Havana at **Roof Garden** ((53-7) 33-8530, Hotel Sevilla, Calle Trocadero No. 55, La Habana Vieja, with international dishes served by almost painfully correct waiters and classical music played by gifted musicians. Views across the city are stunning.

Despite its reputation as the city's most luxurious place to dine, the most impressive thing about **Comedor de Aguiar** ((53-7) 33-3564, Hotel Nacional, Calles 0 and 21, Vedado, is its surroundings, although service is good. Overall, the dishes are both expensive and mediocre, as is the wine list.

Pleasantly located within the marina, **Papa's** ((53-7) 24-1150 to 24-1156 extension 120, Calle 248 and Avenida 5, Santa Fé, Marina Hemingway, is an enjoyable place for lunch or dinner, especially if you feel like escaping the city for a few hours. Seafood dishes are excellent, and can be pricey. You can order a whole roast fish in advance for US$50; while lobster can be prepared in many different ways. Naturally, they serve good *daiquirís* and *mojitos* here, and there's plenty of Hemingway memorabilia.

Located in the leafy diplomatic district, the very popular **El Ranchon** ((53-7) 24-9346 or 25-5838, Avenida 19 and Calle 140, Cubanacán, Playa, has generous servings of Creole and international dishes on the menu, and a jovial atmosphere.

Moderate

La Divina Pastora ((53-7) 62-3886, Parque El Morro-La Cabaña, Habana del Este. This is easily the most romantic place to dine in Havana — perhaps in all Cuba — set among palm trees within the battlements of the city's great fortress, and with sweeping views across the bay. As well as the surroundings, the musical trio that performs here is exceptional: watching the sun smolder across the Malecón as it sets, while drinking a *mojito* and enjoying them perform is an unforgettable experience. Seafood and Creole dishes are the specialty; stick with the simplest dishes on the menu, such as grilled fish. You can always just have a drink at the bar and enjoy the same ambiance.

La Ferminia ((53-7) 24-6555 or 24-6786, Avenida 5 No. 18207, between Calles 182 and 184, Miramar, Playa, is set in a lovely colonial house with extensive paved gardens and tables both inside and out. This is the most relaxed place for formal dining in Havana, and is a must. The extensive menu is traditional and refined, and well-served, with great efforts made to create the impression of European-style elegance.

The traditional Creole food served at **La Bodeguita del Medio** ((53-7) 62-4498 or 62-5156, Calle Empedrado 207 between Calles Cuba and San Ignacio, La Habana Vieja — roast pork or beef, usually accompanied by rice or beans — is good, from the diet-busting *chicharrones*, the *arroz congri* (rice with spiced meat sauce) and the *picadillo* (shredded meat sautéed with garlic, onions, tomatoes and olives).

Located right on the seafront, an eye-catchingly elegant colonial *palacio* has been converted into the partly open-air restaurant **1830** ((35-7) 33-1952 , Malecón and Calle 20, Vedado, which becomes a popular discotheque at night. The atmosphere is more compelling than the food.

La Cecilia ((53-7) 24-1562, Avenida 5 and Calle 110, Miramar, specializes in Creole cooking with mixed grills of seafood and meats, and well-spaced tables in the pretty garden allow unobtrusive enjoyment of the music performed at night. This is a popular dinner-dance spot after 10 PM.

El Barracón ((53-7) 33-4011, Hotel Habana Libre, Vedado, is considered one of Havana's best restaurants for Creole food. Its specialty is roasted pork, or pork in the form of *masas fritas* (fried pork skin), the *yucca con mojo*, and the *frioles dormidos*.

The main attraction of **La Torre** ((53-7) 32-4630, Calle 17 between M and N, Vedado, is the panoramic view from its location on the thirty-third floor of the FOCSA building. In its heyday this was the most swanky joint in town; now it is well worth coming for a drink at the bar.

Al Medina ((53-7) 63-0862, Calle Oficios No. 112, La Habana Vieja, is an Arabic restaurant that *does* have an atmospheric courtyard setting in a traditional, two-story colonial house, but the food isn't all that good. Kitsch amusement value is provided by the psychedelic artwork of ample-breasted maidens and the waitresses, clad in harem pants, who perform belly dances in between serving the kebabs.

Inexpensive

At **Al Aljibe** ((53-7) 24-1583, Calle 24 at Avenida 7, Miramar, the house specialty, roast chicken *con mollo* (with garlic sauce), is reliably good, and the *el aljibe* itself, a combination platter of chicken, beans, rice, salad, meat and dessert, is very good value.

Dos Gardenias ((53-7) 24-2353, Calle 26 at Avenida 7, Miramar, is a complex of restaurants and bars that serve Cuban, Chinese and Italian food, all inexpensive and of unremarkable quality; but it is chiefly known for its **Salon Bolero** that every night stages a tribute to Cuba's much-loved musical form, the bolero. There is also a shop that sells Cuban CDs and cigars.

You should at least have a coffee or a drink at **El Patio** ((53-7) 62-9888, Plaza de la Catedral, La Habana Vieja, for its lively and relaxed setting in a beautiful three-story *palacio* overlooking the cathedral. Inside, light filters through colored stain-glass windows, caged parrots entertain and children watch turtles clamber inside the trickling marble fountain; outside, there's always a fabulous musical ensemble performing, at almost any hour day or night. People-watching is provided with your poison.

La Mina ((53-7) 62-0216, Plaza de Armas, La Habana Vieja, is set in the courtyard of a delightful, colorfully painted *palacio* with crescent-shaped stained-glass windows, rambling plants, and pet roosters; and is alive with vibrant musical performances. This is an enjoyable place that you should visit at least once, perhaps even to sample their *guarapo frío* (cold sugar-cane juice), along with typical Cuban Creole food and coffee.

Located right next to Plaza de la Catedral, the Italian restaurant **D'Giovanni** ((53-7) 33-5566, Calle Tacón next to Calle Empedrado, La Habana Vieja, is not especially authentic; the best thing about it is the pleasant setting in a three-story colonial

house, which also has pretty tables overlooking the harbor.

Los Doce Apóstoles ((53-7) 63-8295, Parque Morro-Cabaña, Habana del Este, located in the Castillo de los Tres Reyes del Morro (very close to the restaurant La Divina Pastora), is a little Creole restaurant that offers stunning views, along with modest, but satisfying, Cuban dishes, such as rice, beans, pork and *yucca*.

Café El Mercurio ((53-7) 62-0216, Lonja del Comercio, San Francisco de Asís, La Habana Vieja, is an excellent place for good coffee, sandwiches and salads, with great fresh fruit shakes.

A Cuban icon: Hemingway's favorite Bodeguita del Medio.

As you might expect, paella is the specialty at **La Paella** ℂ (53-7) 62-3801, Hostal Valencia, Calle Oficios No. 53, La Habana Vieja, and their classic rendition of the dish actually won the Best International Paella prize at the annual contest held in Sueca in Valencia, Spain, in 1996.

A slightly rough-and-ready atmosphere pervades **Café Paris** on Calle Obispo, La Habana Vieja, a popular meeting spot where *habaneros* and foreigners intermingle. It's known for its slabs of pizza and cheap drinks.

best dish is the house *"Cabañas pollo,"* which is chicken cooked with cheese and jam.

La Torre de Marfil ℂ (53-7) 62-3466, Calle Mercaderes, between Calles Obispo and Obrapía, La Habana Vieja serves so-so Chinese food, in a restaurant run by Chinese-*habaneros*.

Paladares

Havana has a large and ever-changing number of *paladares*, or private restaurants, which offer an alternative to the usual government-run tourist restaurants, as well

Café O'Reilly, Calle O'Reilly No. 203, between Calles San Ignacio and Cuba, is a renovated version of one of Havana's oldest cafés and is good place for snacks and coffee.

Hanoi ℂ (53-7) 63-1681, Calle Teniente Rey near Calle Bernaza, La Habana Vieja, is an unpretentious little eatery which serves Vietnamese dishes as well as the usual Cuban ones on a shady terrace. It's a good place to stop if you're tired out from walking around the old city.

Open until very late, the seafront restaurant **Cabañas** ℂ (53-7) 33-5670, Calle Cuba No. 12, next to Peña a Pobre, La Habana Vieja, has a very casual, friendly atmosphere and popular with *habaneros*, who swear that the

as a chance to meet with hospitable and enterprising Cubans. Licensed *paladares* are preferable because they have to observe strict hygiene requirements (as well as pay high taxes). Although meals are generally cheaper, always remember that wine can be surprisingly expensive (especially as its quality is generally not very good), so ask the price first. Reservations are always appreciated.

La Finca ℂ (53-7) 23-5032, Calle 84 No. 1112 between Avenidas 11 and 13, Miramar is run with professional flair and has a popular following for its good Italian and Creole dishes, as well as its evening Happy Hour.

With flowers and candles on its verandah tables, the owners of **La Casa** ℂ (53-7)

34869, Calle 30 No. 865 between Calles 26 and 41, Nuevo Vedado, set in a spacious and modern Vedado home, have managed to create a restaurant atmosphere in their family home. The specialty is Cordon Bleu chicken (stuffed with ham and cheese).

El Elegante ((53-7) 23-8215, Avenida 33 No. 3140, between Calles 34 and 36, Playa, is set in an airy private home that lives up to its name. You can expect excellent home-cooking and solicitous service by Rafael and Joaquín. It is open for lunch and dinner.

Hurón Azul ((53-7) 78-4189, Calle Humboldt No. 153, next to Calle P, Vedado, is a very pleasant *paladar* specializing in Creole dishes; while **Long Sai Li**, Sociedad de Instrucción y Recreo, Calle Dragones No. 313, between Calles Rayo and San Nicolás, Barrio Chino, Habana Centro, run by the descendants of Chinese immigrants, has an unusual mixture of Chinese and Creole in its cuisine and ambiance. On the menu, you'll find the typical Creole *pollo fritto* and the traditional Chinese fried rice served with Hatuey beer, against a backdrop of a large Chinese painting and salsa music.

Dining at Sea

Another option is to have lunch or dinner aboard **El Galeón**, a replica eighteenth-century galleon that is berthed at El Morro and makes forays out into the harbor for lunch and dinner cruises. Ask your hotel concierge to help you make reservations; or call **(** (53-7) 33-8600.

NIGHTLIFE

When the light fades and the streets take on their half-lit hue (both dodgy electrics and power shedding mean blackouts are a regular occurrence), Havana's exuberant nocturnal spirit asserts itself. *Habaneros* take their partying very seriously, even if it just involves assembling around a fragile sound system blurting out high-velocity salsa.

The city's fabled nightlife is what you make of it, whether you chose to have a quiet moonlit drink next to the vine-covered backdrop of an old fort listening to Cuban ballads, or whether you decide to take your partner by the hand and start executing crazy salsa steps with the best of them.

There are cabarets with elaborate dance acts, and many musicians playing salsa, conga and rumba rhythms, as well as live jazz and other types of music. Most hotels and restaurants feature soloists, trios or musical groups. Whatever you do, you will find that one thing is unavoidable: you may develop a newfound interest in rum and cigars, and almost wherever you go, the level of live music will range from the merely infectious to the sublime. You can buy the weekly magazine *Urbe*, which gives listings of upcoming performances and other cultural events. Expect to pay US$15 upwards as cover charge, especially at nightspots located within hotels.

Nightspots

Palacio de la Salsa ((53-7) 33 4501, Hotel Riviera, Vedado, with its 1950s setting, and nightly performances by Cuba's top salsa bands, making it a venue not to be missed.

La Casa de la Música ((53-7) 24-0447, Calle 20 between Calles 33 and 35, Miramar, is the equivalent of Havana's Casa de la Trova, where almost every night you can expect to hear top-quality Cuban musicians amid an appreciative audience. There is also a shop with a good selection of Cuban CDs and cassettes.

From 10:30 PM until midnight, the **Club Turquino (** (53-7) 33-4011, Hotel Habana Libre, Vedado, on the twenty-fifth floor of the Habana Libre, presents a rather lack-luster musical revue, after which it becomes a discotheque. But the views — especially at sunset — are wonderful.

La Maison ((53-7) 24-0126 or 24-1543, Calle 16 No. 701 near Avenida 7, Miramar, set in a white colonial mansion with a large garden terrace, is a magnet for well-connected and moneyed Cubans, who come here to enjoy the nightly fashion shows and cabaret performances, and to drink on into the night. The show begins at 9:30 PM. It is closed on Monday.

The restaurant **La Cecilia (** (53-7) 24-1562, Avenida 5 and Calle 110, Miramar, has a very popular performance show at night, with excellent salsa groups. It is open Thursday to Sunday, from 9:30 PM.

Lounging in a Havana horse carriage.

Café Cantante Mi Habana ((53-7) 33-5713, Teatro Nacional, Paseo and Calle 39, Plaza de la Revolución, features nightly live music showcasing jazz and salsa, and a humorous variety show, although some travelers report having encoutered a rather unsavory crowd. The very small intimate setting of **Bar Nostalgia**, Hostal Valencia, La Habana Vieja, is a great place to watch budding local musicians. Evening performances vary, so check for their latest schedule. **La Zorra y el Cuervo**, Calle 23, between Calles M and N, Vedado, features nightly live "Caribbean jazz," starting at 10 PM. Every Friday and Saturday night, contemporary groups perform rumba and jazz at **Casa de las Infusiones**, Calle Mercaderes 109, La Habana Vieja.

In pre-Revolutionary days, two American brothers ran **Dos Hermanos**, Avenida del Puerto at the corner of Calle Santa Clara, La Habana Vieja, near the Havana docks, and it was a rough-and-ready watering hole for sailors and dock workers. Today, it's a fun, out-of-the-way place to linger and meet Cubans.

Discotheques

There are plenty of discotheques all over the city, and in most of the larger hotels. Some of the most popular include **Aché** ((53-7) 33-3636, Hotel Melía Cohiba, Vedado, currently Havana's hottest discotheque, open from 10:30 PM to 5 AM, every night. The Afro-Cuban group Oni Ire performs here every Friday from 10 PM to 3 AM at **Riviera Azul** ((53-7) 33-8812, Hotel Deauville, Centro Havana. The rest of the week, there's live music, usually salsa or rumba.

You can also try **Discoteca Habana Club** ((53-7) 24-2703, Hotel Comodoro, Miramar, while to go to **Salon Rosando**, at the Jardín Tropical, Playa, is to be immersed in an intensely Cuban night out; you won't see many foreigners. On weekend nights this open-air stadium is packed for popular salsa performances, at this peso-only venue near the Havana stadium.

Cabarets

The **Tropicana** ((53-7) 20-5144, Calle 72, between Calles 41 and 45, Marianao, despite being an obvious monument to 1950s deca-

dence, was one of the symbols of pre-Revolutionary Cuba that was not allowed to die. Night after night, this socialist show, whose slogan is "Paradise under the Stars," goes on, celebrating more than six decades of existence with so much kitsch flamboyance that it is hard to resist, and many of its performers are clearly very talented. Since the Tropicana first opened in 1939, it has been renowned for its scantily clad and outrageously costumed dancers. Its central stage is surrounded by tropical gardens and is open to the sky, which means that a rainstorm cancels the evening's performance. The cabaret is undeniably spectacular, with a huge cast of café-con-leche dancers who manage to be theatrically dressed and seminaked at the same time, sometimes teetering beneath chandelier headdresses that light up on cue; and gyrating to the music of a massed choir and a swing band playing Afro-Caribbean rhythms. As well as the dance ensembles, acrobats perform dare-defeating acts, and the entire performance is delivered at a slick pace. Although the show is meant to begin at 9 PM, it usually does not get going until a half an hour or an hour afterwards. The cover charge is Havana's most expensive (US$40 to $60) and includes a cocktail. If it rains, you can opt for another performance or (apparently) are refunded for your ticket. Closed Monday.

For a traditional hotel floor show, with more than a little touch of Las Vegas, try **Cabaret Parisien** ((53-7) 33-3564, Hotel Nacional, Vedado. The show starts at 10:30 PM and lasts until midnight: after that there is disco music. It is open from Friday to Wednesday.

The less expensive cabaret show at **Salon Rojo** ((53-7) 33-3747, Hotel Capri, Vedado, has something of a following, and presents two shows: one from 10 PM to 11 PM; the other from 12:30 AM to 1:30 AM.

RECREATION FACILITIES

Outside the Hotel Melía Cohiba **BioTop** ((53-7) 24-2377, Avenida 7 No. 2603, Miramar, is the best it gets for pampering in Havana. You can work-out in their small gymnasium and use the jacuzzi; book a massage,

waxing or beautifying session, and stock up on Cuban-made cosmetics and propolis honey products.

For information on swimming, spectator sports, horseback riding, golf and scuba diving, see SPORTING SPREE, page 30.

GETTING AROUND

Havana is a very spread-out city, divided into 15 municipalities, six of which — La Habana Vieja, Centro Habana, Miramar, Playa, Regla and La Habana del Este — are bounded by the sea.

Most museums, historical sites, restaurants, nightclubs and bars are found in La Habana Vieja, Vedado, Centro Habana, Miramar and Miramar Playa, and are usually

well-known to taxi drivers. You should, however, make sure that you confirm that they know the address before you set off. For some areas, such as La Habana Vieja — with its labyrinth of narrow cobbled streets filled with something interesting to see at every corner — it is much better to be on foot.

Havana has two main car rental agencies, **Transautos** and **Havanautos**, which have representatives in the city's main hotels. More details on car rental can be found in GETTING AROUND, page 309 in TRAVELERS' TIPS. If you rent a car, remember that driving around Havana can be hard on the nerves, involving a lot of dodging pedestrians and cyclists. Also remember that the city's traffic

A local musical institution, La Casa de la Música.

lights are confusingly located on the other side of the junction you are trying to cross, which can be hard to see.

If you don't have a rental car, the easiest option is to hail or book a taxi. Havana's two main taxi services are both 24-hour: **Turistaxi** ((53-7) 33-5539, 33-5540 or 33-5541 or the less-expensive **Panataxi** ((53-7) 81-3311, 81-3008 or 81-3065. Turistaxi has stands at every major hotel, and both taxis have a stand near the seafront outside the Plaza de la Catedral and at Calles 17 and L in Vedado, near the gas station. These offi-

or sometimes, several days. Officially, these *taxis particulares* are only legal if they have been licensed, and if you are in an unlicensed car you and the driver run the risk of being pulled over by the Havana police. The driver will always claim that he is driving his "friends" on a sightseeing trip.

You can opt to see some of Havana's sights by tour bus, which can be a useful way of quickly familiarizing yourself with the city, and perhaps returning to some places on your own later. One of the best tours is **Vaivén**, run by Rumbos, which have a fleet

cial taxis operate by meter which drivers are obligated to turn on as soon as you set off. Both taxi services also offer special hourly and long-distance rates. You will also see peso taxis cruising (or rather limping) along Havana's streets; these are generally service taxis operating along scheduled routes, they accept only pesos and generally do not take tourists.

You may want to go for a spin in one of Havana's: *taxis particulares*: the old chariots of chrome from Detroit such as Buicks, Chevrolets, Chevys, or a Lincoln Continental for example. Just remember to negotiate the price beforehand, and try to have a good feeling about the driver before you step in. Prices can be negotiated for a trip,

of Mitsubishi buses offering air-conditioned comfort as you zoom around the city. Rumbos operates from the Hotel Habana Libre ((53-7) 32-9409. Another city tour on offer is operated by **Tour and Travel** ((53-7) 33-9199, which has various minibus tours daily. **Agencia Viejes San Cristóbal** ((53-7) 33-8693, Calle Oficios No. 110, offers daily walking tours of La Habana Vieja. The price of most tours is around US$10 and most hotels should be able to book you a place.

Havana's public transport buses, referred to as *guaguas* ("wah-wahs"), are very often two buses which have been hitched together — nicknamed *camelos* or camels — and they are not recommended for tourists. Many depart from the Parque de la Fraternidad.

Increasingly, tricycle taxis or *"ciclotaxis"* are a feature on Havana's streets, and these can be an enjoyable way to be whisked around, especially around La Habana Vieja and the Malecón.

If you are feeling adventurous, you could experiment with hiring a bicycle, which in Cuba tend to be the Chinese, one-speed "Flying Pigeon" variety. Most hotels will, after some discussion, be able to direct you on how to go about renting a bicycle. **Panaciclo** ((53-7) 45-3746 or 81-0153, at the intersection of Avenida Rancho Boyeros and Santa Ana, near the Plaza de la Revolución, is a subsidiary of Panataxi, and rents out bicycles. But you'll have to be extra-cautious about the risk of reckless drivers, pot-holes, and the possibility of having it stolen, so be prepared for those consequences.

In La Habana Vieja and Centro Habana, the *calles* or streets are named in the familiar mode of any European city — Obispo, Prado, San Rafael, and so on. In Vedado and Miramar, streets and avenues are identified by numbers or letters, First being closest to the seafront, and Third, Fifth, and Seventh located progressively further inland; while in Vedado, streets are known by the letters A through P towards the east, and by even numbers 2 through 28 running west. In Miramar, streets are also labeled with even numbers, from 0 to 100, east to west. Although it is quite straightforward to locate any given address, it is essential that you are sure of the district, to avoid unnecessary confusion.

EXCURSIONS FROM HAVANA

THE HEMINGWAY TRAIL

When he wasn't drinking *daiquirís* at El Floridita or *mojitos* at the Bodeguita del Medio, Ernest Hemingway could most often be found either writing at his home outside Havana or fishing for marlin from his custom-made boat, the *Pilar*, off the Cuban coast.

To follow his trail, ideally you should combine a mid-morning visit to his former home, now a museum, with lunch at La Terraza restaurant at Cojímar, and you will need a taxi or rental car.

Overlooking Havana in the tiny San Francisco de Paula, 15 km (nine miles) southeast of the capital, is **La Finca Vigía**, the handsome white mansion Hemingway bought with the advance from *For Whom The Bell Tolls* in 1940. Here, surrounded by *flamboyán* trees and *areca* palms, Ernesto, as the Cubans called him, spent the last two decades of his life and worked on some of his finest works: *To Have and Have Not*, *For Whom the Bell Tolls*, and dozens of short stories and novellas, including *The Old Man and the Sea*.

Hemingway moved to La Finca with the journalist Martha Gellhorn, his third wife; and was later to live here with his fourth, Mary Welsh, telling her that this was the only place he ever felt at home. Feeling that Cuba was too unstable to live in during the early days of the Castro takeover, the Hemingways left for Idaho where, on July 2, 1961, he committed suicide.

A month after Hemingway's suicide, Welsh received Fidel Castro on La Finca's front porch, and in a brief ceremony she handed the house over to the Cuban government. The next year, Castro turned La Finca into the **Casa-Museo de Hemingway**. Unlike Hemingway's house in Key West, Florida, La Finca remains much as it was left, preserving all his books, papers, personal effects and furniture. His aura is strongly, almost eerily present.

Inside the mansion is the writer's idiosyncratic collection of African fetishes, Picasso sculptures and Goya reproductions, and everywhere are books; more than 5,000 of them, including the intriguingly titled: *Nine Lives Before Thirty*, and another used as a doorstop. Stuffed victims of hunting expeditions stare glassily down from almost every room: impalas and antelopes, buffaloes and brown stags, pronghorns and Grant's gazelles. In the living room, next to his favorite armchair, are empty bottles of Gordon's gin; while next to his bed was the last book he read here, on which his wireframe glasses perch, as though absent-mindedly left behind. On the bookshelf in the bedroom is the Royal portable at which he wrote standing up for the last 17 years of his

The Malecón also serves as a playground for children.

life. In the bathroom are the hieroglyphic-like scrawls of the daily register he kept of his weight, which fluctuated between 190 and 242 pounds, as well as pickled frogs and lizards in a jar on top of the toilet. In the closet are some military-style jackets, and many pairs of worn-but-dashing "war correspondent" leather boots, shoes, and sandals, all Hemingway's size 48, as well as smaller pairs that belonged to Mary, his wife.

In Hemingway's office, unused rounds of ammunition, including a dozen 20-gauge Winchester cartridges, stand upright on his

If you are driving by rental car, take the Primer Anillo de La Habana (Havana's First Ring Road) then follow the Carretera Central to Güines and onwards to San Francisco de Paula, in San Miguel de Padrón. La Finca Vigía is open Monday to Saturday, 9 AM to 4 PM, Sunday, 9 AM to 12:30 PM, and is closed on Tuesday and on rainy days.

As you leave La Finca for Cojímar, get back onto the Primer Anillo de la Habana which joins with the Via Monumental to lead to **Cojímar**, the tiny fishing village where Hemingway used to keep the *Pilar*.

desk. In the last few years of his life, Hemingway frequently tormented his wife and friends by rehearsing his suicide: he would brace the barrel of his Mannlicher Schoenauer .256 against the roof of his mouth and play with the trigger with his big toe.

Although you are only allowed peer inside the mansion from the verandah and through open doors, you can wander through the lush frangipani-fragrant gardens to see the outdoor tower where Hemingway often worked; the swimming pool, which is empty now; the guest-house (guests included Gary Cooper and Ava Gardner) and the cemetery he created for his beloved dogs, Black, Negrita, Linda and Nero. His boat, the *Pilar*, is now on display here as well.

The crescent-shaped bay of Cojímar (pronounced Co-HEE-mar) was the setting for *The Old Man and the Sea*. A pergola shades a bronze bust of the author, smiling, in a fishermen's sweater. A little further on is **La Chorrera**, a seventeenth-century tower-like colonial fort, and the port, where a few boats are moored to a rickety wooden pier, around which barefoot children cast their reels to the sea.

More recently, Cojímar has been notoriously popular as a launching ground for thousands of attempts by *balseros* (rafters) to cast themselves across the Florida Straits — locals still talk about the scandal when two *balseros* were shot as they tried to escape in 1993, and the frenzied scenes in 1994, when a riot in Havana sparked the biggest exodus since Mariel.

Cojímar's most famous resident is Gregorio Fuentes, now a hundred years old, who was Hemingway's longtime fishing-boat captain, and he remains a passionately loyal defender of his friend's memory. Rarely seen without a half-smoked *puro* between his lips, Fuentes's handshake remains strong, he bangs the table with his fist as he makes a point, and good-naturedly poses for the steady parade of tourists who ask to take his photograph. There is plenty of Fuentes's spirit in the fictional character of Santiago, the old man in *The Old Man and the Sea*, which was to win the 1954 Nobel Prize for Literature. "Everything about him was old except his eyes," he wrote of Santiago, and they were the same color as the sea and were cheerful and undefeated." Fuentes's eyes remain a deep blue reflection of the Caribbean.

For the last 30 years, Fuentes has been a guest of honor at Cojímar's seaside restaurant **La Terraza**, where he has a daily meal and a double whisky. With the terrace's windows open to the sea breeze, this is one of the most delightful and relaxed places to while away an hour or two: whether it's just for a *cafecito* and rum, or for their delicious fish soup or seafood paella with Spanish wine. The walls are lined with photographs of Hemingway (with some of Fuentes too) in their glory days.

Where to Eat

La Terraza de Cojímar ((53-7) 63-3471, Calle Real No. 161 next to Calle Candelaria, Cojímar. With wonderful sea views, this was one of Hemingway's watering holes. Its specialties include excellent paella and seafood dishes.

THE PLAYAS DEL ESTE

Once you have reached Cojímar, you are halfway to the **Playas del Este** (Eastern Beaches) the long string of beaches to which *habaneros* traditionally flock during the stiflingly hot months of July and August to escape the humidity of the city.

From Cojímar, the Vía Monumental runs eastwards, turning into the Vía Blanca, the four-lane highway that runs all the way to Matanzas and then to Varadero. Leaving Cojímar, you'll pass the Revolution-era prefabricated apartment buildings made with unpainted cement — known as micro-brigade housing — of **Alamar**, a glum seaside dormitory suburb of Havana, and further east, **Celimar**, another fishing village with similar micro-brigade housing built with the labors of untrained volunteers.

From here begins the undulating expanse of blue water and wide, white-sanded beaches dotted with coconut palms that makes up the Playas del Este. **Bacuranao** is the closest, no more than 20 minutes from Havana. Then comes the seaside towns of **El Mégano**, **Santa María del Mar**, **Boca Ciega**, **Guanabo**, **Jibacoa** and **El Trópico**. Especially during the peak summer months, these beaches have an intensely Cuban atmosphere, with entire families decamped here: old men sticking to their game of dominoes in the shadows; toddlers having their first dip in the sea; and the inevitable rum, cigars and salsa music permeating the beach. Off-season, it's still the best place for a swim close to Havana, although drifting pollution has been reported and beaches are often left littered with trash.

Although the hotel and restaurant facilities are pretty rough, this is a much more gratifying place than the more celebrated Varadero to spend a few days by the sea if you want to meet and mingle with ordinary Cubans. On the downside, prostitution is becoming a much more visible problem here. The beach communities mentioned above are lined with inexpensive tourist resorts catering for both Cubans and tourists, private vacation homes dating from the 1920s and 1930s, cafés, shops and discotheques. However, it has to be said that the gloom of the Special Period can be felt here: the Playas del Este are suffering from the lack of transportation and food supplies, which is why you will see so many people on bicycles.

Where to Stay

If you want to spend a day — or a few days — at the beach at the Playas del Este, Santa

Trying to hitch a ride in the streets of Havana.

María del Mar is probably your best base, and its also has the nicest beach. It has to be said that none of the hotels are especially attractive.

Hotel Atlántico Going One**** ℂ (53-7) 80-2375 to 80-2379 FAX (53-7) 80-2646, Avenida de las Terrazas, Playa Santa María del Mar offers moderately priced accommodations. Despite its cryptic name (not so cryptic when you realize that large numbers of single Italian men flock here), this rather Retro-style hotel could be a good base to hang your beach hat, although a few days may be enough if the constant stream of beach *jineteras* is not for you. It is located right on the beach and in walking distance of most nightspots.

The following hotels offer basic facilities and value at inexpensive price: **Hotel Horizontes Itabo***** ℂ (53) 687-2581 to 687-2589, Playa Santa María del Mar; Laguna Itabo, Boca Ciega, **Horizontes Hotel Tropicoco Beach Club***** ℂ (53) 687-2531 to 687-2539, Avenida Sur and Avenida de las Terrazas, Santa María del Mar; and **Horizontes Aparthotel Atlántico***** ℂ (53) 687-4910 to 687-4919, Avenida de las Terrazas, Santa María del Mar.

Where to Eat
There are plenty of casual eateries and pizza bars along the strip at Playa Santa María del Mar. In adjacent Playa Boca Ciega, try the seafood restaurant, **Casa de Pescador** on Avenida 5 for its simple dishes and beach atmosphere.

Nightlife
The **Horizontes Hotel Tropicoco** is the liveliest dance venue. Walking along the beach and being invited along to gatherings by Cubans may be all part of the fun.

REGLA AND GUANABACOA

Across the harbor from Havana, two historic neighborhoods offer an alternative view of the city.

The easiest and most atmospheric way to reach the maritime hamlet of **Regla** is to take the stalwart ferry which regularly

Santería celebration of the Yoruba god of fire and war.

commutes to and from the Muelle de la Luz dock on Avenida San Pedro (Avenida de la Puerte) across from the Plaza de San Francisco de Asís. Buy a ticket for 10 centavos each way and see Havana from this unique perspective. (But if you drive or take a taxi, you will be able to roam further afield and visit Guanabacoa, which is too far to walk from Regla.) From the boat, you have a wonderful view of Havana Bay, passing under the gaze of the large sculptured Christ figure near the city's observatory in the suburb of **Casablanca** immediately south of La Cabaña. From the station here, the electrified Hershey train runs to and from Matanzas.

When you disembark at the Regla docks, you can't miss seeing (along with the eyesore of a large thermo-electric plant) the harbor-front **Iglesia de Nuestra Señora de Regla**, one of Havana's most important places of pilgrimage. Here, the Virgin of Regla, patroness and protector of all travelers, can be called upon to give her blessings, also in her incarnation as Yemayá, the Santería goddess of the sea. Presiding over a blue-and-white-tiled, flower-bedecked altar, the blue-robed Virgin of Regla is black, although the infant she cradles is white. Every September 8, the Virgin's feast day is celebrated here with both a Catholic mass and Santería rituals. Many have come here to say an emotional farewell to Cuba, or to pray for their loved ones in other countries. A small adjacent museum displays objects and figurines used in Santería practices. The entrance fee of US$2 also covers the Museo del Regla.

From the church, you can wander through Regla's warren of old streets. Here, the traditional tempo of life remains unchanged: there are few cars but many bicycles, children play in the streets and modest wooden houses have a ramshackle quality, many emblazoned with socialist slogans faded along with the paint. The **Museo del Regla**, on Calle Marti between Calles Facciolo and La Piedra, has a good collection of antique religious art, as well as displays relating the neighborhood's history during the Spanish colonial period. A special place has been reserved for the accoutrements of the **Tabla de Ifa**, divining instruments of Santería.

It is open from Tuesday to Friday, 9 AM to 6 PM; Saturday, 9 AM to 7 PM and Sunday from 9 AM to 1 PM.

If you are feeling energetic, you can walk up winding streets and hillside steps to the neighborhood's highest point on **Lenin Hill**. It is graced by a rather surreal sculpture of androgynous post-modernist mannequins hailing the giant deathmask-like face of the Russian revolutionary. Puzzlement over the sculpture is forgotten in the panoramic views of Havana, which also take in the creeping industrialization of the foreground.

The seemingly sleepy, unpretty town of **Guanabacoa** is a few kilometers away, renowned in Cuba for its deep connections with Santería, as well as the other Afro-Cuban belief systems, *Palo Monte* and the secretive *Abakuá*. If a *habanero* has a string of misadventures, he's likely to say, with a laugh, "I'm heading for Guanabacoa!" for a purifying ritual from the *babalao*. From the earliest times of Spanish colonial rule in Cuba, Guanabacoa was associated with the trafficking of African slaves. This painful history is reflected in the name of Calle Amargura (Bitterness Street), where slaves who had been sentenced to death were dragged away to be executed. There are several historic churches and a monastery: the **Par-**

roquial Mayor, founded in 1644, overlooks the main square; and the early baroque Iglesia de Santo Domingo and the monastery complex of the Iglesia de San Francisco, founded illegally by Spanish missionaries, both date from the early eighteenth-century.

One very good reason to visit for anyone interested in Santería is the Museo Historico de Guanabacoa, housed in an attractive colonial house, which has Cuba's most comprehensive display of lore relating to the Afro-Cuban religion, Santería, or goddesses, with dolls dressed as Santa Barbara, bead necklaces, bottles of rum and plastic flowers. You can also browse at the Bazaar de los Orishas, close to the town's main square.

If you have time, make a detour further south along the Autopista Nacional, to reach Santa María del Rosario, a charming town of crumbling mansions and well-established trees founded by the sugar-baron Counts of Bayona. It's barely visited Iglesia de Santa María del Rosario is a beautiful baroque church built in 1776

and other related cults. You can see ritual tools that belonged to some of Cuba's most respected *babalaos*, or priests. Santería dance performances and rituals are frequently enacted in the museum and in the nearby Casa de Cultura. The museum is housed in a colonial eighteenth-century house on Calle Marti between Calles San Antonio and Versalles, and is open Monday to Saturday, 10:30 AM to 6 PM; Sunday 9 AM to 1 PM and closed Tuesday.

Whether you walk or drive through the streets of Guanabacoa, you can feel how steeped it is in Santería: white-clad *santeros*, or initiates, are a common sight, and through open doors, in gloomy interiors, you catch glimpses of shrines to the *orishas*, the gods

which, with its richly carved pulpit and altar, is the most sophisticated rural church interior in Cuba. The paintings are by an artisan from the Canary Islands, José Nicholas de la Escalera. Across the cobblestone plaza is the restored mansion that belonged to the aristocratic Bayona clan. Unfortunately, the church is only open on Sunday between 5:30 PM and 7:30 PM. Cuba's greatest contemporary artist, Manuel Mendive, lives here and you can see his mural on the town's Casa de Cultura opposite the church. Santa María del Rosario lies 19 km (12 miles) southeast of Havana.

The windows of the Palacio del Segundo Cabo decorated with *mediopuntos*.

FURTHER SOUTH OF HAVANA

If you have a day or two to spare and want to see something of the "real" Cuba — as well as to visit un-touristed regions, you might consider combining several of the following places, all easily reached by car and within an hour's drive south of Havana. If you try to use any form of public transportation, you will soon experience how great the daily obstacles faced by many Cubans are.

an centers, a theatre and the Paso Sequito lake, where you can rent boats, but most of these amusements are either closed or in a state of neglect. Hopefully, this park and its many activities will soon be restored and once again operational.

Where to Eat
Las Ruinas ((53-7) 44-3336, Calle 100 and Cortina de la Presa, Parque Lenin, is a 1970s-style restaurant that serves good Creole food at moderate prices and can handle large parties, with an interesting setting that in-

PARQUE LENIN

Due to transportation problems, not many *habaneros* have been going to **Parque Lenin**, a huge recreation park area, which lies off the Calzada de Bejucal in Arroyo Naranjo, 20 km (just over 12 miles) southeast of Havana. If you are driving a rental car, you can reach it by the Vía Monumental, then by the Primer Anillo de la Habana, which traverses La Habana del Este; the park lies southeast of Guanabacoa and just south of Arroyo Naranjo. The park's namesake is commemorated by a giant white marble bust of Lenin; and encompasses an amusement park, Havana's only *autokine* (drive-in cinema), a small aquarium, various equestri-

corporates fragments of an eighteenth-century sugar mill. Located in the park's southeast corner, it is open Wednesday to Sunday.

JARDÍN BOTÁNICO

Further south of the park is the **Jardín Botánico Nacional** (National Botanical Gardens), where you can see an extraordinary array of exotic trees and plants imported from all over the world, as well as those endemic to Cuba itself. The gardens cover some 12 hectares (30 acres) and over 32 km (20 miles) of road. The many varieties of Cuba's palm trees are a specialty, but there is also a charming Japanese garden, and extensive varieties of bougainvillea and orchids. Tours take up to three hours and vary in price — you should be able to book ahead from your hotel. Try, if you can, to visit during the months of April and May, when the gardens are at their most beautiful. The opening hours are Wednesday to Sunday from 8:30 AM to 5 PM.

Further south, beyond the José Martí International Airport, is the small traditional town of **Santiago de las Vegas**, which is primarily of interest for a nearby church, **San Lázaro de San Rincón**. On the night of December 16 every year, El Rincón is the scene of an extraordinary religious procession celebrating San Lázaro's Day, dedicated to one of Cuba's most venerated saints, the patron of the old and sick. Each year, thousands of pilgrims, many of them barely able to walk, gather here in the hope that San Lázaro will answer their prayers. Most make the journey on foot from Santiago de las Vegas. Everywhere, there are cries of "Viva Lázaro," and the church itself is crammed with flowers and candles, with much emotional singing and praying. It is significant that Pope John Paul II chose to visit El Rincón on his landmark visit to Cuba in 1998.

SAN ANTONIO DE LOS BAÑOS

An hour's drive, some 37 km (23 miles) along the Autopista del Mediodía, southwest of Havana, **San Antonio de los Baños** is close enough to the capital that many commute to their jobs in the city; and is the closest thing Havana has to a small country town. Rich in mineral waters, it was a fashionable spa town during the nineteenth century. The advantage of coming here is to see how ordinary, educated Cubans live outside the urban perimeter. It is known for its biennial international humor festival, held in April, when cartoonists and humorists converge to discuss the serious business of satire. At the town's entrance, a sign announces that you have entered "San Antonio del Humor." The **Museo del Humor**, housed in a rose-colored colonial mansion on Calle 60 at Avenida 45, declares itself devoted to the "conservation, study and dissemination" of humor, and has a visual tour of Cuban graphic humor from the first extant Cuban caricature (1848) to the present. Open Tues-

day to Saturday from 2 PM to 7 PM, Sunday from 9 AM to 1 PM, it is closed on Monday.

On the town's outskirts, is Havana's **International School of Film and Television**, located amid leafy, tranquil surroundings. It is often referred to as Gabriel García Márquez's school, since the novelist (and former television scriptwriter) was actively involved in its creation in 1986.

Since then many greats from the film world have offered themselves as visiting professors for the school's workshops, including Márquez himself, Constantin

Costa-Gavras, Francis Ford Coppola (who also cooked pasta for the students), George Lucas, the late Tomás Gutiérrez Alea, Istavan Svebo; actor-director Robert Redford (whose Sundance Institute frequently participates in the annual International Festival of New Latin American Film), and actors Hanna Schygulla and Matt Dillon. The school, which is open to international students — mostly from Latin America, Asia and Africa — and only accepts a limited quota of Cuban students, has a two-year film-making program as well as shorter and experimental workshops.

OPPOSITE: Watching street life from a balcony.
ABOVE: A lovely building converted into broadcasting station.

Western Cuba

WITHIN EASY DRIVING DISTANCE FROM HAVANA, it is possible to explore a highly varied array of places and landscapes within the island's western region, even if you have just a week or a few days to spare.

Travel west, through the lush, tobacco plantation-filled province of Pinar del Río — Cuba's tobacco heartland, to relax amid some of the island's most spectacular scenery, laced with sleepy villages and cigar factories.

Also within western Cuba, yet to the east of Havana, the resort of Varadero may appeal if beach hedonism is what you have in mind.

More adventurous excursions may lead you southeast to the wildlife-rich Zapata Peninsula and Playa Girón (site of the abortive Bay of Pigs invasion), where secluded, translucent waters offer some of the island's best spots for swimming and scuba diving.

PINAR DEL RÍO PROVINCE

This spectacularly beautiful and tranquil mountain province of Pinar del Río boasts some of the island's most dramatic and varied landscapes. Within this region's scenic Valle de Viñales, vegetation-covered Jurassic-period mountains of limestone schist tower over hidden caves, tobacco farms and unexpectedly charming colonial towns. The distinctive *mogotes* or high flat-topped mountains seen here are rarely found in such profusion elsewhere.

you can spare a few days, you will be rewarded by letting the region's relaxing hillstation ambiance seep gradually into a sense of well-being — a rare mood in the heightened rush and blast on the senses that characterizes much about being in Havana. At least that's the idea: the lack of obvious distractions at night is an incentive, so be sure that you have distracting company, a yen to practice your Cuban-Spanish in small village taverns, or at the very least that you are well-equipped with a good book. In addition, make sure you come equipped with some strong insect repellent — the Cuban forest teems with tiny mosquitoes.

BACKGROUND

For centuries, even for much of the colonial era in Cuba, the province of Pinar del Río which occupies the western-most end of the island was a forested backwater. It was the last refuge of the Siboney, Cuba's early tribe of hunter-gatherers who were forced here from other parts of the island by the fiercer Taíno. Later the same mountains — which are riddled with caves and underground rivers — helped conceal communities known as *palenques*, where escaped slaves or *cimarrones* hoped to evade detection by so-called *ranchedores*, the ruthless bounty hunters who were paid to find or kill escaped slaves.

Today, the main attraction of Pinar del Río is simply to admire and explore the shifting moods of its changing landscape. There are plenty of possibilities to walk through its forests, swim in its natural rivers and to enjoy the gentle tempo of life in this predominantly agricultural region. It has to be said that the quality of the food served in Pinar del Río's hotels is generally of a higher standard than elsewhere in Cuba.

This is also the region of the classic *guajiro*, or Cuban peasant farmer, who you are likely to see wearing a weather-beaten straw hat astride his horse, chomping a cigar between his teeth.

Pinar del Río's fertile plantations — especially those in its Vuelta Abajo region — have been renowned for centuries for the exceptional quality of the cigars produced here, adding an additional lure for cigar connoisseurs. Whatever the season, you will see some aspect of the tobacco production process: from freshly tilled red ochre soil, to bright green plantations to the stacking of leaves in palm thatched *vegas*, or tobacco drying sheds.

Although some manage to be whisked through Pinar del Río in a one-day dash, if

LAS TERRAZAS

You may wish to make the delightful Hotel Moka within the forest reserve of Las Terrazas your base for all or part of your stay in Pinar

PREVIOUS PAGES: LEFT: Sandy María La Gorda in the far west. RIGHT: Tending young tobacco plants. ABOVE: Panoramic view of the Valle de Viñales with its *mogotes*, or flat-topped mountains.

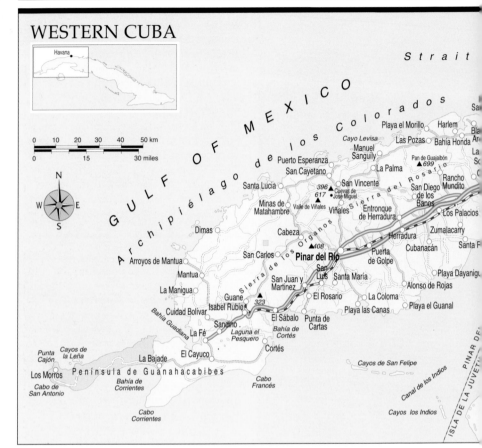

del Río. Located within Sierra del Rosario, the so-called tourist complex of Las Terrazas is also home to a community of some 890 local people, most of whom are farmers and agricultural workers, who live amid what is Cuba's first exercise in sustainable development. The largely self-sustaining community of Las Terrazas was founded in 1968: its low-lying bungalows, apartments, school, clinic and other buildings — including the region's traditional rodeo — lie in a narrow valley around Lake San Juan. Initially, the community undertook large-scale reforestation and the terrace building that gives the region its name. In 1993, the Ministry of Tourism stepped in and created Cuba's first eco-resort, Hotel Moka.

WHAT TO SEE AND DO

The **Sierra del Rosario**, with its upper reaches of thick tropical forest and high-

land rocky outcrops, is one of the most rain-prone regions in Cuba. It is also one of the island's most concentrated habitats for migratory and endemic bird species, including the *zunzuncito* and the *trogon*. The cave-filled hills are home to other endemic species, such as the pygmy boa and an unusual-looking water lizard, as well as sheltering many varieties of trees, plants and flowers. Most of this large reserve is closed to visitors, however there is still plenty to see.

At Las Terrazas, the **Ecological Research Center** can provide maps of the walking trails in the area, which can lead to the splashing cascades of waterfalls and pools perfect for swimming or to the ruins of former nineteenth-century coffee plantations. Walks around the hills reveal an abundance of plant species, including native orchids. You can explore some of these trail by horseback, and ask for a guide to accompany you for longer walks. Both activities can be

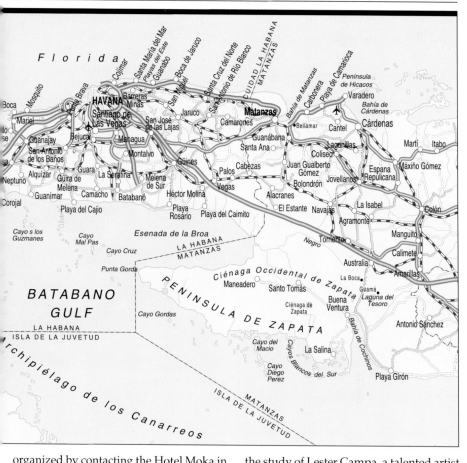

organized by contacting the Hotel Moka in advance.

The most beautiful lookout point in the area is the **Buena Vista**, a narrow ridge from which, on a clear day, you can see both the Florida Straits and the Caribbean Sea. This was a former nineteenth-century coffee plantation, run by a French planter who kept close guard on his 120 slaves: you can see the ruins of the stone barracks they were bolted into at night to the right of the plantation. The planter's house has been turned into a restaurant that specializes in French-Creole food, notably the dish they call "Witch Chicken." It also has outdoor tables so you can appreciate the charming view, which sprawls across vine-canopied forests and blossoming flame-red *flamboyán* trees. The air has an invigoratingly alpine scent and coolness.

When you get back to the Hotel Moka, you may want to ask whether you can visit the study of Lester Campa, a talented artist who was raised in Las Terrazas, and whose detailed landscapes reflect his fascination for nature.

WHERE TO STAY AND EAT

Set amid forested hills, **Hotel Moka** ((53-85) 2921, 2996 or 2694 (/FAX (53-7) 33-5516, Las Terrazas, Autopista Havana, Candelaria, Pinar del Río, is a new and comfortable hotel built in a style that incorporates much of the natural surroundings, as well as using natural woods. A large tree grows up through an open-air atrium in the reception hall and a stream runs through the garden and under the hotel. All the air-conditioned bedrooms have bathrooms faced entirely with glass so you can lie in your bath and look out through the trees. All rooms have safe deposit boxes, satellite television and a refrigerator. Facilities also include a charming swimming pool and tennis court. Horseback riding, fishing, bird watching and guided tours can be arranged.

Apart from the hotel's **Hotel Moka Restaurant**, you should have lunch at the **Cafetal Buena Vista** (it is open only between noon and 4 PM). In the Las Terrazas village, you can try the local *paladar*, **Terraza de la Fondita** in Unit 9, which is a great place to socialize with locals, and the Cuban fare is very good.

HOW TO GET THERE

Las Terrazas is located 75 km (nearly 47 miles) west of Havana, off the Autopista Nacional at Km 51. Look carefully for this marker on the highway, since only one small sign announces the four-kilometer (two-and-a-half-mile) turnoff to Las Terrazas, which enters the green steep hills to reach the guard booth standing where the border of the ecological reserve begins. It is best to advise Hotel Moka of your arrival in advance, so that the guard can expect you and wave you through. Also, drivers should know that a toll of US$3 is exacted from those who pass through this essentially private road for a scenic short-cut to the town of Soroa.

SOROA

Only 18 km (11 miles) from Las Terrazas is the tiny settlement of Soroa, best known for its extensive *Orquideario* or **Orchidarium**, which contains some 750 species of plants, including over 200 endemic to Cuba, all thriving in this lush, humid hillside environment. It was founded in 1943 by a native of the Canary Islands, a botanist named Tomás Felipe Camacho, in honor of his daughter Pilar who had a great passion for

orchids before she died during childbirth. Today it is maintained by the University of Pinar del Río. Look out for the tiny yellow orchids from Thailand, and the "Queen's Clogs" from the Philippines. The gardens are also landscaped with many other plants, including endemic palms and wildflowers. The best months to visit are between November and March when the orchids flower, although the gardens are pretty all year round. Entry costs US$2.

Close by, on the right side of the road you will see a small cafeteria and a sign marking the way to the **El Salto Falls**, which is a ten minute walk away through leafy forest. Should you feel so inclined, you can bathe in the surrounding pools.

Soroa's other main attraction, at the very least a good rest stop or coffee break, is its post modern-gothic style restaurant **El Castillo de las Nubes** (The Castle of the Clouds), which is located at the area's lookout point, from which you can see lushly lovely views of the surrounding countryside, peppered with *flamboyáns*. Within the area, the Manantiales River is renowned for the mineral and medicinal properties of its water.

WHERE TO STAY AND EAT

For inexpensive accommodations, try **Horizontes Villa Soroa (** (53-85) 2122 or 2041, Carretera de Soroa, Candelaria. Located at the crossroads of the valley, this hotel is probably the least appealing of the options listed for Pinar del Río due to its bland *cabaña* rooms. But it is comfortable enough, has a pleasant restaurant and swimming pool and is well located as a starting point for hikes and walks in the surrounding tropical forest.

The restaurant **El Castillo de las Nubes**, Alto de Villa Soroa, Sierra del Rosario, features spectacular views across the valley, and is a good place for lunch, although the former is far more impressive.

TRAVELING WESTWARDS

From here, return to the Carretera Central (Main Highway) and continue westwards. You will pass through the picturesque rural town of **San Cristóbal**, where tumbling-down red-tiled wooden *bohíos*, or cottages, are set against the green expanse of tobacco fields and thatched *vegas*. Here, as you will see throughout Pinar del Río, humped Indian Brahman cows plough the soil in a centuries-old method.

Continuing on, look out for the turnoff for the hamlet of **San Diego de los Baños**, once-popular for its spa waters. It lies on the fringes of another of Pinar del Río's nature reserves, the **Parque Nacional La Güira**, which sprawls across the sloping mountains of the Sierra de los Órganos. The 22,000-hectare (54,000-acre) wilderness of Parque Nacional La Güira remains undeveloped, although perhaps not for long.

It is already on the itinerary of visiting bird-watching groups, and although its trails are limited, they offer satisfyingly predictable glimpses of the resident birdlife, as well as the occasional deer. This reserve is located within the former private estate of Manuel Cortina, whose property was nationalized after the Revolution. You can see Cortina's elegant house and garden, now a museum with his possessions on display. The town's only hotel, **El Mirador**, is a good place to stop for cold drinks or lunch.

On the western edges of the reserve, on the Río Caiguanabo, is **Cuevas de las Portales**, a giant free-standing *mogote*, riddled with cavernous chambers, and an amazing spectacle of stalagmites and stalactites. Just as remarkable is the fact that Che Guevara made these caves his headquarters during the Cuban Missile Crisis in 1962, when he was commander of Cuba's western army.

As you retrace your route back onto the Autopista Nacional en route to Pinar de Río, you have the option of taking a turnoff to the south leading to the sparsely populated coastal settlement of **Maspotón**, notable as Cuba's largest hunting and fishing preserve, where the Horizontes hotel group operates a *Casa de Caza*, or hunting lodge, however this is not recommended as a place to stay. Don't make the disheartening mistake of coming here to birdwatch.

Cigar rollers OPPOSITE are allowed to smoke on the premises LEFT and to take home two cigars a day. RIGHT: Signed labels are meant to counter imitations.

THE PROVINCIAL CAPITAL OF PINAR DEL RÍO

The provincial capital of **Pinar del Río**, 176 km (109 miles) from Havana, is not recommended as a place to stay but, using Hotel Moka or Viñales as your base, you should certainly come here to spend an hour or two touring its cigar factories and museums. Include a walk along Calle Martí between Calles Medina and Colón, which are full of Cuban atmosphere, with bars, cafés and shops.

Since its rapid post-war expansion, Pinar del Río has lost whatever previous claims to charm it may have had, although tucked amid its colonial center you may find the occasional architectural gem.

BACKGROUND

The city's expansion has been largely due to the development of the tobacco industry, signaled by the many tin-roofed *casas del tobaco*, which contain the leaves harvested from the surrounding plantations of Vuelta Abajo and Viñales. The region's tobacco-growing soil and climate is universally recognized as being unsurpassed anywhere. Tobacco production reached its peak in the mid-1970s at 50,000 metric tons per year and then was crippled by a blight of blue mold. Although it nearly recovered in 1990, 1991 saw the first of many poor harvests. Since 1995, production has increased steadily as has foreign investment in the industry.

You can sample the region's famed cigars, in the very factories where they are hand-rolled.

WHAT TO SEE AND DO

Head for the **Fábrica de Tabacos Francisco Donatien** on Calle Antonio Maceo near the Plaza de Independencia, the oldest and most established in the city, housed in a former nineteenth-century jail. Here you can watch the cigar-making process, including leaf selection, cigar rolling and label gluing: over six brands are made here by skilful Cuban workers of both sexes and all ages. As always, a

man at the front of the room reads to the rollers over a loudspeaker: usually the day's news from the official state newspaper, *Granma*.

They also have an excellent shop and well-stocked humidor where you can browse or buy both the local brands, some of which can be very good, as well as the smoother export cigars. A guided tour costs US$2. It is open Monday to Friday from 6:30 AM to 4:30 PM and Saturday from 7:30 AM to 11:30 AM.

Another visit you should not miss is to the **Casa Garay** on Calle Isabel Rubio. Here a production team of garrulous women in white kerchiefs make *Guayabita del Pinar*, the alcoholic liquor made from the local *guayaba* or wild guava plant that grows everywhere in this region. You can tour the plant and sample the sweet and dry forms of this slightly spicy concoction, and if you like, you can buy a bottle. It is closed during the weekend.

Aside from these two factories, it has to be said that little else holds much attraction for visitors, except perhaps the 1909 **Palacio Güasch**, on Calle José Martí. It was designed for a wealthy doctor who traveled extensively and wanted to live in a building inspired by architecture around the world, including Moorish arches and French Gothic spires. It now houses the **Museum of Natural History**, crammed with collections of shells and stuffed birds, fish and animals, as well as an outdoor display of two concrete dinosaurs and a stone *megalon*, a large extinct rodent that was endemic to Cuba. This is a good place to see examples of the archaic corkscrew palm tree (a contemporary of the dinosaur) and a stuffed pygmy boa constrictor, in case you don't see them on your wanders in the wild. Further up Calle José Martí is the **Provincial Museum**, housed in a less dramatic colonial mansion, which has a display of local memorabilia. Across Calle Colón is the decaying Greek Revival-style **Milanés Theater** which does have a pretty, if crumbling, nineteenth-century interior.

As you leave the city, it's difficult not to notice the shabby Soviet-era Hotel Pinar del Río, notable only as a place not to stay.

Where to Eat

Located on the outskirts of the city of Pinar del Río, **Rumayor** ((53-8) 63051, Carretera de Viñales, Pinar del Río, is an Afro-Cuban restaurant whose specialty is smoked chicken. The *cherna frita* (sea bream sautéed in butter, garlic and onions) is also very good. At night, this establishment transforms into an open-air cabaret.

How to Get There

The Autopista Nacional (National Highway) from Havana will get you to the provincial city of Pinar del Río, 176 km (109 miles) away, within three hours. This is a relatively bland route aside from the

great slogans-to-socialism billboards, the agricultural scenes, and the increasing numbers of Cuba's prized palm trees, banana trees, corn fields, and rice paddies along the way.

It's worth knowing that the only decent place to stop at for a break and refreshments (or even a meal, given the lack of appetizing restaurants in the township of Pinar del Río) is the roadside truck stop **Las Barrigonos**, on the north side of the Autopista Nacional, 27 km (17 miles) east of Pinar del Río.

Aside from joining an organized tour, another way to reach Pinar del Río is by train, which has a daily scheduled service

The Mural de la Prehistoria was painted in 1966.

from Havana. The trip is meant to take five hours, but can be much longer. See GETTING AROUND, page 309 in TRAVELERS' TIPS for making reservations through the state railway agency, Ferrotur.

If you have time to spare, you might consider taking the Circuito Norte, the longer, more scenic coastal road which runs parallel to the Autopista to the north. It begins near Havana from the outlying town of Mariel, and follows the coast all the way up to Puerto Esperanza, passing through rustic farming scenes and villages with plenty of opportunities to stop and talk to local people.

VALLE DE VIÑALES

From the city of Pinar del Río, a small two-lane highway (full of bicycles, horse-drawn carts and exhaust-spewing buses) leads north to the Valle de Viñales, 26 km (16 miles) away, formed by the convergence of two mountain ranges, the Sierra del Rosario and the Sierra de los Órganos.

BACKGROUND

It is generally acknowledged that the Viñales valley contains the most breathtaking scenery in the region. This is largely due to the strange, almost primeval spectacle of the landscape's row of free-standing sugar-loaf hills called *mogotes*, which rise sharply from the valley floor to a flat top, with cliff-like flanks covered in green vegetation that tower over everything else in sight.

Found only in Cuba and in parts of China, Vietnam, and the Philippines, these fossil-filled geological formations are the oldest in Cuba, dating back to the Jurassic era, 150 million years ago. They are mainly limestone karst formations, shaped when underground rivers cut through the soft rock, forming caves and cliffs. The generally accepted explanation is that these formations came about by the differential erosion of two types of rocks: slate and limestone, with the latter eroding more easily, so that with time, the action of the water formed the valleys that you see today.

These mountains also conceal spectacular cave corridors, apparently the largest in Latin America, with countless underground streams and gorges. Only 30 cave systems have been charted, and many more wait to be explored, making the area considerably interesting for speleologists. The largest of the caves is the Cueva Santo Tomás, which has more than 45 km (28 miles) of galleries. Particular caves of interest that you can visit include the Cueva del Indio, through which runs the San Vicente River.

WHAT TO SEE AND DO

The main settlement in the valley is the charming town of **Viñales**, whose historically preserved nineteenth-century buildings appear almost frozen in time. The main street is lined with red-tiled wooden houses with verandahs and pine trees. The town's oldest house, Casa de Don Tomás, was built in 1822 and has now been turned into a delightful restaurant and bar. Within the town, a small, white nineteenth-century church and the Casa de Cultura are ringed around the main square's inevitable bust of José Martí.

Aside from Hotel Moka, the two best hotels in Pinar del Río — **Los Jazmines** and **La Ermita** — are located in the mountains surrounding Viñales, both perfectly sited for their panoramic views across the entire valley. The experience of watching dusk fall over the landscape — watching the light fade the shapes of the mountains to stencils against the sky, seeing farmers lead their horses home, and the quiet punctuated only by chattering birds — makes the trip here worthwhile in itself. Needless to say, there are no such views from the town of Viñales itself, given that it lies in the valley bowl.

From Viñales, follow the road west of town for several kilometers to reach the **Valle de Dos Hermanas** (The Valley of the Two Sisters) and the **Mural de la Prehistoria** (Prehistoric Mural), a huge mural depicting the process of evolution, from snails to dinosaurs and from chimpanzees to *Homo sapiens*. Set amid a landscape of such dramatic delicacy that is more reminiscent of a Chinese brush painting, this gauche mural certainly adds an incongruous element to the scene. It was designed by Leovigildo Gonzáles, a former student of the famous Mexican mural-artist Diego Riviera, and completed in 1966, but despite the imposing scale, it is unfortunately an artistic eyesore. A restaurant in the shadow of the cliff provides good Creole dishes for the large tour bus groups that tend to come here for lunch.

North of Viñales, follow the main road between the hills toward Puerto Esperanza, a road which would ultimately take you to the coast. The atmosphere is very rural, with small farming communities clustered in the shadows of the *mogotes*. After crossing Ancón Pass, to your left you will see a sign for the **Cueva de José Miguel** where a bar and discotheque has been built in a dripping cave. On the other side of the cave is one of the largest cave *palenques* in Cuba, where up to 200 escaped slaves managed to survive; you can see a recreation of how they lived here, and perhaps have lunch at the restaurant **El Palenque de los Cimarrones**.

Head for the **Cueva del Indio**, a few kilometers ahead on the right. It was discovered by local farmers in 1920 and takes its name from the burial bones of the Siboney, also known as the Guanahatabeys, the Indian tribe that once lived here. Once you have entered and your eyes have adjusted to the interior, you can explore part of this enormous cave system by foot, and partly by a small motorboat along the underground river, which picks you up inside the cave and takes you on a short tour through a gallery of dramatic stalagmites and stalactites to emerge from the hillside. The cave is some 1,700 m (nearly 5,600 ft) in length, but less than a third of that is open to the public. It is open daily from 11 AM to 5 PM and the entrance fee is US$3. The riverside restaurant here is good, if this is where you feel like stopping for lunch. Watch out for the swarms of tiny mosquitoes however.

From here, after continuing north for two kilometers (slightly over one mile), you will come to **Rancho San Vicente**, a spa-hotel catering mainly for Cubans, who come here for its complex of thermal waters and sulfur baths in search of a cure for various ailments.

WHERE TO STAY

Moderate

Hotel Horizontes Los Jazmines ((53-8) 93-3205 or 93-3206 FAX (53-7) 33-5042, Carretera de Viñales, 25 km (about 15 miles) from Pinar del Rio, is the nicest of the hotels in the Viñales. This attractive pink colonial building with traditional stained-glass windows

has fantastic views across the valley. Apparently, Castro himself suggested the site as an ideal honeymoon retreat. All of the simply furnished rooms are air-conditioned, and have a balcony from which to enjoy the sunset. There is a large swimming pool. Horseback riding can be arranged, or you can explore tracks leading down into the valley by foot. It is prudent to reserve in advance.

Hotel Horizontes La Ermita Motel ((53-8) 93-204 or 93-205 FAX (53-8) 93-6091, Carretera de la Ermita, is two kilometers (slightly over a mile) from Viñales. The best thing about this hotel is its restaurant which

Exotic flora in the Valle de Viñales.

has a large open-air balcony from which you can enjoy another vantage view of the valley: the most spectacular balcony in Cuba, no less. The rooms are comfortable and air-conditioned, and there is a pleasant swimming pool. Make your reservations well in advance.

Inexpensive

Hotel Horizontes Rancho San Vicente ((53-8) 93-200 FAX (53-7) 33-5042, Valle de San Vicente, road to Puerto Esperanza, Viñales, is a small, "no-frills" 20-room hotel with simple, comfortable rooms and facilities including a restaurant and bar and guided tours by horseback or on foot through the nearby mountains and caves. As well as the thermal waters and sulfur baths, the hotel also specializes in mud packs, using local mud which is rich in "algae, marine organisms and biologically active substances." Don't expect a luxury spa.

WHERE TO EAT

Moderate

Casa Don Tomás ((53-8) 93-114, Calle Salvador Cisnero No. 140, Viñales, is set in a charming, two-story wooden colonial house on the main street of Viñales. This is the best place for lunch or dinner in town. You can dine outside or on the verandah. The Creole food and the service is very good. Among its specialties is a rice dish with ham, pork, lobster and sausage. The *tasajo de campesino* (*guajiro*-style dried beef) is another dish of the region.

Aside from this site's dramatic history as a *palenque*, **El Palenque de los Cimarrones** restaurant, Valle San Vicente, Viñales, has been modeled on a Santería theme, with each section inspired by a different *orisha*. The Creole dishes are good, especially the *pollo asado*, *arroz morro* and *yucca*; and be sure to also try their house drink, *chinguirito*, which is a mixture of lemon, rum, honey, mineral water and ice.

Mural de la Prehistoria, Valle de Viñales, is a ranch-style restaurant next to the Mural de la Prehistoria. It caters mainly to large groups, but manages to keep a good standard of service and food, serving regional Creole dishes.

Inexpensive

Paladar Valle Bar ((53-8) 93-183, Calle Salvador Cisneros No. 100, Viñales, is fun at night, when the town's local personalities gather to banter with visitors and play the battered, much-loved piano. They appreciate reservations so they can prepare in advance.

La Casa del Marisco, Cueva del Indio, Valle de Viñales, is a modest establishment, across from the entrance to the Cueva del Indio, it serves Creole food, and its specialty is the freshwater prawns caught in the nearby underground rivers.

Located next to the entrance of the Cueva del Indio, the restaurant **Cueva del Indio**, Valle de Viñales, features charcoal-grilled chicken, *cassava* cakes and *ajiaco*, a meat and vegetable stew.

CAYO LEVISA

Most visitors generally head back from here to their hotels in Viñales. However, it would be a shame to miss one of Pinar del Río's prettiest, secluded beach resorts. Here is the route you take: continue by road beyond San Vicente, turn left at the crossroads toward San Cayetano and soon you will reach **Puerto Esperanza**, a small fishing village which is the nearest point from which to reach the small offshore island resort of **Cayo Levisa**, a 45-minute boat ride away.

Until recently, Cayo Levisa was a destination for day-long excursions, which could include lobster fishing, snorkeling over the rim of coral reefs, and lunch on the beach. Recently, a tourist resort has been developed on the three-kilometer (nearly two-mile)-long island, the **Villa Cayo Levisa**, which specializes in diving and water sports. It is becoming an increasingly popular destination for Spanish and Italian divers, who rave about its offshore black coral formations, and its abundant tropical fish and lobsters. Lounging on its soft, creamy sands is equally pleasant.

From Cayo Levisa, it is easy to arrange (through Villa Cayo Levisa) boat excursions to **Cayo Paraíso**, beloved by Ernest Hemingway, who frequently anchored his

Hotel Los Jazmines ranks among Cuba's most pleasant.

yacht here during the 1940s. Plans are afoot to build a marina for yacht enthusiasts and scuba divers, who swear that diving here — the loveliest *cayo* in the Archipiélago de los Colorades — is nothing less than spectacular.

WHERE TO STAY

To ensure that this small key remains pristine, the well-run resort, **Villa Cayo Levisa** is limited to 20 moderately priced beach *cabañas*, which are comfortable and have satellite television, radio, and a telephone. There is a lively restaurant and bar and a small boutique. Gran Caribe recently took over and plan to expand this into a more luxurious resort. Facilities include basic diving and snorkeling equipment, and arrangements can be made for fishing trips and excursions to Viñales. Advance reservations are advised. To book, contact Manotur ((53-7) 33-1162 FAX (53-7) 33-1164, or Gran Caribe ((53-7) 33-0238, Avenida 7 No. 4210 between Calles 42 and 44, Miramar.

In Puerta Esperanza

The very affordable **Villa Rosario** ((53-8) 9-3828, Granja Rosario, Puerto Esperanza, is housed in a nineteenth-century mansion that once belonged to a wealthy landowner and later housed the area's Communist Party headquarters). This quirky hotel and restaurant is a good base from which to explore this little-visited but very scenic region of small seaside villages and make trips to surrounding keys. There are only four rooms. The restaurant features good home cooking using local ingredients.

WESTERN PINAR DEL RÍO

Not many visitors take the time to travel further westwards into Pinar del Río. However, this off-the-beaten-track region offers some opportunities to appreciate some of Cuba's least developed natural scenery, and contains two important ecological reserves. Distances are short and if you are staying in Viñales you can easily use your hotel as a base.

From the city of Pinar del Río the standard route westwards is the main highway, which will soon lead you through this region's famous tobacco-growing area of Vuelta Abajo where the leaves for Cuba's most prestigious cigars are grown, notably the rustic towns of **San Luís** and **San Juan y Martinez**. The latter, which lies 23 km (14 miles) west of Pinar del Río, is worth a stop to admire its pastel-colored houses.

Depending on the time of year you visit, you will see various stages of tobacco production. During the rainy winter and the early spring growing season, the tobacco plants are shielded from the ravaging effects of the sun by tarpaulins suspended from poles; which en masse appear like a sea of undulating fabric. You'll see countless drying sheds thatched with palm fronds where the precious tobacco leaves are dried in the traditional way to preserve their flavor.

Further on, past the town of Sandino, you'll enter a region of lagoons, where fishermen exist as they have done for centuries, paddling their small boats out and using woven nets. **Laguna de Pesquero** is the most popular.

From here, until the end of the highway, the road cuts through thick forests and swamps, a breeding ground for the region's large crabs, who often swarm out onto the roads.

A secondary road heads from the fishing outpost of **La Fé** for **La Bajada**, the entry point for the Bahía de Corrientes, at the southern-most point of the peninsula, at which you have to pass through a military checkpoint.

Located here is the **María La Gorda International Dive Center**, a diving resort which arranges diving expeditions to pristine reefs and sunken wrecks offshore.

In this area, María La Gorda ("Mary the Fat") has entered local legend. Apparently she was a large Venezuelan woman in the eighteenth century who had the misfortune to be kidnapped by pirates and was later stranded here after a shipwreck. Taking stock of the situation, she soon became a sought-after attraction for passing sailors, and lived on to end her days in comfort at an old age.

On the other side of La Bajada is the **Guanahacabibes Peninsula**, one of the last refuges for the doomed Indian tribe, the Siboney (also known as the Guanahuatebey) during the Spanish colonization of the island. It is one of Cuba's largest forest reserves, and although rather unprepossessingly sparse in parts, is home to a great many endemic plant, bird, insect and animal species, a number of which are in danger of extinction. In theory, you can visit the reserve with a permit from the Cuban tourism authorities. However it is better to contact the Hotel María La Gorda, who can arrange for you to rent a jeep with a driver who can also serve as a guide. Or you can go with your own car, and ask the park ranger at the entrance to accompany you. Entrance is US$10, and you will have to arrange a fee with your guide. It is forbidden to camp here, and you should leave the reserve before nightfall.

The road that passes through the reserve follows a line of deserted sandy beaches along the Bahía de Corrientes before ending at the lighthouse of Cabo de San Antonio, from which all you can see is the endless expanse of the Gulf of Mexico.

WHERE TO STAY

Villa María La Gorda ((53-8) 43121 SATELLITE **(** 683680510 FAX 683680510, Playa María La Gorda, Peninsula de Guanahacabibes, is a fairly simple, inexpensive and practical establishment, designed with divers in mind, but is pleasant enough in its own right if you want a few days of swimming and seclusion. The 20 *cabañas* are comfortable enough (don't expect any frills), and the restaurant serves good meals featuring fresh seafood. The diving instructors and the staff here are very friendly and helpful.

FROM HAVANA TO VARADERO

It is an easy and well-signposted two-and-a-half-hour drive eastwards from Havana to Varadero along the two-lane highway Vía Blanca, which begins when you emerge from the Havana Bay tunnel and passes through the provincial capital of Matanzas.

Past the **Pan-American Village**, and further on, beyond the beaches of Playas del Este as you drive along the coastal highway, your spirits may sink a little (hoping this is not an indication of what may be to come) as you pass plain beaches strung with clusters of plebeian bungalows and dreary cement-block hotels which cater to Cuban workers; the Havana Club rum factory; and then a depressing industrial tract punctuated with dirty oil pumps, shelved with iron rock and carpeted with spiky *sisal* plantations. You may notice that a stretch of oil pumps stand

out because they look new — this is the result of Cuba's joint-venture with a Canadian oil company.

The first moment of truly impressive scenery comes when you reach the **Yumurí Valley**, which lies at the entrance to the province of Matanzas, 80 km (50 miles) from Havana. Here, from the lookout point at **El Mirador**, you can break the journey with a drink (the juice of a freshly cut coconut or a *cafecito*) and survey the fabulous view across the valley, formed as a natural canyon by the Yumurí River and its tributaries. The surrounding landscape is sheathed in green forest, high above which you can see wheeling Cuban vultures, and beyond which coconut palms rim the coast. The valley, which is eight kilometers (five miles) wide and ringed by hills except to the west, is spanned by the **Bacanayagua Bridge**, the highest bridge in Cuba, completed in 1959.

Near Playa Girón, a mid-stream jeep cleaning.

MATANZAS

From here, you are 20 km (slightly over 12 miles) from the historic colonial city of Matanzas, one of Cuba's main agricultural centers and industrial ports, and also known as the vibrant home of many Afro-Cuban musical styles, including the *danzonete*, a variation on the *danzon*, traditionally played by *charanga* bands.

BACKGROUND

By the mid-1800s, Matanzas was one of Cuba's most important trading cities: with its well-situated harbor and its surrounding countryside worked by thousands of slaves, it became the largest sugar exporter in the world, and the magnet for some of Cuba's most prominent intellectuals, scientists, musicians and artists. With its growing population of Creole elite, as well as the merchants and moneylenders who followed, Matanzas was a progressive city that saw the founding of Cuba's first printing press in 1813, its first newspaper in 1828, as well as its first Philharmonic Orchestra and its first public library. Today, you can see many fine nineteenth-century civic buildings and residences dating from this period.

Located around the large curving Bay of Matanzas, surrounded by gently undulating hills and valleys and crisscrossed by the San Juan, Yumurí and Canimar rivers that flow to the sea, the city has a long history of settlement. Originally a Taíno Indian village called Yucayo, the Spanish founded the city in 1693, first trading in cattle, then tobacco and later, sugar. It is not known for sure how Matanzas got its name, which means "place of slaughter": Some speculate that it could refer to the slaughter of cattle, but perhaps, more convincingly, it may refer to an unconfirmed account that 32 shipwrecked Spaniards who were killed here by the Taíno, and in an interesting twist, one of the survivors became the wife of the local Indian chieftain. Certainly, violence seemed to crop up in Matanzas: between 1825 and 1843,

Family on the road for Sunday lunch with friends.

when slaves were revolting and attacking plantation owners, the Spanish colonial masters retaliated by brutally torturing and killing more than a thousand slaves in this region. In addition, the Spanish were particularly forceful in their attempts to proselytize, and consequently, the slaves here developed Christian disguises for their own gods, who they continued to worship. Thus, Matanzas became a key center for the development of Santería, as well as other offshoots of Afro-Cuban beliefs, such as Palo Monte and Abakuá.

WHAT TO SEE AND DO

You could easily spend an hour or two walking around Matanzas looking at its interesting buildings in the city center. Start with the imposing **Sauto Theater**. Built in 1863 and designed by an Italian architect, this was the most impressive theater outside of Havana, and became the model for many theaters around the country. While the elegant five-story structure has a classical design, the ground floor incorporates the Cuban *portal*, into which carriages could drive. It is worth going inside to see the exceptional and beautifully preserved interiors, where every detail was fashionable for its time, including the elaborate paint-

ed neoclassical stage set, which could be raised and lowered mechanically, and the cast-iron seats. Many European touring companies — ranging from classical ballet to Italian opera — and stars, including Anna Pavlova and Sarah Bernhardt, performed here.

Nearby stands the **Matanzas Fire Station**, completed in 1900, which is among the country's first Republican-era civic buildings and occupies a prominent place on the city's original plaza.

Also worth seeing is the **Museo Farmacéutico** and the **Palacio del Junco**, both on the Calle Milanés, next to the Plaza de Armas, also known as the Parque Libertad. Founded in 1882, and housed in its original building, the museum is a fascinating place to visit, with all of the original copper and bronze instruments used for processing medicinal plants and distilling water, alcoholates and essential oils. There is a collection of thousands of labels, jars, tools and formulas, as well as books in four languages that make up its extensive library. The museum is open Monday to Saturday, 10 AM to 6 PM and Sunday 9 AM to 1 PM.

The Palacio, built for a wealthy sugar planter in 1842, houses the **Matanzas Museo Provincial** which recounts the city's history and is open Tuesday to Sunday, 2 PM to 9 PM.

Other nineteenth-century buildings of interest are the **Hotel El Louvre**, a film-set period piece; the 1826 **Aduana** (Customs Building), now the Palacio de Justicia (Courthouse); and the **Casa de la Trova y el Escritor** (House of the Troubadour and the Writer) which, if you are lucky, may be staging one of their memorable music ensembles the day you visit.

On the main square, look out for the early twentieth-century **Casino Español**, a former social club and casino notable for its ornate façade. It is now the municipal library, and you can take a walk inside to admire its marble staircase and the grandiose proportions of its rooms.

You can also see the **Catedral de San Carlos**, the oldest church in Matanzas, which dates to 1730, but was remodeled with neoclassical elements, including the pilasters, during the following century. Both the church of **San Pedro** and the **Monserrat Chapel** are influenced by Italian Renaissance architecture. The chapel's statues were added for a movie set and have remained there.

As you leave Matanzas on the road to Varadero, you will see a signpost on your right directing you to the **Cuevas de Bellamar**, eight kilometers (five miles) away. Discovered in 1861, this 3,000 m (over 9,800-ft)-long cave has an abundance of stalagmites and stalactites, with impressive galleries that drop to a depth of 48 m (157 ft), and a network of underground lakes and rivers. The caves are open daily from 9 AM to 5 PM.

Where to Stay and Eat

Matanzas is not really recommended as a place to stay, as the Cuban government prefers that visiting foreigners stay in the purpose-built resorts further along in Varadero. To this end, although there are three vintage hotels — **Hotel El Louvre**, **Hotel Velasco** and **Hotel Yara** — they are peso-only, and non-Cubans are not encouraged to stay. It's easy to imagine how all of them, especially the Hotel El Louvre, would look quite wonderful if they were restored to their former elegance.

Likewise, there is not much scope for a good meal in Matanzas. If you are desperately in search of a meal or refreshments, try **Mesón La Viña**, on the southwest corner of the main square. **Café Atenas**, opposite the Sauto Theater, is another standby.

As you drive out of Matanzas towards Varadero, at the exit of the town is the **Ruinas de Matasiete**, an open-air establishment which serves drinks and snacks overlooking the bay.

Cárdenas

The sleepy, crumbling colonial town of **Cárdenas** lies just five kilometers (three miles) east of Matanzas. Here, horse-drawn carts bearing bales of hay and straw-hatted farmers atop bicycles outnumber cars. Despite its run-down ambiance and the obvious hardship faced by many of its residents (which may open the eyes of many visitors to the harsh realities faced by many Cubans), there is a charming gentility to this rustic town.

It is known as the "City of Flags" because the Cuban flag was first raised here in 1850, in a failed insurrection.

You should coincide your visit to see the **Oscar María de Rojas Museum**, on Calle Cárdenas. Among its curiosities are an elegant nineteenth-century hearse, two preserved fleas trussed up in dancing costumes and a fountain pen pistol which belonged to a Nazi spy who was captured in Havana in 1942. It is open Tuesday to Saturday, 1 PM to 6 PM and Sunday, 9 AM to 1 PM.

How to Get There

Matanzas is 42 km (26 miles) west of Havana and 98 km (61 miles) east of Varadero. If you are driving, it is worthwhile exploring both Matanzas and Cárdenas en route from Havana, or as you return to Havana. If you are planning to continue on from Varadero to Playa Girón, you will pass through Cárdenas.

If you want to take the train from Havana to Matanzas, you will pull into the new Estación de Ferrocarriles at the city's southern edge. Most national trains pull in here from Havana en route to the island's main cities and towns, including Santiago de Cuba.

If you have set your heart on taking the Hershey Railway, which plies between Matanzas and Casablanca, you need to take the train at another station at Calles 55 and 67 in Versalles, close to the town center. Ticket sales begin an hour before departure.

VARADERO

Many visitors who arrive in Cuba on package tours are pitched directly into Varadero, Cuba's purpose-built premier beach resort, two and a half hour's drive east of Havana, and very often never get to see any other part of the country, let alone the capital. While this may not be surprising, it helps explain the way in which the culture of Varadero can be described as almost surreal: a playground for foreigners that is about as dislocated from the rest of the country as it is possible to be.

Oscar takes a reflective puff in his Varadero home.

BACKGROUND

The Varadero that you see today — with its impressive row of luxury hotels that are best described as landscaped concrete wonders, lined up along an isthmus facing the Straits of Florida and nearly touching the Tropic of Cancer — was developed in the early 1990s as the centerpiece of the Revolution's bid to shore up its failing economy by re-starting the Cuban tourist industry after a long sabbatical.

The Spanish had set up a garrison here to keep watch for pirates and smugglers. As a resort, its popularity began during the late nineteenth century when the well-to-do from nearby Cárdenas began to build summer homes here. Then, in 1920, the pharmaceuticals magnate Eleuthère Irenée Du Pont built a grand mansion here and bought up 512 hectares (1,265 acres) of beachside property, thus encouraging many fellow millionaires to vacation here. Later, during the Second World War, it became fashionable when prosperous Americans looked for somewhere safer and closer than Europe to take a vacation. The Cuban elite also had residences here, including the dictator Batista. After the Revolution, Varadero was just as popular with Cubans as with sun-seekers from the Soviet Bloc countries.

Varadero is said to have the most beautiful beaches in Cuba; certainly the peninsula's 18 km (11 miles) of beaches are blessed with the necessary trio of soft white sands, palm trees, and clear blue seas (with hardly a rock or a weed) to satisfy most basic requirements for a beach vacation. The hotels, a series of some surprisingly tasteful Canadian, German, French, Italian and even Jamaican investments in joint-ventures with the Cuban government, are designed for people who are content to stay within the confines of their hotel, or shuttle between tourist-orientated cafés, bars, restaurants, shopping complexes and now, Cuba's largest, brand-new three-kilometer (nearly two-mile)-long, 18-hole golf course. Meanwhile, planners intend to double the number of hotels here within a decade. Some joke that Varadero is pre-

siding over its very own oil boom, the kind associated with suntans.

Varadero also has a reputation as something of a fleshpot: don't be fooled by the hotel schedules posted up in the lobby which suggest activities for almost every moment of the day, like a Baden-Powell-style British vacation camp. One observer commented that Varadero was the only place he had ever seen prostitutes soliciting in the surf. If you go with your family, this aspect of the resort culture is pretty easy to overlook; indeed many couples and families come to Varadero "for a change" and accommodate some of its problems.

GENERAL INFORMATION

Most hotels have information and tour excursion desks, and the leading hotels often house offices of the main Cuban tour agencies, such as Cubatur and Havanatur.

The **Centro de Información Turistico** (Tourist Information Center) is located at Avenida 1 and Calle 23. It is open daily 8 AM to 8 PM and can help arrange hotel reservations and tours, as well as field general questions.

Asistur ((53-5) 66-7277 or 66-2164, at Avenida 1 and Calle 31, can provide advice and assistance should emergencies strike. For example, they can help arrange medical treatment and insurance, legal advice and special-case cash advances, should you require it. It is open Monday to Friday, 9 AM to noon and from 1:30 PM to 4:30 PM; Saturday, 9 AM to noon.

Varadero's **International Clinic** ((53-5) 66-7710, is located at Avenida 1 and Calle 61, Varadero.

You can get cash advances and cash traveler's checks at the **Banco Financiero International** ((53-5) 33-7002, Calle 32 and Avenida Playa.

WHAT TO SEE AND DO

Not surprisingly, most people prefer to simply lie on the beach, get sand in their paperbacks, gaze at — and swim in — the sea, and perhaps, on an ambitious day, play a few rounds of tennis. Most of the hotels have bars designed around their swimming pools, so that swim-suited sun-worshippers can indulge in rum-based *cuba libres* and get sozzled as they get sizzled. Varadero specializes in sun, sea and sand vacations, with water sports, diving and sailing expeditions by day; and plenty of discotheque and cabaret diversions if you like that sort of thing at night.

This being said, the town of Varadero has a few places of interest tucked away, and you can always visit Matanzas or nearby Cárdenas if you are curious to see some "real" Cuban towns.

be a sort-of "golfing hotel" with comfortable rooms and the exclusive **Las Américas** French restaurant, which features some rooms left as they were and a wonderful Moorish sea-facing terrace with details hand-carved in mahogany and romantic lamps at the corners. Golfers will be interested to know that the golf course was designed by the Canadian firm Golf Design Services, headed by Les Furber who worked with the great Robert Trent Jones. For details about this new complex, contact Esther Hirzal, head of Public Relations at Rumbos

The historic part of Varadero — where the remains of the nineteenth-century Spanish garrison can be seen, now painted pink and green — lies between Calles 42 and 54 and Avenidas 1 and 2, and some of the wooden houses are quite charming. It is worth visiting the **Museo de Varadero**, housed in a candy pink-and-blue painted Key West-style house, set back in a garden by the beach, where all the local lore is documented. It is open Tuesday to Saturday, 9 AM to 6 PM, Sunday 9 AM to noon.

You can't miss seeing the splendid Spanish Revival-style Du Pont family vacation home built in 1926, which now sits within the new 18-hole **Varadero Golf Club**. The Rumbos-operated complex was devised to

((53-7) 66-2113 to 66-2115, at Línea and M, Vedado, Havana.

Parque Josone is a tourist complex, full of restaurants, shops and cafés. Of all Varadero's shops — which include well-stocked supermarkets and casual-wear boutiques like Benetton — the **Casa del Habano**, on Avenida 1, between Calles 63 and 64, is notable as a mecca for cigar-smokers with its stock of Cuba's best brands.

If you want to drive to the end of the peninsula, follow the two-lane Carretera del Sur all the way past the hotel developments, past the Marina Chapelín on your right, and soon all you will see will be

Vegas or tobacco-drying sheds dot the fertile west.

swampy marshes on your right and low-lying shrub to your left. Varadero's Marina Gaviota is located here (the larger Marina Acua lies at the south end of the peninsula). The seafood restaurant here, **El Galeón**, is one of Varadero's best. Further on is the Frontier Guard, a military guard post which is where you have to turn back.

WHERE TO STAY

As a general rule of thumb, accommodation in Varadero is less expensive than in Havana, and most guests stay here on pre-arranged packages at a discounted rate that works out very reasonably by international standards. However, of all Varadero's luxury resorts, the Melía-Varadero stands out: it fulfils most standards of international pampering and, although expensive, is worth it. Otherwise, the less expensive Sol Palmeras and the Internacional hotels are both attractive places to stay.

Varadero's five-star hotels are expensive by Cuban standards, and usually have a variety of restaurants and bars, a discotheque, boutiques, shops, medical services, child care and play areas, as well as facilities for tennis, volleyball, squash, diving and other water sports. The three- and four-star hotels are generally moderately priced, and have a similar standard of amenities, whether they offer rooms or bungalows. Most complexes have rooms which are air-conditioned, with televisions and radios; while facilities include swimming pools, restaurants and bars. Rental villas usually come equipped with a refrigerator. The inexpensive one- or two-star hotels have the basic necessities — rooms with a ceiling fan (air-conditioning if you are lucky), a radio and a safe, and some, such as the Horizontes Pullman, have a swimming pool. Most hotels can arrange car, motorbike and bicycle rentals, and almost all of them rent equipment for snorkeling, windsurfing, catamaran sailing, and other water sports.

Bear in mind that the star rating system indicated here is that of the Cuban tourist authorities, and does not necessarily match up to the international system.

Aside from this, the other important factor is, as always, location. The nicest, soft-sanded beaches are found between Calle 55 and Punta Hicacos, which means that it is worth checking before you book that your hotel is actually located in this more desirable part of the peninsula. The least attractive beaches are located near the Vía Blanca and Avenida Kawama areas. It is at least useful to know in advance why you may have been given such a good rate on hotels and villas located on the way into Varadero, such as Villa Kawama and Hotel Paradiso Puntarena.

Expensive
Hotel Melía Varadero***** ((53-5) 66-7013 FAX (53-5) 66-7012, Carretera del Sur, Playa Las Américas is still the undisputed queen of Varadero's deluxe resorts. You may feel quite content to simply commute between your room, the beach, the swimming pool and the buffet table without really feeling the need to leave. You can stay in a bungalow or a sea-facing terraced suite (which comes equipped with a minibar, satellite television, and VCR). Among its restaurants, the Fuerteventura is reputedly one of the best and most expensive in Cuba. The only drawback is that while the hotel beach is very pleasant, it is truthfully not the best on this strip of coastline.

Located alongside, **Hotel Melía Las Americas******* ((53-5) 66-7600 FAX (53-5) 66-7625, Carretera del Sur, Playa Las Américas, is another luxury hotel in the same mold, run by the same joint-venture as the above, with a similar standard of amenities and services.

Moderate
Hotel Sol Palmeras**** ((53-5) 55-7009 FAX (53-5) 66-7008, Carretera del Sur, is located next to the Melía Varadero and is an attractive place to stay, with its seashell-shaped main building, prettily landscaped and brightly colored stucco bungalows, good facilities and excellent service, with direct access to the beach.

Varadero's first luxury hotel, the faded pink, concrete 1950s classic **Hotel Internacional****** ((53-5) 66-7038, or 66-7039 FAX (53-5) 66-7246, Carretera Las Americas, is located on one of the loveliest beaches in Varadero, which makes it much easier to tolerate the hotel's idiosyncrasies and only average service and facilities, although this has improved with a recent renovation. The beach alone, as well as the slightly shady atmosphere at the beach bar, makes this hotel, along with the Melía Varadero, a great place to stay in Varadero. If you only plan to come to Varadero for the day, you can rent one of their beach cabins as a place to change, rest, and shower for a nominal fee.

The recently built Gran Caribe venture, **Hotel Arenas Doradas****** ((53-5) 66-7810 or 66-7811 FAX (53-5) 8159, Carretera del Sur, Punta Hicacos, is located towards the end of the peninsula, away from Varadero's main hotel strip. Attempts have been made to integrate the hotel with its natural surroundings, and there are plenty of thatched umbrellas on the pretty, soft-sanded beach.

Hotel Sol Club Las Sirenas**** ((53-5) 66-8070 FAX (53-5) 66-8075, Carretera Las Américas and Calle K, Reparto La Torre, is a brand-new hotel likely to be popular: like the Sol Palmeras, it is attractively landscaped and generally tasteful, with excellent sports facilities (including a miniature golf course) and attention to service. To book, you can also contact the Gaviota office in Havana at ((53-7) 22-7670 FAX (53-7) 33-2780.

The Jamaican joint-venture **Varadero Superclub Resort****** ((53-5) 66-7030 FAX (53-5) 66-7005 E-MAIL clubvar@clubvar.var.cyt.cu, Carretera Las Américas Km 3, has all the kinds of organized fun and sports activities you might expect of this all-inclusive hotel chain: here the set price includes your accommodations, all meals, free bar and hotel services, and windsurf and catamaran rental.

The large **Hotel LTI Tuxpan Resort****** ((53-5) 66-7560 FAX (53-5) 66-7561, Carretera Las Américas, offers comfortable accommodations with standard facilities, including a range of restaurants, boutiques, shops and convention rooms. **Hotel LTI Bellacosta Resort****** ((53-5) 66-7210 FAX (53-5) 66-7205, Carretera Las Américas is a good, well-located hotel, close to a nice stretch of beach, with excellent buffet meals.

Hotel Gaviota Caribe**** ((53-5) 66-7280 to 84 FAX (53-5) 66-7194, Calle G, Reparto La Torre, is a relatively small complex, made up of comfortable and pleasantly landscaped

hotel rooms and cabins within steps of a pretty beach. **Hotel Gaviota Cascada****** ((53-5) 66-7280 FAX (53-5) 66-7194, Calle K, Reparto La Torre is another nicely landscaped small-scale hotel, set in a main building with large rooms, some with balconies, close to the beach.

Villa Punta Blanca**** ((53-5) 66-7090 or 66-8050 FAX (53-5) 66-77090, Avenida del Mar, Avenida Kawama is run by Gran Caribe. You can choose from a selection of private villas and houses, as well as several restaurants, facing a secluded and relatively undeveloped part of Varadero.

Hotel Paradiso-Puntarena**** ((53-5) 66-7120 or 66-7121 FAX (53-5) 66-7728 E-MAIL hpp@rlparad.gca.cma.net, Avenidas Kawama and Final, consists of two ugly, stalwart-looking seven-story hotels buildings which are known locally as the "Twins" and are located on an unattractive beach at the end of Punta Kawama, and are not particularly cheap either. The two hotels are linked by an outdoor walkway and swimming pool.

Moderate

The salmon-pink **Hotel Cuatro Palmas Resort***** ((53-5) 66-7040 FAX (53-5) 66-7208, Avenida 1 between Calles 61 and 62, is set in lush vegetation, with its rounded *portales*-style arcades, balustrades and pillars; it has a pleasant Cuban atmosphere. Importantly, it is located on a lovely stretch of beach, is also close to the commercial district and has good water sports facilities.

Villa Cuba*** ((53-5) 66-7065 or 61-2952 FAX (53-5) 66-7207, Carretera Las Américas, is located near the Du Pont mansion. These pleasant one, two or three-bedroom apartments — some more luxurious than others — are an excellent choice for families — but can be private and secluded as well. The beach is very lovely.

The Spanish-style (think Costa del Sol) complex-village **Villa Kawama***** ((53-5) 61-3015 or 66-7295 FAX (53-5) 66-7334, Avenida Kawama and Calle O, is unexceptional, although not entirely without charm, with two-story, divided-up bungalows close to a palm-dotted if uninspiring stretch of beach, which, not surprisingly, is quite private.

Inexpensive

Hotel Horizontes Pullman** ((53-5) 66-7161 FAX (53-5) 66-7495, Avenida 1, between Calles 49 and 50, is the nicest of Varadero's inexpensive hotels, renovated in a quirky mansion, and located close to both downtown Varadero and the beach.

WHERE TO EAT

As well as an abundance of restaurants, pizza bars and cafés that have sprung up along Varadero's beachfront stretch, you can consider the following recommendations.

Expensive

Fuerteventura ((53-5) 66-7013, Hotel Meliá Varadero, has to be Varadero's most exceptional restaurant, with excellent Spanish cuisine from Basque specialties, to creatively prepared paella and lobster.

Las Américas ((53-5) 66-7750, Carretera Las Américas, Reparto La Torre, the former Du Pont mansion, was Varadero's most elegant expatriate mansions in its day, and much of the atmosphere lingers on: sections of the mansion have been preserved, with family photographs and book-lined rooms. It has to be said that the food and the prices are not up to the surroundings. However, it is still worth a visit.

Moderate

El Palacete ((53-5) 6-2933, Avenida 1 and Calle 56, is one of Varadero's most creative and interesting restaurants, with a changing menu of international dishes and house specialties, such as home-made pâté. Upstairs, a band plays bolero music under the stars.

Set within this peaceful marina with sea views, **El Galeón** ((53-5) 66-3712, Marina Gaviota, Carretera del Sur, is a pleasant place to have lunch, with excellent seafood dishes.

La Campagna ((53-5) 66-7224, Retiro Josone, Avenida 1 and Calle 58, is a pleasant rustic-style tavern which serves good Creole food, with meats and seafood grilled over hot coal. It is located within Varadero's most popular restaurant complex, which also includes a small lake, several other restaurants and El Rincón de los Enamoradas (Lover's Corner) where trios or classical musicians perform every evening.

Mesón del Quijote ((53-5) 66-7796, Carretera Las Americas, serves Spanish food of unexceptional but reliable quality, and the surroundings are pleasant, overlooking a nineteenth-century Spanish lookout tower. **Casa del Queso Cubano** ((53-5) 66-7747, Calle 62 and Avenida 1, is not for the calorie-conscious, the specialties of this restaurant being cheese, meat and chocolate fondues. Whatever else, it is certainly unique in Cuba. **La Barbacoa** ((53-5) 66-7795, Avenida 1 and Calle 64, serves barbecued meats and seafood in a baronial-colonial atmosphere.

Inexpensive

The best place for typical Creole and Cuban dishes is **El Bodegón Criollo** ((53-5) 66-7784, Avenida Playa and Calle 40, with inexpensive prices and an entertaining musical trio. For good seafood and international dishes amid rustic beach surroundings and palm trees, try **Mi Casita** ((53-5) 61-3787, Camino del Mar between Calle 11 and 12. **Lai-Lai** ((53-5) 66-7793, Avenida 1 and Calle 18, is regarded as Varadero's best Chinese restaurant.

It is fun to visit the so-called "Honey House" or **Casa de la Miel**, Avenida 1 between Calles 26 and 27, where you can sample intriguingly prepared dishes, sweets, juices and herb teas sweetened with honey and royal jelly — as well as cocktails with a honey and rum sting.

NIGHTLIFE

Cabaret Cueva del Pirata ((53-5) 66-7130, Carretera Las Morlas, is located in a limestone cave, a dramatic, if somewhat claustrophobic setting, lit up with flashing strobes and dry ice. After the nightly cabaret show which begins at 10:30 PM, dancing is *de rigueur*. The show at the **Cabaret Varadero** ((53-5) 66-7130, Vía Blanca towards Carretera Cárdenas, tries to rival that of the Tropicana in Havana, and becomes a popular discotheque after midnight.

Nightly Latin music and dancing, as well as live bands, have made **Discoteca La**

Bamba ((53-5) 66-7560, Hotel Tuxpan, Carretera Las Americas, one of Varadero's most popular venues.

At **El Rincón de la Salsa**, across from Parque Josone, Avenida 1, you never quite know what Cuban band may appear here next. This is a great place to hear live salsa music, with dancing long into the night. From the cocktail hour onwards the **Piano Bar Hotel Melía Varadero**, Carretera Las Americas, is a civilized place to enjoy musicians perform traditional Cuban songs and Afro-Cuban jazz.

The main roads lengthwise are the Avenida Kawama, Avenida 1 (the peninsula's main commercial strip), Carretera Las Américas and the Carretera del Sur (Southern Highway) which runs all the way to the end of the peninsula. Calles (streets) run perpendicular to these main avenues and are numbered from 1 to 69; while the calles in the residential Villa Cuba section run from A to L.

A popular way to get around the relatively small confines of Varadero town is by rented motorcycle or bicycle (although renting bicycles on this lengthy beach can be

GETTING AROUND

Getting orientated is not difficult. Varadero is located on the Hicacos Peninsula, and is a long, narrow isthmus of rocks and sand surrounded on both sides by sea, pocked (on the non-swimming side) by mangrove swamps and sand bars. The distance from the peninsula's entrance at the drawbridge over Paso Malo lagoon to its easternmost tip at the Punta de Hicacos is almost 20 km (about 12 miles) and its average width is no more than 700 m (about a half a mile); at its most bulbous point at the Punta de Hicacos, it is only 211 km (131 miles) from Key West, with a clear reception from Florida radio stations that is somewhat surreal.

a nightmare), allowing you to cruise along to different parts of the peninsula, stop at whatever beach looks inviting and investigate the town's cafés, restaurants and shops. Try the rental office on Avenida Primera, opposite the entrance to Retiro Josone. Horse-drawn *calesas* are another option.

Most hotels have rental agencies where you can rent cars, four-wheel drive vehicles and motorbikes, although be forewarned that you should do this well in advance to ensure availability. Otherwise, try the central office of **Habanautos** ((53-5) 66-7094, Avenida 1, No. 5502, between Calles 55 and 56; another is at the airport.

Playa Girón, known for the aborted Bay of Pigs invasion, features many billboards and slogans.

You will have no trouble finding agencies to book catamaran, sailboat or launch cruises. The best known is the catamaran **Jolly Roger**, which can be booked for half-day, full day or sunset cruises. Varadero has three main marinas, the Marina Acua, the Marina Chapelín and the Marina Gaviota, all of which offer tailor-made and scheduled excursions such as so-called sea-safaris, yacht and sailboat rental, snorkeling, and rod-and-reel fishing expeditions, all for a fee.

How to Get There

The Juan Gualberto Gómez International Airport is located 16 km (10 miles) west of Varadero. See GETTING THERE, page 298 in TRAVELERS' TIPS, for information about international and domestic airline flights to Varadero, as well as its main ports of entry.

From Havana, there are various options for reaching Varadero by road. Aside from renting a car, you can opt to make the journey on a minibus: this service is offered by Havanatur's Tour & Travel as well as by almost all Cuba's leading tour operators and costs about US$30 each way. Any hotel desk or tour agency will be able to make a reservation for you. Contact **Tour & Travel** in Havana ((53-7) 33-3433 at Avenida 5 No. 8409, at the corner of Calle 86, Miramar; and in Varadero ((53-5) 66-3713 at Avenida de la Playa No. 3606, between Calles 36 and 37.

If you want to travel by taxi, the cost will be about US$80 each way.

THE ZAPATA PENINSULA

Within several hour's drive from Varadero is an exceptional region on the southern coast of western Cuba, encompassing **Playa Girón** — a region more memorably known as the Bay of Pigs, site of the abortive invasion of Cuba by exiles and mercenaries in 1961 — and the immense **Zapata Peninsula** — the island's finest nature preserve and its largest area of pristine wetlands, which has been turned into a national park that also offers isolated beaches, crystal-clear waters, beautiful limestone *cenotes* (sunken lagoons) as well as exceptional fly fishing opportunities.

You can explore this area — which lies on the sparsely populated south coast of Matanzas Province — within a few days, perhaps setting out from either Havana or Varadero.

From the southern coast of Matanzas, you can continue onwards to explore central Cuba; from here you are within several hour's driving distance of both Cienfuegos and, further on, Trinidad.

The easiest way to reach this region is to take the main exit for Playa Girón from the Autopista Nacional, near the intriguingly named town of Australia. If you are driving from Varadero, via Cárdenas, you will be on secondary roads that pass through scenery that becomes increasingly lush, dominated by its *llanos*, its flatlands, fecund with a patchwork quilt of sugarcane, orange and

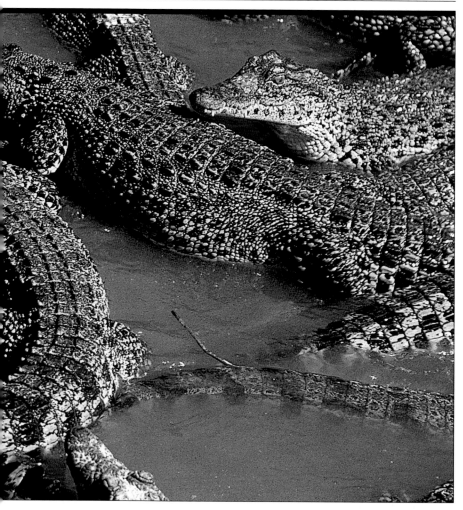

malanga plantations, rimmed by a distant horizon of royal palms.

As you drive along, scenes of small town life flash by: women with curlers in their hair tending horses; old trucks wheezing by crammed with plantation workers; the entrance to a military training camp and the Russian-design agricultural camps, where schoolchildren are sent to learn the ways of the field.

WHAT TO SEE AND DO

After you have exited the main highway for Playa Girón (which goes through Playa Larga first), you can't miss the roadside **Fiesta Campesina**, a tourist village where air-conditioned tourist buses usually make a

scheduled stop. A miniature zoo has been constructed here, with lizards, baby crocodiles, pre-historic pike or *majuani*, the rodent-like *jutias* and even guinea pigs on display in tiny thatched enclosures and ponds. The house specialty is delicious Creole coffee, served in a small clay cup with a stick of sugarcane, or the other typical drink of the region, the *fiesta campesina*, made with sugarcane liqueur and rum. If for no other reason, this is a convenient rest stop.

The town of Australia is notable for its hulking giant of a **sugar mill**, which Castro used as his personal headquarters as he and his Revolutionary Armed Forces staged their

Watchful crocodiles at La Boca Crocodile Farm in Ciénaga de Zapata.

defense during the Bay of Pigs invasion. That victory is commemorated by a row of solemn concrete tablets that rise from the side of the road, sporadically at first, and then peppering the roadside, en route to Playa Larga. They honor Castro's troops, of whom 161 died in action, and they stand where the soldiers fell during the three-day battle in April 1961.

As you near the entrance to Playa Larga, you will see to your left the entrance to the **Laguna del Tesoro** (Treasure Lake), Cuba's largest natural lagoon, which spans 92 sq km (over 35 sq miles) and is tightly ringed with bulrushes and dense with mangrove swamps and thick palmetto-shrub forest. Aside from the increasing annoyance of mosquitoes, you could assume this scene was the picture of implacable serenity. Not quite; for as you are just about to discover, this area is also home to one of Cuba's few potentially deadly creatures: the Cuban crocodile.

As the Spanish went about colonizing Cuba, this was one of the few regions that they largely left alone. Christopher Columbus mentioned in his missives that these rivers and swamplands were inhabited by large quantities of "enormous monsters." However, within a few centuries, indiscriminate hunting turned them into an almost extinct species, and only those that managed to hide away in intricate areas of the swamp system survived. Since a protection campaign was begun in 1961, thousands of the reptiles have been bred at the adjacent **La Boca Crocodile Farm**.

At La Boca, you can walk around a large circular enclosure where about fifty of the crocodile equivalent of teenagers and mature adults lurk in small swamps, hide out under rocks, and gaze up longingly at visitors leaning over the wooden platforms, making sudden lunges at any movement. Watching feeding time — which takes place twice weekly — is a gruesome experience. If you miss feeding time, it is still quite an experience to peer down at these sluggish beasts as they eye you back, flex their jaws and make the odd lunge at each other. Although these crocodiles can live up to 150 years, they rarely do, and often end up being attacked and eaten by another crocodile.

Smaller enclosures contain younger, smaller crocodiles that do not appear so threatening: one of the musicians of the inevitable trio that performs in the entrance of La Boca puts a tiny crocodile through its cabaret paces: you can get your photograph taken with one if you like.

If you want to see even more crocodiles, you can ask to see the nearby **crocodile nursery** across the road. Although it is not open to the public, if you are traveling independently, and are prepared to give a donation, ask the keeper if he can arrange a guided visit. At the nursery, some 45,000 or so crocodiles have been nurtured, after emerging from their egg, through each stained-glass stage of their "childhood." They are held in steel pens divided up by age and size, and released at the age of 17. The workers who look after them know all sorts of crocodile stories, and some will hold out a munched arm or scarred stomach to show their own personal experience. Crocodiles, they say, can run up to 60 kph (37 mph) for short spurts, and they don't recommend spear fishing in the shallow waters around here. No one is exactly sure how many crocodiles are "out there" now; apparently many escaped from the nursery when Hurricane Lili devastated the area in 1996.

Also at La Boca is the embarkation point for **Guamá**, a resort village that is quite unique in Cuba, situated on a series of islands connected by wooden walkways deep in the Laguna del Tesoro. The boat ride — accompanied by good-natured musicians — takes you through the lagoon for several kilometers, then approaches the resort, which is supposedly sited on what was once a Taíno Indian village. According to legend, when the Taíno realized that the Spanish had finally discovered their home, they hid all their gold and valuable possessions in the lagoon, hence its name.

It was Celia Sánchez, Castro's revolutionary companion, who was inspired to create the Guamá resort, and *El Jefe* himself has often visited (having acquired a first-hand in-depth knowledge of the surrounding topography during his rout of CIA-backed Cuban exile mercenaries), tending towards adventurous fishing expeditions. On an island near the resort you can

explore the **reconstructed Taíno village** with its life-size sculpted figures depicting Taíno Indians by Cuban sculptor Rita Longa; sample *saoco* (rum and coconut water); and wander through the complex of thatched *cabañas* connected by pathways and bridges. It is unquestionably a beautiful place to visit, and you can linger at the restaurant for an hour or so and take the next boat back, but bring strong mosquito repellent regardless.

Fishing enthusiasts will be interested to know that the lagoon is rich in trout, haddock, carp, and the local Cuban *biajaca* as well as the alligator-gar or *manjuarí*, one of the most ancient of Cuba's endemic fish, as are caimans, a pygmy species of alligator.

The only blot on the experience of visiting Guamá is the environmentally unfriendly diesel exhaust emitted by the boats, fuel shortages being as dire here as everywhere else in Cuba.

WHERE TO STAY AND EAT

Hotel Horizontes Villa Guamá*** ((53-59) 7125, Laguna del Tesoro, Peninsula de Zapata, is unique in Cuba: a series of circular thatched *cabañas* made from native woods, perched on stilts above the lagoon and surrounding swampy marshes, and linked together by wooden walkways. The moder-

Aquatic plants cover the Ciénaga de Zapata marshes.

ately priced *cabañas* may look rustic, but they are comfortable: they are air-conditioned, with a bathroom and telephone and television. The complex has a restaurant and a discotheque (be warned that the nightly music may defeat your desire for tranquility), as well as fresh-water fishing supplies, binoculars for bird watching, and row boats to explore the lagoon. The Villa Guamá also arranges three-hour-long guided fishing trips on Laguna del Tesoro. The food is not very good, aside from freshly snared grilled fish you may catch.

Overlooking the lagoon at **La Boca** is a ranch-style restaurant of the same name, which serves excellent Creole dishes as well as roast crocodile tail, said to be an aphrodisiac.

PLAYA LARGA AND ZAPATA NATIONAL PARK

From La Boca, continue by road through the marshlands until you reach the beach resort of Playa Larga, 14 km (about nine miles) away. Lying at the head of the Bahía de Cochinos (Bay of Pigs), this was the secondary landing site during the Bay of Pigs invasion. Playa Larga is not the loveliest beach in the region, however, it is the entry point to the Zapata Peninsula's **Parque Nacional Ciénaga de Zapata**, (Zapata National Park), the vast swamp which is Cuba's most important bird reserve. The modest-looking **International Bird Watching Center** is based here, close to Buena Ventura, the reserve's entrance, and operates bird-watching tours.

The reserve's designated fishing areas are also becoming something of a mecca for fly fishing enthusiasts: primarily for its tarpon and bonefish.

No unauthorized access to the sanctuary is allowed, and all visitors — including bird watching and fishing groups — must be accompanied by government tourist guides assigned here. Consequently, many visitors, including ornithologists, stay at the modest **Hotel Playa Larga**, set on a fairly nondescript beach. From here, you can make individual or guided forays into the reserve, which has a well-established network of day and night observation sites and walkways.

GENERAL INFORMATION

Try to book a guide in advance, to lead you through the Zapata reserve, when you make your accommodation reservation. The Hotel Playa Larga runs excursions starting at US$20 per person. You can discuss with the staff the type of excursion you'd like and negotiate your guide's time and fees. Guides can also be hired through the Fiesta Campesina complex: ask for the manager.

You can contact the government agency **Cubatur** ((53-7) 32-4521 FAX (53-7) 33-3104, Calle 23 No. 156, Vedado, Havana, for their information pamphlet on bird watching, as well as their bird watching excursions in the Zapata Peninsula. In the United States, the specialist tour company, **Wings of the World** US TOLL-FREE (800) 465-8687, 1200 William Street, Suite 706, Buffalo, New York 14240, offers eight-day bird-watching tours to this region (as well as La Güira National Park in Pinar del Río) from January to March, at a cost of US$2,295.

The best time to visit the reserve is between April and October, when vast numbers of birds arrive for the migratory season.

WHAT TO SEE AND DO

Within easy reach of Playa Larga, the reserve's densely lush scenery is a paradise for some 190 species of birds, the majority of them migratory. Those that you will see most commonly are rosy flamingos, black-necked stilts, white ibises, parrots, wildfowl, and migratory birds such as warblers, herons, terns, swallows, and several birds of prey. Of Cuba's 23 endemic bird species, 18 inhabit these swamps. If you are lucky, you may see the *zunzuncito;* the *trogon* or *tocororo;* the Gundlach hawk, the blue-headed quail dove; the reclusive gnome owl and the island's rare species of woodpecker as well as many Cuban parrots.

Most birding excursions make their first stop at **Santo Tomás**, about 30 km (19 miles) west of Playa Larga, where spoonbills and flamingos gather during migratory season.

One of the most beautiful journeys in the reserve is to visit **Las Salinas** (which lies near the coast about two hour's drive southwest from Playa Larga), a huge expanse of marshes, flatlands and islets where many communities of birds make their home. To reach it, you have to take a dirt road which winds and twists its way through what feels like (and is) true wilderness: sometimes the road gets flooded, and crocodiles are known to live in the surrounding marshes. It is compulsory (as well as both a comfort and an education) to have a guide along with you here. There are plans afoot to make this reserve more accessible for eco-tourists.

two designated fishing areas — Laguna de Salinas and the 200-m (650-ft)-wide Río Hatiguanico, which snakes through mangrove swamps to the sea, branching out into many cross-streams. See SPORTING SPREE, page 38, for details about arranging fishing trips here.

WHERE TO STAY

Although **Hotel Horizontes Playa Larga**** ((53-59) 7225 or 7219, Playa Larga, Peninsula de Zapata, is a good base for exploring the

It's interesting to know that within the Zapata Peninsula, in which the reserve occupies large tracts, a 70 km (43-mile)-long limestone crevice snakes through this landscape, riddled with *cenotes* or semi-circular sunken lagoons, as well as underwater cave systems. Washed by both sea and fresh water, these mysterious caverns teem with all sorts of life, including crocodiles, *manatees* and aquatic reptiles. Having just seen those crocodiles at La Boca, you might want to take your guide's advice about which *cenotes* are swimming- and spelunking-friendly, if this is what you have in mind.

If you are a fly-fishing enthusiast, you will be interested in this area not only for its scenic beauty and birdlife, but also for its

Zapata National Park, it has a fairly Spartan atmosphere and is not a place to linger beyond meals and after a day's outing. However, it has to be said that the local staff are very friendly and make an effort to ensure you are looked after.

EN ROUTE TO PLAYA GIRÓN

From Playa Larga, the historic town of **Playa Girón** lies 33 km (about 20 miles) away on the peninsula's eastern coast. En route there are several places worth stopping at. Along the road, the scenery is spectacular, with clear blue lapping up against mangrove

Crocodiles are raised at a nursery across the road from La Boca Crocodile Farm.

forests and small rocky beaches, and dotted by secluded coves, some of which have tempting *cenotes*.

If you weren't too impressed with Playa Larga, you might want to stop at **Caleta del Rosario**, about three kilometers (nearly two miles) from Playa Larga, an excellent little bay with good swimming. You may want to drive five kilometers (three miles) on to have lunch at **La Casa del Pescador**, a tranquil spot which serves simple seafood and Cuban dishes. Its balcony overlooks one of the most impressive cenotes along the coast: **El Cenote**, in which you can dive or snorkel amid schools of brightly colored tropical fish, which sparkle like gems in the dazzlingly ice-blue water. Adjacent, the small diving center attached to El Cenote rents equipment and gives advice about what to see. According to local lore, an unexploded projectile, dating from the Bay of Pigs invasion, is wedged within the depths of the *cenote*.

Further along (15 km or nine miles from Playa Larga), the **Cueva de los Pesces** is another impressive *cenote* and a perfect place to return for an afternoon of scuba diving. It drops to a depth of 70 m (230 ft), and its flooded caverns are filled with fish.

PLAYA GIRÓN

As you drive on to Playa Girón, which lies at the mouth of the Bahía de Cochinos, Site of the Bay of Pigs invasion, giant billboards announce that you are entering a politically charged zone. "Playa Girón: The First Rout of Imperialism in Latin America!" says one. During the rainy months of May and June, this is where you will see masses of insect-sized crabs swarming across the pavement, their shells black and their legs vermilion, and make driving an act of mass crab homicide, if not dangerous, with sudden slippery skids.

BACKGROUND

In the early seventeenth century, these coasts were the domain of a notorious French pirate, Gilbert Girón, whose ultimate fate was supremely gory: he was decapitated by a Spanish captain, who then displayed the head in a jar of brine in order to claim a reward from the Spanish Crown.

Playa Girón is best known as the main site of the April 17, 1961 invasion by some 1,500 Cuban exiles, backed and trained by the CIA, who code-named themselves Brigade 2506. Within a day, Castro's pilots were bombing the invading army's boats and planes, and had the bay surrounded by a volunteer army of 20,000 soldiers and peasants, led by Castro himself. By dusk on April 19, 1,200 of the 1,500 exiles had been taken prisoner and were eventually exchanged for more than US$50 million worth of medicines and supplies from the United States.

GENERAL INFORMATION

Facilities are few. The small town of Playa Girón has a pharmacy and a dollar-shop opposite the museum, and a few modest fast-food *paladares* have sprung up.

Rental cars, as well as bicycles and mopeds are available at the **Transauto** office opposite the Villa Horizontes.

WHAT TO SEE AND DO

The **Museo Girón** is housed in a well-kept bungalow, with its lawns rightly mowed and everything almost self-consciously spic-and-span. Outside stands a British-made Sea Fury fighter that was flown by the Cuban air-force, and the remains of the Brigade 2506 aircraft.

Inside, the museum displays dioramas charting the hour-by-hour progress of the invasion and the counter-attack, with detailed maps and photographs of the invading mercenaries as well as the martyrs of the Bay of Pigs, whose 30-year-old bloodstained garments, weapons, letters, and other possessions can be seen here. It also documents the Revolution's efforts to improve the living conditions of residents of this region, many of whom are descended from poverty-stricken charcoal-makers. The museum is open Tuesday to Sunday, 9 AM to 5 PM.

Facing the pretty Playa Girón beach is the **Villa Horizontes Playa Girón** resort, which has simple *cabañas* with basic facilities, but the azure coast makes staying here a more attractive prospect than Playa Larga. There are two beaches, both stony as opposed to sandy — Playa Girón itself, which is not very big, but has safe calm waters, and another known locally as Enamorados (Lover's Beach) which is more secluded and unspoiled, both popular with Cuban vacationers.

The potential for scuba diving in the waters off Playa Girón is beginning to attract much attention. You are likely to see *manatees* as well as many species of tropi-

cal fish, and the submarine *cenotes* that are such a feature of this region provide opportunities for the adventurous for underwater spelunking. Contact the **International Scuba Diving Center** at the Villa Playa Girón.

Where to Stay

Villa Horizontes Playa Girón*** ((53-59) 4118 or 4110 FAX (53-59) 4117, Playa Girón, Peninsula de Zapata, offers inexpensive accommodations. Here, almost 300 rooms and small concrete bungalows are spread out facing the beach, each equipped with a refrigerator and a television. There is a choice of restaurants, tennis courts, a swimming

pool, and tourist facilities such as a shop, doctor's office, car and motor-bike rental. Its International Scuba Diving Center may well be the reason you stay.

Caleta Buena

Having come this far, you should not miss spending a day or half-day at one of loveliest swimming spots in the area, **Caleta Buena**, which lies eight kilometers (five miles) east of Playa Girón at the end of a long coral road along the coast. This idyllic, sheltered sea lagoon is perfect for swimming and lazing, with natural pools and transparent waters alive with multi-colored fish that are ideal for snorkeling — and further out, for scuba diving, with an ocean floor carpeted with corals, gorgonians and sponges. A small restaurant run by friendly locals serves snacks, cold drinks or lunch, and you can use their facilities as a changing room. Deck chairs and thatch umbrellas have been discreetly spaced to ensure privacy. On a beautiful day, this place is simply perfect, and long may it stay that way.

How to Get There

If you are interested in visiting this region, but don't wish to rent a car, you may want to join an organized tour from either Havana or Varadero, which offer reasonably priced overnight packages to Laguna del Tesoro, the Zapata Peninsula and Playa Girón. Contact **Tour & Travel** ((53-7) 33-2433, Avenida 5 No. 8409 at the corner of Calle 86, Miramar, Havana; or ((53-5) 66-7279, Avenida Playa No. 3606 between Calles 36 and 37, Varadero.

Western Cuba is renowned for its quality tobacco.

The
Cuban
Heartland

CIENFUEGOS

SPREAD AROUND A DRAMATICALLY WIDE harbor, Cienfuegos, which means "a hundred fires," was earmarked for rapid industrial development under the Revolution, and is now Cuba's most important port, with the country's largest cement and plastic factories, a sugar terminal, and an oil refinery plant. Still, the surrounding sea and the seaside life of its citizens, strolling and cycling along the Malecón, make Cienfuegos one of the prettiest provincial towns in Cuba.

Known as "La Perla del Sur" ("the Pearl of the South"), Cienfuegos has another advantage of not being full of tourists, *jineteras*, or scrums of urchins. Its unsightly edifices are more than offset by its magnificent setting, boulevards, and mansions. Located 250 km (155 miles) from Havana, Cienfuegos is a good place to stop for a night or two if you are traveling further into central Cuba; be sure not to miss the beauty of the light under the coconut trees just before twilight.

BACKGROUND

The history of Cienfuegos is inseparable from its sweeping natural harbor, Bahía de Cienfuegos. Remains of a large settlement of aboriginal Siboney Indians have been found here. The Spanish recognized its potential from the beginning. Christopher Columbus sailed through the bay on his second expedition to Cuba in 1494, and a decade later, the conquistador Sebastián de Ocampo made a careful survey of the bay during his exploration of the island. Pirates and smugglers were lured here from the Isle of Pines (now known as Isla de Juventud) and Jamaica, by the prospect of plundering ships moored off the bay. In order to protect the early colonial settlement from attack, the Spanish constructed the Castillo de Jagua in the mid-eighteenth century, a small fortress which still dominates the harbor's entrance.

As a city, Cienfuegos has the unusual distinction of having attracted an intrepid mixture of early immigrants, including many of French and Spanish descent from Baltimore, New Orleans, Jamaica, and other Caribbean cities. Merchants, shippers and money-lenders soon followed the expansion of the sugar industry in the region, and the city quickly gained the reputation of having the highest concentration of wealthy families in the country. It was founded in 1819 by Louis de Clouet, a Creole trader from New Orleans, who named the city Fernandina de Jagua in honor of King Fernando VII, but also out of respect for the native name for this site. As the city grew, settled by a colony of French planters from Louisiana, it was soon renamed Cienfuegos after Cuba's then-governor, José Cienfuegos.

GENERAL INFORMATION

The best the city has to offer in the way of tourist information services is the modest **Buro de Turismo** at the Hotel Jagua's front desk. If you need medical treatment, legal advice or emergency cash advances, contact **Asistur** ((53-432) 66-6190, located in the Hotel Jagua.

Banco Financiero Internacional is located on the southeast corner of Parque Martí. It is open Monday to Friday, 8 AM to 3 PM.

If you need medical treatment, the **Clínica International** caters to foreigners. It is located opposite the Hotel Jagua, on Calle 37 No. 202. It has a doctor and nurse on 24-hour call.

WHAT TO SEE AND DO

If you are staying at the Hotel Jagua, then you are already in the heart of **Punta Gorda**, a small peninsula on a sliver of land lapped by the sea at the other end of the city. This peaceful settlement, dotted with palm trees and tiny piers, is characterized by wood-frame, gingerbread houses, many of which were prefabricated in the Gulf Coast of the United States and assembled here at the turn of the century.

Immediately opposite the hotel, the **Palacio de Valle** is perhaps the most extraordinary sight of all in Cienfuegos. This exuberantly ostentatious, neo-Moorish confection was commissioned by Aciclio Valle in 1890, who enlisted the help of Moroccan craftsmen to create this curious marvel of elaborate fretted interiors, stained-glass windows and balustraded rooms, and was completed in 1917. The Valle family fled Cuba after the 1959 revolution, and since 1990 its ground floor has been converted into the city's top restaurant. You can wander through its many rooms and up its winding iron staircase to the rooftop bar, which has magical views across the bay at sunset.

Since Punta Gorda is some two kilometers (slightly over a mile) from the city center, you will need to continue your tour by a taxi or car, passing along the seafront Malecón. As you leave the sea, the Malecón becomes the **Paseo del Prado**, the city's central boulevard, which is lined with colonnaded colonial houses and monuments and crossed by streets in a regular fashion. This is the best place to begin your stroll, admiring close-up the colored façades, porticos and balustrades of these houses, painted in a rainbow of hues. You'll see that many of the ground-level houses have been transformed into peso- and dollar-shops, ice-cream and fast-food parlors and *paladares*. Numerous horse-drawn carts — referred to as *mulos* by locals — act as service taxis along the bustling Paseo del Prado, which is the center of commercial activity in Cienfuegos.

Turn right on Avenida 56, known as El Boulevard, a pedestrian section lined with dollar-shops that has become a main meeting point for young Cienfuegans. Continue to walk four blocks and you will reach **Parque José Martí**, the city's beautiful historic center, with its ensemble of nineteenth- and early twentieth-century buildings that are collectively considered a national monument. At one end, the park's entrance is guarded by two white marble lions on high pedestals; while a triumphal arch, a statue of José Martí and various monuments complete the sense of civic pomp.

At one corner stands the yellow-tinged **Catedral de la Purisma Concepción**, built in 1819, which is notable for its particularly fine stained-glass windows depicting the 12 apostles. To the right, as you leave the cathedral you will find the **Teatro Tomás Terry**, an elaborate theater named after the sugar- and slave-rich Venezuelan philanthropist who built it for the city in 1890. Make sure you see the elegant *fin de siècle* interior, with its three-tiered auditorium, mosaic murals and painted ceiling. The legendary Enrico Caruso once performed here, among other famous performers. Although it is now seriously dilapidated, national dance and folklore productions are still staged here.

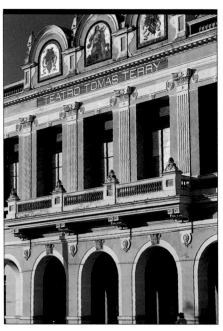

Continuing counterclockwise around the square, there are various notable buildings to observe: you will see the **Biblioteca Provincial** (Provincial Library) and the **Galeria de Arte**, housed in an early colonial building. Across the park is the **Palacio de Ferrer**, a strikingly ornamental building: once a residential mansion, it is now the **Casa de la Cultura**, and is worth exploring for its grand winding staircase and elegant rooms lined with gilt mirrors. Likewise, the nearby **Museo Provincial**, displays antique furniture and memorabilia to recreate the by-

PREVIOUS PAGES: Trinidad's Plaza Mayor LEFT, a colonial-era gem. RIGHT: Vividly-hued houses in Cienfuegos. ABOVE: The 1890 Teatro Tomás Terry.

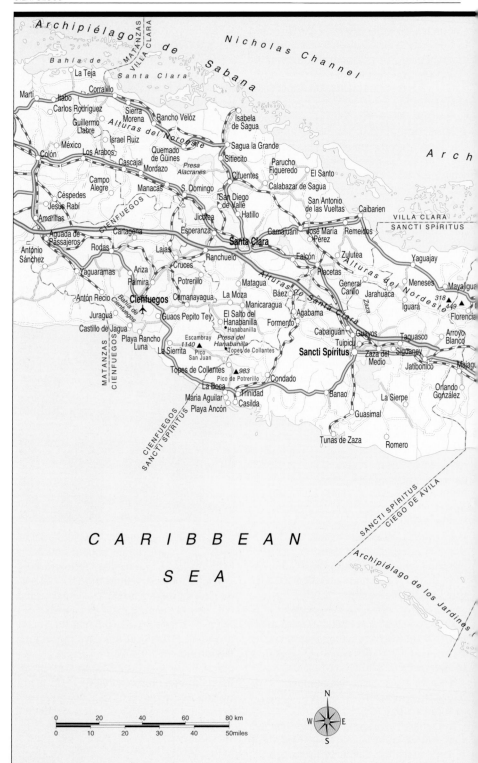

THE HEARTLAND

Havana

ATLANTIC OCEAN

ago

ayo llermo

Cayo Coco

San Rafael

Morón

Loma de Cunagua ▲ 338

Bolivia

Cayo Romano

La Nueva de Manga Larga

Primero de Enero

Velazco

Pesqueria

de Ávila

Colorado

Gaspar

guá

Mamanantuabo

Esmeralda

Brasil

Jiquí

Playa Jigüey

Palma City

Cayo Guajaba

Playa Piloto

Cubitas

Sola

Cayo Sabinal

Santa Lucia

Carlos Manuel de Céspedes

Piedrecitas

Presa Caonao

Noel Fernández

Lugareño

Nuevitas

Bahía de Nuevitas

Florida

San Antonio

Minas

Playa de Florida

Camagüey

Jimaguayú

Camalote

Puerto Manatí

Manatí

LLANURA MERIDIONA

Vertientes

Contramaestre

Siboney

Sibanicú

Cascorro

Hatuey

Concordia

Martí

Laguna Lamar

Cuatro Compañeros

Najasa

Guáimaro

Bartle

Colombia

Las Tunas

Calixto

Jobabo

Cándido González

Haití

Amancio

Sábalo

Vado del Yeso

CAMAGÜEY LAS TUNAS

Santa Cruz del Sur

Playa Habanero

Cayos de Sevilla

LAS TUNAS GRANMA

Guamo

Río Cauto

Cauto Embarcadero

la Reina

CAMAGÜEY

GUACANAYABO GULF

Cayos Manzanillo

Manzanillo

de

Camagüey

ducing trees, 241 medicinal plants, 200 types of cactus, 89 different rubber plants, 69 varieties of orchids and 23 types of bamboo. From Cuba itself, it contains 23 species of the *mariposa*, Cuba's national flower, as well as a complete collection of Cuban palm trees, including the "pot belly" palm and the "cork" palm, considered to be a living fossil. The entrance fee of US$2 includes a guided tour, and there is a refreshment bar near the parking area. It is open from 8 AM to 4 PM daily.

The Jardín Botánico Soledad is located along an unmarked road and can be tricky to find. If you are not going in a taxi, which will cost up to US$40 for a round trip, or by tour bus, the following directions will help you find it. From the Hotel Jagua, follow Calle 37 to Avenida 18. Turn right and continue four blocks to Calle 45, then make a left until you reach the municipal stadium. Look out for a sign marked Clínica Estomatológica, which is your cue to turn right onto Avenida Cinco de Septiembre. This is the main road to the Rancho Luna beach. On the outskirts of Cienfuegos this is lined with micro-brigade estates and communal gardens. Take the turnoff onto the Circuito Sur (Southern Ring Road) and look out for the entrance to the garden before the Pepito Tey sugar mill between the villages of San Antón and Guaos.

You may wish to stop off en route to see the charming **Tomás Acea Cemetery**, easily spotted along the Avenida Cinco de Septiembre a short distance outside the city. It has a monumental marble portico designed as a replica of the Greek Parthenon, supported by 64 columns. Set among gravel pathways and trees are elaborate funerary statues and mausoleums which reflect the fashionable tastes imported by the city's French colonial inhabitants.

Another suggested excursion from Cienfuegos is a visit to the Spanish-built **Castillo de Jagua**, located at the entrance to the city's harbor. Completed in 1745, it was intended as a defense against roving pirates, however it never came under serious attack. Now restored, its main attraction is the roving view from its parapets, which takes in small seaside villages and the wide sweep of the sea and the bay. There is a bar and

gone ambiance of homes owned by the city's wealthy nineteenth-century bourgeoisie. The **Colegio de San Lorenzo**, also in the square, was inaugurated in 1927.

This may be your cue to have a coffee or cold drink at **El Palatino**, right on the square, for a brief respite, as well as to enjoy its colonial atmosphere of this tavern, which has been renovated from a building dating from 1842, and has high vaulted roof, tiled floors, and stools made from rum casks.

EXCURSIONS FROM CIENFUEGOS

Outside Cienfuegos, there are several worthwhile places to visit, making a morning or afternoon's excursion. Lying 18 km (11 miles) east of the city, the **Jardín Botánico Soledad** is one of the true highlights of visiting Cienfuegos. Indeed, this garden is the most beautiful — and the oldest — of its kind in Cuba. It is laid out across nine kilometers (five and a half miles), and was originally founded by the American sugar millionaire Edwin F. Atkins, then taken over as a research center by Harvard University. Chosen for its ideal climatic conditions, one of the initial tasks of its founders was to create new, more profitable varieties of sugarcane. It soon expanded to include some 2,000 tropical and sub-tropical plants from all over the world, including 400 types of cactus, 248 timber-pro-

restaurant within the castle and the surrounding settlement has some very charming colonial mansions near the water's edge. However, it is hard not to be dismayed at the ugly sight of the nearby Chernobyl-era Juraguá nuclear plant and the equally ugly Ciudad Nuclear, built as residential quarters for the plant's workers. Cuba's only nuclear power station was begun in 1983 with the help of the Soviet Union, then abandoned before completion in 1992. It is now in development limbo waiting for fresh foreign investment.

A rather Gothic legend is attached to the Castillo de Jagua, dating from the time of its first commander, Juan Castilla Cabeza de Vaca. According to the story, the guards became alarmed when, every night, a blackbird would swoop around the fort and then, upon alighting, would turn into a lady dressed in blue robes and wearing a vengeful expression. All the men were too terrified to stand guard at night, but one night, a soldier dared. The next morning, he was found prostrate on the floor, clutching his sword and surrounded by pieces of blue cloth. Apparently, he was left a gibbering wreck and spent the rest of his life in an asylum, and the mystery was never solved. Some said that the unearthly visitor was the commander's beautiful wife, whose remains are buried under the castle's chapel floor.

You can reach the Castillo de Jagua by road, after about an hour's drive from Cienfuegos. Or, perhaps more fun, you can take a peso-only ferry, which leaves from the jetty at Muelle Real, Avenida 46 and Calle 25 at intervals throughout the day. The trip takes 40 minutes and stops off at several small seaside fishing villages and the ugly Pascabello Hotel en route, which, incidentally, should be avoided. The most enjoyable place for lunch or dinner in the area is the **Casa de Pescador** in the seaside village of Perché.

Also within an hour's drive from Cienfuegos along a road lined with mango plantations is **Playa Rancho Luna**, a sheltered, crescent-shaped and soft-sanded beach with calm shallows. There are several hotels and marked scuba diving areas in the vicinity, but the best place to stay is the **Hotel Horizontes Rancho Luna**. As you drive there you may notice the collective farm, Comunidad "Martires de Barbados," which is named in honor of the 80 Cuban athletes who died when anti-Castro terrorists bombed a Cubana de Aviación airline mid-air over Barbados in 1976.

WHERE TO STAY

There is only one hotel reserved for foreigners in Cienfuegos itself; otherwise there are several alternatives by the beach, within an hour's drive of the city.

Moderate
Built in the 1950s, **Hotel Jagua****** ((53-432) 32-3021 to 32-3026 FAX (53-5) 66-7454. Calle 37, Punta Gorda, is the best hotel in or around Cienfuegos, converted from a Batista-era gambling haven. Peacefully located in the leafy peninsula of Punta Gorda, the Jagua has panoramic views from its upper rooms across the bay and the city from the terraces of its 145 rooms, and also overlooks and operates the Palacio de Valle next door. It has a saltwater pool and a nightclub, which stages a cabaret most evenings. The hotel has a Turistaxi stand as well as horse-drawn carts.

Inexpensive
Horizontes Rancho Luna Hotel*** ((53-432) 48120 to 48123 FAX (53-432) 33-5057, Carretera Rancho Luna, is located 16 km (10 miles) east of the city, on its own small but pleasant beach, with simple accommodation provided by a terraced red-tiled concrete row of rooms set in landscaped gardens. There is a restaurant, cafeteria, bar and shop, as well as a car rental office.

Located close to Playa Rancho Luna, the small **Cubanacán Faro Luna***** ((53-432) 5532 or 48168 FAX (53-432) 33-5059, Carretera Rancho Luna, has 24 sea-facing rooms each with a small terrace. It has a saltwater swimming pool and scuba diving facilities.

Although **Hotel Pascabello***** ((53-432) 09-6212 or 09-6280, Carretera Rancho Luna, has a dramatic location located overlooking Castillo de Jagua, the dismal Soviet-era design of this large 180-room hotel makes for a grim prospect, and rooms face away from the sea. Twenty-five kilometers (over 15 miles) east of Cienfuegos, it has a restaurant, bar, swimming pool, and a shop. Avoid, if at all possible.

WHERE TO EAT

Moderate
Right next to the Hotel Jagua, the flamboyant palace **Palacio de Valle** ((53-432) 6366 and 6910, Jardines de Hotel Jagua, has been converted into the city's best and most expensive restaurant, serving a wide variety

of dishes. The main dining room used to be the Valle family's drawing room, and has a resident pianist, a grande dame, Carmen Iznaga, a niece of Nicolás Guillén. The rooftop terrace bar is perfect for cocktails. It closes at 10 PM.

The **Casa de Pescador** ((53-432) 8160, Punta La Milpa, Carretera de Pascabello to La Milpa, Perché, is tucked into the entrance to the bay, with a view of the Castillo de Jagua, making it a charming place for lunch. The fresh seafood — such as fish, shrimp and lobster — served here, is the best you will find in Cienfuegos. Open for lunch until midnight.

La Finca Isabela, ((53-432) 7606, Carretera de Rancho Luna, a former colonial estate set among mango plantations several kilometers from the city, has been restored as a *campesino*-style restaurant for tourists, with roast pig, Creole dishes and evening performances.

Inexpensive
Located directly opposite the Hotel Jagua, **La Cueva del Camarón** ((53-432) 8238 specializes in seafood; the bar terrace is popular with local Cienfuegans and is open late.

GETTING AROUND

To contact **Turistaxi**, call ((53-432) 9-6256 or 9-6212. Or, like the majority of Cienfuegans, you can experience transport aboard a horse cart, nicknamed *mulos*.

You can also opt for a sightseeing cruise of the bay. **Puertosol** in Marina Jagua, offer various cruises, including one that stops at the Castillo de Jagua.

Rumbos ((53-432) 9645, Calle 20 No. 3905 between Calle 39 and 41, Punta Gorda, offers a city sightseeing tour, as well as excursions to Trinidad, nature walks from El Nicho in the Sierra del Escambray and other destinations.

HOW TO GET THERE

Cienfuegos lies 250 km (155 miles) southeast of Havana. The city's **Aeropuerto Internacional Jaime Gónsalez** is five kilometers (three miles) northeast of Cienfuegos. Aerotaxi, Aerogaviota and Aerocaribbean make scheduled flights to Cienfuegos, but Cubana de Aviación does not. For more information on international charter and domestic flights, see GETTING THERE, page 298 in TRAVELERS' TIPS.

There are daily trains from Havana, which is a seven-hour journey on the Havana-Santiago train, and the **Terminal de Ferrocarriles** is located at Avenida 58 and Calle 4, almost adjacent to the bus station.

The cruise ship **Melía Don Juan** — which runs cruises of various lengths to Santiago de Cuba, Jamaica and the Gran Cayman Islands — is based in Cienfuegos. See GETTING THERE, page 298 in TRAVELERS' TIPS for more information.

FURTHER AFIELD

Although most of Cienfuegos Province is relatively flat, it encompasses the lush, green Sierra del Escambray to the east, one of Cuba's three largest mountain ranges. If you are driving, you may can either make a day trip into the Sierra del Escambray's Lake Hanabanilla area from Cienfuegos, or you could make this excursion the first stop en route to Trinidad. Other excursions into the Sierra del Escambray are best made

Lake Hanabanilla, which spans 36 sq km (about 14 sq miles), is man-made; formed by a large dam across the Hanabanilla River. Surrounded by gentle forests, with beautiful, winding passages, the lake is a popular fishing spot for bass. The **Hotel Hanabanilla**, located right on the lakeside, is a good base for fishing expeditions. Depending on the time of year, the hotel is either reached by road or by launch as some times, the road may be flooded over. (You can expect to pay up to US$4 per person for the launch trip.)

from Trinidad, and are covered in that section.

To reach Lake Hanabanilla, leave Cienfuegos on Avenida 64, which is the main highway to Trinidad, and take the turnoff toward Cumanayagua, which you will see after several kilometers on your left. The lake is roughly equidistant — about 48 km (30 miles) — from both Cienfuegos and the provincial capital Santa Clara. It's an interesting drive, passing first through undulating tobacco plantations and a military air base, then climbing into a mountainous region dotted with small agrarian hamlets, where at every turn, astride their horses, men have the weather-beaten faces of true *gauchos*, their mouths clenched on *puros*.

As well as Lake Hanabanilla, there are some wonderful walks, hidden limestone caves, waterfalls and natural swimming pools to be found in the surrounding mountains, notably at **El Nicho**, near the small village of Camilo-Che set amid coffee plantations. Up from the village, there is a row of rough bungalows that have been used by Cuban army troops undergoing specialized guerilla training by visiting North Vietnamese commandos; apparently the bungalows may be converted into a base camps for tourists who want spend a few days here exploring the many trails in the area. A guide

Cienfuegos offers fine examples of art nouveau, such as the Palacio de Ferrer OPPOSITE, along with neo-classical detail ABOVE.

from the village can lead you through the lush forest to the magical **El Calvo cave**, filled with calcified limestone shapes, to a beautiful clear (and cold!) natural waterfall pool.

Along the way, look out for what the locals call the *chichicates* or "smoking trees," which you can watch sending plumes of pollen, as though it was blowing out smoke. There is also a simple place to have lunch, *campesino*-style.

WHERE TO STAY AND EAT

Hotel Hanabanilla** ((53-42) 86932, Salto del Hanabanilla, Muncipo Manicaragua, Villa Clara, is an inexpensive Soviet-style resort run by Isla Azul, which specializes mostly in Cuban vacations. It is very popular for romantic getaways and "honeymoons." The rooms are very simple and the food can be good. From here, you can easily explore the lake with boat and fishing trips, and there are some beautiful lakeside walks.

Río Negro is a lakeside ranch-style restaurant which makes an excellent base for fishing expeditions, and its fabulous setting makes it one of the highlights of a visit here. It can be easily reached by launch from the Hotel Hanabanilla. Perhaps oddly, considering that the lake is renowned for its bass, the house specialty is *pollo saltón a la piña* (chicken with pineapple), but the chef may be amenable to serving bass if he has some in stock.

TRINIDAD

A colonial-era gem, much of Trinidad feels as though it has remained unchanged for centuries, as though one is stepping back to a fragile, untouched world. It is unquestionably charming and tranquil, with a warren of narrow, often steep streets lined with brightly-colored, thick-walled town houses adorned by porticoed windows and red tile roofs. Amid streets hazily lit by wrought-iron lamps, restored mansions have been polished up as museums; while horse-drawn carriages clip-clop lazily over the cobblestones. Often as you walk

Shady arcades and a *paladar* in Cienfuegos.

through the back streets people will invite you out for a local coffee and a tour of their house. Some of these old houses are fascinating, packed with antiques, most of them with an interesting story attached to them.

Preserved to an astonishing degree, Trinidad has a decidedly baroque air, unsullied by much of the usual tourist tat that often accompanies such full-scale restoration. Much less hectic than other major Cuban towns, Trinidad is also very manageable. From *palacio* balconies or nearby hillsides,

apogee — when it became known as a kind of El Dorado — occurred during the seventeenth and eighteenth centuries, when sugar plantations mushroomed in nearby Valle de los Ingenios (Valley of the Sugar Mills) and Trinidad became one of Cuba's richest trading ports, exporting one-third of the island's sugar to Europe, South America, the United States and Spain.

The *criollo* (Creole) bourgeoisie, as well as the new influx of French planters from Haiti, flourished on the steady flow of sugar and contraband, as thousands of black

expansive views sweep across green marshlands to the glittering Caribbean Sea and the surrounding, flower-splashed mountains of the Escambray.

BACKGROUND

Trinidad is Cuba's third-oldest settlement. It was founded in 1514 by Diego Velázquez, who was initially lured by reports that local Taíno Indians had struck gold in nearby rivers.

After quickly subjugating the large Taíno population in the region, the Spanish set about establishing their fortunes, first by gold mining, then cattle ranching, tobacco farming and slave trading. The town's

African slaves toiled. The colonial *Trinitarios* established elaborate homes, the wealthiest vying to out-do each other's monogrammed Meissen and Limoges collections, and intent on copying the latest fashions from Paris. They were also proud of such cultural institutions as their newspaper, language school (teaching English, French and Italian), and an academy for music, dance and theatre.

However, by the end of the nineteenth century three factors contributed to Trinidad's ruin: the collapse of the slave trade, the establishment of Cuba's new republic, and the growth of vast sugar estates elsewhere on the island. Opportunistic incursions by roving pirates created even more

The Cuban Heartland

dismay. Trinidad was soon all but deserted, and for almost a hundred years, existing buildings were left to slide into dilapidation: nothing new was added to the town's historic architecture. Due to its economic collapse, Trinidad was left alone, and ultimately untouched in architectural terms. Restoration work did not begin here until after the Revolution, when the new Cuban government declared it a national monument. Later, along with Havana, Trinidad and the Valle de los Ingenios became designated World Heritage Sites by UNESCO.

You can easily spend two days or three days in and around Trinidad, including a visit to the Valle de los Ingenios and to the nearby beach resort of Playa Ancón. Don't leave Trinidad without sampling its unique cocktail, a delicious concoction with a melodic name: *la canchánchara*, made of honey, lemon juice, and distilled fermented sugarcane brandy, or *aguardiente*.

GENERAL INFORMATION

The one-stop office for making tour bookings and for any general queries is **Rumbos** ((53-419) 3355, 2436 or 4204, Calle Gustavos Izquierdo (de La Gloria) at the corner of Calle Simón Bolívar. They can arrange reservations and transportation for the Valle de los Ingenios *tren turistico*. You can also book city tours and excursions at **Agencia de Ventas de Opcionales** ((53-419) 4414, at the corner of Calle Antonio Maceo (Gutiérrez) and Calle Francisco Zerquera (Rosario).

Your hotel is your best option for changing foreign currency and making telephone calls. If you need to hire a taxi or car, ask at the Hotel Las Cuevas. Otherwise the rental offices for Turistaxi, Havanautos, and Transautos are all located at the **Hotel Ancón**, Playa Ancón. Should you need any medical attention, try the Clínica Internacional, Calle Lino Pérez (San Procopio), at the corner of Calle Anastasio Cárdenas.

It's worth mentioning that most museums in Trinidad share the same opening hours. Most are open from Tuesday to Saturday, 9 AM to noon, 2 PM to 6 PM; Sunday, 9 AM to 1 PM; and closed on Monday. Consequently, Monday is not a great day to visit Trinidad.

You'll also notice that many of Trinidad's streets are known by both their pre-Revolution and post-Revolution names. As you follow the walking tour, you will see the most frequently used name listed here, with its alternative in parentheses.

WHAT TO SEE AND DO

Trinidad is a place that can be easily explored on foot — its steep, winding and narrow cobblestone streets defy any other method of getting around. Many are slant-

ed towards the middle to drain away rain water. As you walk over the large, uneven paving stones, it may interest you to know that many of them originated as ship's ballast, transported to the town from New England. This being said, the first thing to recommend is a comfortable pair of shoes.

The obvious place to begin is the **Plaza Mayor** (Parque Martí) in the heart of the town. All around, impressive colonial buildings reflect the growth in fortunes of the town's sugar-rich grandees, many part of the original settlement founded by the Spanish. In the eighteenth century, the original

OPPOSITE: Trinidad's Cuban-style colonial church.
ABOVE: One of Cubaís varied means of transport.

square was embellished with the addition of square palm gardens, decorative iron fences, statues, classical urns, and bronze greyhounds.

The only two-story building on the square is the canary-yellow **Palacio de Brunet**, on Calle Fernando Hernández Echerrí (del Cristo). This classically beautiful, carefully restored, colonial residence set around a plant-filled inner courtyard houses the **Museo Romántico**, perhaps the most interesting and charming of Trinidad's many museums, and also a popular venue for marriage ceremonies. It meticulously recreates the coquettish atmosphere of its erstwhile inhabitants: Count Brunet and his household, which included 12 children and some 20 slaves, who lived here during the nineteenth century.

The building itself dates back to 1740, although the upper floor — a great rarity in Trinidad — was built much later. Unusually large for a provincial town, it evokes the *palacios* of Havana. Many of the *palacio*'s 13 rooms are decorated with grandiose fresco paintings and trompe l'oeil, and furnished with a collection of exceptional period antiques as well as utensils in its perfectly recreated period kitchen. Especially look for the cedar wood ceilings, the mother-of-pearl-studded bed, mahogany staircase, marble floors, scalloped windows, and the stunning views from the balcony across the main square, which literally make you feel you have walked back into the eighteenth century.

To your left as you leave the museum is the cream-colored, vaguely Gothic-looking **Iglesia de la Santísima Trinidad**. As it stands, this church was built in the late nineteenth century, although an earlier version had occupied this site since 1787. Built in an archetypal Cuban style, with three naves each fronted by a door, it is worth visiting for its venerated *Cristo de la Vera Cruz*, carved in Spain in 1731, which has an unusual history. The figure of Christ was carried on a boat from Spain to Mexico, which stopped in Trinidad's port: three times the boat left to complete its journey only to be swept back by heavy storms. Ever since, the Christ figure has remained here, believed by locals to have sanctifying powers.

As you continue around the Playa Mayor in a clockwise direction you will come to the **Museo de Arquitectura Trinitaria**. Not only does this museum showcase a remarkable collection of colonial architectural construction techniques and styles, it is a distinctive building in its own right, made up of two former homes (one built in 1738, the other in 1785) that were joined together in 1819, sharing a beautiful patio. It was the townhouse of the Sánchez-Iznaga family, who owned and operated large plantations in the region. The timber roof is worth seeing alone. Unlike other museums in Trinidad, it is closed on Fridays.

Continuing clockwise, still on Playa Mayor, to the left is the **Casa de Alderman Ortiz**, now an art gallery which exhibits works by contemporary Trinidadian artists.

Opposite, on Calle Simón Bolívar (Desangaño) stands the **Museo de Arqueología Guamuhaya**, a restored eighteenth-century mansion which displays archeological finds and Indian artifacts, notably utensils, tools, decorations and ceramics constructed by early Indian settlers. A somewhat macabre addition are exhumed skeletons taken from an African slave cemetery on the Iznaga sugar plantation in the Valle de los Ingenios. According to local historians, the house that originally occupied this site was lived in by the conquistador Hernán Cortéz before he left to conquer Mexico.

Heading away from the Playa Mayor, walk down the main cobbled thoroughfare of Calle Simón Bolívar, formerly the most fashionable address for Trinidad's colonial elite. To your right is the **Palacio Cantero**, now the **Museo Histórico Municipal**, with a collection that traces the town's history. It was owned by Justo German Cantero, paterfamilias of one of Trinidad's wealthiest families and owner of six sugar mills, but also a doctor, poet and aesthete. This impressive *palacio* includes a large central courtyard with shaded patios and spiral stairs leading up to a rare watchtower. The careful specialty and neoclassical decoration of the formal salons — with delicate, gilt-etched and exuberant patterns set against pale walls, Bo-

OPPOSITE: Colonial Trinidad has been well-restored and maintained. RIGHT: Detail of the eighteenth-century Museo de Arquitectura Trinitaria.

hemian chandeliers and gleaming mahogany furniture — evoke the sensation that this residence has remained untouched for generations. Off the central patio, the kitchen is distinguished by an enormous oven and chimney system built of plastered *mamposteria*. The climb up the watchtower is rewarded by stunning views, not only across the plaza and the town, but across to the Iglesia de la Popa, a ruined eighteenth-century church.

Close by, along Calle Gustavo Izquierdo (de la Gloria), you can walk inside the newly

is **La Canchánchara**, a charming rustic-style building with an interior patio garden that serves the house drink of the same name.

Returning to the Plaza Real del Jigüe, walk down Calle Piro Guinart (Boca). To the left, at 302, are the remains of Trinidad's old town hall and jail. Further down at the next corner is the **Archivo Histórico Municipal**, interesting especially for its documents tracing the story of early immigrants from Manila, Macao, Philadelphia, Buenos Aires, Boston, New Orleans, Amsterdam and Belgium.

restored **Palacio Iznaga**, another of Trinidad's few two-story buildings. You'll notice stalls displaying hand-made embroidered lace, wooden carvings and curios for sale along surrounding streets here.

From here, walk towards Calle Piro Guinart (also known as La Boca) and turn right to reach **Plaza Real de Jigüe**. A native tree — the *jigüe* — and a plaque commemorate the site where Diego Velázquez and his band of fellow expeditionaries held their first Christmas Mass in 1513, a year before Trinidad was founded. An attractive tile-studded colonial house shaded by the *jigüe* tree is now an elegant restaurant, **El Jigüe**.

Around the corner, after turning left on Calle Ruben Martínez Villena (Real de Jigüe)

On the adjacent square, between Calles Fernando Hernández Echerrí and Piro Guinart, stands a former eighteenth-century **Franciscan convent** notable for its four-story bell-tower, which is in fact all that remains of the original structure, and from which there are marvelous views across Trinidad. This former home for novices now houses the **Museo de Lucha contra Bandidos** ("The Museum of the Struggle Against the Bandits"). It graphically illustrates the verve with which the Castro government condemned and crushed the band of counter-revolutionary rebels who held out in the nearby Sierra del Escambray mountains. The fascinating exhibit includes photographs, clothes, weapons, maps, pieces of a U-2 reconnaissance plane and even a hammock that Che Guevara slept in.

From here turn left, back along Calle Fernando Hernández Echerrí and continue along until you reach Calle Ciro Redondo (Calle San José). To your left, you will find **La Luna**, a friendly tavern that has been a fixture of Trinidadian society since the nineteenth century.

Turn right on Calle Jesús Menéndez (Alameda) to reach Plaza de Segarte. Here you will find Trinidad's delightful **Casa de la Trova**, located in an eighteenth-century house, where there are almost daily performances by local musicians. At the end of the patio there is a music shop and a small bar where you can enjoy a drink while you listen to the music.

Leaving the Casa de la Trova, you will see to your left, along Calle Fernando Hernández Echerrí, the house where the great German naturalist Alexander von Humboldt stayed during his time in Trinidad in 1801. Across the street is the so-called **Mansión de los Conspiradores**. In the mid-nineteenth century this was the surreptitious meeting place of La Rosa Cubana, a revolutionary group. To the right, there is a stairway which leads you back to the Plaza Mayor.

Beyond its historic center, Trinidad's other sights are more spread out. If you are staying at the Hotel Horizontes Las Cuevas, you can't miss catching sight of the **Plaza Santa Ana**, which lies at the hotel's entrance gate. Here, next to the ruined **Iglesia de Santa Ana**, the former prison has been painted a strident yellow and turned into the city's largest cultural center: Trinidad's Folk Ensemble regularly performs Afro-Cuban music and dances for visitors within the cobbled courtyard, which is also ringed by an art gallery, a handicrafts bazaar and a shop run by the Cuban Cultural Heritage Fund. There is also a lookout bar and a restaurant.

Elsewhere, away from Trinidad's tourist sights, the **Parque Central** (about ten blocks south of Plaza Mayor) is a good place to take the town's pulse. This is where you will find Trinidad's peso-shops and markets, government ration dispensaries and the **Iglesia San Francisco de Paula**.

Several kilometers outside Trinidad, is the **Finca María Dolores**, set along the banks of the Guaurabo River, which organizes horse treks through the surrounding countryside. It also has simple accommodations and a popular restaurant which often hosts a "Fiesta Campesina," or "Farmer's Night" featuring spit-roasted pig, Creole dishes, hearty rum cocktails and *guateque* (folk) performances.

WHERE TO STAY

Moderate

In Trinidad itself, the best place to stay is **Hotel Horizontes Las Cuevas***** ((53-419) 4013 to 4019 FAX (53-419) 2302, Finca Santa Ana. Located on a hill overlooking Trinidad as well as across to the Caribbean Sea, this hotel has stunning sunset vistas, so ask for a room with a balcony view. Its villa-style bungalows are spread across the hillside around a central bar and swimming pool area. The rooms are fairly basic, although you can ask to stay in the group of newer villas which are more comfortable and spacious, with pleasant balconies. Meals — included in the room rate — are not especially good. The main advantage of staying in Las Cuevas is its proximity to Trinidad, which is a fairly short walk down a steep hill away. The hotel takes its name from the numerous caves nearby, one of which houses a popular discotheque.

Inexpensive

On the outskirts of Trinidad, another Accommodation option is the **Finca María Dolores*** ((53-419) 3581, Carretera Circuito Sur. Rustic, retreat-style accommodations are offered here, with 20 small and simple concrete and thatch bungalows. This complex also organizes horse-treks.

WHERE TO EAT

Moderate

Trinidad Colonial ((53-419) 3873, Calle Antonio Maceo (Gutiérrez) at the corner of Calle Colón, is housed in an attractive restored colonial mansion and is considered Trinidad's finest. The specialties are Creole-style fish and seafood dishes, al-

Nineteenth century French porcelain in the Museo Romántico, former palace of Spanish Count Brunet.

ways accompanied by *fufú de platano* (fried bananas).

Located in an eighteenth-century building, the partly open-air, vine-covered tavern **La Canchánchara** ((53-419) 4345, Calle Ruben Martínez Villena between Calles Piro Guinart and Calle Ciro Redondo, is a charming place to visit at any time of day. There is usually a high-spirited performance of traditional music going on, and deftly made *cancháncharas*, made with *aguardiente* (local brandy), honey, lime juice and ice. Apparently this drink was invented by the *mambisas*, the revolutionary guerillas who fought for independence against the Spanish in the nineteenth century. According to the manager, it is guaranteed to cure colds, especially if served hot according to the original version of the recipe. Accompanying Creole-style snacks are also served.

Mesón de Regidor ((53-419) 3756, Calle Simón Bolívar between Calles Ruben Martínez Villena and Gustavo Izquierdo, shaded by bougainvillea, is a pleasant courtyard restaurant and bar that is open all day and serves delicious Creole food, including, if you request it, lobster. You will often be entertained by Trinison, a talented band of three brothers on the guitar, bongos, flute and baracas.

El Jigüe ((53-419) 4136, Calle Ruben Martínez Villena, is in another historic courtyard, this time in a prettily-tiled colonial house on the square where Trinidad's first Christmas Mass was celebrated in 1513. The house specialty is chicken à la Jigüe.

If you are in the mood for a somewhat orchestrated good time, **Fiesta Campesina** ((53-419) 3581, Finca María Dolores, Carretera Circuito Sur, can be fun, and the food is always abundant.

Inexpensive

Vía Reale, Calle Ruben Martínez Villena near Calles Piro Guinart and Ciro Redondo, serves Italian food served within an attractive colonial mansion, with good pasta and pizza.

Las Begonias, Calle Antonio Maceo, is named after Trinidad's ubiquitous flower, and is housed in Trinidad's Museo de Histórico Municipal. This restaurant serves good seafood dishes.

NIGHTLIFE

Aside from the Casa de la Trova, where you can hear excellent live music by seasoned traditionalists as well as well-known Cuban bands, there are two other places to put on your list. **Bar Daiquirí**, Calle San Proscopio between Calles Gracia and Jesús María, is a friendly and relaxed place to have a drink under the night sky, and perhaps meet some locals, since this is a popular gathering place. **Ruinas de Segarte**, above Trinidad, near

the Hotel Horizontes Las Cuevas, is Cuba's most bizarre discotheque, tucked within a huge natural limestone cavern, with underground walkways that lead to a strobe-lit clearing that functions as the dance floor, with a bar area to one side. It is very popular with young locals, who come here to dance into the night, and perhaps to meet foreigners. As you leave the cave, you'll notice a Santería shrine.

HOW TO GET THERE

Located 82 km (51 miles) from Cienfuegos and 462 km (287 miles) from Havana, Trinidad is best reached by road — there is no train service. For such a popular destination the air service is fairly skeletal: two Cubana de Aviación flights a week from and to Havana.

TRINIDAD'S BEACHES

Located some 12 km (seven and a half miles) from Trinidad near Casilda Bay, both **Playa Ancón** and **Playa Costa Sur** and have white sandy beaches fringed by palms with hotels of the same name. This can be a good base for exploring Trinidad and enjoying the beach as well. Sheltered by a sandy peninsula, the bay's Caribbean waters are warm and clear, and are quite shallow close to the shore, although coral reefs are fairly close by. By wading out about a hundred meters (a hundred yards) you can snorkel around coral and rocks to see many different types of tropical fish, and you may see a lobster or two.

Next to the beach is the **Marina Cayo Blanco**, run by Marinas Puertosol, where you can rent equipment for scuba diving and snorkeling. It also offers scuba diving, fishing, and daily boat expeditions to nearby coral reefs and tiny islets, including Cayo Blanco, and more distant excursions to the Archipiélago de los Jardines de la Reina. Prices for such excursions range from US$50 per day to US$400 for the latter option.

Another beach option is **La Boca** which lies five kilometers (three miles) west of Trinidad. During the weekends especially, La Boca is a popular and relaxing place for locals to gather.

WHERE TO STAY AND EAT

Moderate
Hotel Ancón* ((53-419) 4011 or 3155 FAX (53-5) 66-7424, Playa Ancón, Carretera María Aguilar, is a large and somewhat austere hotel, but the beach it stands on is very pleasant and helps take the edge off the shortcomings of the hotel. Rooms are comfortable, and of course, you should request a sea view. Facilities include a bar, restaurant, cabaret, swimming pool, water sports, currency exchange, shop, and a car and bicycle rental office. Right next to the Hotel Ancón is the open-air **Grill Caribe** restaurant, which specializes in grilled seafood.

Inexpensive
Hotel Horizontes Costa Sur Hotel* ((53-419) 3810 or 3491, Playa María Aquilar, Casilda, is located on another of the bay's soft-sanded beaches, and is prettily landscaped with *flamboyán* trees. This hotel is otherwise fairly uninspiring and basic. It is preferable to stay in one of the 20 beach bungalows next to the main hotel complex, some of which have nice beach views. Buffet meals are nothing to get excited about, and the swimming pool can be less than tranquil. There is a tennis court.

EXCURSIONS FROM TRINIDAD

You cannot miss visiting the nearby **Valle de los Ingenios** (Valley of the Sugar Mills), which lies 12 km (seven and a half miles) from Trinidad. You can easily explore its sights within a day, perhaps partly by steam train if you are so inclined. Along with Trinidad, the valley is an UNESCO World Heritage Site, and aside from its architectural value it is an extraordinarily lush rural spectacle, with a patchwork of greens as the eye follows the horizon to the Sierra del Escambray mountains in the distance.

Portraits of Trinidad old-timers.

BACKGROUND

Trinidad's wealth is easily explained by just one statistic: by 1827, some 56 sugar mills in this valley were producing over 7,000 tons of sugar a year. Today, the valley is a vast open-air museum with some 65 sites of historic interest, including the remains of many steam-powered *ingenios*; 15 plantation mansions in various states of restoration; a village that was once home (or shall we say more correctly, prison) to generations of African slaves; sugar warehouses; and a bell tower at the Manacas-Iznaga plantation, from which the slaves were called to work. Eventually these sites will form what is being planned as a giant open-air Museum of Slavery, still under development. While you can miss seeing many of these sites, make sure you manage to see those described below.

WHAT TO SEE AND DO

Within the heart of the valley, you should first visit the eighteenth-century **Hacienda Manacas-Iznaga**, one of the best preserved and most impressive *palacetes* or country mansions in the area. It belonged to the wealthy Iznaga family, who owned several townhouses in Trinidad, and it was from here that they ran their large sugar plantation and mills. Now the hacienda contains a modest museum that details the history of the region's sugar industry. Apparently, when the Valle de los Ingenios Museum of Slavery is completed, this will contain much more information about the history of slavery within Cuba, and in the Caribbean in general. A section of the hacienda has been turned into a delightful restaurant, (presumably where family members used to have their meals). According to the manager, the back steps here contain small niches in which slaves were chained as punishment.

By now you will have noticed and perhaps already explored the nearby **Torre de Manacas-Iznaga**. This baroque, seven-story look-out tower — which is almost 44 m

The Sierra del Escambray mountains overlook a patchwork of greens in the fertile Valle de los Ingenios, with its many sugar cane plantations.

(144 ft) high — has spectacular views across the valley, and was used to keep an eye on the slaves working on the surrounding plantations.

Also within the valley, you should see the **Casa Guachinango**, further along on the Carretera Sancti Spíritus. This modest eighteenth-century plantation house has been turned into a restaurant, with tables along its broad verandah. Inside are a beautiful and unusual array of fading frescoes under restoration, depicting mythological beasts and figures, that were painted in the eighteenth-century by an Italian artisan.

You could spend a day exploring the valley from here by horseback, accompanied by a local guide.

It is worth mentioning that the Valle de los Ingenios, with its many working sugar plantations, is a good place to witness the *zafra*, or sugar harvest. You can ask Rumbos in Trinidad for more information about visiting plantations, or simply drive through the valley, taking any road alongside the fields where you see sugarcane being cut. The *zafra* begins around December 15 and goes on through around June 15.

WHERE TO EAT

Restaurant Hacienda Manacas-Iznaga ((53-419) 7241, Carretera Sancti Spíritus, is a charming, moderately priced restaurant that serves excellent regional dishes and good coffee, perfect for contemplating the outstanding views across the valley. You can dine indoors or outside on the verandah.

HOW TO GET THERE

It is possible to make a day trip to the valley from Trinidad by the Valle de los Ingenios *tren turistico*, a vintage steam-train, which makes stops at various historic sites, including Hacienda Manacas-Iznaga and Casa Guachinango. Check with the Rumbos office in Trinidad for details. It costs US$13 for the trip alone, or US$23 including lunch. Officially, the train runs on Wednesdays, Friday and Sunday, but departures often vary depending on the ebb and flow of large tourist groups. It is worth checking to see if you can coincide this trip with your visit.

TOPES DE COLLANTES

If you need a change of scene from Trinidad's historic charms and its beaches, you may wish to make an excursion into the nearby Sierra del Escambray mountains. You should know that parts of this region have been sectioned off as a military zone, definitely off-bounds to tourists. For this reason, you are advised to have a Cuban guide or driver with you.

The logical place to head for is the mountain's main hill station, **Topes de Collantes**, at an elevation of 771 m (about 2,530 ft), located within a large national reserve. Here, there are two hotels from which to set out on nature trails amid coffee plantations, hidden caves, waterfalls and dense vegetation. This very fertile has its own micro-climate, which encourages swathes of giant ferns, endemic palms and native orchids.

Although Topes de Collantes lies only 19 km (12 miles) away, the road requires slow going as you wind up steep inclines with countless hair-pin turns. The higher the road goes, the more you notice a profusion of sweet-scented eucalyptus trees and Caribbean pines. This is really the only way to reach the Topes de Collantes at present, since the other road, which leads from Manicaragua on the other side of the Sierra del Escambray, is too risky a proposition for most rental cars, or even jeeps, especially during bad weather.

BACKGROUND

Topes de Collantes was developed during the 1950s Batista-era as a sanatorium for sufferers of tuberculosis and other respiratory ailments. It is rather hard to ignore this fact if you check into the Kurhotel Escambray, a decidedly institutional health resort run by Gaviota, in which foreign tourists mingle bemusedly with Cubans undergoing treatments on health sabbatical. More inspiring is the Hotel Helechos, which caters to regular tourists.

The entire Escambray range spans an area that is 90 km (56 miles) long and 40 km (25 miles) wide, in which the highest peak is Pico San Juán (1,156 m or 3,793 ft), with a lower peak, Pico de Potrerillo (931 m or 3,054 ft), that is frequently the goal of hikers in the region.

WHAT TO SEE AND DO

Aside from Pico de Potrerillo, one of the most popular trails is to the **Caburní Falls**, which is a fairly arduous hike three kilometers (nearly two miles) down the ravine (even more arduous is the return, uphill effort) to the bottom of the 75-m (246-ft)-high falls, which are deservedly beautiful when you get there. This is a strenuous climb and not recommended unless you are in good physical condition.

A much less difficult excursion is to drive six kilometers (about four miles) to the **Finca Codina**, a turn-of-the-century ranch that belonged to a Spanish coffee grower. From here, an easy and extremely beautiful trail wanders past mountain caves and luxuriant forest, alive with butterflies, *zunzuns* (bee hummingbirds) and an incredible variety of plants and flowers, including many medicinal plants, orchids and the fragrant *mariposa*, Cuba's national flower. Back at the Finca, you can try their delicious cocktail, made of ginger root, honey and rum.

Make sure that you come equipped for the changes in temperature and the sudden downfalls of rain. You will probably find that rain gear, a change of warm clothes, and mosquito repellent are all essential, even though none of the above might seem important while you are basking in Trinidad's strong sunlight.

It is well worth asking the hotel staff to arrange a local guide to accompany you on the nature trails in the area, someone who can point out and explain the fascinating medicinal properties of the region's plants, explain local history, and make sure you don't get completely lost in the dense forest.

WHERE TO STAY

Los Helechos* ((53-42) 4-0180 or 4-0301 FAX (53-42) 4-7317, Topes de Collantes, Escambray, Sancti Spíritus. This is a far better proposition than the Kurhotel, located close

The palm is a ubiquitous feature in Cuba, where hundreds of varieties can be found.

by. It has 38 quiet comfortable rooms with mountain views, a pleasant restaurant, a swimming pool, sauna, shop, and car rental facilities.

Kurhotel Escambray**** ((53-42) 4-0117 or 4-0330 FAX (53-42) 4-0288, Topes de Collantes, Sancti Spíritus, is an admirable national institution where many Cubans come for rest and treatments for various ailments, and as such it functions as a sanatorium, with patients using the swimming pool, jacuzzis and steam baths as therapeutic treatment. However, as a hotel for tourists it cannot exactly be recommended: it has a distinctly institutional quality and is much dingier and more depressing than it sounds. Running into color-coded track-suited patients in the corridors and elevators, you may start to feel like a patient yourself. There are over 200 rooms, most of which have a mountain view, with television and radio, and there are two restaurants, one for patients and one for tourists.

HOW TO GET THERE

In theory, you could take the daily bus from Trinidad, however, this is not necessarily a viable option unless you wish to stand upright on the open back of a truck. It is always full with villagers trying to get home.

Driving is your best option, or you can negotiate a fee with a taxi particular from Trinidad.

To reach Topes de Collantes, take the Carretera de Cienfuegos out of Trinidad, and after crossing the Guaurabo River, just before the town of Piti Fajardos, take the turnoff to the right, then continue on the main road which you will notice starts to climb steadily. Regardless of how you get there, for this trip, you need to be in a vehicle with functioning brakes.

VILLA CLARA

Most visitors speed by the province of Villa Clara, bypassing its sights as they travel through on Cuba's main highway, the two-lane Carretera Central. The province lies in the center of the island, directly north of Trinidad, and is one of Cuba's most traditional agricultural beltways, with vast plantations of sugarcane and rice interspersed with fields of maize, beans, *yucca*, citrus fruits and cattle farms.

After Pinar del Río, Villa Clara is Cuba's biggest producer of high-quality tobacco, and you will see countless tobacco fields, as well as shaggy thatched *vegas* where the leaves are dried. Driving through this region, the enduring images are those of giant sugarcane rising above the road like green waves; and work-weary *guachos* astride their horses, driving herds of bullock. During the tobacco harvest (between December to March), many farmers are happy to welcome visitors; it is interesting to see them working in the fields, they'll give you a visit of the drying houses if you ask.

SANTA CLARA

The Provincial capital, Santa Clara, was founded in the 1570s, after its Spanish settlers had to flee their original site, the town of Remedios, which being on the coast, was constantly threatened with pirate raids. Like the rest of central Cuba, Santa Clara's independence fighters suffered greatly during the Wars of Independence. In recent history, Santa Clara is best known as the city whose capture by Che Guevara on December 28, 1958 played a decisive factor in bringing Fidel Castro to power. It is also where the remains of Che's body were laid to rest in 1997, after almost 30 years of lying in a hidden mass grave in Vallegrande, in the Bolivian mountains.

With its ochre-tiled and thick stucco colonial houses and the occasional *palacio*, Santa Clara in many ways has the feel of a small Spanish town, and it definitely merits a visit, at least for an hour or so. In the distance, the foothills of the Sierra del Escambray are easily visible. Santa Clara is also a university town, and young students make up a large section of its residents.

WHAT TO SEE AND DO

You cannot miss one of Cuba's most idiosyncratic museums, the **Tren Blindado** ("the Armored Train") which stands next to the main highway to Remedios, at the very site where it was attacked and derailed by

Che in late 1958. The train, which was crammed with Batista's soldiers and weaponry, is now a museum: you can peer inside the old wagons and muse over the exhibits and historical documentation.

In Santa Clara's massive **Plaza de la Revolución**, a monument honors Che Guevara, with a large statue of the iconic revolutionary posed for action with a machine gun above his words, "Hasta La Victoria Siempre" and a stone tablet bearing the complete letter that Che wrote to his comrade Fidel. There is a small **Museo de la Revolución** here.

Parque Vidal is Santa Clara's main civic square, and it is lined with some interesting buildings, overlooking a leafy cobbled square with a central gazebo. Housed in a colonial mansion, the Museum of Decorative Arts has a charming collection of eighteenth- and nineteenth- century furnishings from the city's wealthier households. The **Teatro de la Caridad** is one of Cuba's outstanding theaters, built in 1884 and funded by a local philanthropist, Marta Abreu du Estevez. Painted allegorical figures the interior dome, under which such greats as Enrico Caruso sang when he made a tour of Cuba.

Also facing the square is the **Palacio Municipal** (Town Hall) and the **Hotel Santa Clara Libre**, the city's best hotel, although not recommended as a place to stay. The exterior is pock-marked with bullet holes from the battle that proved so crucial to Cuba's history.

WHERE TO STAY

Hotel Cubanacán La Granjita*** ((53-422) 26051, Carretera de Maleza, Santa Clara, located on the outskirts of Santa Clara, has for its slogan "A Step in Nature's Direction." This refers to the rustic-style theme of the thatched bungalows, landscaped by palms. With pleasant surroundings and good food, this is a good place for an overnight stop. The swimming pool is nice.

Hotel Horizontes Los Caneyes*** ((53-422) 4512 or 4515 FAX (53-7) 33-5009, Avenida de los Eucaliptos and Circunvalación de Santa Clara. This hotel is also styled as though Johnny Weismuller, the actor famous for his Tarzan role, might walk in at

any moment, with *faux* Indian-style thatched *cabañas*, and surrounded by lush foliage. A large billboard-size Indian welcomes you at the entrance with a "How." Both of these hotels are moderately priced.

WHERE TO EAT

1878 Restaurant Colonial, Calle Máximo Gómez between Calles Marta Abreu and Independencia, is an inexpensive restaurant housed in an old colonial mansion a block from the Parque Vidal. The food is unexceptional, but the surroundings are pleasant enough. Also inexpensive is **Restaurante Renancer** ((53-22) 2-2272, Calle J.B. Zayas No. 111, between Calles Eduardo Machado and Tristá. Set in a colonial-style house, this *paladar* can provide more substantial dishes, and can often offer lobster and meats not on the "official" menu. There are two menus, one in pesos and the other in dollars.

HOW TO GET THERE

Aside from stopping in Santa Clara while driving or going along on an organized tour, it is more practical to travel here by train, rather than by bus. There are daily trains from Havana, Matanzas, Cienfuegos, Sancti Spíritus and Santiago de Cuba. The **Estación de Ferrocarriles** is located to the north of the town, off Calle Luis Estévez.

REMEDIOS

Located near Villa Clara's northern coast, Remedios, which lies 43 km (27 miles) east of Santa Clara, is one of Cuba's best-preserved late-colonial towns. In many ways, it is just as interesting architecturally as Trinidad, for although it lacks such grand *palacios*, it possesses an almost eerily time-warped ambiance. Most of its surviving colonial buildings date from the eighteenth and nineteenth centuries, and are fairly modest and provincial, and a church tower is the highest vantage point over low-lying red-tile roofs and sleepy, narrow alleyways. Few tourists come here, and there are virtually no cars (except vintage American cars in various stages of decay), just horse-drawn carts and bicycles.

Remedios was not one of the seven *villas* or settlements established by Diego Velázquez, but it is still one of the oldest colonial towns in Cuba, founded in 1524.

WHAT TO SEE AND DO

At the town's center is the **Plaza Martí**, around which the main civic administrative buildings are arranged. On the eastern side of the square is the extraordinary **Iglesia de San Juan Bautista**, which was originally built in 1578 but was significantly remodeled in the seventeenth century. Inside, there is a magnificent Churrigueresque-style altarpiece which was carved of cedar and encrusted with gold leaf. The walls are covered with iconographic carvings and religious paintings, including a rarely depicted image of the pregnant Virgin Mary.

When you walk outside the church, you might want to stop at one of two local nearby bars, both of which have interiors that look as they have not changed for at least a century.

On the north side of the square, the **Museo de Música Alejandro García Cartula** is a shrine to the town's most famous musician, Alejandro García Cartula, housed in the elegant nineteenth-century mansion that was the musician's birthplace. Cartula, who was both a musician and a judge, scandalized *le tout* Remedios when he lived openly with his black mistress and was inspired to incorporate Afro-Cuban musical traditions in his compositions; and he was murdered in mysterious circumstances.

Opposite is the **Hotel Mascotte**, the town's only hotel. In 1899, this was where General Máximo Gómez met with an aide of American President McKinley to negotiate the retirement of the *mambisas*, the independence fighters who had fought in the Spanish-American War.

Leaving the square, a short walk along Calle Máximo brings you to the **Museo de las Parrandas Remedianas** (Museum of the Frolics of Remedios), dedicated to Las Parrandas, the unique festival of the region, held each year, which dates back to the early nineteenth century and was apparently con-

cocted by the local parish to try and drum up more attendance for the Midnight Mass on Christmas Eve. Along with the Carnival in Santiago de Cuba and the Charanga de Bejucal in Havana, Las Parrandas is one of Cuba's most important historical fiestas.

For months before Las Parrandas takes place, on the last Saturday of the year, two sections of the town each secretly prepare a huge float, called *trabajos de plaza*, which are premiered to great fanfare of the night of the fiesta, paraded through the town accompanied by musicians playing the polka, firework displays, and townspeople dressed-up in outrageous costumes carrying banners. Traditionally, efforts by each camp to sabotage or outdo the other's efforts in order to come up with the most spectacular display have caused as much hilarity in the town as the celebration itself.

Since the beginning of the Special Period, Las Parrandas, sadly, has been cancelled. You can get a good idea of the festival from the museum's displays of float models, photographs, costumes and lanterns. It is open Tuesday to Saturday, 1 PM to 6 PM, Sunday 9 AM to 1 PM and is closed on Monday.

On the main square, **La Fe** serves only traditional drinks such as mango juice and an intriguing concoction made with anise; while **El Louvre** serves a few light snacks along with the traditional shots of rum and Hatuey beer.

By road, Santa Clara is 45 km (28 miles) away. Buses — or rather re-constituted trucks — ply between the towns several times a day.

SANCTI SPÍRITUS

If you are planning to continue along the Carretera Central onwards into central Cuba through the largely agricultural province of Sancti Spíritus, you may wish to stop briefly in the provincial capital, which takes the same name.

WHAT TO SEE AND DO

Founded in 1514 by Diego Velázquez, and once an affluent sugar capital, Sancti Spíritus has faded into sleepy gentility, and now

---

Traces of Spanish colonial founders in Sancti Spíritus.

ugly industrial factories and sugar mills are encroaching on its fringes. Head for the **Parque Central**, a large square surrounded by nineteenth-century neoclassical buildings, some of which were very ostentatious in their day, with the ubiquitous bust of José Martí, and old men dozing on park benches under the trees. If you look closely at many of the historic buildings, you can see traces of classically inspired motifs; many house exteriors were painted in a trompe l'oeil masonry pattern and have elaborate cornices.

Also seek out the **Iglesia Parroquial Mayor del Espíritu Santo**, which dates from 1512, and is considered to be Cuba's oldest extant church, although much of its construction dates from later centuries. The narrow streets surrounding the church contain many well-preserved colonial mansions.

From the church, Avenida Jesús Menéndez continues southwest two blocks to the Yayabo River, from which you should take the first right, on Calle Placido, to reach the **Palacio Valle Iznaga**, which once belonged to the sugar-wealthy family from Trinidad, whose townhouse and plantation estate you may already have seen if you have already visited that town. Today it is the **Museo de Arte Colonial**, which houses the usual display of colonial furniture, but is beautiful to behold. Nearby, the Yayabo River bridge, built in 1522, is the only remaining arched stone bridge from the early colonial period to be seen in Cuba.

It is pleasant to take a stroll through the main core of Sancti Spíritus, looking at houses and buildings to appreciate how the influence of early twentieth-century French and Italian styles, as well as art deco, can be seen alongside traditional colonial architecture, even in Cuba's provincial towns. In particular, look out for the grand, three-story nineteenth-century **Hotel Perla de Cuba**, which is being renovated.

WHERE TO STAY AND EAT

For inexpensive accommodations, try **Villa Rancho Hatuey***** ((53-412) 6015, Carretera Central, Sancti Spíritus. Lying five kilometers (three miles) north of town, this is the best place to stay in the area, and top Cuban government officials often stay here too. It has a swimming pool and a decent restaurant. You can also try **Hotel Horizontes Zaza**** ((53-412) 6012 or 5334 FAX (53-5) 66-8001, Finca San José, Lago Zaza, Sancti Spíritus. Ten kilometers (six miles) southeast of town, located on El Zaza, a man-made lake and popular trout-fishing spot, this hotel makes a good rest stop.

There's not a lot of scope for finding a good meal outside the hotels recommended above. The best place to head for is the **Restaurante 1514**, Calle Céspedes Norte No. 52, which has a very basic menu amid fairly Spartan surroundings.

HOW TO GET THERE

If you are driving directly from Trinidad, Sancti Spíritus lies 55 km (34 miles) away, and so makes a convenient rest stop, although tourists rarely stay long. However when the Autopista Nacional currently under construction is completed, it will not pass through the city as the Carretera Central does.

CIEGO DE ÁVILA

As you drive onwards through central Cuba, you enter the province of Ciego de Ávila, another mainly agricultural region, with an unbroken succession of cane plantations, pineapple farms, banana groves and citrus orchards; the air is rich with Cuba's inescapable smell of jasmine.

Its capital, **Ciego de Ávila**, which lies 76 km (47 miles) east of Sancti Spíritus and 108 km (67 miles) west of Camagüey, has a quiet and suburban feel, and is usually only visited by tourists because it is located on the main east-west highway and makes a good rest stop.

However, it can be used as a base if you plan to explore the **Archipiélago de los Jardines de la Reina** — an archipelago of unspoiled keys surrounded by clear waters with beautiful coral reefs, abundant fish and close to shore, many migratory birds — found off the province's south coast, since many fishing and diving excursions to the keys originate from Ciego de Ávila.

However, the goal of many visitors who pass through Ciego de Ávila Province is to head across to the north coast to the exotically named **Cayo Coco** and its neighbor, **Cayo Guillermo**, which have become popular, if remote, beach resorts, and also happen to be one of Cuba's most important bird sanctuaries.

WHERE TO EAT

Ciego de Ávila is not a great place for eating out. If you want refreshments and

addition, Cubana de Aviación flies here from Havana.

You can get there by train from various points in the island, including Havana, Matanzas, Holguín and Santiago de Cuba. The **Estación de Ferrocarriles** is located six blocks southwest of the town center.

TO THE CAYS

En route, you will pass through a town by the unlikely name of **Morón**, the epitome of

snacks, try the **Rumbos 12** cafeteria on Parque Martí.

One of the better *paladares* is the **Mesón El Fuerte**, Avenida Las Palmas, opposite Plaza Camilo Cienfuegos. Set in a historic Spanish arms house, it is open for dinner only. It's a good idea to ask around for recommendations for any *paladares* that may have opened recently.

HOW TO GET THERE

Ciego de Ávila's new **Aeropuerto Internacional de Máximo Gómez** is located at Ceballos, 25 km (nearly 16 miles) north of town. Many charter flights from Canada arrive here, with visitors bound for Cayo Coco. In

rural life in Cuba, and notable for its large metal rooster programmed to crow at dawn and dusk. Nearby, a road winds the scenic and bass-filled **Laguna de la Leche** which earned its name from its milky waters, created by lime deposits at the lake's bottom. It is a beautiful sight when flamingos flock here in large numbers. Further on, the smaller **Lago La Redonda** is also popular — Horizontes Hotels have a lodge here, the delightfully named **Horizontes La Casona de Morón** ((53-7) 33-4563, Cristóbal Colón No. 41, Ciego de Ávila. This lodge is well-equipped and situated for fishing excursions.

The Sancti Spíritus library was a casino in the 1920s.

Several kilometers after leaving Morón you'll see the surprising apparition of an entire farming community, constructed as if it were a hamlet in Holland, complete with peaked roofs, chimneys and windmills. It's named the **Communidad Celia Sánchez**, and was created by Fidel's longtime confidante and private secretary after she returned from a trip to Holland and declared herself besotted with Dutch architecture. The plump cattle you see grazing here are result of an artificial insemination program, crossing European breeds with local livestock.

Coco and the neighboring Cayo Guillermo, which are the most developed islands within the **Archipiélago de Sabana**.

At times it feels as though you are literally driving over the sea itself, and in the right season you will see flocks of flamingos, pelicans, diving birds, and flying fish on either side.

Cayo Coco

Cayo Coco is named, not for the coconut palms seen here as you might expect, but for

Cayeria del Norte

From the mainland and onwards to the keys beyond lies a 34-km (21-mile)-long stone-fill causeway across the Bahía de Perros (Bay of Dogs) known as the **Cayeria del Norte** (also known as the "Pedraplen") that was completed in 1989, partially built on water and one of the most complex engineering feats of the Cuban roadway system. Environmentalists worry that the landfill bridge has cut off the sea's current and the waters are becoming stagnant, causing the mangrove swamps to rot, and that birdlife will suffer.

The drive along this causeway is one of the most memorable parts of a visit to Cayo

the bird the locals call "coco": the long-legged white ibis. It also has the island's largest flamingo colony, estimated to be at least several thousand strong. This mangrove-dense region is an important migratory retreat for many thousands of birds and is also home to 158 year-round endemic species including sea swallows, herons, egrets and the Cuban cuckoo.

More than half of this 22-km (14-mile)-long cay is covered in mangrove and bracken forest where wild horses, wild boar and wild livestock roam free, but for how long is the question. Initially, only ornithologists, scientists and biologists came out to this region to study the fragile inter-dependency of this mangrove and marine ecosystem.

The Cuban government seems to be going ahead with its plan to develop the area's beaches as its next Varadero, and is poised to complete an airport. (The nearest airport is currently at Ciego de Ávila.)

Certainly, the Sabana archipelago — with its hundreds of keys and sandbars spread over hundreds of kilometers, most unexplored, connected by a vast underwater system of reefs — is widely regarded on the island as one of Cuba's last great unspoiled frontiers for snorkeling and diving. Other parts of the archipelago, such as **Cayo Romano** and, much further east, **Cayo Sabinal**, will likely be developed in future.

Today, Cayo Coco has two large tourist resort complexes, which between them share about a thousand hotel rooms, and apparently the government plans to build as many as 20 more hotels on its northern Atlantic-facing coast in the near future.

When you approach the end of the causeway and arrive at Cayo Coco, the road branching northwest will lead you past the main resorts. Close to the main beach of **Playa Larga**, you'll find the **Coastal Ecosystems Research Center**, run by Cuba's Academy of Sciences, and part of a United Nations Development Program which studies the region's ecology and biodiversity. Visitors are welcome.

Beyond the airport, another causeway leads 17 km (over 10 miles) across tiny stepping stones of mangrove-covered islets to the much smaller **Cayo Guillermo**. Like the Cayeria del Norte, this dyke has also caused a disruption in the ecology of these islands.

ACROSS TO CAYO GUILLERMO

If you have read Ernest Hemingway's *Islands in the Stream*, you will recognize the author's description of this sketchy patchwork of sandy coves, dark green mangroves, and soupy lagoons filled with rosy-colored flamingos. This is where he led his protagonist, Thomas Hudson, in search of Nazi soldiers, based on his real-life adventures patrolling for German U-boats off this coast in his boat *Pilar*, accompanied by his captain, Gregorio Fuentes.

The **Marina Puertosol** is located on Cayo Guillermo's **Playa El Paso**, along with the cay's two modestly sized hotels. It's a very peaceful and relaxing place in which to stay, admire the birdlife, and scuba dive amid the offshore reefs which teem with rich and varied marine life.

WHAT TO SEE AND DO

There is plenty of nature to enjoy, and you can decide what sort of pace appeals to you, and whether you like the sound of hotel-organized excursions or prefer to do your own exploring. You can either swim on the beach in front of the hotels or venture to other

beaches within the keys. The information desk at your hotel can advise and give you a map for the many local bird watching sites, nature trails and swimming lagoons in the keys, as well as the tourist-orientated facilities set up by Rumbos, notably on Cayo Coco where a series of attractions such as beachside restaurants, a horseback-riding ranch and trails have been landscaped throughout the cay.

You can rent bicycles, mopeds and, if necessary, cars, from both the Tryp hotel complexes. These resorts also offer a range of special events and excursions, such as cruises retracing Hemingway's fishing trips, sunset cruises and moped tours across the keys.

Marina Puertosol can arrange scuba diving, fishing (for bonefish, mackerel, pike and marlin) and snorkeling trips — as can your hotel — and there are plenty of coral reefs and gardens to explore in the area.

OPPOSITE: Colorful plazas and antique cars abound in Cuba. ABOVE: On the road to Ciego de Ávila.

Further offshore, dolphins are a common sight.

WHERE TO STAY

Expensive

The 458-room tourist complex **Hotel Tryp Cayo Coco******* ((53-33) 30-384 to 30-388 FAX (53-33) 30-166, Caribbean Poblado, Cayo Coco Beach, Ciego de Ávila, is an entire village fashioned against what used to be empty mangrove swamps. Apartment-style condominiums (some complete with Jacuzzis) are linked by a walkways which lead to an array of swimming pools, bars, restaurants, cafeterias and shopping centers, designed to create the idea that you are in some sort of unnatural beach village. The beach *is* lovely, with soft sands and plenty of space to roam. You can rent equipment for a full range of water sports, including jet skis and water skiing, and explore surrounding beaches by boat. Make sure you request a room with a balcony facing the sea.

The recently completed 507-room hotel complex **Hotel Club Tryp Cayo Coco****** ((53-33) 30-1311 FAX (53-33) 30-1386 E-MAIL ht@club.tryp.cma.net, Caribbean Poblado, Cayo Coco Beach, Ciego de Ávila, has replicated the village theme of its neighbor, and is located within easy walking distance along the beach. Style-wise, they are fairly interchangeable and not to everyone's liking. Both are managed by the Spanish Tryp hotel chain.

Villa Vigía**** ((53-33) 30-1760 FAX (53-33) 30-1748, Cayo Guillermo, Ciego de Ávila, is a good luxury choice if you want to be away from the two huge tourist villages above.

Moderate to Expensive

Villa Cojímar**** ((53-33) 30-1012 FAX (53-33) 33-55540, Cayo Guillermo, Ciego de Ávila, is a fairly luxurious, all-inclusive resort with a secluded atmosphere, good facilities for water sports and scuba diving, and a white-sand beach that is very pleasant to loll on. It is an Italian-Cuban joint-venture, meaning that the food is much better than usual. It is being expanded to 750 rooms.

Note that Spanish-Cuban joint venture, the luxury 270-room **Hotel Sol Club Cayo Coco****** ((53-33) 30-1280 FAX (53-33) 30-

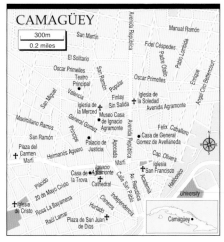

1285 E-MAIL solclub.caycoco@melia.solmelia.cma.net was recently completed along the beachfront at Cayo Coco. On Cayo Guillermo, the 312-room **Hotel Gregorio** is also nearing completion.

WHERE TO EAT

Aside from the hotels (which, in the case of the all-inclusive Tryp hotels offer non-guests a day pass for their restaurants), there are several places worth considering. Rumbos has various beachside and roadside eateries, the best of which is **Parador La Silla**, located in one of the small islands before you reach Cayo Coco, which has a lookout for flamingos.

Cueva del Jabalí, five kilometers (three miles) west of the Hotel Tryp, is a popular nightspot. Its restaurant and bar have been constructed within a cave. Although atmospheric, it can be a little damp and mosquito-prone. It's open for dinner only.

HOW TO GET THERE

In keeping with the rapid expansion of tourist facilities, an airport is scheduled to open on Cayo Coco, and will receive both domestic Cubana de Aviación and international charter flights, primarily from Canada.

By road the only way to get there is by car, unless you are arriving as part of a tour, or by airport shuttle bus from Ciego de Ávila airport.

JARDINES DE LA REINA

Some 80 km (50 miles) off the south coast stretch the **Archipiélago de los Jardines de la Reina**, an extensive chain of secluded low-lying coral islets rimmed by beautiful, if small, white sand beaches and reefs; and a pristine habitat for a spectacular array of marine life as well as birds. The Jardines de los Reina sprawl across the offshore boundaries of Ciego de Ávila and Camagüey provinces.

BACKGROUND

The provincial capital of the same name, but originally called Santa María del Puerto del Príncipe, was among the seven townships founded by Diego Velázquez. The original settlement was founded in 1514 near the present port of Nuevitas on the north coast, but after constant attacks from pirates, it was moved inland to its present site in 1528. Camagüey's settlers soon thrived from new-found prosperity in marketing

The only way to reach the keys is as part of an organized excursion from **Marina Júcaro**, 24 km (15 miles) south of Ciego de Ávila, or aboard your own private yacht. These diving packages can be organized from Puertosol ((53-7) 33-4705 or 33-4708 FAX (53-7) 33-4703, Calle M and L, Edificio FOCSA, Vedado, Havana (see SPORTING SPREE, page 30.)

CAMAGÜEY

Cuba's largest province, Camagüey has a tough cowboy reputation, famous throughout the island for its horse-adept *vaqueros* and its immense flatlands of sugarcane plantations and grazing cattle.

contraband livestock to nearby French, Dutch and English Caribbean islands. Soon, the notorious English pirate Henry Morgan got wind of the treasures that were piling up, and he and his men ransacked the city mercilessly in 1668; another pirate attack followed a decade later.

Fear of pirates is evident in Camagüey's resultant early-colonial architecture: its inner core is surrounded by a labyrinthine network of winding streets, abutting in squares of all shapes and sizes, blind alleys and forked streets — and all with only one exit. Should the city find itself under siege, the plan went, the assailants would find the tables turned

Horse-drawn carriage transports tourists at Playa Santa Lucía.

on them once they were trapped in this so-called "City of Squares."

The city is also known for its trademark bulbous clay pots, called *tinajones*, used to store precious rainwater for times of drought. A family's prosperity was measured by the number of *tinajones* they possessed, and the pots have since become a symbol of the city. An old legend has it that if a young woman from Camagüey gives a visiting stranger water from a *tinajón*, he will find himself so smitten with her that he will be unable to tear himself away from the city.

For anyone driving eastwards through central Cuba, Camagüey is an inevitable place in which to make an overnight stop. Despite the fact that it is very spread out — this is Cuba's third largest city — once you get to the colonial center, which has recently been named as a national monument, you can easily spend several enjoyable hours wandering around its maze-like and intensely traditional streets.

You will notice that most of the colonial buildings that line Camagüey's streets are very modest-looking, neither brightly painted or embellished with any form of decoration. However, the most attractive feature of these houses lies unseen behind discreet doors: the courtyard patio, which in Camagüey is the center of the home. Planted with shady trees, these courtyards are traditionally surrounded by roomy galleries, or in the case of less wealthy homes, supported by unembellished wooden eaves. Large pots of medicinal plants, flowers and herbs are also a traditional touch, as are the *tinajones*.

Servi Cupet-Cimex gas stations, located on the Carretera Central to the south of the city, close to the district of La Caridad.

GENERAL INFORMATION

There is little in the way of facilities geared for visitors in Camagüey. However, you'll find a **Banco Nacional** on Plaza de los Trabajadores, and a **Banco Financiero Internacional** two blocks south.

There is no Clínica Internacional, although the city has several hospitals and there's a 24-hour pharmacy, the **Farmacia Alvarez Fuentes** at the corner of Calles Oscar Primelles and Avellaneda.

Havanautos has a car rental office at the Hotel Horizontes Camagüey. There are two

WHAT TO SEE AND DO

Start by heading for downtown Camagüey, where you can leave your car behind to navigate your way through the city's narrow one-way streets on foot. Like many rustic capitals in Cuba, you may see more horse-drawn carriages and bicycles in these streets than cars.

You can begin at **Plaza de los Trabajadores** (Worker's Square), which in the nineteenth century was used to stage bullfights. You can't miss the enormous placard of Che Guevara. Just off the square, off

The Cuban Heartland

Avenida Agramonte, lies the **Museo Casa de Ignacio Agramonte**, the birthplace and home of one of Cuba's most revered military revolutionaries and Camagüey's hero, General Ignacio Agramonte (1841–1873). He was renowned for many feats of bravery, and took part in an estimated 45 battles while commanding troops during the Wars of Independence. His favored military strategy — much admired by Castro — involved using a small detachment to distract the enemy, then to simulate a retreat, only to lure the enemy troops into the thick of his army — much like the design of Camagüey itself. Although only the piano was an original possession of the Agramonte family, the house has been furnished to create the impression that the general has just stepped out.

The museum is open Monday and Wednesdays through Saturday from 1 PM to 6 PM and Sunday from 8 AM to noon; it is closed on Tuesday.

Directly opposite is the **Iglesia de la Merced**, built in 1748 and restored after a 1906 fire. Although the exterior has a stern, almost fortress-like quality, the interior is ornate: an altarpiece made of carved wood, silver and marble is startlingly impressive. To the left, a side chapel contains an image of the Infant Jesus of Prague, much revered by locals. Elaborate confession boxes face the courtyard of the adjacent convent.

From here, walk westwards along Calle Valencia for two blocks and look for the marble façade of the **Teatro Principal**, built

Happy rodeo spectators.

The Cuban Heartland

in 1850 and the home of the Camagüey Ballet, which, after Havana, is the second most prominent ballet in Cuba. As you return to the square, look for Calle Salvador Cisneros. This will lead you into the labyrinthine maze that can be found at the city's heart; the streets here are lined with colonial-era houses.

Further along Calle Salvador Cisneros to reach the **Palacio de Justicia** (Court House), a notable mid-eighteenth-century construction housed in a former seminary. Nearby, the **Centro de Promoción Cultural** often

stages exhibitions by Cuban artists as well as jazz concerts, and is usually a lively place to visit. From here turn right on Calle Hermanos Aguero, where on the corner, is the birthplace of the Cuban poet Nicolás Guillén, which is open to the public as a small library. Keep walking until you reach the **Plaza de Bedoya**, unusual for its row of bright pastel-painted colonial houses — a sudden splash of welcome color. At the end is the run-down **Iglesia del Carmen**.

From here, take your bearings and head for Avenida Martí, immediately parallel, which will lead you onto the **Parque Agramonte**, between Calles Independencia and Cisneros. Here, a 1916 statue of General Agramonte brandishing his sword and flanked by a sculptured relief of his cavalry soldiers presides over the square. The four palm trees at each corner of the square are also monuments in a sense: they commemorate four Cuban independence fighters executed by the Spanish in 1851, and were planted by locals as a secret homage to their slain compatriots unbeknownst to the colonial authorities. To the south side of the square is Camagüey's cathedral, the **Nuestra Señora de la Candelaria**. On the square, on Calle Salvador Cisneros, you will also find the city's **Casa de la Trova**.

A short walk three blocks south on Calle Cisneros, and then left on Calle Hurtado brings you to one of Camagüey's gems: **Plaza de San Juan de Dios**. Built in the eighteenth century, it is easy to see why this cobble-stoned square is a national monument. Since it has been restored, its red-tiled houses painted in their original colors, it looks straight out of a film set. It is flanked by the **Iglesia de San Juan de Dios**, built in 1728 and the first hospital of similar vintage that was the first to be established in the town. Inside the cobbled square, you can visit a ceramics workshop, and perhaps, buy a *tinajón*. Within the square, two colonial-style restaurants, **Parador de los Tres Reyes** and **Meson La Campaña de Toledo** are the city's most inviting places to dine.

From here, you may want to climb aboard a horse-drawn *calesa* to get back to your starting place on this tour.

If you have time for one last sight on your visit to Camagüey, see the lovely baroque **Iglesia de la Soledad**, built in 1775 with impressive fresco paintings in its interior. It lies at the corner of Avenida Agramonte and Avenida República, south of the railway track.

As you leave Camagüey, you can't fail to notice the ornate **Palacio de los Matrimoniales**, the yellow and white mansion that once belonged to a wealthy family (long-gone to Miami, one supposes) and is now used to officiate civil weddings. The **Parque Casino Campestre** is where the city's school-children go to play; there is a small amusement park and donkey rides. At the park's entrance, a statue commemorates the two Spanish pilots, Barberan and Collar, who completed their flight from Seville to Camagüey in 1933, a unique achievement, and the first direct flight between Cuba and Europe.

Where to Stay

Hotel Cubanacán Maraguán*** ((53-322) 7-2170 or 7-2017 FAX (53-322) 36-5247, Camino de Guanamaquila, Circunvalación Este, is a modest and pleasant hotel, built as a series of stone cottages on the outskirts of the city, and probably best suited as a rest stop for those traveling by car as it is some distance from the center. The buffet meals are very good. Facilities include a small swimming pool and a bar.

Another inexpensive hotel, the 1970s-style **Hotel Horizontes Camagüey***** ((53-322) 7-2015 or 7-1970 FAX (53-7) 33-5699, Carretera Central Este, Jayamá, has seen many a tour bus come and go and the rooms are lackluster. It is redeemed by the friendliness of its staff, the attempts to brighten up the place with artistic ceramic sculptures by a local artist, and the talented musical trio who entertain here. Right next door, Camagüey's cabaret nightclub puts on a nightly show.

Located close to Camagüey's rail station, **Hotel Plaza***** ((53-322) 8-2413 or 8-2415, Avenida Von Horne, is an idiosyncratic, turn-of-the-century hotel that has a lot of old-fashioned charm and is a good choice if you want to be located within the city center and don't mind going without some comforts. You can request a room with air-conditioning and a private bathroom.

Where to Eat

La Campaña de Toledo, Plaza de San Juan de Dios, is a moderately priced eatery housed in an attractive colonial house, with tables set outside on the cobbled courtyard overhung with vines. This is the most enjoyable and atmospheric place to dine in Camagüey. Spanish-style dishes are served, including the local dish, *ajiaco Camagüeyano*, a stew which has a little bit of everything, including corn. It is open from 9 AM to 5 PM.

The charming tavern **Parador de los Tres Reyes**, Plaza de San Juan de Dios, is a pleasant place to unwind and has a very local at-

mosphere. It is the best place to sample the local beer, Tínima, along with *chorizo* sausage.

How to Get There

Camagüey Ignacio Agramonte Airport lies 14 km (about nine miles) northeast of the city. There are direct charter flights from the United Kingdom and Canada. There are regular scheduled flights with Cubana de Aviación from Havana and Santiago de Cuba.

By train, Camagüey is a main stop on the daily Havana-Santiago railway service. The

Estación de Ferrocarriles is located at Calles Avellaneda and Finlay, opposite the Hotel Plaza.

PLAYA SANTA LUCÍA

On Camagüey's north coast, the beach resort of Playa Santa Lucía is a perfect place to spend a day or two recuperating if you are driving across Cuba. Over the past few years it has become popular destination for the pale hordes of tourists who arrive on sun-seeking packages during the winter months, most arriving by direct charter flights from Britain, Canada, Holland, Germany, Fin-

Bright colonial houses OPPOSITE in Camagüey, an area with a tough cowboy reputation ABOVE.

land, and Argentina at either Camagüey or Holguín, the nearest international airports. It has to be said that most visitors simply come for a beach vacation and barely get out to see much of the rest of Cuba from here.

From Camagüey, the 112-km (70-mile) journey takes a couple of hours and follows a road that heads northeast and winds through Wild West-style pasturelands and pan-flat fields rimmed with bulrushes, where cattle ranches are overseen by brawny-looking cowboys or *vaqueros*, who frequently trot along the road with horses or cows in

relaxing beach experience than, for example, Varadero or Cayo Coco: it is still not as developed, and has a much more Cuban atmosphere. Just three kilometers (nearly two miles) west of Playa Santa Lucía, you should not miss a visit to the characterful little village of **La Boca**, with its own beach and seaside restaurants run by friendly locals.

Playa Santa Lucía's main bay is protected by a coral reef close to the shore, and its enticing, clear blue and warm waters make it an excellent site for snorkeling and scuba diving, with more than 15 dive sites; the

tow, cigar at the mouth, with a tip of the hat to passer's by. You should by-pass the ugly industrial port of Nuevitas and head straight on to Santa Lucía, which now has five resort hotels which among them have all the usual resort facilities, including an international diving center and horseback excursions.

WHAT TO SEE AND DO

Although the little settlement of Santa Lucía looks like nothing more than a shabby shantytown, Playa Santa Lucía is an exceptionally pleasant beach, with soft white sands stretching for more than 20 km (12 miles), fringed by palm trees and shrubs. In many ways, Playa Santa Lucía offers a much more

surrounding reefs are home to more than 50 different coral species, including vivid bright orange sponges and black coral, as well as many species of mollusks, fish, gorgonians, and crustaceans. Divers report that nurse sharks and barracudas can often be seen, but they are not described as posing a serious threat. Schools of dolphins are also frequently seen, as are flying flamingoes, who settle in seasonal flocks alongside the lagoon behind Playa Santa Lucía.

As a staging area, Santa Lucía is increasingly being promoted as an access base to Cuba's northern Sabana archipelago, evidenced by numerous diving expeditions to outlying keys that can be arranged through the major resorts here.

Another diving excursion can include dives to shipwrecks within the Bahía de Nuevitas, including the steamship *Motera*, which sank in 1898, and lies just meters below the ocean surface; now embalmed with colorful coral, and home to turtles, fish and the odd shark.

Snorkeling and scuba-diving excursions — as well as specialized and beginners courses — are offered at both the Golden Tulip hotels and the Hotel Cuatro Vientos. These hotels also offer chartered sport-fishing trips — for *macabí* and *sábalo*.

Nearby, there are several beautiful beaches are to explore. **Playa Los Cocos**, at the mouth of the Nuevitas Bay, is a good swimming beach, with a broad strip of white sand protected from the ocean winds. It also has several simple, yet atmospheric, seaside restaurants.

Through your hotel in Playa Santa Lucía, you can also arrange a visit to **King Ranch**, a working ranch, where you can watch local *vaqueros* herding cattle, stage a rodeo show, and eat at a *campesino*-style restaurant. You can also rent horses and go riding. The ranch, which was owned by the Texan owners prior to the Revolution, lies just west of the entrance to Santa Lucía.

Separated from the mainland by a narrow inlet with shallow waters that can be reached from Playa Santa Lucía by excursion ferry, **Cayo Sabinal** has a 33-km (over 20-mile) stretch of lovely beaches, including aptly named **Playa Bonita**, and inlets which attract flocks of migratory flamingos. Casual beachside restaurants, camping grounds and diving huts have been set up to make an excursion to Cayo Sabinal more tourist-friendly. In fact, the Cuban government plan to do more than that: a recent study on the tourism potential of Cayo Sabinal estimated that the area has a tourism capacity for 12,000 hotel rooms. Developers have been placing their bids.

Where to Stay

Moderate to Expensive

Located directly on one of the nicest stretches of the beach, **Golden Tulip Club Caracol****** ((53-32) 3-6302, 3-6303, or 3-6428 FAX (53-32) 36-5153, Playa Santa Lucía, is made up of a cluster of small buildings. Rooms are quite luxurious, with the usual amenities for this range of accommodation, including a small living room area, a mini bar, and a beach view. Good facilities for children include an activities program. There is a large swimming pool, a cabaret with dance area, a water sports and diving center, car rental, horseback tours, shops and a hair-dresser.

Golden Tulip Club Coral*** ((53-32) 3-6265 FAX (53-32) 36-5153, Playa Santa Lucía, is the larger of the two resorts. This hotel complex also caters mainly to package tourists, and of the two, this is more orientated towards younger clients, rather than young children. It has the same facilities as its neighbor, but also has a discotheque and a beachside restaurant and bar. Every morning, a catamaran departs to cruise out to a nearby coral reef, allowing scuba divers and snorkelers to explore, and then to have an Italian pasta and lobster lunch on board.

Moderate

Hotel Cuatro Vientos**** ((53-32) 3-6317 FAX (53-32) 36-5142, Playa Santa Lucía, was recently renovated and is another possibility along the same beachfront strip. Compared to the two hotels recommended above, this hotel does not offer the same high standard.

Inexpensive

Although **Club Amigo Mayanabo***** ((53-32) 3-6184 or 3-6369 FAX (53-32) 36-5176, Playa Santa Lucía, is not in the same league as the two Golden Tulip hotels, it is another all-inclusive resort, with the rate including all buffet meals, drinks and non-motorized water sports.

How to Get There

Almost all visitors to Playa Santa Lucía arrive on package tours, and therefore are ferried here on resort shuttle buses from Camagüey, 112 km (70 miles) away. There is one daily bus service between Camagüey and Santa Lucía.

Resident of the Bahía de Naranjo, Holguín.

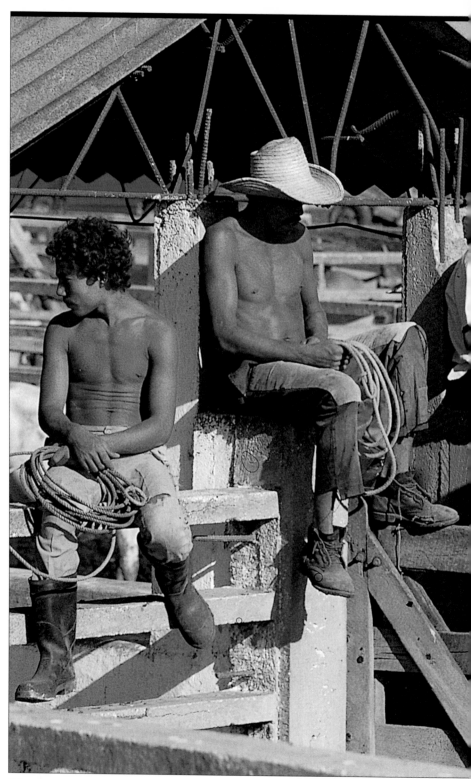

Eastern
Cuba

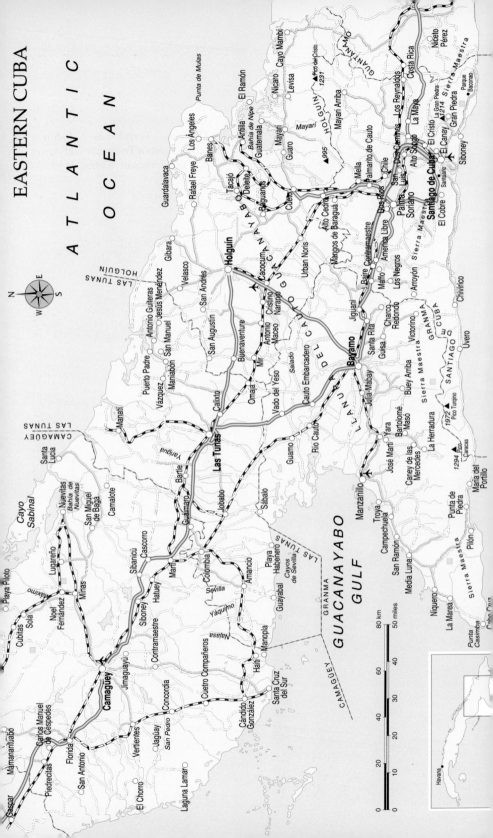

HOLGUÍN

NOT AN ATTRACTION IN ITSELF, the provincial capital of Holguín is an inevitable stop on the main highway from Las Tunas on the way to Bayamo. It is also a transit point for the many tourists who fly into its international airport to reach the nearby beach resort of Guardalavaca. Few foreign visitors linger long here: yet as the country's fourth-largest city, Holguín is a good place to stop to explore for an hour or two, simply

GENERAL INFORMATION

Generally speaking, you are best advised to go directly to the Hotel Pernik's information desk if you need directing for any practical needs. The Hotel Pernik has a doctor's office, and it also has a **Transautos** office for car rental. The **Havanautos** office is located in Motel El Bosque. The **Servi Cupet-Cimex** station is located three kilometers (nearly two miles) outside town, on the Carretera Central en route to Las Tunas.

to appreciate the street life and the reality of existence for many Cubans, away from places tourists would usually visit. It's not recommended as a place to stay overnight, unless you are recuperating from an international flight into Holguín's airport.

During the late colonial period many Spanish and Creole ranch owners settled here, and the city has its own brand of reserve and conservatism. Cubans regard Holguín as having a rich cultural and intellectual life: since the revolution, the province of Holguín has benefited from the creation of research institutes, universities and the modernization of its sugar industry.

WHAT TO SEE AND DO

The best place to start is **Plaza Calixto García**, a desultory colonial park encircled by colonnaded houses, named for Holguín's most celebrated denizen, General Calixto García, a formidable rebel commander during the Second War of Independence. In dusty patches of sunlight, sitting in chairs and drinking *cafecito*, you'll see the proprietors of various small shops and of the local museum and art gallery (Casa de la Trova) debating the latest gossip. Tradition has it

PREVIOUS PAGES: Resting *vaqueros* or cowboys LEFT and a *guajiro*, or traditional Cuban farmer RIGHT. ABOVE: Green pastures line the roads in Holguín Province.

that for generations, amorous assignations and marriages were inspired around this small green square, during a weekly ritual in which the whole town would stroll here at dusk, men promenading in one direction, women in the other.

Facing the park, on Calle Frexes, the **Museo Provincial de Historia** was built in 1868, first used as a grand house and venue for elaborate parties and later as the seat of the municipal government. It has been called *La Periquera* ("the Parrot Cage") ever since the first War of Independence, when

rebel forces, known as *mambisas*, besieged the Spanish infantry here, whose flamboyant uniforms could be glimpsed behind the building's barred windows. "Come out of your cage, you parrots," the *mambisas* are said to have jeered. The museum is worth visiting for its archeological and historical exhibits as well as its section on Santería, the Afro-Cuban religion, which displays a mock shrine. Open Monday to Saturday, noon to 7 PM, closed on Sunday.

On nearby Calle Maceo, just south of the park, is the **Carlos de la Torre Museo de Historia Natural** (Natural History Museum), which has Cuba's most outstanding collection of brilliantly colored *polymita* snail shells, which are endemic to the coasts of Eastern Cuba. There is also a display of stuffed birds and mammals; sponges, conches and shells. It is open Tuesday to Saturday from 8 AM to 6 PM, Sunday from 8 AM to noon, and is closed on Monday.

As you walk along Calle Maceo to the Parque de San Isidoro, you will see the **Iglesia de San Isidoro**, built in 1720 and dedi-

cated to the city's patron saint. Inside, the altar was transported here on foot by slaves from Bayamo, after the church there was burned to the ground. Outside, in the square stands a statue of Karl Marx.

Elsewhere, life revolves around the **Plaza de la Revolución**, in which stands a bronze statue and an imposing mausoleum containing the remains of General Calixto García. The general's birthplace, now a museum devoted to his life and times, is located nearby at the intersection of Calle Frexes and Calle Miró.

On the northern outskirts of Holguín, a fairly strenuous climb up 450 steps leads to the lookout at **Loma de la Cruz** (Hill of the Cross), with a cross that was placed here in 1790, and a bird's eye view across the city below. Every May 3, the Day of the Cross is celebrated by a pilgrimage here.

Another scenic view is from the **Altura de Mayabe** (Mayabe Heights), eight kilometers (five miles) southeast from the city. A tourist complex, the **Mirador de Mayabe**, which features restaurants, bars, shops and a small motel, marks the lookout point, from which you can look across at the beautiful Mayabe Valley, with its clusters of palm trees, sugarcane plantations and *bohíos* (the traditional wooden houses of the Cuban countryside). The star attraction here is **La Taberno Pancho**, home for many years to a donkey called Pancho, famed for his beer-drinking exploits, who is now on display, stuffed.

WHERE TO STAY AND EAT

Inexpensive to Moderate
Hotel Horizontes Pernik*** ((53-24) 48-1011 or 48-1667 FAX (53-24) 48-1371, Avenida Jorge Dimitrov and Avenida XX Aniversario, Holguín, is named after the birthplace of the Bulgarian national hero, Geogry Dimitrov, whose country was partly responsible for its construction. This hotel exudes classic Soviet-era style, with a huge mausoleum-like lobby, poorly maintained facilities, and a cafeteria dining hall. Despite these surly appointments it offers the city's best option for a comfortable stay. Be careful using the elevators, which are known to break down regularly.

Inexpensive

Cubanacán El Cocal** ((53-24) 46-1924, Carretera Central, is located seven and a half kilometers (just over four and a half miles) from Holguín. Set amongst lush tropical vegetation, this is the best option for an overnight stay outside the city, with simple, two-story bungalow buildings arranged around a swimming pool. It is conveniently located near the airport.

Motel El Bosque** ((53-24) 48-1012, Avenida XX Aniversario near the Hotel Pernik, is much less impressive but has modest, budget accommodation, and also has a popular nightclub, El Pétalo. However, the noise and lack of value for money may make you wish you had chosen the Hotel Pernik instead.

As for eating in Holguín, all roads in this respect tend to lead to the Hotel Pernik, which is not hugely exciting. Otherwise, the most enjoyable place to eat is the Mirador de Mayabe, where a limited but reliable repertoire of simple Cuban dishes are served under a thatched roof.

How to Get There

Holguín's new **Frank País International Airport** terminal lies 13 km (eight miles) south of the city center. Regular direct charter flights arrive here from Germany, the Netherlands, and Canada (see GETTING THERE, page 298 in TRAVELERS' TIPS). Cubana de Aviación has daily scheduled flights from Havana.

Holguín is a main stop on the railway network, and is connected daily by train services from Havana and Santiago de Cuba. The Estación de Ferrocarriles is located to the south of the city center, on Calle V Pilar.

EN ROUTE TO GUARDALAVACA

For many arriving in Holguín, the real goal of their journey is **Guardalavaca**, 50 km (31 miles) away on the northeast coast.

GIBARA

If you are driving, it is well worth including a detour to the small port and fishing town of **Gibara**, 32 km (20 miles) directly

north of the provincial capital. Both routes meander through cultivated fields and small towns, and especially in the case of the latter, some dirt track roads lined with cacti fences.

Gibara remains almost completely unvisited, and is an unspoiled haven of crumbling colonial shipwrecks of houses, narrow cobbled lanes, sleepy fishermen's bars, and barnacle-encrusted fishing boats. A certain has-been grandeur seems part of its salty air: Gibara's claim to fame is that it was the crucible of many sea-borne for-

tunes when it served as a key port along Cuba's eastern coast during the nineteenth century. It is also the birthplace of the prolific, exiled novelist and essayist Guillermo Cabrera Infante.

While you are in Gibara, wander along the waterfront which is bounded by the small **San Fernando Fort**, built in 1817, and find the main square, **Plaza de la Iglesia**, named for the nearby Church of San Fulgencio. Also visit the **Museo de Arte Colonial**, on Calle Independencia, the town's main street, which has all the classic decorative features of a nineteenth-century colonial home as well

OPPOSITE: Horse-drawn carts transport tourists in Guardalavaca. ABOVE: A child dwarfed by the sugar cane in Holguín Province.

as Art Deco embellishments, including distinctive fan-shaped stained-glass windows. It is open Tuesday to Saturday from 8 AM to noon and 1 PM to 5 PM; Sunday 8 AM to noon.

For lunch, try **El Faro** restaurant on the waterfront, which offers a variety of seafood dishes, including lobster, at reasonable prices.

CAYO BARIAY

Whether or not you make the detour to see Gibara, you can include another stop as you

suitable for a rough ride along the unpaved road, which dips in and out of small streams in places.

Located at the narrow tip of Cayo Bariay, on a forested beach scattered with coral rock, the monument — built in 1992 to coincide with the 500th anniversary of Columbus's discovery of America — is strikingly eccentric, with its row of truncated neoclassical-style columns and ochre-colored sculptures resembling indigenous Indian gods and amulets. Although there are plans to embellish the site, to build a café and improve

drive en route to Guardalavaca: the place where Christopher Columbus first sighted and then set foot on Cuban soil, after he sailed into **Cayo Bariay** on October 28, 1492. Although historians have argued about where exactly the explorer landed, his diary entries unmistakably describe the Silla de Gibara (Saddle of Gibara), a giant mountain outcrop that does indeed resemble a saddle that dominates the horizon.

The turnoff to visit the **Landing Place Monument** starts from Rafael Freyre, a town known for its hulking, antediluvian sugar mill fed by the bushels of sugarcane ferried from surrounding fields by steam locomotives. Although it's barely a twenty minute drive away, be sure your vehicle is

the roads, few visitors actually come here and the friendly local guide (who seems to stride up from nowhere) is delighted to have an audience. A small pathway leads to a series of rock pools by the shore, almost entirely comprised of ancient brain coral fossils. Historians have also speculated that Columbus may have visited an Indian village across the bay at nearby Punta de los Gatos.

More interesting than visiting the monument itself, is seeing the Cuban families, *guajiros* (rural workers) and small children of this area going about their lives: sitting on rocking chairs in front of their wooden *bohíos*, listening to transistor radios, or mending fishing nets, loading vegetables on makeshift trucks, with an entourage of farm pigs, dogs, horses and chickens. Any hint of a genuine wave or smile from strangers, and they reciprocate with friendliness.

Near Cayo Bariay, **Playa Don Lino**, where a modest hotel complex sits on a small, white-sanded beach, has long been a favored destination for government officials. It's not recommended as a place to stay.

However, several beach resorts along this coast located on the **Bahía de Naranjo**, within the **Parque Natural Bahía de Naranjo** — as well as on the outlying island of **Cayo Saetía** — offer an enticing alternative to staying on the main beach of Guardalavaca.

Back on the main road, you will soon reach Guardalavaca.

GUARDALAVACA

Following close on the heels of Varadero, Guardalavaca is a popular and ever-growing beach resort. As beaches go, these are pretty enough, with soft blond sands fringed with plentiful palm trees to loll under. Although you may hear that this is one of the loveliest beaches in Cuba, it is in fact merely very pleasant, its azure waters still clear despite creeping seaweed, and its warm, swimmable shallows are suitable for keeping an eye on small children.

In fact, the most beautiful beaches along this coast — much more deserving of such a claim — are found close by, especially Playa Esmeralda in the Bahía de Naranjo, which has superb landscapes lined with coconut palms and the best hotels.

It has to be said that the scale of hotel development in Guardalavaca seems somewhat out of proportion with the size of the beach, given the fact that there are few other attractions in the vicinity. Still, for many of the foreign tourists who visit Guardalavaca on package tours from Canada and Germany, it is luxury enough being away from cold winters at home. Not surprisingly, with all this focus on tourism development, the resorts here are designed to be as self-contained as possible. Few tourists venture beyond the beach once they have disembarked from Holguín airport, and consequently see little, if anything, of the rest of the country, just the way Fidel likes it.

Rather than a destination in itself, Guardalavaca is a good place to recuperate if you are on a driving expedition around the country.

GENERAL INFORMATION

In Guardalavaca, hotels cater to most practical needs. For medical assistance contact the resort town's 24-hour **Clínica Internacional** ((53-24) 03-0291.

There is a **Banco Nacional de Cuba** opposite the Hotel Guardalavaca and a **Banco Financiero Internacional** in the resort's only **Centro Commercial**.

There are car and moped rental offices at the Delta Las Brisas Club Resort, Hotel Guardalavaca and Hotel Atlántico. There is a **Servi Cupet-Cimex** station between Hotel Cubanacán Turey and Hotel Sol Río de Mares.

WHAT TO SEE AND DO

Guardalavaca's main beach is a fairly relaxed scene, with vendors selling coconuts, cold drinks and snacks. Further afield, you can also explore the beaches and coves around **Playa Estero Ciego** in Bahía de Naranjo several kilometers southwest. The best way to explore these beaches and coves is by rented car, moped, or bicycle.

Aside from swimming, there are plenty of opportunities for diving and snorkeling around offshore reefs and outlying coral keys, especially around the Bahía de Naranjo. The waters in this marine reserve are renowned for spectacular diving, as well as the many large and colorful sponges and deepwater gorgonians. Swordfish and barracuda are commonly seen off a sharp cliff drop well known to diving guides here.

Most hotels can arrange diving trips or will send you to Guardalavaca's **Marlin Watersport Base**, which offers certification courses.

You can also contact the **Marina Naranjo**, four kilometers (two and a half miles) southwest of the Sol Río de Luna and Sol Río de Mares resorts, which organizes diving and fishing charters.

Volleyball on the beach in Guardalavaca.

You can also visit the tucked-away beauty haven of **Cayo Saetía**, reached by helicopter.

WHERE TO STAY

As you will have discovered, it is a challenge to find inexpensive accommodation in any of Cuba's tourist destinations. Guardalavaca is no exception. It is worth checking in advance for any low season discounts. In the Bahía de Naranjo, **Playa Estero Ciego** (also known as Playa Esmeralda) is rapidly becoming a small beach resort in its own right, and is located close enough to Guardalavaca to be included in this section.

Expensive

With rooms overlooking the sea, the all-inclusive **Delta Las Brisas Club Resort****** ((53-24) 3-0218 FAX (53-24) 3-0018 or 3-0755, Playa Guardalavaca, Banes, offers a higher level of comfort and better buffet meals and is better value for money than you will find elsewhere on the beach. It also has one of the nicer stretches of sand. Otherwise it has all the standardized features that any veteran of these types of resorts will expect, including orchestrated entertainment programs, diving excursions, water sports, tennis court and volleyball games in the free-form swimming pools. There is also a massage center. Parents may appreciate the children's activity programs, and there is a good variety of bars and restaurants. The hotel's travel desk can arrange excursions and bicycle and car rental.

Serious divers will appreciate the well-equipped international diving center at the modern resort **Sol Club Rio de Luna****** ((53-24) 03-0030 to 03-0034 FAX (53-24) 03-0035, Playa Estero Ciego, Carretera Guardalavaca, Rafael Freyre, Banes, which also offers PADI-licensed courses for beginners. Run by the Gaviota group, this all-inclusive resort has a range of restaurants, bars and sports activities, a sauna, and two swimming pools, one for children. Many of its rooms face the beach and the suites have jacuzzis. Bicycle, moped and car rental is available.

Slightly larger than its sister resort, the **Sol Rio de Mares****** ((53-24) 33-7013 FAX (53-24) 33-7162, Playa Estero Ciego,

Carretera Guardalavaca, Rafael Freyre, Banes, is pleasantly landscaped overlooking the bay, and also offers luxury suites with Jacuzzis, as well as two handicap-adapted suites, in addition to its standard rooms. It is not an all-inclusive resort, but otherwise has an identical array of facilities and services (excepting the international diving center) as the above resort.

Only five *cabañas* — each with air-conditioning, satellite television and a refrigerator — and one suite comprise the hideaway resort **Villa Cayo Saetía****** ((53-24) 2-5350 or 33-5571, Cayo Saetía, Mayarí, located on this idyllic small bay, which is reached by helicopter. Meals are served on your balcony or at the resort's small restaurant. Perfect for a peaceful retreat and exploring the island's wilderness.

Moderate

The recently renovated **Cubanacán Turey****** ((53-24) 03-0195 or 03-0293 FAX (53-24) 03-0265, Playa Guardalavaca, Banes, is made up of low-slung, two-story wine and vanilla painted villas which are linked by landscaped pathways, one of which meanders to the nearby beach. It has a low-key relaxed atmosphere, and its array of facilities include a swimming pool. It is a little smaller than the other hotels which are geared for large groups of package tourists.

Cubanacán Atlántico** ((53-24) 03-0180 or 03-0181, Playa Guardalavaca, Banes, is large and modern with comfortable facilities. This hotel's main advantage is its large pool with a swim-up bar and a restaurant which serves reasonable Italian dishes and seafood. Ask for a room with a sea-facing view. It is quite close to the beach and can arrange car, bicycle and moped rental. Activities include horseback riding, water skiing, windsurfing, diving and fishing.

More than its neighbors, **Cubanacán Guardalavaca**** ((53-24) 03-0121 or 03-0145 FAX (53-24) 03-0221, Playa Guardalavaca, Banes, feels especially tailored for large groups, with its cafeteria-style dining hall rather unromantic to say the least. Its rooms are comfortable, with bath and air-conditioning, grouped in rows of bungalows around the swimming pool. It is located a short distance from the beach.

WHERE TO EAT

El Ancla sits on an outcrop at the western end of the beach overlooking the sea and is undoubtedly the most pleasant of Guardalavaca's restaurants, especially as the sun sets. It has a varied seafood menu, including lobster dishes and is a good place to linger for cocktails.

Two other restaurants on the beach, **El Patio** and **El Cayuelo**, are also within easy strolling distance of all the Guardalavaca hotels, and offer simple, local cuisine.

NIGHTLIFE

Disco music is pumped out with strobes on the sands at the beach nightclub of **La Rocha**, which is a magnet for local Cubans, while at Delta Las Brisas Hotel, **La Piazza** is more of an up-market, yet predictable nightspot.

HOW TO GET THERE

The only way to get to Guardalavaca is by road. You can take your chances on the bus service from Holguín. In theory, this bus service connects with the arrival of the daily train from Havana, departing from the station. A taxi from Holguín will cost about US$40 each way.

Relaxing at Playa Esmeralda, on the Bahía de Naranjo, one of Cuba's loveliest coastlines.

EXCURSIONS FROM GUARDALAVACA

Each of the following three suggestions are day trips. Aside from the visit to Cayo Saetía, which needs to be booked in advance, these excursions are within convenient driving distance.

You can also contact **Fantástico Tours**, which operates a tour desk in the Delta Las Brisas, and offers a range of local excursions, including helicopter tours to Cayo Saetía and a "seafari" within the Parque Natural Bahía de Naranjo, as well as further afield to Cayo Coco, Trinidad, Santiago de Cuba and Havana.

CAYO SAETÍA

It is easy to arrange a helicopter day trip from Guardalavaca to the "island" of **Cayo Saetía**, which has some of the most beautiful beaches in this region of Cuba. Until recently, this pristine cay (which lies at the end of a narrow causeway off the easternmost side of the entrance to the Bay of Nipe), was off-limits to visitors because it was a favorite retreat for top officials, including Fidel.

Exotic animals such as zebras, antelope and ostriches were imported to breed and to become targets within this hunting preserve, which in Cuban doublespeak is also referred to within the same breath as a "wildlife reserve."

You can visit for the day and explore by jeep safari or horseback, and swim from the cay's perfect white sand beaches.

You may be interested to know that the helicopter service is run by Gaviota, the tourism company ultimately administered by the Cuban military. Ask at your hotel or at either of the Gaviota-run hotels at Playa Estero Ciego for booking arrangements.

BAHÍA DE NARANJO

This large, protected bay is one of Cuba's loveliest areas of coastline, with a magnificent landscape of sweeping coconut palms circling a pristine bay. It also lies within the **Parque Natural Bahía de Naranjo**, one of the island's important marine reserves,

most notable for its main beach, **Playa Esmeralda** (also known as Playa Estero Ciego). Even if you are not staying here, it is worth visiting, and is just four kilometers (two and a half miles) away from Guardalavaca. Its soft, scrunchy white sand makes it one of the best swimming beaches in the area.

Also within the Bahía de Naranjo area is a recently created Gaviota-run **marine complex** which includes a **dolphin aquarium**, sail and motor boats for sea tours and a seafood restaurant. Call ((53-24) 03-0132 for the aquarium schedule. The site of the aquarium is superb, reached by boat, and the dolphin and sea lion shows are fantastic: a must see.

THE CHORRO DE MAITA ARCHAEOLOGICAL SITE

Two of the country's best archaeological museums are located close by. Just five kilometers (three miles) south of Guardalavaca, a turnoff on the road to Banes leads to one of Cuba's most important archaeological sites, the **Chorro de Maita Site Museum**, a Taíno Indian burial ground thought to have been used between 1490 and 1540. Some 108 skeletons have been discovered here, making this the largest aboriginal burial site in the Antilles. Part of the site has been turned into a museum, with more than 50 skeletons visible in the exact position they were found. Glass cases display offerings that were left alongside the dead; mostly shell and bone objects and ornaments. Anthropologists have speculated that one of the female skeletons, numbered "57," belonged to a young woman of high rank, since a rare gold idol, as well as copper ornaments, were found draped on her remains. Also, equally interesting, is the presence of a Caucasian skeleton, presumed to be a Spaniard, who appears to have lived with the Taíno community. Most of the Taíno dead were buried in the fetal position, yet some were found arranged horizontally, with arms crossed over the chest in the Christian manner, suggesting further evidence of contact with Europeans. It is open Tuesday to Saturday from 9 AM to 5 PM, Sunday from 9 AM to 1 PM and is closed on Monday. Across the road, a replica village has been built with displays on the lifestyles and times of the Taíno Indians.

BANES

Continue along the same road for another 30 km (just over 18 miles) if you are interested in going to the small, unassuming town of **Banes**, once the site of a large Taíno Indian settlement and worth visiting for its compelling archeological museum.

Banes is also something of a quirk of history, for in more recent times, it was found-

used by the Taíno Indians to induce vomiting before taking hallucinogenic potions. The museum is open Tuesday to Saturday, noon to 6 PM, and Sunday, 2 PM to 6 PM; it is closed on Monday.

FROM GUARDALAVACA TO MAYARÍ

If you are planning to venture further into the countryside, perhaps stay overnight in the mountains, then do make time to visit the beautiful hill station of **Mayarí**, which

ed in 1887 by North American planters and became the headquarters for the United Fruit Company, a United States conglomerate, with its "Barrio Americano" (modeled on a North American town complete with golf course and country club) for its expatriate executives.

Located off the main square of Plaza Martí, on Calle General Marrero, the **Museo Indocubano** offers a fascinating collection of ceramics, utensils, jewelry and other objects unearthed in this region, some dating back more than 5,000 years. One of the prized exhibits is a distinctively Mesoamerican gold figurine of a woman with a feather headdress holding a bowl. It is easy to miss the innocuous-looking *espátulas vómicas*, which were

is a two-hour drive east from Guardalavaca and a good base for walking excursions. From Mayarí, it's impossible to continue without a four-wheel drive vehicle with which to head up into the **Sierra del Cristal mountains** along bumpy, unpaved roads. The tranquil views, scents and wilderness of these mountains are worth the effort.

As you ascend these mountain roads, you'll notice the distinctive color of the soil, which changes from light brown to a soft red to a dark, densely iron-rich rust red — referred to by locals as *mocarrero*. Plantations of pine trees and coffee are grown up here — the coffee that grows in this rich soil is

Cold drinks for sale on the beach.

famous in Cuba for its taste. Famous also are the varieties of orchids that grow here along mossed slopes and out of rock clefts.

Visit the Scientific Station at regional national park, **Jardín de Pinare**. The park has set out trails, one of which leads you through 12 different ecosystems, from cacti shrubland to clearings amassed with small waterfalls, flowers and coffee plantations. Look out especially for the *cupey* plant, whose thick, waxy leaves were used by revolutionaries as paper to send messages during the War of Independence against the Spanish.

WHERE TO STAY AND EAT

Set against a breathtaking landscape, the mountaintop **Hotel Pinares de Mayarí**** ((53-24) 05-3157 or 05-2131, Mensura, Pinares de Mayarí, Mayarí, is built in the rustic style of traditional Cuban houses, with rough-cut timber and natural stone walls. There are 25 rooms and nine larger cabins. A restaurant, bar and a swimming pool are part of the complex.

GRANMA PROVINCE

Named for the famous leaky yacht that carried Fidel and his 81 fellow revolutionaries safely ashore in this region on December 2, 1956, Granma (literally, "Grandma") is in many ways the quintessential Oriente Province. Drama permeates both its history and its landscape. Over the past two centuries some of the most decisive moments in Cuban history have been played out here, against the cinematic backdrop of giant camel-toned Sierra Maestra mountains hinged against an unruly, boulder-strewn coastline and a sparkling, marine-blue Caribbean sea. Its people seem carved from the same rough-hewn mold and they pride themselves on their tough self-reliance in this blisteringly difficult environment. Rain is a rarity in this southwestern region, which is the country's hottest and driest.

There's a reason many Cubans jokingly refer to this part of the country as "The Wild West," for a discernable frontier spirit remains intact. If you make the effort to travel through this sparsely populated, poor and fiercely traditional region, you can pride yourself that you are seeing one of the few authentically unspoiled parts of the country.

To appreciate the best the province has to offer, you should spend a few hours in Bayamo, and then head along the southwest coast to stay at the beach resort of **Marea del Portillo**, perhaps making sorties to explore the magnificent **Gran Parque Nacional Sierra Maestra**; and enjoy the drive through sugarcane country and small coastal towns in this easy day's drive.

BAYAMO

Capital of Granma Province, Bayamo makes an interesting place to stop for hour or two, before pressing on to explore the rest of the province. If you do want to stay overnight, it has reasonable facilities for visitors.

BACKGROUND

In 1513, San Salvador, as it was first named, was the second colonial township (known as a *villa*) to be founded by the expeditionary Diego Velázquez on behalf of the Spanish crown. The original site beside the Yara River was moved inland soon afterwards to its present location, and was called San Salvador de Bayamo, a name that was eventually shortened. As soon as the local church and the town council were installed, this was the town from which Velázquez set forth to capture and colonize the rest of Cuba.

Snuggled against broad flatlands on the banks of the Cauto River, the longest in Cuba, and protected from pirates due to its inland location, Bayamo was well placed to become a key trading center. It followed that when the Spanish Crown imposed heavy new restrictions on commercial traffic, Bayamo prospered as an active smuggling depot for French and Dutch contraband, with manufactured goods and fabrics from Europe being exchanged for meat, leather, indigo, sugar and coffee.

Although Bayamo is one of the earliest colonial towns, there is little evidence of that fact in the colonial architecture you will see here. During the first War of Independence in 1869, the townspeople of Bayamo deliberately started a fire to destroy their city, so that the Spanish troops who were massed to take it over would have nothing to seize except a smoldering ruin. In effect, Bayamo was the epicenter of the independence movement, and it was the provisional capital of the new republic before it was razed to the ground. One of the most famous figures in the town's history was Carlos de Manual Céspedes, so-called "Father of the Nation," whose call for independence and abolition of slavery from *La Demajagua*, his sugar mill near Manzanillo, set the revolt in motion.

everyday transportation, and you'll see everyone using them, from schoolchildren to police officers.

The place to begin your short walking tour is the **Plaza de la Revolución**, around which, as with all Cuban towns, life revolves. This square is a little different, however. Not only was it the first square in the country to be given this title, it commemorates the uprising against Spain that began in 1868, rather than Fidel's Revolution in 1959. At the square's center stand statues of Bayamo's two most famous figures:

GENERAL INFORMATION

Many of the facilities for visitors, such as the **Servi Cupet-Cimex** station, the **Hotel Sierra Maestra** and the **bus station**, are located on the Carretera Central, southeast of the town center. The **Banco Nacional de Cuba** is at Calles Saco and General García.

WHAT TO SEE AND DO

One of the first things you will notice about Bayamo are all the horse-drawn carriages in use, many of them looking little changed since the nineteenth century. Bayamo is one of the Cuba's few cities, like Cárdenas and Remedios, which retain these carriages for

first, Carlos Manuel de Céspedes, and second, Perucho Figueredo, the author of Cuba's national anthem. It was on this square, in the former town hall, that Céspedes signed the decree abolishing slavery.

One of the few structures that survived the fire was **Céspedes's birthplace**, also on the square. This two-storied mansion has been turned into a museum, and each of its 12 rooms contain displays of memorabilia relating to his life as well as the history of Bayamo and the struggle for independence. You can also see his printing press and copies of his *Cubano Libre* ("Free Cuban"), the first independent newspaper

Cuba's beaches are well-equipped for water sports.

to circulate in Cuba after the capture of Bayamo. It is open Tuesday to Saturday from noon to 7 PM, Sunday from 9 AM to 1 PM, and closed on Monday. Admission is free.

After you emerge from Céspedes's house, to your right is the **Museo Provincial de Granma**, which has all sorts of relics and displays relating to the history, geography and natural sciences of the province. There are mangled remains from the fire of 1869 and the original copy of the national anthem. The simple colonial building in which it is

pendence fighters. Tradition has it that the author was so overcome by the moment that he jotted the words down on the nearest thing that came to hand — on the back of his saddle. On one corner of the square, at No. 36, is the **Casa de la Nacionalidad**, a colonial building which houses a historical research center.

As you leave Bayamo's old quarter, try to at least drive by **Plaza de Patria**, the city's huge gathering place for political rallies and meetings, where a large sculpture honors the nation's revolutionary heroes.

housed was the home of Manual Muñoz, who composed the tune for the national anthem as well as Bayamo's much-loved song, *La Bayamesa*.

If you continue along the same street, you come to the **Iglesia de San Salvador**, Bayamo's main church. Although it was first built in 1613, virtually nothing remains of the original except the baroque Dolores chapel, which dates from 1740 and survived the 1869 fire. Adjacent to the church is **Plaza del Himno** (Anthem Square). This is apparently where Perucho Figueredo was inspired to write the lyrics for the national anthem as he watched a triumphant Céspedes ride into Bayamo on October 20, 1868, having just claimed the city for the inde-

WHERE TO STAY AND EAT

For inexpensive accommodations, try **Villa Bayamo**** ☎ (53-23) 42-3102 or 42-3124, Carretera via Manzanillo and Mabay Road, Bayamo. Although located at a distance from the city, this small spread-out complex is a more comfortable place to stay overnight than the Hotel Sierra Maestra. With a restaurant (specializing in roast pork and chicken), a bar area, and a swimming pool, this is not too bad.

Hotel Sierra Maestra** ☎ (53-23) 48-1013, Carretera Central, is a dismal hulk of a hotel that quite likely has seen better days. Despite the fact that it has a restaurant, bar, swimming pool, shop, tourist office and nightclub, none of these are very inspiring.

In the Plaza del Himno, there are two places to rest and have lunch. Try **Bodega de Atocha**, (next to the Casa de la Nacionalidad) which has a friendly atmosphere, simple meals and the chance to try the local wine. If you just want a light snack, coffee or fruit juice, try **La Casona**, located nearby.

NIGHTLIFE

Head for the Plaza de la Revolución, where you can see what is playing at the **Casa de la Trova**, **Café de Cantante** or **Las Ruinas**, where you can sit and dance among the ruins of a colonial house.

HOW TO GET THERE

By air, Bayamo is linked by Cubana de Aviación with Havana three times weekly. Bayamo's **Carlos Manuel de Céspedes Airport** is located four kilometers (two and a half miles) north of town on the road to Holguín.

By rail, there are daily train services to Bayamo from Havana, Camagüey and Santiago de Cuba. The **Estación de Ferrocarriles** is at Calles Saco and Línea, one kilometer (slightly over half a mile) east of town.

FROM BAYAMO TO MAREA DEL PORTILLO

As you'll see from your map, there are two roads leading to Marea del Portillo, both of which branch from Yara.

The recommended main route road passes through sugarcane plantations, historic small towns and beautiful coastal scenery, with some worthwhile stops and sights along the way. From Bayamo, the first main town you'll encounter is **Yara**, 33 km (slightly over 20 miles) away. This was where Velázquez originally founded San Salvador. Yara is also famous in Cuban history books as the place where the Indian chief Hatuey began his uprising against the Spanish in 1512, and where, legend has it, he was burned at the stake rather than convert.

THE GRAN PARQUE NACIONAL SIERRA MAESTRA

It's not a good idea to take the more direct route which cuts across the Sierra Maestra mountains, despite the fact that it is marked on the map as a paved main road, unless you have Indiana Jones-style nerves and a four-wheel drive jeep. However, if you have come prepared, this is the route to take to explore the Gran Parque Nacional Sierra Maestra, the largest protected reserve in Cuba.

In 1956, returning from a one-year exile in Mexico, Fidel Castro, his brother Raúl, and the young asthmatic Argentinean doctor Che Guevara, along with 79 other men, were shipwrecked along the coast of this province, and battled their way up into these seemingly impenetrable peaks. Only about 15 men, (including Fidel, Raúl and Che) survived the journey. Traditionally one of the country's most isolated regions, the Sierra Maestra became a battlefield between 1956 to 1959, during which Castro's guerilla campaign gained control of the ever-expanding area they called "Free Territory."

OPPOSITE: Freshly harvested coffee beans: the *cafecito* is an important Cuban institution.
ABOVE: Banana farm worker in Bayamo.

The park is scattered with rebel bases, including Castro's own headquarters, which has been preserved and can be visited.

From Yara, a steep road runs south to the park's entrance 32 km (about 20 miles) away. Your first stop should be at **Santo Domingo** (reached via Bartolomé Masó), which was a key rebel camp during Castro's guerilla campaign in the late 1950s. Located in the heart of the park, it is now a tourist complex, with cabins for an overnight stay. From here, you can contemplate the site's history, swim in a nearby river, or take walking or horseback trails through the mountains.

Or you can hike up **Pico Turquino**, which at 1,973 m (6,470 ft) is Cuba's highest peak. Located in the Parque Nacional Pico Turquino, this trail is a full day's hike, and it can be very steep in parts. While you are still climbing the mountain's lower, shrub-covered pastures, you are likely to pass herds of goats, bells tinkling, and even see wild horses grazing at a distance. As you climb higher up the mountain flanks, the forest paths lead through ever-denser enclosures of mahogany and cedar trees, and if you are lucky, you may see a wide variety of butterflies, insects, birds and some wildlife. When you reach the summit, the rewards are tremendous views in all directions, across the surrounding mountains and over the Caribbean.

Where to Stay and Eat
Horizontes Villa Santo Domingo ((53-23) 59-5180, Bartolomé Masó, Santo Domingo, offers inexpensive accommodation. This is the base camp for hiking to the Pico Turquino summit and La Plata command post. There are 20 cabins with bath and air-conditioning. There is a simple restaurant and bar.

MANZANILLO

The port city of **Manzanillo**, 56 km (nearly 35 miles) from Bayamo, is the second-largest city in the province, but despite the certain dilapidated elegance of some its colonial buildings, it has little to delay the stranger. Its people, however, make this a very friendly and charming place. The city is also credited with being the birthplace of

son, Cuba's famous traditional musical style, and its orchestra, La Orquesta Original de Manzanillo, is known throughout Cuba as one of its best exponents.

As for places to stop by, try the Moorish-influenced gazebo, known locally as **La Glorieta**, in **Parque Céspedes**, the main square. Parque Masó, with its promenade along the sea, is the best place to watch the sunset across the Gulf of Guacanayabo.

You should to see the **Celia Sánchez Memorial**, located seven blocks southwest of Parque Céspedes. Born in nearby Media

Luna, this intriguing, courageous woman was one of the legendary figures of the Revolution. She was Fidel Castro's assistant in the Sierra Maestra and later in Havana, and was the closest companion *El Jefe* ever had until her death from cancer in 1980. Although her grave is in Havana's Colón cemetery, this memorial, whimsically shaped like a staircase and decorated with sculptured sunflowers and doves, touchingly shows how much she was loved in this province.

Where to Stay and Eat
The inexpensive **Hotel Guacanayabo***** ((53-23) 5-4012 or 5-4590, Avenida Camilo Cienfuegos, is located right on the seafront. This is the best place to stay in Manzanillo,

and its rooms have a view of the bay. It has a selection of restaurants and cafeterias and a swimming pool.

SOUTH FROM MANZANILLO

About 10 km (just over six miles) from Manzanillo, on the road to Marea del Portillo, is the turnoff to **Parque Nacional de Demajagua**, where Cuba's first War of Independence was launched. It can be difficult to find: turn south along the road to Niquero after the Servi Cupet-Cimex station and after

devoted to Celia Sánchez. From here, if you are interested, you can make a 20-km (12-mile) detour through Niquero to **Playa las Coloradas**, the narrow, mangrove-covered beach famous as place where the *Granma* landed on December 2, 1956.

As Che Guevara recounted, "It wasn't a disembarkation, it was a shipwreck." Off-course, behind schedule, and seasick, Castro and his band had to abandon the leaking six-berth cabin cruiser and wade for two hours through mosquito-infested mangrove swamps before they reached dry land. A

driving for about 15 minutes, you should see the park's entrance.

La Demajagua was the name of the hacienda and sugar mill owned by wealthy landowner Carlos Manuel de Céspedes. It was here, on October 10, 1868, that Céspedes first urged his fellow Cubans to fight for independence and the abolition of slavery. The ruins of La Demajagua form an open-air museum, which displays such objects as the bell with which Céspedes gathered his slaves to set them free and to launch his rebellion.

Back on the main road onwards from Manzanillo, the road hugs the coast until you reach the village of **Media Luna**, with its painted wooden houses and small museum

monument marks the actual landing place of the famous yacht, and a long wooden pathway across mangrove swamps to a jetty apparently follows the route taken by the rebels as they waded ashore. Three days later, the men had their first encounter with Batista's troops — at Alegría de Pío, south of Niquero.

After visiting Playa las Coloradas, you will probably want to retrace your way back to the main coastal road. Otherwise, you could continue down to **Cabo Cruz**, where a 1877 lighthouse marks the very tip of the western peninsula of Granma Province. Dramatic, layered marine terraces are a

Guardalavaca offers the complete Caribbean resort experience.

feature of this coastline, some rising from sea level to more than 200 m (650 ft) high. The surrounding densely forested region, which extends as far as the eye can see, is the **Parque Nacional Desembarco del Granma**, also known as *El Guafe*.

Before the arrival of the Spanish, this was a Siboney Indian settlement, and an intricate network of cave dwellings, burial grounds and archeological remains have all been uncovered here — most notably a cave containing an idol carved from a stalagmite. Signposted walkways are being gradually established with the aim of creating an ecological reserve here, but at present you need a guide to explore, otherwise it is very easy to get lost.

MAREA DEL PORTILLO

Continuing along the main coastal road from Media Luna, it's a 40-km (25-mile) drive across the hills of the Sierra Maestra to **Marea del Portillo**. The road leaves behind the wide expanses of sugarcane plantations which are lined with queues of tired workers waiting at train crossroads. The landscape becomes more arid, with tussocky bleached grass, horse farms and small hamlets. Rain is rare in this region, which is one of driest and hottest parts of the country. Along the route, you'll see giant billboards with illustrations and slogans which elaborately recount the progress of the rebels as they made their way up into the mountains.

At first glance, this small, black-sanded crescent of a beach, tucked alongside mangrove swamps and flatlands dotted with coastal palm trees, looks like an unpromising location for a resort. However, as you may discover, the particular charm of this place takes a little time — at least a few hours — to percolate. There is something special about Marea del Portillo, and it is easy to see why many of the foreign tourists (mostly Canadians) who come here return again and again. The appeal is that, unlike so many destinations in tourist-apartheid Cuba, this resort manages to be genuinely relaxing, and a palpable sense of goodwill, as well as many friendships, has been built up between the local community and the tourists.

It makes the perfect place to stop for a few days of relaxation if you are driving around this part of Cuba.

WHAT TO SEE AND DO

The black-sanded beach is pleasant enough to look at from your balcony, and at sunset, the view across the bay is ravishing, burnishing the sea red. But it's not recommended as a place to swim. Indeed, this coast is reknowned for its sharks. Instead, at set intervals during the day, a minibus and ferry connection takes guests to nearby **Cayo Blanco**, which the three hotels in the area use as their main beach. This perfect little island has soft white sand and natural sun umbrellas formed by sea-grape trees, and it is

lapped by a clear, blue sea with good visibility for snorkeling. A delicious barbecue lunch is served on the island each day, and you can choose to be as sociable or private as you like.

Ask the hotels about their guided, all-day excursions by jeep or horseback into the lush foothills of the nearby Sierra Maestra mountains, along tracks exploring small villages, low-lying forest and waterfall havens where you can picnic and swim. It is worth mentioning that many routes that used to be taken for horseback rides in this area are now off-limits for military reasons.

There are plenty of rewarding opportunities for scuba diving in and around the offshore keys in the area, with some 25 established diving spots. These include visits to dramatic calcified limestone sea terraces, the wreckage of a Spanish galleon and to a site off *El Guafe* and Cabo Cruz where you are almost guaranteed to see *manatees*, grouped in small herds of six or seven, an endemic and protected species in Cuba.

The mangrove swamps that surround the main beach at Marea del Portillo support a thriving number of oyster beds, which are farmed by local state-controlled co-operatives. You can watch fishermen working from their catamarans (silently, so as not to disturb the oysters) and take a catamaran ride yourself through the mangroves to visit an oyster bar, open seasonally, where freshly shucked oysters are served with beer or wine.

A traditional rodeo in Holguín Province.

WHERE TO STAY AND EAT

A recently formed joint venture between the Canadian company Journey's End and Cubanacán means that all three hotels in Marea del Portillo have been renovated and improved. Although they vary in price, all operate as all-inclusive resorts.

Moderate

Farallón del Caribe**** ((53-23) 59-7081, Carretera Granma, Pilón, is attractively landscaped on a hill facing the black-sanded bay on one side and the Sierra Maestra mountains on the other. This modern hotel is the most luxurious of the three recommended and has become a favorite with Canadian visitors for its relaxing atmosphere and excellent value. All of the pleasantly furnished rooms have sea views, balconies and satellite TV. The US$50 daily rate per person is all inclusive. Facilities include a bar, shop, restaurant, swimming pool, and games rooms.

   Punta Piedra** ((53-23) 59-4421, Carretera de Pilón, located close to Cayo Blanco, set on the hillside overlooking the bay, is made up of 12 private cottages, including four suites, all with television. It is private, has a nice restaurant, and is very pleasant if you prefer to be away from the crowds and don't mind not having all the facilities.

Inexpensive

Located on the beachfront, the recently renovated **Marea del Portillo***** ((53-23) 59-4201 FAX (53-23) 59-4134, Carretera Granma Km 12.5, Pilón, has comfortable rooms with balconies from which you can step directly onto the sands. There is a restaurant, cafeteria, shop, and a palm-thatched outdoor bar around the pool. The resort has a large pet iguana called "Guana" who is tame and eats mosquitoes, but is often tempted from a variety of his hiding places to eat pancakes, watched by admiring visitors.

HOW TO GET THERE

Most visitors reach Marea del Portillo by hotel bus, having arrived at Manzanillo's **Sierra Maestra Airport**, 110 km (68 miles)

away, on a charter flight from Canada. Cubana de Aviación flies to Manzanillo twice weekly from Havana.

DRIVING TO SANTIAGO DE CUBA

The 196-km (122-mile) drive from Marea del Portillo to Santiago de Cuba is one of the most spectacular in Cuba, and being less-traveled than other stretches in the country, has a certain maverick quality to it. It is made for those who enjoy solitary adventures: you will often find yourself completely alone on these roads, rarely seeing another car. A new paved road has recently been completed, and apparently the Castro government is planning to open this remote area up for tourism development. At present, facilities are few and the local inhabitants are often very shy, but always friendly. If you stop to talk with those you see on their long mountain treks by the roadside, always offer food and water as a friendly gesture, which will be greatly appreciated. Allow about four hours for the drive.

   The road winds around the coast and is full of starkly beautiful vistas: sparkling sea vistas and black-shingle sand on one side, with increasingly vertiginous arid tussock-grass mountains and sporadic impoverished-looking hamlets on the other. Herds of goats and grazing horses are a common sight, and villagers sometimes emerge by the roadside seemingly in the middle of nowhere. Further on, the mountain sides become huge calcified limestone cliffs, with big boulders lapped by the sea.

   Don't be unduly alarmed if you are stopped at an impromptu check point made with a string and rags: locals with rifles slung over their chests are apt to check passing vehicles to make sure that farmers from the region are not heading to town with pigs that might spread an African pig disease that has been rife in this area. Although the men look like vigilantes they make these checks with the blessing of the Cuban armed forces, and if they see tourists, will wave them on.

   En route, you will pass through the town of **Uvero**, where Fidel Castro's revolutionary guerillas won a decisive battle on May 28, 1957. Further on is **Chivirico**, a tidy little town on the water's edge, its tree-lined streets busy with perky horse-drawn *calesas*. Chivirico has two popular beach resorts, one of which has an international diving center.

Two of the nicest swimming beaches in the area are **Playa Sevilla** and **Playa Blanca**. Further on, the road will lead you to Santiago de Cuba.

WHERE TO STAY

Distances are given from Santiago de Cuba, from which these hotels are within an hour or so's easy driving distance.

center (with catamarans, windsurfing, and snorkeling equipment), day and nighttime tennis, a medical center, shops, and car and bicycle rental. There is a large free-form swimming pool with a water-slide and a swim-up bar. This is probably the best beach resort catering for young families: even children as young as two can be looked after at the Kids Kamp, which has a playground, a swimming program, Nintendo, nightly movie and cartoon programs, and water sports and other activities for older children.

Expensive
Terraced up a mountainside of lush tropical forest, the all-inclusive **Sierra Mar Club Resort****** ((53-22) 2-9110 FAX (53-22) 2-9007 or 2-9116 E-MAIL sierrmar@smar.scu.cty.cu, Carretera Chivirico, Km 60, has a beautiful beach. It is unquestionably luxurious by Cuban standards, and is virtually a fully self-contained village in its own right, with elevators down to the beach and a walkway out to a thatched stilt-bar. Rooms and suites are very comfortable and soothingly pastel. The higher up the mountain, the more dramatic the view from your balcony. Aside from the excellent international diving center here, facilities include a Nautilus equipment-stocked gym, a water sports

Moderate to Expensive
Los Galeones* ((53-22) 2-9110 FAX (53-22) 2-9007 or 2-9116, Poblado de Chivirico, Km 72, near Guamá town, is a quiet 34-room all-inclusive resort perched on a nearby hilltop near the ocean and has wonderful views over the Caribbean Sea and the Sierra Maestra mountains. It is much more intimate than the Sierra Mar, and better for couples or serious divers. It has a small private beach and unlimited access to all facilities at Sierra Mar Club Resort.

An example of a Spanish-Cuban joint venture resort hotel at Playa Esmeralda.

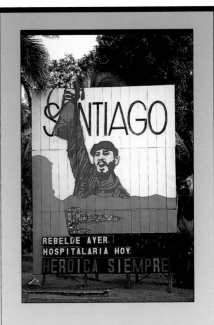

Santiago de Cuba and the Far East

Opción
Café   0.40
Fritura 1.00

SANTIAGO DE CUBA

IT'S EASY TO UNDERSTAND WHY SANTIAGO is called the most Caribbean of Cuba's cities. Not only is it more tropical in temperature here but, due to its geographical location, it has always had close links to neighboring islands in the Caribbean. More predominantly *mulatto* than Havana, this influence also goes some way to explain the extraordinary tradition of musical innovation for which the city is celebrated. It has also helped make the city's legendary Carnival Festival, which brings performers from all over the Caribbean, the most exuberant in Cuba. The Carnival has been suspended in recent years due to the Special Period, but there is expectation that this side of the city's soul will be revived.

BACKGROUND

At first glance, as you drive in from the airport, Santiago has the feel of a lush, heat-opiated backwater. In fact, it is Cuba's second largest city, with more than 400,000 inhabitants, and it was the island's original capital. With its rolling hills ranged around a wide, easily navigable harbor, Santiago was an obvious location for a strategic port within Spain's empire, despite proving somewhat earthquake-prone.

Santiago was founded in 1515 by the island's first governor, the conquistador Diego Velázquez. Another famous conquistador, Hernándo Córtez, used the settlement as his base for expansionist forays into Mexico and Central America. At that time, Santiago's fortunes had closer ties to what was then Hispaniola (now Haiti and the Dominican Republic), the North Caribbean and parts of South America than to the rest of Cuba, as inland communication and transport were hampered by a natural barrier of formidable mountain ranges. Santiago remained the capital until 1607, when that status was transferred to Havana.

Santiagüeros are also proud of their city's historical and cultural importance: "Hero City" and "Cradle of the Revolution" are the post-Revolutionary titles given to Santiago, and you'll see them proclaimed by ubiquitous roadside slogans. Support among its people was crucial during the nineteenth-century War of Independence, and it was also here that Fidel Castro and his rebels staged a daring attack on Moncada Barracks, thus setting in train the sequence of events that were to make him *El Jefe*.

Santiago's colonial core is an intriguing mélange of early Spanish colonial administrative buildings and dandified mansions constructed by French plantation

owners who settled here after fleeing the slave revolt in Haiti during the 1790s. Although Santiago cannot compete with Havana's architectural splendors and the cosmopolitan outlook (and is clearly suffering considerably from shortages and power cuts during the Special Period), the city's intimate scale, not to mention the gutsy brinkmanship of its people and their passionate relationship with all aspects of music, make this one of Cuba's most special places.

PREVIOUS PAGES: LEFT: View from the road in Baracoa, Guantánamo Province. RIGHT: Billboard announces the entrance to Santiago de Cuba. OPPOSITE: Children tempted by roadside sweets. ABOVE: A young woman celebrates her coming of age on her fifteenth birthday.

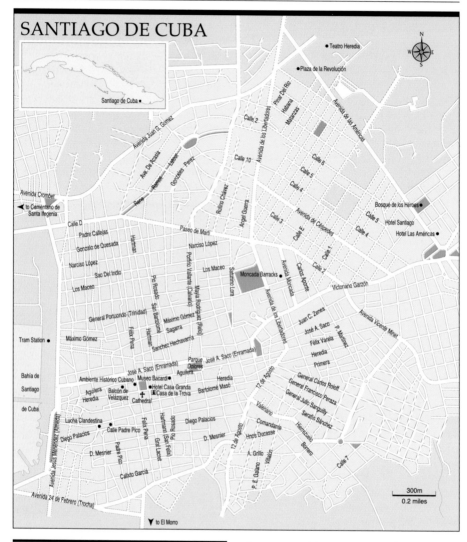

SANTIAGO DE CUBA

to El Morro

GENERAL INFORMATION

Apart from the tourism desks in most of the hotels, you can consult the **Buro de Información Cultural** ((53-226) 2-3302 or 2-3267, Plaza de Martí, which is open daily from 9 AM to 8 PM.

You should pay a visit to the city's **Casa de la Cultura**, just off Parque Céspedes, at Calle General Lacret No. 651 and Calle Aguilera, to check their information desk and bulletin for upcoming cultural events and concerts that you otherwise may not hear about. In particular, try to see one of the city's greatest dance ensembles, the **Ballet Folklórico Cutumba**, which per-

forms an exciting repertoire of Afro-Cuban dances.

Another cultural institution, the **Casa del Caribe** ((53-226) 4-2285 FAX (53-226) 4-2387, Calle 13 No. 154, at the corner of Calle 5, Vista Alegre, is a good place to ask about *casas particulares* or private home-stays.

Rumbos Travel Office and Tours ((53-266) 2-2222, opposite the Casa Granda Hotel on Calle Heredia. This office can help with most queries and arrange tours both in and around the city, as well as to Parque Baconao and Guantánamo Province.

The **Banco Nacional de Cuba** is located at the corner of Calles Aguilera and Lacret, on Parque Céspedes, and is open Monday to Friday, 8 AM to noon. Otherwise, exchange facilities are available at all the main hotels, it's worth mentioning that hotels in Santiago tend to charge exorbitant commission to cash traveler's checks.

Should you need any medical attention, if it is not too serious, try the doctor's office at the Hotel Santiago de Cuba. Otherwise, go to the **Clínica Internacional Cubanacán Servimed** ((53-226) 4-2589, Calles 13 and 14, Vista Alegre, which has been set up specifically to cater to foreigners. It offers a 24-hour service and, as well as doctors, a dentist is also available.

WHAT TO SEE AND DO

A Walking Tour

The obvious place to begin is **Parque Céspedes**, a tree-dotted square from which you can easily explore much of central Santiago by foot. You could begin with a *cafecito* on the expansive balcony of the colonial-era **Hotel Casa Granda** at the corner of the square in the shadow of the cathedral. From here, feeling bathed in the flowering scented space and chatter floating up from the park, you will surely see almost all of the city's personalities parade by eventually: wizened men gather to exchange gossip over their walking sticks; a double-bass soloist gives an impossibly brilliant, impromptu performance; shoals of children pass by in either mustard or red uniforms; flirtatious hustlers of both sexes wave and beckon with outrageous directness.

The Casa Granda itself is a city landmark. For decades leading up to the revolution, it was a playing ground for the Cuban elite, a magnet for intrigue, assignations and international spies. Now it is so gleamingly restored by a major hotel group that the *louche* atmosphere described by Graham Greene in 1957 has almost been expunged. Greene, who arrived in Santiago hoping to interview Castro in his Sierra Maestra hiding place, sprinkled his book *Our Man in Havana* with recollections of his Santiago stay, sending his character Wormold on an espionage mission disguised as business trip here.

On the balcony, unsteady *turistas* clad in "I love Cuba" T-shirts may be on their first

mojito of the day, recovering perhaps from a night at the Santiago Tropicana, while a deaf-mute magician and his Lycra leopard skin-clad assistant move from table to table. Yet if nattily dressed in crumpled linens and Panama hat you will not feel out of place. The top floor offers yet another excuse for a *cuba libre* (in keeping with Santiago's fabled revolutionary zeal) and mesmerizing views across the red-tiled roofs out to the harbor. Next to the Casa Granda is the **Casa de Cultura**, which is a good place to see local artists exhibit their work, and sometimes to

meet them. Look out for the work of Luis Rosaenz, a talented artist whose paintings fuse primitive colors and a distinct, Santeria-influenced naive style. Upstairs, the **Casa de Matrimonio** is where civil marriages are officiated; some no-nonsense affairs, others with as much wedding pomp as can be managed.

Within the center of the square is a monument to Carlos Manuel Céspedes, the former Cuban plantation owner who by freeing his slaves and fighting for independence against the Spanish was dubbed "Father of the Nation." Ranged around it are some of Santiago's most historic and inter-

A Santiago de Cuba street scene.

esting buildings. Imposingly large, the yellow and cream **Cathedral** is dominated by a statue of the Angel of Annunciation, blowing her horn, apparently on the verge of flying away in a burst of Márquezian magic realism. The original church built on this site — the Santa Iglesia Basilica — dates back to 1523, yet many successive versions have since been built, having been destroyed by earthquake and pillaged, with sections rebuilt as recently as 1810 and 1922. It is said that Diego Velázquez was buried in the original cathedral, but his remains have never been found. Inside, an ecclesiastical museum documents the history of Catholicism in Cuba. The sacred and profane mingle at street level, where the cathedral encompasses various dollar-shops, including a bookshop, and one selling uninspiring arts and crafts, and now, a Benetton shop. You will also find the **Heladería Coppelia**, where, as well as the ice-cream, you can sample *pru*, a local concoction of various roots and vanilla.

As you walk clockwise around the square, on Calle Félix Peña, you come to the **Museo de Ambiente Historico Cubano** (Museum of Cuban History) also known as the Casa de Velázquez. This is Cuba's oldest residence, built between 1516 and 1530 as the home of Diego Velázquez. You can still see many original details and some furniture from that period: the entrance pavestones and heavy doors, and the ornately decorated cedar ceiling on the upper floor, (reminiscent in scent and design of a Kashmiri houseboat) and fresco designs that adorn the upper floors that were Velázquez's living quarters. Moorish-style fretted wooden balconies add a distinctly Oriental effect. The ground floor was a frenzy of activity; functioning as the island's Office of Commerce, as well as a foundry where gold ingots were smelted and then shipped off to Spain.

Velázquez's quarters now house a collection of furniture from the sixteenth through to the eighteenth centuries; such items as an original wall hanging bearing his personal coat of arms; Spanish ceramics and paintings; and eighteenth-century silver and gold ornaments from Germany, Mexico and Cuba. The Spanish-style kitchen still contains some of the original utensils and ceramics. Dur-

ing the nineteenth century, the residence was used as a hotel, with a new wing added, along with the playful crescent-shaped stained-glass windows and fresco decorations popular with the French *haute bourgeoisie* who settled in Santiago de Cuba after fleeing Haiti. These rooms give a good impression of a wealthy planter's home of that period, with Bohemian chandeliers, Murano glassware, Napoleonic and Franco-Cuban *palisandro* furniture (made with a type of local wood with the appearance of dark mahogany), and rattan rocking chairs — then a recent invention deemed perfect for the tropics. The museum owes its existence to one man: Dr. Francisco Prat, a Professor of Cuban Art at the Universidad de Oriente (University of the East). When, in 1965, the building had fallen into such disrepair that the city ordered its demolition, Dr. Prat fought for its restoration, and it is his donated personal collection that makes up most of the museum's exhibits. The staff who conduct guided tours are very friendly and informative; they also speak English. It is open Monday to Saturday from 8 AM to noon and from 2 PM to 6 PM, and Sunday from 9 AM to 1 PM.

Further up Calle Félix Peña, you'll see the local office of the **Partido Comunista de Cuba**, the **Casa de Galicia** cultural association and the **Academia Municipal de Ajedrez** where chess players gather throughout the day and into the evening to play beneath the whirring fans, rum at hand. Nearby is the Cine Rialto movie-house and an open-air nightclub popular with *santiagüeros* where avid flirtation and frenetic dancing occur most nights.

On the north-end side of Céspedes Square is the **Ayuntamiento**, or Town Hall, a large white colonial building with blue wooden balconies. The original structure on this site was built by Hernándo Cortéz, however there have been several reconstructions. Variously used as the headquarters of the Spanish crown and later the American military government, it now houses the city government offices. It was from this central balcony that Fidel Castro made his first victorious speech as the nation's leader on January 1, 1959, to a crowd of cheering thousands.

From here, a web of cobblestone alleys and avenues branch out, any one of which will plunge you into Santiago's heady street life. Life spills out, voyeuristically, from the open doors and fretted balconies of wooden houses; a band rehearses from the recesses of a dusty schoolroom and with them, a clear alto voice soars with shiver-inducing melancholy; Lycra-wearing women with their hair in curlers shoot quizzical glances; a crowd jostles to fill bottles with rations of *aguardiente* (a cheap liquor); unseen, a pig's squealing is suddenly silenced and red

magicians and dancers to entertain, a spectacle not to be missed.

Further down Calle Heredia at No. 304, near the intersection with San Félix, is Cuba's best loved **Casa de la Trova**, an inevitable destination. Whether you are an aficionado of popular Cuban music or not (yet), spending a few hours listening to Santiago's famed veteran troubadours perform here is one of the most memorable experiences to be had to in Cuba, the tropical afternoons and evenings alive with almost continuos, intoxicating sound. The traditional ballad

frothy blood trickles into the gutter; the smell of cigar smoke mixes with the scent of the sea. In the still of a hot afternoon, a siesta-shuttered inertia takes hold.

One of the oldest streets is **San Basilico**, a cobblestone row still illuminated by antique gas lamps (used on occasion to hang suspected revolutionaries by Batista's hit men), while one of the prettiest is **Padre Pico**, with its historic steps. However, start with the liveliest street, **Calle Heredia**, east of the square, just off the Hotel Casa Granda, which is lined with colonial mansions, many with traditional ironwork balconies, some of which have been turned into art galleries, shops and offices. On weekends, this street is closed to traffic to allow musicians, actors,

form (*trova*), a blend of African percussion and Spanish guitar rhythms with passionate lyrics, originated in Santiago.

An eclectic and unpredictable range of performers take the stage here, ranging from talented amateur musicians to established professionals. The "stage" is a simple raised platform, with rows of fold-up chairs in the front, surrounded by walls covered with paintings of famous performers of time gone by, including the Trio Matamoros. Sometimes it has a party atmosphere, with the audience breaking into an impromptu chachachá. Weekends are the best time to come, but music plays through-

Santiago de Cuba's neo classical Palacio Provincial.

out the week. Within the complex, a shop sells compact discs and cassettes of groups that have performed here, as well as musical instruments and souvenirs. Recently, the Casa de la Trova was given a makeover from its original bohemian and history-steeped setting and the result by contrast lacks character. However, the music is still wonderful.

On Calle Heredia, the **Casa del Vino** may be worth noting for visiting later on — although it is open most of the day. It is a very popular local haunt that serves unusual alcoholic concoctions, such as their house specialty, a "wine" made from grapefruit. Further along, **Casa Heredia** is the museum-birthplace of the Santiago's most famous poet, José Maria Heredia (1803–1839), after whom the street is named. Heredia was one of the first Cubans to speak out against the Spanish in favor of independence. Here you can find a small library of the poet's works as well as other Santiago writers. One of the more interesting shops along Calle Heredia is the **BFC Liberia**, a small shop, run by the affable Eddy Tamayo, selling second-hand books, songs by Pablo Milanes, atlases of Cuba, histories of the revolution and selections of compact discs. You might want to ask directions for the UNEAC (Union of the Writers and Artists), a large hall located on Calle Heredia, where art shows, literary discussions and lectures take place.

Across the Calle Pío Rosado, on the next block, at Heredia No. 303, is the **Museo de Carnival**, housed in a former prison. The phenomenon of carnival in Cuba began at the end of the seventeenth century during the Spanish colonial period, and has undergone many mutations of form and content since. Nowhere else is it celebrated with as much gusto as in Santiago, where it officially began. Originally called *Fiesta de las Mamarrachos* (roughly translates as a "festival of the masked grotesques") it took place on the feast days of Epiphany and Corpus Christi before it came to be held in July.

There is a diverting display of masquerader costumes (ranging from glittery bikinis for *mulatta* beauties to androgynous Pierrot attire), ornamental capes, giant

Santiago de Cuba and the Far East

papier-mâché heads, musical instruments, banners, and drums used by competing bands over the past century. It is open Tuesday to Sunday, 9 AM to 6 PM, and closed on Monday.

Next door, lawyers may be intrigued to peer in at the **Casa del Jurista** which functions rather like a bar association, where lectures and meetings are held, and the legal community meet to gossip over subsidized rum. Also, look out for the **Jesuit college**, a block to the east, where Fidel Castro attended high school.

ple, is José Martí's tuxedo, and the blood-stained campaign hammock and scarf in which Antonio Maceo, one of Cuba's most feted national heroes, was fatally shot.

Elsewhere, even prosaic displays of nineteenth-century doctor's kits (complete with alarmingly large syringes) and clothes and shoes made from plant fibers are interesting.

Tinseled crowns date from one of the few celebrations allowed African slaves by their plantation owners — the annual "Day of Three Kings" — during which a slave king

From here, retrace your footsteps to the Calle Pío Rosado. At the intersection with Calle Aguilera is the **Museo Bacardí**. This unmistakably imposing structure is the oldest museum in the country, built for the purpose in 1899 by the rum clan's patriarch, Emilio Bacardí Moreau (1844–1922). When not presiding over the family fortune (or wearing his other hat as Santiago's mayor), Bacardí was a tireless collector and made the creation of this museum one of his passions. At entrance level, a section documents Cuba's early colonial history, with much memorabilia — some of it fascinatingly personal — belonging to a phalanx of leaders in Cuba's War of Independence against the Spanish. Here, for example,

was crowned for the night. (Some of those elected may well have been actual descendants from African kings or chieftains in their homelands, thus for many this was a bitter mockery of their patrimony.) Look out for the hand-made *mambisa* torpedo crafted in 1895 by Cuban rebels intent on blowing up Spanish ships moored in Santiago Bay.

In the adjourning courtyard is Callejón Bofill, a cobblestone row of preserved colonial houses typical of the Santiago's colonial era, with authentic colors, intricate ironwork, wooden doors, stained-glass windows, and street lamps. Upstairs, one of Cuba's most important collections of Eu-

OPPOSITE: The Museo Bacardí traces Cuba's colonial history. ABOVE: School in Santiago de Cuba.

ropean and Cuban colonial paintings from the sixteenth to the nineteenth centuries is displayed (many of which have aroused much interest and been authenticated by the Prado Museum), including distinctive works by the well-known portrait artist of the Cuban colonial period, Federico Martinez Matos. A small wing displays contemporary Cuban art and sculpture, notably by Lucia Victoria Bacardí and Alberto Lesay, whose striking sculpture of Che Guevara dominates the room.

A separate entrance in the building leads to the archaeological hall, which includes a collection of mummies from Egypt and South America. Bacardí (who seemed to have a taste for the macabre) is said to have personally removed the elaborate head-dress of the Egyptian mummy — said to be a 25-year-old princess who lived more than 2,000 years ago — who now lies unwrapped alongside her mummified crocodile, ibis, and cat. Other exhibits include a pair of Peruvian mummies, a man and a woman whose skin and bodies have petrified together as if hewn from a tree, and the 400-year-old shrunken head of a 23-year-old woman from the Amazonian Tsantsa de Jibaro tribe. After this, the Cuban archaeological exhibits dating from the aboriginal Taíno Indian period seem somewhat tame: bones, shells, carved idols, ceremonial seats made for Indian chiefs, and deformed skulls that show how inhabitants of the time successfully used wooden slats to mold the foreheads of infants to create a desired gorilla-like slope-effect. Open Tuesday to Saturday, 9 AM to 6 PM, and Sunday, 9 AM to 1 PM, the museum is closed on Monday.

After a morning's exploring, you will need a break. As you walk up Calle Aguilera, you'll come to a pretty square known locally as **Plaza Dolores**, located between Calles Calvario and Reloj. At the intersection with Calle Calvario is **La Isabelica**, which serves only coffee, which patrons tend to take spiked with Cuban rum or *marasquino*, a sweet liqueur. As usual, the popularity with tourists of this characterful institution means that dollar prices are inflated. Otherwise, the plaza contains an array of restaurants — **La Perla del Dragon**, **Terressina**, **Casa de Don Antonio**, and

the **Café Matamoras** — as well as an ice-cream parlor, set in restored colonial houses — all exceptionally well-managed by the tourist company Rumbos, which won an award for the plaza's restoration. The church on the square has been converted into a concert hall and this is the best place to hear classical music performed in Santiago, usually at the weekend.

As you stroll back along Calle Aguilera to Calle Pío Rosado, look for Calle Saco, better known as **Enramada**, Santiago's main commercial thoroughfare. Dilapidated signs from long-gone cabarets, restaurants, and hotel still flap in the tropical breeze; while lackluster shop windows and a grimy cinema showing a kung-fu movie attract long lines. The main commercial activity seems to be the demand for *cafecitos* or *rallado* (shavings of ice dribbled with syrup). Men play dominoes in the neighborhood café, alternately long-faced then grinning as they tell *chistes*, jokes, to pass the time. The Hotel Venus, one of the most popular pre-revolution bars in Santiago and reputedly where the *daiquirí* had its commercial debut, is off the side street as you approach the Casa Granda. Like its mascot, an eye-less, armless Aphrodite placed glumly in the front window, it is a moldering wreck.

Walk two blocks down to reach Calle Heredia once more, but this time, continue in the opposite direction. In the second block on the right, between Calles Corona and Padre Pico, is the **Casa de Orfeon Santiago**, a paint-peeling colonial mansion with a courtyard and interiors that are worth a look. Occasional evening musical performances take place here — this was once the home of Cuba's most prestigious choral society.

To the left, a little further along is **Calle Padre Pico**, the famous street of stone steps that climbs to the top of a steep hill where the views across the city and bay are spectacular. The swaying hips of the women who climb these steps was supposedly the inspiration for a local ballad. As you ascend, houses are stacked, higgledy-piggledy, many of them helter-skelter incarnations of earlier abodes dating back to the sixteenth-century, some sweet-looking, balconies aflow with rambling plants. This district, known as **El Tivolí**, was originally the home of French settlers.

At the top of the steps, to the right, is the **Museo de la Lucha Clandestina** (Museum of the Underground Struggle), on Calle General Jesús Rabí. On November 30, 1956, a group of Castro's revolutionaries led by Frank País fire-bombed this building, which was then the Santiago police headquarters and often used for interrogations. The attack was meant to divert attention away from the planned landing of the *Granma*, en route from Mexico with Castro, Che and other

was used to keep watch over the arrivals and departures of galleons. Its beautiful setting is now used by the typically musical-minded *santiagüeros* as the city's Peña del Tango (Tango Club). From here, you are only a block away from Parque Céspedes.

En Route to El Morro

Although the first suggested city tour is designed especially for those on foot, the other excursions suggested here require a car, as you will need to cover quite a lot of distance.

comrades on board, however, it was mistimed. Many of those who took part were gunned down, some of them on the Padre Pico stairs.

Inside this former colonial mansion, you'll see an exhaustive exhibition devoted to the underground struggle against the Batista regime. It is open Monday to Saturday, 8 AM to 6 PM, and closed on Sunday.

When you return to the stairs, instead of going down, take the next street, leading to the old tramway-lined Calle Corona. Look out for an archway at the corner of Calle Bartolomé Masó: it leads to a small open cobbled square lined with flowering plants called the **Balcón de Velázquez**. During the early Spanish colonial era, this lookout

Begin at the **Hotel Santiago**, even if you aren't staying here. For many Cubans, this Canadian-designed hotel represents the apex of privilege, and party members are awarded short stays here as incentives. Across the avenue, is the much less salubrious **Hotel Las Américas**.

As you drive along Avenida de las Américas — the city's main boulevard — you'll see a number of Universidad de Oriente faculties, and pass the **Bosque de los Héroes**, a monument commemorating Che Guevara and his band of Bolivian guerillas. Further along are a series of structures, rather sternly utopian, all commissioned by Fidel Cas-

A slogan heralds the *zafra,* or sugar harvest.

tro in preparation for the Fourth Communist Party Congress in 1993. Here you'll see the monumental **Teatro Heredia**, used for such events as Fidel's annual July 26 speech; the Sala Polivalente gymnasium and the **Estadio de Béisbol Guillermón Moncada** which can hold some 350,000 people, where regular baseball games, frequently starring Santiago's own "Orientales," are staged. It all leads to the **Plaza de la Revolución**, where an immense futurist bronze monument to Antonio Maceo (whose nickname during his heyday was "Titan of Bronze") depicts the hero astride his rearing horse amid a circle of 23 red machetes that point victoriously towards the heavens, symbolizing March 23, 1878, the day he resolved to continue his spirited campaign against the Spanish. At the base of the monument is a very strange, small museum which contains holographic representations of icons symbolizing each stage in Cuba's evolution to revolution.

Turn left just before the monument and continue along the same street to reach the corner of Portuondo and Moncada, off Avenida de los Libertadores. You may need to ask directions to the **Moncada Barracks**, since it is not well signposted. Surrounded by mustard-yellow stucco walls, this bullet-splattered garrison represents one of the most crucial events in the remarkable story of Castro's rise to power. (The bullet holes are reconstructions based on historical photographs, since Batista's men filled them in after the attack.)

On July 26, 1953, a 26-year-old then little-known lawyer named Fidel Castro, and 125 militants, made an assault on Moncada, at that time, during the Batista era, one of the island's most important military installations. Although daring, the attack was an unmitigated disaster in which most of the assailants were either machine-gunned down or later brutally tortured to death. However, Castro himself survived to stand trial, and to make his first famous speech, which became the basis for his new revolutionary manifesto, the Movimiento 26 de Julio, known in revolutionary shorthand as M-26.

Now known as the July 26 Historical Museum, the collection is an exercise in

revolutionary patriotism, with sections devoted to the nineteenth-century War of Independence; the guerilla struggle led by Castro throughout the 1950s and followed by the glories and achievements of the Cuban republic. The assault on Moncada is scrupulously documented, and the blood-stained uniforms of those who died taking part in the siege are particularly graphic. Some of the military equipment used by the Castro-led M-26 movement in the Sierra Maestra mountains can be seen here, including hand-made weapons and grenades, Castro's khaki uniforms and sharp-shooter rifle and Che Guevara's mud-stained boots. Outside, a large part of the barracks has been turned into a school complex, known as "School City July 26." The museum

is open Monday to Saturday, 8 AM to 6 PM, and Sunday 8 AM to noon.

Retrace your route and head for Avenida Jesús Menéndez, which curls around Santiago's desultory dockfront, warehouses, custom offices and the Parque de la Alameda with its slumbering, horse-drawn *calesa* drivers. Close by, **La Trocha**, a district cluttered with dilapidated wooden houses, is considered to be the site of the original Santiago carnival, as it was here, during the colonial period, that slaves were permitted to celebrate once a year. Continuing on, as you pass the train station, if by chance the Havana train has pulled in you will witness scenes of near-hysteria as relatives and lovers wave farewell or greet passengers.

Santiago de Cuba and the Far East

Just north of the train station is **Barra del Ron Caney**, Cuba's oldest rum distillery, opened in 1862 by an astute Spanish immigrant called Don Facundo Bacardí. The Bacardís were among the wave of wealthy business clans who hastily left Cuba after the revolution, and having left Cuba, continued to rebuild their rum empire in various other countries, including the Bahamas, Puerto Rico, Canada, Mexico and Spain. Until the mid-1960s, the Cuban government, having nationalized the industry, continued to market rum under the Bacardí label, but when the state tried to export the rum the Bacardí family filed a trademark infringement claim in the World Court

PREVIOUS PAGES: The fretted wooden windows at Casa Velázquez. ABOVE: View of El Morro parapet.

— and won. Now the rum that is produced here is labeled "Havana Club," and it is regarded by many rum purists as a better product than the original Bacardí. Some 60 percent of the rum produced here is exported to Canada and Spain, and the rest consumed in Cuba. Factory tours have been suspended but the shop here is a good place to buy 15-year-old Havana Club rum, difficult to find elsewhere.

As you continue north, past a giant replica of a rum bottle, there are two places of interest in the area. The **Yarayó Fort**, a small,

of the Moncada Barracks attack are also buried here.

From here, retrace the route to La Trocha, and turn right on Avenida Eduardo Chivás, which becomes the road to **El Morro Fortress**, eight kilometers (five miles) away. As you scan the horizon from the stalwart, honey-slate colored Spanish fortress, it is obvious why this spectacular location, with its commanding views across the seas at the entrance to Santiago Bay, was chosen. Completed in 1633, during the governorship of Pedro La Roca, its construction was master-minded

unprepossessing, yellow and tile building, was the first of 116 fortifications built by the Spaniards. From here, turn left, and follow the Avenida Combret to the **Cementerio de Santa Ifegenia**. A necropolis of marble angels, crosses and extravagantly wrought tombs, this is one of Cuba's oldest and most interesting cemeteries, once strictly segregated by social rank and race. It is also the burial place of Cuba's revered heroes of the independence movement. Among those buried here are José Martí, Carlos Manuel de Céspedes and Tomás Estrada Palma (the first president of an independent Cuba). A tomb shaped like a small mock castle contains the remains of those who died in the war of independence, while the victims

by Battista Antonelli, the same Italian architect known for Havana's famous fortress.

Once inside the main drawbridge, an elaborate labyrinth of time-scoured stone passageways, stairwells and alcoves reveal the headquarters from which generations of commanders strove to protect Santiago from a string of savage attacks. (In 1662, however, the fortress was briefly besieged by the English pirate Henry Morgan, after which additional fortifications were added.) Wonderfully atmospheric, its small blue-washed chapel contains its original wooden cross carved in the sixteenth century; while tiny cramped dungeons once housed African slaves in transit as well as hapless prisoners. During the War of Independence, the

Spanish authorities imprisoned many Cuban rebels here, among them Emilio Bacardí Moreau.

Restored in 1978, and then again in 1997, the fortress now contains the **Museo de la Piratería** (Piracy Museum). Here, a colorful history of Caribbean piracy (remember that it was Cuba's Isle of Pines, now called the Isla de la Juventud on which Robert Louis Stevenson modeled his *Treasure Island*) is juxtaposed with a bristling display of the "contemporary piracy" as practiced by the United States military today. A captured CIA rubber raft makes up part of the display. The museum is open Monday to Friday, 9 AM to 5 PM, and during weekends, 8 AM to 4 PM.

After visiting the fortress, the nearby **La Taberna del Morro**, an open-air patio, sheltered by vines, which overlooks the sea from the bluff, is a good place to relax. It's located just before you reach **El Faro**, the lighthouse.

WHERE TO STAY

For details on price categories, see TRAVELERS' TIPS, page 314. Make sure you have booked in advance during July, when the carnival festivities can attract a considerable influx of tourists.

Expensive

Much local pride has focused on the monolith **Hotel Santiago de Cuba***** ((53-226) 8-6666 or 4-2612 FAX (53-226) 8-6270 or 8-6170, Avenida de las Americas and Avenida Manduley, which towers like a steel barnyard strangely out of context with the otherwise low-lying, historic neighborhoods of the city. Unlike the Casa Granda, do not expect colonial charm. For a time it was considered the country's most luxurious hotel, but now, with the proliferation of competitive new joint-venture hotels in Cuba, it seems distinctly dated. However, for Santiago, its facilities are still good and include a health club, three swimming pools, a sauna, an array of bars and cafeterias, a shopping complex, conference facilities, child care, car rental and travel agency and a doctor's office. There are several restaurants and an array of bars and cafeterias, and an always-

bustling nightclub. The rooftop terrace bar on the fifteenth floor offers stunning views and the chance to hear some of Santiago's most talented musicians.

Hotel Casa Granda** ((53-226) 8-6600 FAX (53-226) 8-6035, Calle Heredia No. 201 next to Calle Lacret, is located on Plaza Céspedes, facing the Plaza des Armas. The Casa Granda is to Santiago what the Hotel Nacional is to Havana. It has been completely renovated after years of lingering between picturesque decay and near squalor. It has 58 rooms (described by the manage-

ment as decorated in "Renaissance and Neo-Classical style"), including one for handicapped guests, with all the amenities to be had in Cuba. Even if you are not staying here, it has the best restaurant and bar in town, including excellent coffee. Aside from its other facilities — boutique, rental car agency and travel office — it has the best postcard selection outside of Havana.

Moderate

The 68-room **Hotel Las Américas*** ((53-226) 4-2011 or 4-2695 FAX (53-226) 8-6224, Avenida las Américas and Calle General

OPPOSITE AND ABOVE: Two views of El Morro Fortress, which holds a commanding position at the entrance of Santiago Bay.

Cebreco, pales somewhat beside the Hotel Santiago, just across the road. However, it is a cheaper alternative: the rooms are comfortable and air-conditioned, and service is friendly, if not quite as efficient.

If you are content to stay slightly outside the city, there are several alternatives, all ranged around Santiago's nearby hills, and about ten minutes drive from the center. These include **Villa Gaviota*** (** (53-266) 4-1368 FAX (53-266) 6-1385, Avenida Manduley No. 502, Reparto Vista Alegre. This small resort hotel consists of a series of villas, each consisting of three to five rooms, which can be taken separately or all together, and has a pleasant, private atmosphere. Amenities include satellite television, minibar, a swimming pool, and a baby-sitting service.

Located near the airport in a leafy, residential neighborhood, the newly renovated **Versalles Hotel*** (** (53-266) 9-1016, 9-1504, or 8-6603 FAX (53-266) 8-6145, Alturas de Versalles, is a good choice for a peaceful stay. Its landscaped row of rooms and bungalows are air-conditioned and have small balconies. There is a swimming pool and a small shop.

Inexpensive

The ex-Motel Leningrado, **Villa San Juan*** (** (53-226) 4-2478 or 4-2490 FAX (53-226) 8-6137, Carretera Siboney and Parque San Juan, is located at the foot of historic San Juan Hill, with concrete rows of suites ranged around a swimming pool in a peaceful park-like setting.

Set on a cliff above the Caribbean close to El Morro, the setting of the 1960s-era **Hotel Balcón del Caribe*** (** (53-226) 9-1011 or 9-1544 FAX (53-226) 9-1011, Carretera del Morro, is clearly lovely. There are drawbacks, however: sluggish service and uninspiring rooms. It is difficult to climb down to the sea, and the swimming pool is not much consolation. With an overhaul, this hotel could be much nicer.

WHERE TO EAT

Expensive

Restaurante Tocororo ((53-226) 4-1410, Avenida Manduley, Vista Alegre, is named

for Cuba's national bird. This expensive but elegant restaurant has a pleasant setting in an old colonial house close to the Hotel Santiago. It has an extensive menu, and serves lobster and imported wine for a price.

Moderate

Located in a nineteenth-century mansion that was once the Santiago home of the Bacardí family, **1900 Restaurant (** (53-226) 2-3507, Calle San Basilico 354, between Calles Pío Rosado and Hartmann, is a haven of faded rococo that serves good Creole dishes of veal, rabbit and turkey amidst giant chandeliers and antique furniture. There is a charming leafy roof terrace upstairs for cocktails. It is open from 7 PM until midnight.

Located next to the Morro Castle, **La Taberna del Morro (** (53-226) 9-1576 is a must on a sunny day, when the views from this cliff-top restaurant are perfect. Try to avoid the crush of tourist coach traffic though, arrive early or much later, or stay for sunset cocktails. Try a *morro helado*, the special cocktail of the house. It is a blend of rum, crushed ice, and lemon whisked with an eggwhite, then flavored with a dash of cinnamon and Angostura bitters. Creole/Cuban food is the specialty; generally a simple *prix fixe* meal at US$10.

The **Plaza Dolores** located at Calles Aguilera and Reloj, has been transformed into a pedestrian complex of restaurants, each with their own specialty, as well as a 24-hour cafeteria, ranging from moderate to inexpensive. You can choose from the following. **Taberna de Dolores (** (53-266) 2-3913, is charmingly arranged in an old colonial house, with tables in the courtyard. The Dolores specializes in roasts and is open from 7 PM until midnight. **Don Antonio (** (53-226) 2-2205, serves international dishes in a hacienda setting with hospitable service and a saloon-style bar and quirky jukebox. They are open noon to 11 PM. **La Perla del Dragon (** (53-226) 5–2307, serves unexpectedly good Chinese dishes (chopsticks on request), with a Chinese chef in residence, and is open noon to 11 PM. The decor and design of the waiters' costumes at **La Terressina (** (53-226) 5-2307 are apparently inspired by the fact that "La Traviata" was sung in Santiago by the Cuban opera singer Teressina Paradi at the end of the nineteenth century, and an elegant effect is strived for.

Restaurant Matamoros ((53-226) 2-2675, Calle Calvario next to Calle Aguilera, has historic status in Santiago: the Trio Matamoros once played here, and the band that now plays their songs is good too. You can choose to eat in a cafeteria-style section, or in a more elegant, candle-lit setting. The food is simple but well-priced and they serve from 10 AM to midnight.

Inexpensive
Casa del Vino, Calle Heredia No. 254, is a small traditional place usually frequented by Cubans. Tables are reserved and it's popular, so go early to secure a table, and arrive on time, as you are only allowed for 45 minutes. Only wine and cheese are served.

NIGHTLIFE

While your first stop should be **Casa de la Trova** (see in WHAT TO SEE AND DO, above), just about anywhere you go at night in Santiago will reveal why this city has such a reputation for its talented musicians and infectious dancing.

Nightspots
As well as the Casa de la Trova, you should definitely come here to hear traditional Cuban music played every evening from 10 PM onwards in the relaxed, open-air terrace setting of **Patio Los Dos Abuelos**, Calle Francisco Perez Carbo No. 5, Plaza de Marte.

Not in the same league as the famous Casa de la Trova, **Café Cantante (** (53-226) 4-3178, Teatro Heredia, Avenida de las Americas, is nonetheless worth a visit for its evening performances, where favorite Cuban songs through the ages are sung with great gusto and warmth.

As for **La Maison (** (53-226) 4-1117, Avenida Manduley, Vista Alegre, which is set in a beautiful colonial-style building, the main allure of this chintzy restaurant and bar is its nightly parade of fashion models displaying the latest Cuban fashions. Prices are somewhat inflated.

Discotheques
Espantasueño, located in the Hotel Santiago, is the most popular night club outside of Havana, considered the most sophisticated nightspot in town, with its flashing lights, video panels, and relatively up-to-date dance music. It is thronged with young *santiagüeros*, many of whom wait for hours outside, hoping to be beckoned in. Tousled, skimpily clad *jineteras* shimmy with each other under the strobes, darting their gaze in search of available foreign men, who aren't usually hard to find. It's open every night from 8 PM and closes at 3 AM. Entry is US$5 or free for hotel guests.

Cabaret
Located on Carretera del Morro, one and a half kilometers (almost a mile) out of town, **Tropicana (** (53-226) 9-1287 is Santiago's version of the popular Havana cabaret, and though it lacks the professional flair and imagination of the original (nor are the performers quite as glamorous), it still puts up an energetic show with a large cast sashshaying about in flamboyant and titillating costumes, or performing magical tricks and acrobatics. The cabaret is staged in a large

Hotel Santiago de Cuba, a somewhat dated monolith.

custom-built stadium (designed by the same architect responsible for the Hotel Santiago) with an attached piano bar and restaurant. Tickets are US$35.

GETTING AROUND

Car rental is available at the **Cubanacán** desk at the Hotel Santiago, **Havanautos** at the Hotel Las Américas and **Transautos** at Villa San Juan.

You'll find the main tourist taxi stand in front of the Hotel Santiago de Cuba; there

destinations (see GETTING THERE, page 298 in TRAVELERS' TIPS).

Cubana de Aviación has several daily direct flights from Havana, and a thrice-weekly flight from and to Baracoa. Contact **Cubana de Aviación** ((53-226) 2-4156, Calle Felix Peña, between Calles Heredia and Bartolomé Masó.

Aside from flying, Santiago is also easily reached from many points of the island by train (see GETTING THERE, page 298 in TRAVELERS' TIPS). The **Terminal de Ferrocarriles** is near the port, west of the city.

is another taxi stand outside the Hotel Casa Granda in Parque Céspedes. You will also notice *taxi particulares,* or private taxis, who hire themselve out for short rides around the city, and in some cases, you can negotiate a daily rate with the driver. They tend to congregate around the Plaza de Marte.

HOW TO GET THERE

Santiago de Cuba's **Antonio Maceo International Airport** is located seven kilometers (four miles) south of the city. Although most visitors fly to Havana first, and then make a connecting flight, it is possible to fly directly here from many international

EXPLORING SANTIAGO'S ENVIRONS

CAYO GRANMA

While flying into Santiago de Cuba, or looking across the bay from El Morro, you will catch sight of this tiny, pretty island just off the coast.

Formerly known as Cayo Smith, for the wealthy English slave trader who owned it, the island was later renamed for the famous leaky boat that carried Castro and his men to Cuba from Mexico in 1956. It is worth exploring, if only to experience the tranquillity of this picturesque backwater, with its single circular path leading from the ferry pier past ramshackle wooden houses swallowed in foliage and flowers. There are no cars, hotels and few amenities on the island, but it has a charming restaurant — El Cayo, which has a verandah that is one of the most relaxing places to idle in Santiago.

Where To Eat

Charmingly located, **El Cayo**, on Cayo Granma, serves moderately–priced seafood and Creole dishes. This is a nice place to stop for coffee or a cocktail, even if you

Cubans, and the other (run by Marlin Marinas) for tourists. It's worth a visit, especially if you coincide your trip with lunch.

LA BASILICA DEL COBRE

Tucked away in the small hillside town of **El Cobre**, 16 km (10 miles) from Santiago, the basilica of **La Virgen de la Caridad del Cobre** (Virgin of Charity of Cobre) is Cuba's most important religious pilgrimage site. The Virgin is the island's patron saint, officially named as such in 1916 but regarded

don't have lunch here, and is open from noon to 9 PM.

Located on the hillside overlooking Cayo Granma, close to the ferry, this peaceful out-of-town location is good for the Chinese dishes with a Creole influence served at **Kiam Sands Restaurant (** (53-226) 9-1889, Carretera de Punta Gorda. You can sit on the shady terrace or in air-conditioned Chinese-style interiors. It is open from noon to 11 PM.

How to Get There

To reach Cayo Granma, you have to catch a ferry from Punta Gorda, several kilometers from Santiago. There are two ferries — leaving from different piers — one for

as a miracle-worker for centuries. During his visit here in 1998, Pope John Paul II blessed the Virgin with a papal kiss. Thousands of pilgrims from all over Cuba come here every year to worship and pray on September 8, when her festival is held. Many regard this destination as a Cuban Lourdes.

Background

El Cobre itself seems thick with history: it was the first open *cobre* (copper) mine in the Americas, the first mine opening in 1550 with slave labor, and much later in 1731 (perhaps fortified by their belief in the protective powers of La Caridad), this was

OPPOSITE: Santiago musician Emilo Cavailhon. ABOVE: Traveling to the city by carriage.

where the largest slave rebellion in Cuba took place.

The legend of La Caridad begins in 1608, when two Indians and a young slave named Juan Moreno, all mine workers, were at sea off the Bay of Nipe, on Cuba's northern coast, on a salt-collecting expedition. The wind swelled high, and they feared for their lives, when from their boat they saw something floating in the sea. When they fished it out, they saw that it was a small statue of the Virgin on a wooden plank engraved with inscription: "I am the Virgin of Charity." The swells then subsided, and they returned to safety. When they bought the statue back to El Cobre, it was decided to built a new chapel for her at some distance away from town. In the three years that followed, the statue disappeared from its altar, only to mysteriously re-appear at the top of El Cobre hill. The slaves decided this was a sign from above, and built a new chapel for her on that spot, where she became the patroness of the slaves working below. From that moment on, she became famous for her miraculous powers. The Virgin is frequently invoked as Ochún, one of the most powerful of the Yoruba goddesses in the Santería religion — and few Cubans would be so rash as to omit her in their prayers, especially in times of trouble.

Built in 1927, the present church — the only one in Cuba with the rank of basilica — rises from the nearby foliage with its three yellow towers topped by red cupolas. A long staircase leads to the main entrance, lined with street lamps. The statue of La Caridad del Cobre holding an infant Jesus is displayed in a glass case above the altar — her saffron and copper robes are also the color of Ochún, goddess of sexuality and love, protector of pregnant women.

Over the years, visitors have left offerings to the Virgin in a side chapel that is deluged with flowers, little scraps of cheap jewelry and cloth, wooden crosses, hand-written letters, autographed baseball bats, leg-braces, crutches, police badges, military medals, and all manner of other souvenirs from those who sought blessing here.

One of the most famous offerings, unfortunately, cannot be seen. After Hemingway was awarded the Nobel Prize in 1954,

he turned over his gold medallion to the people of Cuba, requesting that it be displayed at the El Cobre basilica. After it was stolen in 1988, only to surface several days later when the culprits were caught, it has been held by the Archbishop of Santiago. Also in safekeeping, perhaps considered too politically contentious, is the Catholic amulet given to the El Cobre basilica by Fidel Castro's mother as she prayed for her son's protection.

Unless you arrive very early, you will undoubtedly be approached by gangs of determined, sometimes quite aggressive, touts trying to sell you lumps of pretty but not very enticing pyrites that have been churned up in the nearby mines. They are best avoided.

EXPLORING SANTIAGO DE CUBA PROVINCE

You don't have to travel a great distance to appreciate the charms of this small province. Within a day or two you can easily explore some spectacular mountain scenery, see one or two quirky museums, and still be able to spend the afternoon by the sea, contemplating the sunset with the inevitable *daiquirí*.

There are a range of fairly modest places to stay in this area, east of Santiago. However, the two nicest beach resorts within driving distance are in fact located to the west of the city. Both the **Sierra Mar Club Resort** and the **Los Galeones**, are listed under DRIVING TO SANTIAGO DE CUBA, page 244 in EASTERN CUBA.

Santiago de Cuba and the Far East

PARQUE BACONAO

Encompassing 80,000 hectares (almost 200,000 acres), Baconao is the largest park in Cuba, stretching 52 km (32 miles) from the outskirts of Santiago to Baconao Lagoon, and from the dense mountains of the Sierra de la Gran Piedra to the sandy beaches of the Caribbean coast. A theme-park in the communist mold, the park was partly the brainchild of Celia Sánchez, Castro's long-time companion and ally, and was originally developed as a recreation center for Cubans, but has since come to embrace international tourists as well.

El Cobre, whose basilica draws pilgrims.

Part of the park has been designated a Biosphere Reserve by UNESCO, and represents an attempt to reforest Cuba with many endemic species of flora and fauna — it is a beautiful wilderness, crisscrossed with walking paths. Elsewhere, the park comprises a long series of beaches, some with hotels and restaurants, a so-called "Prehistoric Valley," and numerous museums and other attractions. It is well worth a day's visit from Santiago, which can easily include a mountain walk and an afternoon by the sea, or you can stay within the park for several days.

As you leave Santiago along the Avenida de las Américas, take Avenida Pujol for Baconao Park. You will see, on your right, the **Loma de San Juan** (San Juan Hill), the site of the last battle in the War of Independence, an event ingrained on generations of United States schoolchildren. For all the hype, the hill itself is very small. There's a small Spanish fortress near the Hotel San Juan, and a large *ceiba* tree. It was under these branches that, on June 16, 1898, Spanish troops surrendered to the United States Army, handing Cuba over in a ceremony at which not a single Cuban was present. At the top of San Juan Hill, a row of memorials commemorates the *mambisas*, the soldiers who fought for Cuba's independence, and there are also some in honor of American soldiers who died here.

The main memorial mentions the blood "of the brave and true Cuban insurgents and that of the generous American soldiers who sealed a covenant of liberty and fraternity between the two nations." Nowhere on San Juan Hill is there any mention of Teddy Roosevelt and his famous Rough Riders, who led the American invasion in 1898.

From here, the road heads for Baconao Park. This route has history branded into it: it was taken first by the invading Americans in 1898, and then later in 1953, by Castro and his revolutionaries on their way to the Moncada Barracks. As you drive along, you'll see 26 stone memorials lining the road — Fidel's superstitious number "26" — in commemoration of the rebels who died in the aftermath of that assault. Incidentally, the number does *not* correspond to the body count of those who died.

LA GRAN PIEDRA

About 10 km (six miles) east of town, before reaching the beach town of Siboney, a well-signposted turn-off marks the route to **La Gran Piedra**, an enormous boulder that perches almost supernaturally on a peak in the northern Sierra Maestra mountains. As the road winds ever upward (this is one of the steepest inclines you are likely to encounter in Cuba), a breathtaking landscape unfolds with each curve: myriad hues of green trees and vines are splashed with fiery orange *flamboyán* blossoms and fragrant *mariposa* flowers; butterflies and birds flit through coffee and guava plantations; and views towards the coast grow increasingly spectacular. The heat of the coast subsides,

and the air becomes cooler, fresher and moist from the tiny waterfalls trickling out from the side of rocks. The road itself is sometimes prone to landslides, and its steepness requires cautious driving — watch out for hikers, locals, and wandering animals. (This is not really a trip to attempt on a day when there is a torrential downpour.)

Shrouded in pine forest, La Gran Piedra, literally the "great rock," looms some 1,234 m (4,113 ft) above sea-level. It's a 432-step climb to the top, with plenty of places to rest and look at the exotic vegetation and lizards. Look out for the spiky *pandanao* tree, with its large nugget-sized seeds striped in Reggae tri-colors which smell just like a banana.

From the top of La Gran Piedra, it's said, you can see Haiti and Jamaica on a clear day

— or at least their reflected lights in the sky at night — but others scoff at this as fancy. You can see as far as the naked eye can stretch in all directions, however: dazzling views southwards to the coast, and undulating green valleys to the north.

There are many mountain pathways to take for long walks through the Sierra Maestra, during which you may catch glimpses of the rare, tiny bee hummingbird, known as *zunzuncito* (a frenetic flash of blue, green and red feathers), and the exquisite *Greta Cubana*, one of two clear-winged butterfly species in the world. You can ask at the Cubanacán La Gran Piedra Hotel about arranging a visit to the nearby botanical

Guajiros, or traditional farmers, at work.

gardens, where seedlings are planted for reforestation.

If you stay up here, remember to bring a pair of good walking shoes, a jacket for cool evenings, and mosquito repellent.

Where to Stay

Cubanacán La Gran Piedra** ((53-226) 5-1154 or 5-1098, Carretera La Gran Piedra, 14 km (nine miles) from Santiago, can't be missed as you drive along the main road to La Gran Piedra. A refuge from the heat of summer, this is a very private, beautifully located Cubanacán resort; each of the 22 stone *casitas* have wonderful views (each have their own terrace). There is a restaurant, bar and games room, and horseback riding and walking tours can be arranged.

La Isabelica

Having come this far as the Gran Piedra, don't miss driving just a little further along the mountain-side to reach **La Isabelica**, an early nineteenth century French coffee planter's estate that is now a museum. The Spartan stone hacienda is a moving sight, its walls alive with a creeping flame-colored lichen echoed by the surrounding red blossoming *flamboyáns*.

It was built in 1810 by Monsieur Victor Constantin Cuzeau, who set about re-building his fortune in this vertiginous and isolated place after fleeing the slave revolution in Haiti, bringing his slaves with him by force. An early daguerreotype shows him to be a tall, stern and maniacally alert figure in a top hat and suit. Yet he was obviously not without passion: he named his plantation for Isabel Maria, his slave mistress, who lived with him as slaves toiled below in their chains. The museum encompasses the hacienda, coffee drying beds, and plantation grounds, with displays of heavy tools and shackles. Delicious coffee is served for the US$1 donation or entrance fee. It is open Tuesday to Saturday 9 AM to 5 PM, Sunday 9 AM to 1 PM.

From the Mountain to the Coast

As you return to the coast, take the turning along the main highway to Baconao Park to

Santiago de Cuba and the Far East

La Granjita Siboney, located just before the beachfront town of Siboney. This is the farmhouse Fidel Castro and his comrades — disguised as chicken farmers — rented in 1953, a few weeks before their July 26 attack on the Moncada Barracks. Some 135 men loyal to Castro gathered here on the eve of the attack, and most had only hours to prepare themselves with the details of what their mission would entail. Despite warnings from Castro about the risks involved, most set off on the doomed assault with their leader's words ringing in their ears: "We will be free men or martyrs." Later, the farmhouse was the scene of grisly torture and butchering as many of those who participated in the raid were brought here by the Batista forces. Inside the museum, blood-stained khaki uniforms and objects retrieved from the Moncada assault tell the story. It is open Tuesday to Sunday, 9 AM to 5 PM, and closed on Monday.

Continuing on, Siboney's beach is very popular with young *santiagüeros*, but there are nicer beaches further. A road to the left at the junction just south of Granjita Siboney heads east to Laguna Baconao. Several kilometers on, you reach **El Oasis**, an artist's community, and to the north, you will see a large thatched restaurant and bar — **Finca Guajira Rodeo** — where you can watch rodeos on Tuesdays, Thursdays, Saturdays and Sundays at 2:30 PM, or rent horses for rides.

Back on the main road, a few kilometers to the east is the turnoff for the **Club Amigo Bucanero**, a resort hotel built into the rocks next to a pretty little cove.

After some 10 km (six miles) along the main highway, you will reach Damajayabo Valley, otherwise known as the **Valley of Prehistory**. A bizarre sight greets the visitor: the dusty landscape is dotted with almost a hundred life-like (well, almost, from a distance) replicas of prehistoric dinosaurs, mammals and Stone Age *Homo sapiens*, all frozen in action poses. (None of them were endemic to Cuba.) Wandering around them and posing alongside for wonderfully kitsch photographs takes about half an hour, with an optional drink in the Fred

Roadside flowers on the way to Gran Piedra.

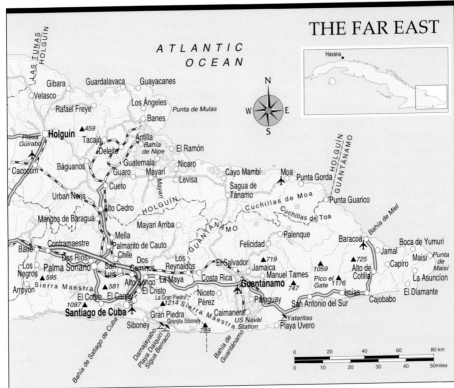

Flintstone-style cave. Admission is free, but you are expected to pay a US$1 parking fee. The valley is open Tuesday to Sunday, 8 AM to 5 PM.

From here, the road heads towards the coast towards Playa Daiquirí, one of the nicest beaches in the park.

Before you get there, though, you'll pass a delightful **Museum of Transport**, which is well worth a stop, either on the way there, or on the way back. It's really more rewarding than visiting the fake dinosaurs. This collection of antique cars was once a private personal collection. Among its stars are the smallest hand-made car in Cuba, Beny Moré's Cadillac, the 1956 Ford Thunderbird that belonged to Angel Castro (Fidel's father), Batista's 1948 blue Oldsmobile and 2,070 miniature cars displayed indoors that trace the history of car design.

FOLLOWING THE BACONAO COASTLINE

From here, the road forks right and leads to **Playa Daiquirí**, site of the 1898 landing by Roosevelt and his Rough Riders, and now a relaxed seaside resort. After swimming, the seaside restaurant here is a very pleasant place to have lunch, under palm umbrellas, with feet in sand.

The marvelous group of musicians who busk on the sands are a tale of modern Cuba: all are former academics — one a former doctor, and every day, they struggle to transport their heavy instruments — including a double bass — long distances in the hope of making a few dollars.

In the area, the **Hotel Cubanacán Daiquirí**** ((53-226) 2-4859 or 2-4735, Carretera Baconao, eight and a half kilometers (five miles) from Santiago, is the only choice should you wish to stay in the area a little longer. It's said that the *daiquirí* was invented here, named for a nearby ore mine, after American soldiers adopted the local habit of mixing rum with sugar and water. With their addition of crushed ice, the drink became famous the world over.

The main advantage of this Spartan complex is its location close to one of the nicest beaches in Baconao park. A small diving school is based here.

You'll notice, beginning at Playa Daiquirí, the layered pancake-like rocks by the sea. This geological phenomenon can be seen all the way along the coast until you reach Baracoa. From here, the road leads to the entrance to a reserve, closed for the moment. There are plans for it to become a zoological park in the future.

Further along is the **Balneario de Sol Hotel**, next to a spray-drenched natural rock pool. At the nearest beach to the hotel, Playa Sigua, you'll find the two best restaurants in the park, **Los Corales** and **Casa de Pedro el Cojo**.

If you have a meal here, be sure to spend a few hours exploring some of the area's sights. The road continues east through the **Jardín de Cactus**, which contains more than 400 cacti, then to **Jardín Marino**, a marine aquarium. The next cove along, **Cazonal**, has soft white sand. Nearing the end of the park, you'll reach **Baconao Lagoon**, where crocodiles can be seen in their natural habitat at a crocodile farm.

Where to Stay

Club Amigo Bucanero* ((53-226) 5-4596 or 2-8130 FAX (53-226) 8-6070, Carretera Baconao, Arroya la Costa, is the best choice of the hotels available. Located atop a clifftop facing the sea and the mountains, this all-inclusive Cubanacán resort has small private beach nearby perfect for swimming. All rooms have air-conditioning, satellite television, phone, and minibar. Facilities include a choice of restaurants, a bar and nightclub, sports activities, and a shop.

The main feature **Balneario del Sol*** (53-226) 2-8130 or 5-4596 FAX (53-226) 8-6070, Carretera de Baconao, is a large saltwater swimming pool that crests above the reefs — the main beach, Playa de Sigua, is a few hundred meters away. It's a pleasant location, with the usual Cubanacán facilities.

LTI Carisol Resort Hotel* ((53-226) 2-6005 or 2-6894, Carretera de Baconao, Cazonal Beach, is a well-maintained and comfortable hotel in a secluded location: a good choice for families with children, with daily recreational programs and a range of sports activities. The twin, but slightly larger **LTI Los Corales Resort*** ((53-226) 2-7202 or 2-7191, Carretera Baconao, Cazonal Beach,

has good facilities including diving lessons and car, bicycle, and moped rental.

Where to Eat

Los Corales ((53-266) 2-7204, Playa de Sigua, is set on a wonderful location on a cliff overlooking the coast and is a must for fresh seafood. **Casa de Pedro el Cojo** ((53-226) 39-8160, also located at Playa de Sigua, has an equally loyal following for its excellent Creole dishes, most notably roast pig.

How to Get There

The easiest way to explore is by rental car or taxi, and of course, you'll need to negotiate rates in advance. Renting a car, or arranging a day away with a car and driver is easily done, either through a car rental agency or from the taxi stand at Plaza de Marte.

Otherwise, the best option for exploring the Parque Baconao is to take an organized excursion run by one of the main tour agencies from Santiago de Cuba. Rumbos has offices opposite the Hotel Casa Granda and in the Hotel Las Américas.

THE FAR EAST

Once you enter Guantánamo Province, be assured that you have strayed firmly off Cuba's beaten track. The province has much more to offer than just the controversial United States military base, and the drive to Baracoa, Cuba's oldest colonial town, along La Farola highway, is one of the island's most spectacular journeys.

GUANTÁNAMO PROVINCE

The remote and unpopulous province of Guantánamo runs from Santiago de Cuba to the easternmost tip of island, which is the least visited part of the island. The capital, also called Guantánamo, which lies 90 km (56 miles) east of Santiago, is a fairly unattractive prospect, with its bleak housing estates and swirling dust bales. Everyone in Cuba, and perhaps a great many people around the world, can recognize this as the province that is celebrated in the song *Guantánamera*, which is also the name of the famous Cuban director Tomás Gutiérrez Alea's last film.

BACKGROUND

Guantánamo is equally well known for the United States Naval Military Base here, which is one of Cuba's great political oddities. In 1902, when Cuba was declared Republic, the price for the end of military occupation by American troops was that the naval station at Guantánamo be leased "in perpetuity." The continuing presence of the naval base has been a constant source of aggravation for Fidel Castro's government. As you enter Guantánamo town, you see a huge billboard which pronounces: "No Son Negociables" — Not Negotiable.

The Guantánamo naval installation is the largest in the world, spanning 72 sq km (about 28 sq miles), and is separated from Cuban territory by a 27-km (nearly 17-mile)-long fence and many thousands of Cuban and American landmines. It houses 2,000 military personnel and about 1,500 civilians within a community of suburban houses and split-level ranches tidily housed on well-lit roads, along with administrative offices, shopping malls, recreation areas, a hospital, a church, a port, and two airfields. The base was the setting for the film, *A Few Good Men*, starring Tom Cruise, Demi Moore, and Jack Nicholson.

Every year the United States sends the Cuban government a nominal rent check for about US$4,000, but since Castro came to power in 1959, these checks have never been cashed, for the Cuban government is incensed by the situation and adamant that the United States should go. It is strictly forbidden for any transit to occur between the United States naval base and the rest of Cuba, although a dwindling number of graying Cuban employees — now entering their twilight years — still retain jobs on the base which they have held since before 1959; and they are the only personnel allowed to come and go. Meanwhile, only approved United States military personnel and their families are allowed in from the United States.

WHAT TO SEE AND DO

With prior permission or by joining an organized tour (ask at your hotel in Santiago)

you can enter the Cuban military zone and drive to a lookout located on a hill overlooking the base, **Mirador de Malones**, a restaurant and bar operated by Gaviota. From the military checkpoint, a road winds upward through dry plains and thick forests of prickly cacti, many of which were planted by the Cuban army as a "cactus curtain" to prevent Cubans from trying to seek political asylum in the base. From the lookout, it is a surreal experience to look through the powerful binoculars (made in Fairhope, USA) set up here, and survey all that the eye can see of the base, from American soldiers in their watchtowers to trucks unloading at the docks, all the while aware that everything on your side is also being avidly scrutinized.

During the summer of 1994, when unprecedented numbers of Cubans were trying to flee in order to seek automatic political asylum in the United States, many of them were intercepted by United States coastguard patrols and returned to the Guantánamo base, which served as a United States detention camp while the United States government tried to figure out what to do with them. Haitians fleeing turmoil in their country were also detained here: 40,000 of them; a quarter of whom were sent back to Haiti. The detention camp was closed down, and at present Guantánamo continues its usual duties of training the entire United States Atlantic Fleet.

To the southeast of Guantánamo town is the small, sleepy fishing village of **Caimanera**, bordering the naval base. This is a restricted zone, and generally, the remaining Cubans who work on the base commute from here. Many Cubans have tried to swim into the base from here, and you need to pass through a checkpoint to enter, however you will only be allowed to pass if you have a reservation at the Hotel Caimanera here.

In the bizarre-atmosphere stakes, this is a great place to stay: you can watch the lights of the naval base twinkle away nearby across the stretch of sea.

WHERE TO STAY AND EAT

The small, 17-room **Hotel Caimanera***** ((53-21) 9-9414 or 9-9416, Loma Norte, Caimanera, is a good place to break your journey and it's far more scenic than anywhere in Guantánamo town. It has a nice swimming pool and the staff are very friendly.

How to Get There

Guantánamo's **Mariana Grajales Airport** is located 16 km (10 miles) southeast of the town center. Cubana de Aviación has daily flights from Havana.

By rail, there are daily train services connecting Guantánamo to Santiago de Cuba, Holguín and Havana. The **Estación de Fer-**

Playas Yateritas and **Imías**, near the village of the same name.

Just after Imías the road turns inland and heads north towards the mountains. Then begins the winding ascent of **La Farola** ("The Beacon"), a 30-km (nearly 18-mile)-long roadway which was finished in 1968 and is one of Cuba's greatest engineering feats. It snakes and winds its way across this region's steep mountain passes, and in many places is supported by columns. As you climb, you enter dense untouched tropical forest and a rarefied, almost alpine coolness

rocarriles is on Calle Pedro A. Pérez, just north of Parque Martí.

FROM GUANTÁNAMO TO BARACOA

From Guantánamo, the road continues for a time across empty arid hills and then along the empty southern coast, which is bordered cacti-covered hills with deep ochre cliffs that are thrashed by unruly waves. Small towns here sustain themselves on fishing and farming salt and mangoes, and although this is a poor region it becomes increasingly lush and beautiful, splashed with bougainvillea and hibiscus plants. Along the route a few sheltered sandy coves are tempting places to stop for a swim, especially

chills the air. Clouds permeate the lush scenery and views across the coffee and cacao plantations of small villages and tropical vegetation are breathtaking (and at some vertiginous moments, a little nervous-making). *Guajiros* on horseback are a common sight. From the highest point, you can see both the northern and southern coasts of Cuba.

From here, the road twists and winds its way downwards to Baracoa's lush coastal flatlands. Be sure to drive across La Farola only during daylight hours and during good weather, as the roads are treacherous enough even by day, with switchbacks, sharp curves and steep hills.

A family on the road among Guantánamo cactus.

BARACOA

For many years, Baracoa remained a very isolated part of Cuba, and in many ways this sultry backwater seems pickled in a peculiar unreality all its own. Tropical vegetation licks at its edges, and its air is sweet with the smell of damp plants and salt-sea. It is an intriguing place to visit, with its lonely colonial fortresses and enveloping provincial life. Further afield, you can visit rural villages, swim in deserted beaches and perhaps even kayak or raft through forested stretches of river.

BACKGROUND

Located at almost the easternmost tip of the island, Baracoa was the island's first settlement; founded in 1512 as the first of seven cities founded by Diego Velázquez, and for a very brief period Cuba's capital. Baracoa sits beside the rounded curve of Porto Santo inlet, the second place Columbus stopped on his first voyage to America, and where he planted (so it is believed) a wooden cross, said to be Cuba's oldest relic, which can now be seen in Baracoa's Nuestra Señora de la Asunción church. Columbus admired the surrounding landscape and commented on the unusual square-shape of **El Yunque**, 575 m (1,886 ft) high, the remains of an ancient limestone mesa which dominates the horizon, and on the beauty of the nearby Río de Miel, the so-called "River of Honey," as well as the Toa and Duaba rivers.

Many in Cuba regard Baracoa as the cradle of the island's civilization: it was home to a large settlement of Taíno Indians, evidenced by the quantities of Taíno pottery, objects made from sea shells and ancient human skeletons found here. After the conquest of Cuba, many Taíno Indians took refuge here (together with slaves who managed to escape from plantations), and they are believed to have survived longest here, explaining why many Baracoans have Taíno qualities, being short of stature, with smooth, light bronze skin. The region's forested mountains are rich in pre-Columbian archaeological sites, and Baracoa itself has one of the best museums in the country and one of Cuba's most active centers of archaeological research.

Baracoa's strategic foothold location required fortresses and towers to protect its early Spanish colonists from pirates at sea, most of whihc were built during the mid-eighteenth century. One of the fortresses, the Seboruco, sits high on a hill and has been turned into **Hotel El Castillo**, a comfortable hotel with unmatched views across the Bahía de Miel in one direction, and across another sea of green forest to El Yunque in the other. There are fortresses at both ends of Baracoa: the Matachín and La Punta: one is now the Matachín Museum and the other provides a dramatic setting for a restaurant.

GENERAL INFORMATION

Baracoa has little infrastructure for tourists, beyond its two main hotels, El Castillo and Porto Santo, and you will probably have to rely on them for essentials such as cashing traveler's checks and changing currency as well as for post and phone calls. Hotel Porto Santo has a **Havanautos** car rental office.

You can check with the **Agencia de Reservaciones e Información (** (53-21) 2337, at Calle Antonio Maceo No. 149, easy to find beside the church. They run excursions within Baracoa and to surrounding nature reserves, working farms and beaches, as well as kayaking trips down the Río Toa, and visits to Finca Duaba. They can arrange accommodation at the Villa Maguaná.

If you are interested in arranging to spend more time in the region's wilds, you should contact **Horizontes Hoteles (** (53-7) 33-4042 FAX (53-7) 33-3722, Avenida 23 No. 156, between Calles N and O, Vedado, Havana, which can arrange white-water rafting and kayaking trips. **Alcona SA (** (53-7) 22-2526 FAX (53-7) 33-1532, Calle 42 No. 514, Havana, can arrange guided nature walks.

Should you need medical attention, one can only hope that it is not serious: the nearest well-equipped hospital is at Guantánamo, 150 km (93 miles) west, a journey that should not be made after dark. **Baracoa**

A wooden shack stands amidst luxurious vegetation near Baracoa, Guantánamo.

Santiago de Cuba and the Far East

Hospital, despite its well-trained doctors, is a study in the impact of the United States embargo.

WHAT TO SEE AND DO

Baracoa is small enough to explore on foot, especially if you are staying at Hotel El Castillo, which lies at the heart of the town. Most of the town's houses are dilapidated, red-tiled and made of wood, and are not very old, yet there is a strongly colonial influence in Baracoa's layout of streets and

beautiful polymites, or snail shells, especially the *polymita Pictas*, which is unique and endemic to this region. Baracoa's well-respected city historian, Alejandro Hartman, has his office in the museum and has an encyclopedic knowledge about the region.

You should definitely visit the church of **Nuestra Señora de la Asunción de Baracoa** (Our Lady of the Assumption), which stands on Baracoa's Parque Central. Inside is the famous **Cruz de la Parra**, the cross that Columbus is believed to have planted when

squares, in its small parks and its long seafront Malecón.

Whatever direction you take, it seems you are plunged into some vignette of neighborhood life: laughing children running in their blue Pioneer uniforms, housewives throwing buckets of water in the gutter, factory buses picking up workers, old men and athletic young boys playing dominoes, side by side.

You could start with a visit to the **Museo Matachín**, housed in the Fuerte Matachín, at the entrance to the town. The museum showcases discoveries (and Taíno skeletons) from some 56 archaeological sites from the area. Another collection of much interest is the museum's display of the

he landed in nearby Porto Santo. Apparently he placed it at the mouth of cove, with rough stones heaped around it, where according to legend it was found under a vine in 1510 by Diego Velázquez's expeditionaries. Made of dark wood, about a meter (a yard) high and adorned with silver-plated metal, carbon dating has confirmed the antiquity of the cross, which is believed to have been made of wood from the area's native seascape tree. Over the centuries, it has survived unscathed — despite the fact that Baracoa's original church, founded in 1512, was twice destroyed, first by pirate attacks and later by fire.

Within the Parque Central stands a statue of the Taíno Indian chief, Hatuey, who the Spanish burned alive at the stake because he refused to become a religious convert.

From here, a block east takes you to Calle Antonio Maceo, one of the town's main streets, which is a good place to wander, passing the **"Socialismo o Muerte" bakery** and perhaps stopping at the **Casa del Chocolate** on Calle Calixto García, which sells cups of hot chocolate and locally made chocolate bars. You may see a few shops selling handicrafts for the *turistas*, made of natural fibers native to the area, coconut husks, shells, and seascape wood carvings.

debarked and left his cross. This complex is Baracoa's most relaxing place to unwind, with its roomy bungalows, a large pool area with a swim-up bar, and a nearby beach. It also has an outdoor restaurant and a cabaret.

Both the above hotels have recently been taken over by Gaviota, the tourist group run by Cuba's Ministry of Defense, and may be upgraded soon.

Inexpensive

The mustard-colored hotel right on the Malecón, **Hotel La Rusa*** ((53-21) 4-2102,

WHERE TO STAY

Moderate

With its commanding position and marvelous views across Baracoa and the harbor from its swimming pool deck, **Hotel El Castillo***** ((53-21) 4-2103 or 4-2125, Calle Calixto García, Loma, is an easy choice if you want to be in walking distance of the town. The hotel's stairs, protected by two old towers, lead up to an elevation where the fortress was built, while the rooftop bar has an excellent lookout. Rooms are simple but comfortable, and the restaurant food is good.

Hotel Porto Santo*** ((53-21) 4-3578 or 4-3590, Carretera al Aeropuerto, is across the bay, close to the beach where Columbus

Calle Máximo Gómez, is named for the colorful Russian lady who established it, Magdalena Monasse. She was a fervent *Fidelista*, who settled here, perhaps preferring the climate. Fidel and Che stayed here in the past. Don't expect luxury.

WHERE TO EAT

La Punta, located within the historic fort, right at the entrance to the harbor, is Baracoa's easily best restaurant, with delicious, inexpensive cuisine served up in a casual atmosphere, with tables outside if you

OPPOSITE: Typical Baracoa wooden houses.
ABOVE: A Baracoa girl celebrates her fifteenth birthday.

prefer. Try the *pescado coleche de coco* (fish cooked in coconut milk), the *chatino* (fried green bananas) and the *arroz con coco* (coconut milk-cooked rice).

In deference to the local coconut industry, you should sample *vino de coco*, which is rather nice and tastes a bit like a sweet retsina, served with ice. It is also hard to resist the local *cucurucho*, a delicious soft, sweet coconut candy that is served wrapped in palm leaves.

Don't miss a visit to the **Casa del Chocolate** on Calle Antonio Maceo, where you can a drink of cup of locally-produced chocolate.

NIGHTLIFE

At night, darkness settles across Baracoa almost eerily, after the nightly visual symphony that is the sunset is enacted across the sky: honeying the sea and seemingly turning the surrounding forest into liquefied green.

From El Castillo's balcony bar, all the sounds of the town float up; you might hear the unmistakably unique tones of the *nengón* and the *kiribá*, instruments which are rarely heard these days in Cuba, and the frenetic chants which accompany the Afro-Cuban *Yambú Akalé* dancers. You can ask about attending one of these ceremonies, which are usually private.

Competing salsa music blares forth from the town's only discotheque, an open-air affair on the rooftop of a dreary building that is the social focus for miles around.

HOW TO GET THERE

In an effort to promote tourism to this province, Cubana de Aviación has recently begun operating thrice-weekly flights to Baracoa from Havana via Santiago de Cuba or Guantánamo at a nearby modest landing strip — the **Gustavo Rizo Airport** — which ends abruptly at the harbor's edge at Porto Santo. Contact **Cubana de Aviación (** (53-21) 4-2171, Calle José Martí No.181.

By road — whether you come by rental car, tour bus or hitching a ride on an old truck — Baracoa lies 150 km (93 miles) northeast of Guantánamo. You'll see Baracoa's sole

Servi-Cupet at the entrance to the town as you drive in from Guantánamo.

EXCURSIONS FROM BARACOA

From Baracoa, there are two possible routes along the coast to explore: westwards towards the mining area of Moa; and eastwards to the very tip of Cuba at Punta de Maisí.

WEST FROM BARACOA

To the west, the road first passes the inlet of Porto Santo, and then passes through a spectacular stretch of lush coconut plantations, Banyan-like *jagüey* trees, and inlets hiding unspoiled beaches.

Some, like **Playa Duaba**, near Porto Santo airport, have a decent swathe of beach; others are merely slivers of sand tucked between dense foliage. At Playa Duaba is a commemorative tablet marking the spot where Antonio Maceo, the great independence fighter, put ashore with a band of like-minded companions and joined the War of Independence.

Within the district — a short distance inland — is the **Finca Duaba**, which stages *campesino*-style meals for tourists and is also a great place from which to swim in the Río Duaba. Visitors are welcome daily, but the *finca*'s managers prefer to have advance bookings (see Baracoa GENERAL INFORMATION, page 279) so that they know to prepare food that day.

En route, it is interesting to see various stages in one of the region's main industries: coconut farming. The palms are harvested from a seed banks set up by the Ministry of Agriculture, with as many as 19,000 coconut palms in each seed bank.

Further on, about 12 km (seven and a half miles)outside Baracoa, is the turnoff to **Playa Maguaná**, one of the best beaches in the area, with rounded and bay. Located here is the Villa Maguaná, a simple, four-bedroom house which can be rented privately and inexpensively, with a cook and a maid to service the villa at an additional cost. Contact the Agencia de Reservaciones y Información in Baracoa (see Baracoa GENERAL INFORMATION, page 279.)

Not many people drive onwards to **Moa**, further around the coast to the northwest. This arduous journey involves a fairly bumpy ride across a mostly dirt road, and is an alternative route to traveling back into central Cuba, if you are heading for Holguín or Guardalavaca perhaps. The initially scenic landscape of rustic villages and plantations becomes a harsh, sunbaked realm of burgundy-colored soil and almost visibly metallic trickles of water. Here, three huge mines — including a brand-new mine that is a Cuban-Dutch joint-venture named after Che Guevara — are progressively mining Cuba's largest deposits of nickel. Not hugely recommended as an overland route.

On your way back to Baracoa from Playa Maguaná, take the turnoff to the **Cuchillas del Toa Ridge** which climbs for about two kilometers (just over a mile) to a lookout point which offers dazzling views across the Alturas de Sagua-Baracoa, the Cuchillas del Toa and the Cuchillas de Moa, as well as El Yunque. All around, for some 220 sq km (85 sq miles), the surrounding virgin rainforest is a protected nature reserve: the **Cuchillas del Toa Biosphere Reserve**, through which runs the Río Toa. Saved from the loggers, this reserve is one of the most beautiful, yet least-visited in Cuba, but correspondingly, it is the island's richest in endemic flora and fauna, with its many varying habitats and ecosystems. Those in the Cuban government who had the foresight to protect this area should be gratified that its success stories are many: the virtually-extinct large ivory billed woodpecker, seen almost nowhere else, lives here as does the endangered royal woodpecker; and Cuba's tiny endemic frog which is no bigger than a fingernail. Just as tiny, multi-colored polymite snails live here amid the forest floor's mosses and lichens.

As yet, there are few trails through the reserve (also referred to as the **Parque Nacional Alejandro Humboldt** Cuchillas del Toa Biosphere Reserve), but take any opportunity to see whatever you can of Cuba's outpost of untouched wilderness. Both Hotel El Castillo and Hotel Porto Santo arrange guided tours.

EAST OF BARACOA TO THE TIP OF CUBA

The most popular place to visit east of Baracoa is **Yumurí**, which lies 25 km (under 16 miles) away and is named after the river which snakes through it. It is a beautiful hour-long drive along a good road, which winds through the hills and then down to the coast, where you pass an array of idyllic little black-sanded beaches.

The village of Yumurí itself is very rustic and relaxed, but the scenery here is

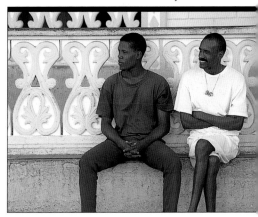

breathtaking, with a towering backdrop of forested cliffs. The drive back is equally impressive for its vistas of El Yunque.

Should you wish to continue on (preferably in a four-wheel drive vehicle), another 20 km (about 12 miles) on a bumpy dirt road brings you to **La Punta de Maisí**, the very easternmost tip of Cuba, 1,280 km (795 miles) from Havana, which has a small track leading to a lighthouse and a windswept, isolated village.

Local men enjoy a joke in Baracoa.

The
Cuban
Islands

ALTHOUGH IT IS GENERALLY REGARDED as a single island, Cuba is in fact surrounded by over 4,000 (mostly tiny) islands and keys fringed with white sand and coral reefs. Most lie within four archipelagos that encircle the mainland: the **Canarreos**, to the island's southwest; the **Jardines de la Reina** to the southeast and the **Sabana** to the north, both reached off Ciego de Ávila and Camagüey provinces; and **Los Colorades**, off Pinar del Río Province. Most of those islands that can be visited fairly easily are already mentioned in this book within the relevant province or closest town from which they are most easily reached, such as Pinar del Río's Cayo Levisa; Ciego de Ávila's Cayo Coco and Cayo Guillermo.

However, two larger islands stand out as destinations in their own right, and for that reason they merit a chapter of their own: **Isla de la Juventud** and **Cayo Largo**. Both are located within the **Archipiélago de los Canarreos** (Archipelago of the Canaries) — which is made up of some 350 islands in total, lying 100 km (62 miles) off the southwest coast of Cuba in the Gulf of Batabanó.

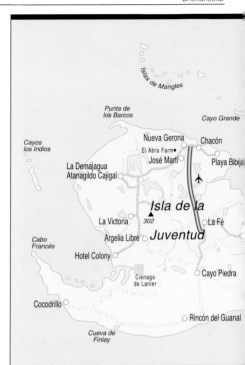

ISLA DE LA JUVENTUD

The second largest island in Cuba, the cauliflower-shaped Isla de la Juventud (Island of Youth) lies 138 km (just under 86 miles) southwest of Havana. It is 327 km (203 miles) long and spans 58 km (36 miles) at its widest point. Some 70,000 people live on what they term "La Isla" which is a special municipality, not a province.

It is an unlikely version of the so-called "paradisiacal island" — with its low-lying shrublands (the pine trees it was once named for have largely vanished); harboring wild boar, *jutias* and indigenous crocodiles in its southern reaches. Yet many believe the island's offshore diving sites, especially those lying in the southeast, to be among the most outstanding and ecologically intact in the Caribbean.

BACKGROUND

Formerly named Isla de los Pinos ("Island of Pines"), Isla de la Juventud had a fearsome reputation during the seventeenth and eigh-

teenth centuries as a hideout for pirates and roving speculators from all latitudes, among them Sir Francis Drake and Henry Morgan; and it was also a shady place of exile for runaway slaves. It seems from all accounts that when Robert Louis Stevenson wrote *Treasure Island* he was writing about what is now the Isla de la Juventud, based on spectacular stories of buried treasure stolen from Spanish galleons, as well as the usual rum-running, slave-trading, and smuggling activities that went on here. The island's first inhabitants were the Siboney Indians, who left behind a series of elaborate cave paintings in a cave at Punta del Este, in the southeastern part of the island. However, when Christopher Columbus discovered the remote, pine-covered island in 1494, on his second voyage to America (baptizing it with the short-lived name, Evangelista) he noted that there were few indigenous tribespeople remaining.

In 1826, the Spanish decided to establish a penal colony here, where they could dispatch political prisoners along with dangerous criminals for a lengthy, perhaps indefinite stay. Cuba's famous independence leader, José Martí, was sent here while still

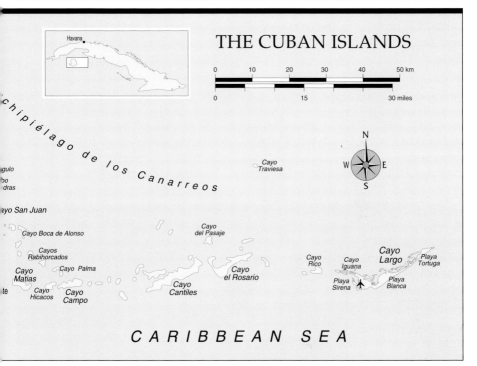

THE CUBAN ISLANDS

Havana

| 0 | 10 | 20 | 30 | 40 | 50 km |

| 0 | | 15 | | 30 miles |

Archipiélago de los Canarreos

gulo
bo
dras

ayo San Juan

Cayo Boca de Alonso

Cayos
Rabihorcados

Cayo
Matias   Cayo Palma

te   Cayo   Cayo
     Hicacos Campo

Cayo
del Pasaje

Cayo
Cantiles

Cayo
el Rosario

Cayo
Traviesa

N
W E
S

Cayo   Cayo
Rico   Iguana

Cayo
Largo

Playa
Sirena

Playa
Tortuga

Playa
Blanca

CARIBBEAN SEA

in his late-teens. In 1925, then-President Gerado Machado ordered the construction of his huge so-called Model Prison here. Later, its most famous prisoner was Fidel Castro, who was imprisoned here in a solitary cell for his attack on Moncada barracks in Santiago de Cuba.

After the Revolution, Castro set about turning the island into a vast educational work camp for young people, and thousands of "volunteer workers" were sent here to transform the newly named Isla de la Juventud into a major citrus-producing region.

In and around the main town of **Nueva Gerona**, over 60 secondary schools were built, typifying the extensive prefabricated complexes designed according to Cuba's centralized plan for education facilities throughout the country, and named for Cuban and communist heroes, Soviet cosmonauts, and revolutionary dates. During the 1970s, some 18,000 students studied here each year, many from socialist-friendly African, Latin American and Asian countries that shared international programs with Cuba. Since Cuba has been in the grip of the Special Period, that number has declined

to less than 10,000 students. Still, Nueva Gerona has a noticeably large population of young-faced students, many of them from Africa.

Today, much of the island is still wilderness. The chief attraction for foreign visitors are its almost untapped opportunities for diving, fishing and exploring the natural scenery. This is also where Fidel Castro — a great outdoors enthusiast as well as an avid diver — has a country retreat, a modern ranch-style house in an isolated part of the island.

NUEVA GERONA

Isla de la Juventud's main town and administrative center is Nueva Gerona, located in the north of the island. Although it is not especially attractive, it has a piquant port atmosphere, and it's liveliest around its downtown historical core of two-story, weather-beaten wooden houses with characterful verandahs, mostly centered along Calle 39 (Calle Martí). It is not recommended

PREVIOUS PAGES: LEFT: A stretch of Cuba's beautiful coastline. RIGHT: View of the tranquil Punta Francés beach.

as a place to stay; noisy industrial quarries (mostly for marble) are located on the town's outskirts.

General Information
You will not find any facilities for visitors within the town of Nueva Gerona, beyond the usual practical necessities.

The **Banco Nacional de Cuba** is at Calles 39 and 18. Try to attend to all your banking needs before you arrive, as efficiency and cash-availability are not strong points of the island. The car rental agency, **Havanautos**

with interior rings of cells was based on the design on a penitentiary in Joliet, Illinois, in the United States, allowing prison authorities to see and control every aspect of the inmates' existence while remaining unseen themselves. It was designed to house some 6,000 inmates, among them Cuba's most dangerous criminals and political prisoners. It was closed as a prison in 1966, and is now a museum. It is open for inspection from Tuesday to Sunday, 9 AM to 5 PM.

Another museum now dedicated to a once-imprisoned leader is the **El Abra Farm**,

((53-61) 2-4432, is located at Calles 32 and 39, while an alternative agency, **Nacional**, is based out of the Villa Isla.

There is a pharmacy at the corner of Calles 39 and 24; and a police station at Calles 41 and 54.

The **Cubalse Supermarket** at Calle 35 between Calles 30 and 32 is the best place to stock up on provisions. It is closed on Sunday.

What to See and Do
A road east of town brings you to one of Cuba's oddities, the **Presidio Modelo**, or "Model Prison," completed in 1926 and now a national monument. This foreboding complex of four enormous circular structures

located a short distance from Nueva Gerona on the Carretera de Siguanea which runs along the coast southwest to the Hotel Colony. It was owned by a Catalonian farmer who convinced the local authorities that he could keep the youthful rebel under his charge, rather than sending them into a forced labor camp. Martí arrived in October 1870, and spent two months here. You can see some of his personal belongings and the room where he stayed. It is open Tuesday to Sunday, 9 AM to 5 PM.

Where to Stay
Villa Isla* ((53-61) 2-3290 or 2-4486, Carretera Nueva Gerona — La Fé, is located two kilometers outside Nueva Gerona on the

road to the fishing village of La Fé. This Gaviota-run establishment has 20 rooms and a swimming pool.

Where to Eat
There are several good restaurants in Nueva Gerona. You'll also find a number of *paladares* along Calle 39. **El Río** ((53-61) 2-3217, Carretera La Fé, between Calles 32 and 35, specializes in excellent Cuban fish and seafood dishes. **El Corderito**, Calle 39 at the corner of Calle 22, next to El Cochinito, features lamb dishes as well as typical Creole food, while **El Cochinito** ((53-61) 2-2809, Calle 39 at the corner of Calle 24, has made roast pork and Creole dishes their specialty.

Nightlife
Due to the number of foreign students on the island, Nueva Gerona has a number of venues which play live music, and some which stage cabaret performances. Located on or just off Calle 39, **Cabaret El Patio**, **Café de Cuba** and **Café Nuevo** all have live salsa bands during weekends.

You may wish to check listings for upcoming events at the **Casa de Cultura**, at Calles 37 and 24. The Isla's best band — **La Tumbita Crilla** — often perform their version of *sucu-sucu*, the local dance rhythm, at this venue.

THE WEST COAST

Elsewhere on the island, the **Hotel Colony** on the west coast is one of Cuba's most popular diving resorts and the base of the island's **International Diving Center**, which is fully equipped for serious diving and has one of Cuba's few decompression chambers, as well as a pool for practice dives.

From here, the hotel arranges diving excursions to various offshore locations, notably along the six kilometers stretch between **Punta Francés** and **Punta de Pedernales**, on the southwestern tip of the island, is the so-called **Costa de los Pirates**, whose offshore waters are lined with spectacular dive spots, including the Gulf Cliff, which teems with exotic coral formations, turtles, and many species of fish. This offshore area

is a marine reserve and by law can only be accessed if you are with an official Cuban guide.

Where to Stay
Hotel Colony**** ((53-61) 9-8181, Carretera de Siguanea, is undoubtedly the best place to stay on the Isla de la Juventud. This colorful Retro-style hotel dates from a 1950s effort to bring foreign tourists to what was then called the Island of Pines. With its blue post-Art Deco edges, it looks straight out of South Beach Miami.

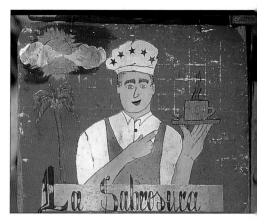

Sitting on a superb beach to the southwest of the island, 41 km (just over 25 miles) from Nueva Gerona, it has 77 rooms overlooking the sea, a swimming pool, a night club, a good restaurant, and facilities for other water sports besides the excellent facilities offered by its International Diving Center. Overbooking can be a problem. Many guests arrive on special diving packages, inclusive of all transport, accommodation and dives. **Wings of the World** US TOLL-FREE (800) 465-8687, 1200 William Street, Suite 706, Buffalo, New York 14240, organizes week-long scuba diving tours here from the United States.

From the Hotel Colony, a taxi to Nueva Gerona or to the island's airport costs about US$30 each way.

PUNTA DEL ESTE

You can also seek out the island's seven pre-Colombian caves, which contain ancient

OPPOSITE: Statue dedicated to a record-winning milk cow, Isla de la Juventud. ABOVE: Isla de la Juventud snack-bar sign.

cave paintings thought to have been executed by the Siboney Indians. Most of them are located at **Punta del Este** at the southeast point of the island. The best known caves were discovered by a shipwreck survivor in 1910, and are notable for their mysterious black and red pictographs and symbols, with some 253 pictographs in total. Some speculate that the paintings may represent an ancient solar calendar. They are regarded as the most important cave paintings in the Caribbean. You can reach the caves by road from **Punta Piedra**, but many of the tracks are unmarked and it is best to go there with a guide.

The caves are located 59 km (just about 37 miles) southeast of Nueva Gerona. You will need a car or a taxi to reach them.

CRIADERO COCODRILO

Another attraction you may be interested in seeking out in Isla de la Juventud is the Criadero Cocodrilo, a crocodile breeding farm, 30 km (almost 19 miles) south of Nueva Gerona on the coast. Here, more than 500 crocodiles live and breed amid a small settlement of wire pens. Ask at the Villa Isla and the Hotel Colony about tours.

HOW TO GET THERE

Make sure you bring your passport, which you will need to clear customs and immigration when arriving at Isla de la Juventud.

By air, Cubana de Aviación flies twice daily from Havana, and the smaller airlines, Aerocaribbean and Aerogaviota also make charter flights here from Havana and Varadero, while Aerotaxi flights operate between Pinar del Río and Nueva Gerona. Nueva Gerona's **Rafael Cabrera Airport** is located 15 km (just over nine miles) south of town.

By sea, there are various options — passenger hydrofoil, ferry or car barge — all reaching Nueva Gerona's ferry terminal from Havana from **Surgidero de Batabanó**, 60 km (37 miles) south of Havana. The hydrofoil service runs between Nueva Gerona and Surgidero de Batabanó twice daily; the journey takes two hours. You can catch a connecting train to Surgidero de Batabanó

from Havana's **Estación de Ferrocarriles** however, this service itself takes up to three hours and is frequently delayed. Call the Surgidero de Batabanó ferry terminal ((53-62) 8-5355 for hydrofoil, ferry or barge reservations.

CAYO LARGO

The undisputed queen of Cuban beach resorts, **Cayo Largo** is as close to most people's concept of a tropical island paradise as it gets. With its perfect snow-white sands, dazzlingly clear turquoise waters, and comfortable resort hotels, this is a far more beautiful place for the relentless pursuit of beach lounging and water sports than, for example, Varadero. It is, however, as un-Cuban

a place as you are likely to find in Cuba; and Cuban tourists are not allowed to come here, adding a surreal sense of tourist apartheid.

BACKGROUND

Cayo Largo is situated at the eastern end of the Archipiélago de los Canarreos, 177 km (about 110 miles) southeast of Havana and 114 km (about 71 miles) east of the Isla de la Juventud.

Cayo Largo is only 27 km (about 17 miles) long, and has been developed exclusively for tourism. Until recently the island was the uninhabited habitat for colonies of migratory birds, including flamingos, pelicans, and storks, as well as sea turtles and iguanas, and apparently the Cuban government has

pledged not to develop this ecological preserve too much or too fast. The maximum number of hotel rooms has been set at 3,000. Already, the development seems quite enough for such a pristine environment, so try to go soon before more construction mars the ambiance.

GENERAL INFORMATION

The Complejo Isla del Sur has an information desk and the island's only medical center. Opposite the complex, you will find a telecommunications center, which includes a post office and an international telephone and fax service.

Boxing matches are held in a Nueva Gerona town park.

WHAT TO SEE AND DO

Cayo Largo has some of the best beaches in the Caribbean — wonderful for diving, fishing, swimming and lazing — and has fewer than ten hotels along its main seven-kilometer (just over four mile)-long beach, **Playa Blanca**.

You can explore the island's many beaches, some of which can only be reached after a long walk along the shore. **Playa Sirena,** at the western tip of the island, is the most

fly and deep-sea fishing) can be arranged through your hotel or at the marina. Costs for these activities are not inexpensive, but are still quite reasonable by international standards. The hotels offer a range of restaurants and welcome outside guests. There are a couple of shops near the hotels on Playa Blanca selling basic provisions.

WHERE TO STAY AND EAT

Complejo Isla del Sur**** ((53-95) 21-0407 FAX (53-95) 21-0408 is made up of a group of

popular swimming beach, blessed with warm, sheltered waters, while **Playa Tortuga** at the eastern end of the island is home to a seasonal colony of sea turtles. Excursions can include a boat ride to nearby **Cayo Iguana**, a nature reserve with hordes of meter (yard)-long iguanas, or to the archipelago's other nature reserve, **Cayo Cantilles**, where there are monkeys along with other wildlife.

Facilities offered by the hotels include water sports, and yacht, boat, bicycle, moped, and car rental (the road through the key runs from the marina past the airport and hotels and follows the beach: it is only 10 km (six miles) long, so you may want to think twice about renting a car). Horseback riding, scuba diving, and fishing (both saltwater

several different hotels (listed below) landscaped around the island's southern Playa Blanca and Playa Lindamar beaches, all operated by the Gran Caribe group. You can book an all-inclusive package if you wish, or book a room and pay for food, water sports, and diving excursions separately.

The Complejo Isla del Sur has extensive facilities for diving and water sports, and you can rent bicycles to explore the beachfront roads. Buses run regularly from the complex to the marina stopping at each of the hotels, as well as stopping at the small airport.

Expensive

The only conventional-style hotel is the **Hotel Isla del Sur**, which has 59 rooms set in a two-story building built behind the beach, and was the first hotel to be built on the island. It has a swimming pool in its central courtyard, and a complex of hotel bars, a buffet restaurant, an information desk, and various shops. Guests staying at other hotels come here to book many organized activities, such as scuba diving, horseback riding, and deep-sea fishing trips.

Hotel Pelicano has 324-rooms, all with sea-facing terraces or balconies. Facilities include several restaurants, a disco, a gym and a swimming pool. Activities include

facing the sea, which are perfect if you are looking for rustic accommodation, with hammocks and shady porches. Its **Blue Marlin Restaurant** is Cayo Largo's most attractive and popular restaurant. The **Hotel Lindamar** has 63 air-conditioned, thatched, natural-wood *cabañas*, situated within a few yards of the beach.

How to Get There

There are daily Cubana de Aviación flights from Havana and Varadero, and weekly

basketball, volleyball and water sports. It has a car, moped, and bicycle rental office.

Moderate

Within the Complejo Isla del Sur, you have a choice of four other hotels. All have en-suite shower rooms, air-conditioning, satellite television, and a fridge. Within the complex are a variety of restaurants and outdoor bars, some right on the beach.

The **Villa Coral** complex is made up of 60 simple but pleasant rooms landscaped along a coral pathway above the beach. The **Villa Iguana** has 52 brightly painted two-story bungalows. The **Villa Capricho**, the most secluded of the properties, has 75 thatched *bohíos*, with sand verandahs

flights from Camagüey and Santiago de Cuba. Flights to the island are also operated by Aerocaribbean and Aerogaviota. A growing number of direct charter flights have begun operating from Canada, Italy, Mexico and the Grand Cayman Islands.

Because Cuba has designated Cayo Largo as a free port (with full customs facilities and duty-free) if you arrive in Cayo Largo on an international charter flight you do not (at time of writing) need a visa: as long as you do not plan to travel to other parts of Cuba you will be granted a 30-day visa upon arrival, for a US$20 fee.

OPPOSITE and ABOVE: Crocodile breeding farm on Isla de la Juventud.

Travelers' Tips

THE TOURISM BOOM

UNTIL 1959, CUBA WAS A HOT DESTINATION for tourists, especially Americans. After the Revolution, tourism was condemned as the epitome of Batista-era decadence. Only since the early 1990s has Cuba welcomed the industry back like a long-lost lover, a shift towards revolutionary pragmatism forced by the collapse of the Soviet Union, which left the island badly in need of hard currency. Although the new Ministry of Tourism was

only set up in 1994, tourism has become the top priority sector within the Cuban economy, destined to become the country's most important source of revenue. Meanwhile a hotel construction boom is sweeping the island.

Now, in the island where socialism meets salsa, communism with a dash of capitalism is becoming a heady brew. Upwards of a million international visitors a year have been arriving in Cuba, mostly from Canada and Europe, and particularly Spain, Italy and France; even Americans, for whom spending money here is a serious offence back in the United States, punishable by as much as a quarter-of-a-million-dollar fine under the Trading with the Enemy Act.

Spanish companies are the major source of capital for tourism projects, having pioneered joint-venture hotels on the island. By the end of the decade, it is estimated that Spanish companies will have poured US$300 million into Cuba. The Grupo Sol (the Sol Melía chain) Europe's third-largest hotel chain, has been creating joint-ventures with the island's largest tourism organization, the government-owned Cubanacán. Among them are the Melía Cohiba in Havana, the Melía Varadero, the Melía Las Americas and the Sol Palmeras in Varadero — all five-star hotels.

Cubanacán also has joint-ventures with other foreign companies, including the Canary Islands CIHSA group, the Catalan company Guitart, LTI International Hotels of Germany, the Amsterdam-based Golden Tulip group, Canada's Delta International and Commonwealth Hospitality chains, and Jamaica's Superclub resorts. Club Med is rumored to want to build a 300-room hotel in Varadero, and to be seeking two other sites — for a Club Med and a lower-category Club Aquarius — in Cuba.

Meanwhile, three Cuban chains run hotels, in some cases contracting out management to foreign partners. Gran Caribe (four- and five-star hotels) and the unintentionally amusingly named Horizontes (two and three stars) and the domestic tourism chain, Isla Azul. The Gaviota group, is perhaps the most unusual of the Cuban tourist enterprises — a subsidiary of the Cuban Ministry of Defense, it often uses former armed-forces facilities, and offers specialist vacations involving, for example, hunting or fishing.

The state-owned company Habaguanex develops and runs hotels, restaurants, and shops and offices in La Habana Vieja: a mini-capitalist empire which brings in millions, a percentage of which goes to reinvesting in its projects while the rest goes to the state.

It's helpful to understand the backdrop to the tourist industry in Cuba — it explains why you can expect somewhat elevated prices, and why there is such a wide disparity between the dollar economy and the Cuban

PREVIOUS PAGES: LEFT: Tourist stops for a roadside shot in Baracoa. RIGHT: Local cookout in Santiago de Cuba Province. ABOVE: A resort hotel in Baracoa. OPPOSITE: A view from La Habana Vieja.

Travelers' Tips

peso economy: an average meal served in a tourist restaurants can represent more than the average Cuban might earn in a month.

It is also helpful to remember that the industry is new, and prices tend to change with disconcerting regularity: Cuba is only learning the tourism business, so you cannot always expect the same precision of information or thoroughness of service as you may find at more established destinations. To enjoy your travels in Cuba, we recommend a dash of tolerance combined with a good dose of humor.

GETTING THERE

BY AIR

Almost all visitors arrive by air. Havana's José Martí International Airport is generally where most flights arrive, however there are also international airports at Varadero, Cayo Largo, Camagüey, Manzanillo, Santiago de Cuba, Holguín, and Cienfuegos.

Cubana de Aviación is the national airline, and its fleet of Soviet-era planes (mostly Ilyushin IL-62s) currently flies regularly to 35 destinations in 26 countries, including South and Central America, Canada, and Europe.

If you are flying to Cuba from closeby, including the United States, you'll need to fly via either Mexico, Nassau in the Bahamas, or Jamaica. Mexico has the most frequent connections to Havana, with daily flights from Mexico City and frequent departures from Cancún and Mérida with Mexicana de Aviación, Aerocaribbean, and Cubana airlines. Taesa also flies from Mexico.

Within the Caribbean, if you are island-hopping, Air Jamaica and Cubana have regular scheduled flights between Montego Bay to Havana, and additional connections to Varadero and Santiago de Cuba are being established, while Cubana also flies from Kingston, Nassau, Grand Cayman, Santo Domingo in the Dominican Republic, St. Martin, Curaçao, Fort-au-France in Martinique, and Pointe-à-Pitre in Guadeloupe. Another option is to take an Air France flight to Havana on their weekly connections (originating in Cayenne in French Guyana) which stop in Fort-au-France and

Pointe-à-Pitre. Aerocaribbean has weekly flights between Puerto Plata in the Dominican Republic and Havana. The Venezuelan airline Aeropostal has twice-weekly flights between Santiago de Cuba, Aruba and Santo Domingo. ALM Antillean Airlines has twice weekly flights between Havana, Curaçao and Amsterdam.

From Canada, Cubana flies directly from Montreal and Toronto to Varadero, and Royal Airlines, Canadian Airlines, and Air Transat fly from Toronto to almost all the other international airports in Cuba except

Havana: namely Varadero, Ciego de Ávila, Camagüey, Manzanillo, Santiago de Cuba and Holguín. Almost all flights from Canada, with the exception of the Cubana flights, are charters, so you will have to contact a local travel agent for specific details. Very few of these charter flights go to Havana.

From the United States, clearly at present there are no scheduled flights to Cuba. However for Cuban-Americans, direct charter flights have been reinstated between several cities in the United States and Cuba, as well as between Miami and Havana.

Although you can call airlines such as Mexicana and Air Jamaica in the United States to inquire about flight availability and prices, you will need to book your flight by contacting the airline or a travel agency at their office outside the United States.

See TAKING A TOUR, page 59 in YOUR CHOICE for a list of travel agencies outside the United States who can help arrange your trip and obtain your Cuban tourist card.

It is important to check with your Cuba-bound airline that you can buy a Cuban tourist card once you arrive in the airport from which you will be traveling onwards to Cuba. In both Mexico City and Cancún airports for example, the Mexicana office can sell you the necessary Cuban tourist card

via Curaçao. From Germany, Lufthansa and the Dusseldorf-based LTU International Airways fly weekly from Dusseldorf to Havana, Varadero, Holguín, and Santiago de Cuba, with connections from Munich. In addition, Cubana flies to Havana from Barcelona, Berlin-Schoenfeld, Brussels, London-Stansted, the Canary Islands, and Moscow. Lastly, Aeroflot flies to Havana weekly from Moscow, St. Petersburg, Stockholm, and Luxembourg.

Your travel agent may suggest a package with one of the popular charter airlines from

for US$15 (see PASSPORTS, TOURIST CARDS AND VISAS, below).

From Europe, Madrid is the only European city which offers daily departures to Havana on either Iberia or Cubana. Iberia has daily flights from Madrid, and plans to substitute a modern Airbus 340 instead of its longstanding DC-10 models. Spainair recently opened direct weekly flights to Cuba in a Boeing 767 between Madrid and Varadero. Presently, AOM (with its DC-10 aircraft) and Cubana share four regular weekly flights between Paris and Havana. Air France may begin regular direct flights to Cuba from France. From Amsterdam, Martinair Holland flies weekly to Varadero and Holguín, or you can fly with KLM

European cities, such as Viasa, Lauda Air, Condor, and Premair. Various charter carriers operate from Gatwick and Manchester, mostly intended for people on all-inclusive packages. The flight from Europe takes about 10 hours.

From Central and South America, Cubana has twice-weekly flights to Havana from Panama City, Caracas, and Lima; while Lacsa, the Costa Rican national airline, flies from San José to Havana three times a week. From Caracas in Venezuela, Viasa has six weekly flights to Havana, while Aeropostal has twice-weekly flights to both Havana and Santiago de Cuba. From Santiago de

OPPOSITE: Naïve painting by unknown artist.
ABOVE: Schoolchildren in a bus on Isla de la Juventude.

Chile, the Chilean airline Ladeco Airlines flies twice weekly to Havana via San José or Bogota in Columbia. From Guatemala City, Aviateca flies to Havana weekly.

From Australia and New Zealand, the most direct route is via Hawaii or Los Angeles and then Toronto, on Air New Zealand. In Toronto, you can then connect with one of the Cuba-bound airlines described above. Alternatively, you can fly to Mexico City from Los Angeles and then onwards to Cuba. From Sydney, Aerolíneas Argentinas flies weekly from Sydney to Buenos Aires,

fuegos and operated by the Spanish Sol Melía chain, plies Cuban destinations Montego Bay and Grand Cayman. See GETTING AROUND, below, for more details.

If you plan to enter Cuba by private yacht or cruiser, you don't have to arrange a prior visa, but you will have to purchase a Cuban tourist card if you plan to stay longer than 72 hours. As you approach Cuban waters — 20 km (12 miles) away — it is essential that you make radio contact with the Cuban port authorities over channel 16 (VHF), or with the National Coast

from which you can make a connection to Havana on Viasa.

BY SEA

Due to the United States blockade, few cruise ships call into Cuba's ports and there are no scheduled passenger ships that stop in Cuba. However, things may change soon. Two cruise ships have put Cuba on their itineraries, linking it to other Caribbean destinations. The first, Costa Playa, has its home port in Havana, and visits the Isla de la Juventud, Santiago de Cuba, Montego Bay, Grand Cayman and Cancún — it is operated by the Italian-Cuban joint venture, Cubanco SA. A more recent venture, Melía Don Juan, based in Cien-

Network over 2760 HF (SSB), before you cross the water boundary. Given the tense situation between Cuba and the United States, it is vital that, if you don't make contact immediately, you keep trying at regular intervals. You will then need to follow their instructions for clearance. When approaching, you need to give the name of your yacht, the type and color of the vessel, its flag, port of registration, last port of call, and the estimated time of arrival and number of people on board. If possible, you should try to fax your target port of entry in advance.

Cuba's official points of entry are the Marina Hemingway in Havana; Marina Puertosol Dársena and Marina Gaviota in

Varadero; María La Gorda International Scuba Diving Center in Pinar del Río; La Marina Marlin Cayo Coco in Ciego de Ávila; Base Nautica Gaviota Bahía de Naranjo in Holguín; Marina Marlin Punta Gorda In Santiago de Cuba; Marina Puertosol in Cienfuegos; and Marina Puertosol Cayo Largo in Los Canarreos Archipelago.

PASSPORTS, TOURIST CARDS AND VISAS

Aside from a valid passport, you need a tourist card or *tarjeta de turista* to enter Cuba. Tourist cards are available for US$20 from any Cubanacán-affiliated travel agents, Cuban tourist offices, or consulates. You can also purchase them from the relevant airline office at the airport where you are making a connecting flight on that same carrier onwards to Cuba. In theory, you can purchase a tourist card on arrival in Cuba, but in practice this may cause problems and it is recommended that you make this arrangement before you arrive.

The tourist card is valid for 30 days, and the date of departure is filled in by the official according to the return date of your ticket.

Although the tourist card is all most visitors require, you may need to apply for a special tourist visa if you intend to stay with a Cuban family (although this is the policy, it is unpredictably enforced), or if you are intending to do business, study or do research.

For lost passports while in Cuba, contact your embassy or consulate. If you do not have diplomatic representation in Cuba you will have to throw yourself on the mercy of your country's nearest (friendly) neighbor or political ally. For example, if your country is a Commonwealth country, excepting Australia and Canada, you should contact the British Embassy. However, Australia is represented by the Mexican Embassy. If you are an American who has entered Cuba illegally and then has either lost your passport or had it stolen, don't panic unnecessarily. You have no choice but to go to the United States Interests Section in Havana (see under EMBASSIES IN CUBA, below). The State Department warns that it may be difficult to assist distressed United States citizens, should emergencies arise. Hopefully, after a series of for-

malities, they will issue you a new passport. You may face problems relating to your stay in Cuba later though, when you return to the United States.

ENTRY FOR AMERICANS

Contrary to popular belief, the United States government does not prohibit Americans from traveling to Cuba. It merely prohibits Americans from spending United States dollars there, under the Trading with the Enemy Act. Although these regulations are rarely enforced, the situation is unpredictable. Additionally, the Helms-Burton Act has raised the potential penalties on Americans who go to Cuba as tourists to US$250,000 in criminal fines and US$55,000 in civil fines. According to the United States Travel Advisory Consular Information Sheet, attempts to enter or exit Cuba illegally are punishable by jail terms of up to five years. To date, the Treasury Department has brought 10 criminal indictments for violations related to travel to Cuba in the past 15 years, and the possibility of civil fines is small, but real. Penalties of US$1,500 to US$2,000 have been assessed in 44 civil cases since 1994.

Nevertheless, tens of thousands of United States tourists are expected to enter Cuba through a third country over the coming year. Travel agents in Toronto, Cancún, Mexico City, Nassau and Montego Bay frequently arrange round-trip flights, accommodations, and the necessary tourist card (see TAKING A TOUR, page 59 in YOUR CHOICE).

Journalists, students, academics, missionaries, and relatives of Cubans with "circumstances of extreme hardship" are among those who can seek special Treasury Department permission to enter Cuba legally. People who meet this criteria need to apply for a license from the Treasury Department's Office of Foreign Assets Control (OFAC) and have to provide evidence on their return to the United States that they have spent no money in Cuba due to their "fully-hosted" status. Further information is available from the OFAC in Washington, DC ((202) 622-2480 or in Miami ((305) 530-7177. For those in such

The Havana Harbor.

categories, Marazul Tours based in New Jersey (see TAKING A TOUR, page 59 in YOUR CHOICE) can arrange flight and hotel reservations. You will have to apply for a Cuban visa or tourist card from the Cuban Special Interests Section in Washington, DC.

If you are American — or even if you are any other nationality and don't want the tell-tale visa in your passport causing problems with your travel to the United States — be sure to ask the Cuban immigration official (politely) not to stamp your passport. They can look intimidating, but they are savvy about State Department restrictions and will usually comply and stamp your tourist card instead. If you have American-issued credit cards, you will find them impossible to use in Cuba. See MONEY, below, for more details.

If you want to extend your permit to stay in Cuba, or to change your immigration status or marry a Cuban, you should contact the **Consultoria Juridica Internacional** ((53-7) 33-2490 or 33-2697 FAX (53-7) 33-2303, Calle 18 No. 120, at the corner of Avenida 3, Miramar, Playa, Havana.

CUSTOMS

Along with personal belongings, Cuban customs allow visitors to bring in one of each of the following: camera; binoculars; baby's stroller; musical instrument; tape recorder; portable computer; tent; fishing rod; bicycle; canoe, kayak, or surf board (under five meters long); and other sports equipment (not firearms). Be prepared to declare all the items above (although it is likely you will not have to) and, if declared, they will have to be produced as you leave the country. You are also permitted to bring in as gifts that do not exceed the value of 100 Cuban pesos, and up to 10 kg (22 lb) of medicine (excluding blood-based or veterinary medicines). If you are over 18, you can bring in three liters (quarts) of liquor, plus a choice of either 200 cigarettes, 50 cigars or 250 grams of uncut tobacco.

The import of any flora and fauna specimens, live animals, or unprocessed food (including fresh fruits and vegetables) is restricted. Items that are forbidden to import into Cuba include narcotics, explosives, motorized vehicles, pre-recorded video cassettes, and any pornographic or "morally offensive" material.

CUBAN EMBASSIES ABROAD

Australia: Cuban Consulate-General ((61-2) 311-4611 FAX (61-2) 311-1255, 16 Manwaring Avenue, Marouba, NSW 2035.

Belgium: Cuban Embassy ((32-2) 343-0020 FAX (32-2) 344-9691, Robert Jonesstraat 77, 1180 Brussels.

Canada: Cuban Embassy ((613) 563-0141 FAX (613) 563-0068, 388 Main Street, Ottawa, Ontario K1S 1E3, Canada.

Cuban Consulate-General ((416) 234-8181 FAX (416) 234-2754, 5353 Dundas Street West, Suite 401, Etobicoke, Ontario M9B 6H8, Canada.

Cuban Consulate-General and Trade Commission ((514) 843-8897 FAX (514) 982-9034, 1415 Pine Avenue West, Montreal, Quebec H3B 1B2.

France: Cuban Embassy ((33-1) 45-67-55-35 FAX (33-1) 45-66-46-35, 16 rue de Presles, 75015 Paris.

Germany: Cuban Embassy ((49) 228-3090 FAX (49) 309-244, Kennedy Allee 22, 53175 Bonn.

Italy: Cuban Embassy ((39-6) 575-5984, Via Licinia 7, 00153 Roma.

Mexico: Cuban Embassy ((52-5) 280-8039 FAX (52-5) 280-0839, Presidente Masarik 554, Colonia Polanco, 11560 México DF.

Netherlands: Cuban Embassy ((31-70) 354-1417 FAX (31-70) 352-0159, Prins Mauritslaan 6, 2582 LR Den Haag.

Cuban Consulate (/FAX (31-10) 412-8970 Stationsplein 45, 3013 AKRotterdam.

Spain: Cuban Embassy ((34-1) 458-2500, Paseo de La Habana 194, Madrid.

United Kingdom: Cuban Embassy ((44-171) 240-2488 FAX (44-171) 836-2602, 167 High Holburn, London WC1V 6PA.

United States: Cuban Special Interests Section ((202) 797-8518, 2630 16th Street NW, Washington, DC 20009.

American citizens wanting to apply for a license to travel to Cuba can contact the Licensing Department, Office of Foreign Assets Control ((202) 622-2480 FAX (202) 622-1657, United States Department of The Treasury, 1500 Pennsylvania Avenue NW, Treasury Annex, Washington, DC 20220.

TOURIST INFORMATION

ABROAD

Canada: Cuba Tourism Board ((416) 362-0700 FAX (416) 362-6799, 55 Queen Street East, Suite 705, Toronto, Ontario M5C 1R6.

Bureau de Tourisme de Cuba ((514) 857-8004 FAX (514) 875-8006, 440 Boulevard René Lévesque Ouest, Bureau 1402, Montréal, Québec H2Z 1V7.

France: Office de Tourisme de Cuba ((33-1) 45-38-90-10 FAX (33-1) 45-38-99-30, 280 Boulevard Raspail, Paris 75014.

Germany: Cuban Tourist Board ((49-69) 288-322 FAX (49-69) 296-664, An der Hauptwachb 7, 60313 Frankfurt.

Italy: Ufficio di Promozione ed Informazione Turistica di Cuba ((39-2) 66981463 FAX (39-2) 669-0042, Via General Fara, No. 30, terzo piano, 20124 Milano.

Mexico: Cuban Tourist Board ((52-5) 574-9651 FAX (52-5) 574-9454, Insugentes Sur No. 421, Complejo Aristos, Edificios B, Local 310, Mexico City 06100 DF.

Spain: Officina de Promoción e Información Turística de Cuba ((34-1) 411-3097 FAX (34-1) 564-5804, Paseo de la Habana 27, Madrid 28036.

United Kingdom: Cuban Tourism Office ((44-171) 379-1706 FAX (44-171) 240-6656, 167 High Holborn, London WCL.

Locals play dominoes on a Santiago de Cuba street.

WEB SITES

The Cuban government runs two travel-oriented web sites: www.cubaweb.cu and www.cubatravel.cu. The Republic of Cuba's web site is: www.unipr.it:80/davide/cuba/home.html.

TravelNet! has a Cuba menu at: www.sky.net/~eric/t/carcub.htm. CaribNat at www.caribnet or www.cpscaribnet.com has information about Caribbean destinations including Cuba. For information call in the United States ((809) 413-0415 FAX (809) 429-5903 E-MAIL info@caribnet.net.

Cuba Internet Resources is at: ix.urz. uni-heidelberg.de/~pklee/Cuba. Other general information sites include: qqq.com: 80/dtt/country/cuba/index.html and www.cris.com/~wm/cuba/index.html.

French subscribers can access "Tourisme à Cuba: operation survie" at pauillac.inria.fr/~maranget/volcans/juin/dossier/cuba.html.

IN CUBA

Asistur ((53-7) 62-5519 or 63-8284 FAX (53-7) 33-8087, Paseo del Prado No. 45, La Habana Vieja, is a Cuban company specializing in assistance to international visitors. They can help if you require any of the following: emergency medical or dental treatment; repatriation; legal aid; help with tracing lost baggage; or new travel documents.

Less urgently, they can also help you with providing information and making reservations for tours, hotels, restaurants, night clubs, excursions, transportation, and performances.

You can also contact the main office of Cuba's largest tourist organization, **Cubanacán SA** ((53-7) 21-9457, 20-0569 or 24-6006, Calle 68 next to Avenida 5, Miramar, Postal 16046, Zona 16, Havana.

TOUR AGENCIES ABROAD

IN THE UNITED STATES

Wings of the World US TOLL-FREE (800) 465-8687, 1200 William Street, Suite 706, Buffalo, NY 14240. For more information on this company see TAKING A TOUR, page 59 in YOUR CHOICE.

Marazul Tours Inc. ((201) 319-9670 FAX (201) 319-9009, Tower Plaza, 4100 Park Avenue, Weehawken, NJ 07087. This is a unique travel agency that operates tours to Cuba — only available to United States citizens who satisfy all the requirements under United States government regulations. This means you will need written permission from the United States Treasury Department. United States citizens who can book their travel to Cuba through this agency may include United Nations or United States government officials, reporters traveling on assignment, academics and teachers on research assignments, and those visiting for humanitarian reasons; such as visiting a sick relative or attending a funeral. Due to United States regulations, participating visitors cannot spend more than US$100 per person per day in Cuba.

IN CANADA

Alba Tours ((416) 746-2488 FAX (416) 746-0397, 790 Arrow Road, Suite 1000, Mississauga, Ontario L4V ITI.

Canadian Holidays ((416) 620-8687 FAX (416) 620-9267, 191 The West Mall, Sixth Floor, Etobicoke, Ontario M9C 5K8.

Hola Sun Holidays ((905) 882-9444 FAX (905) 882-5184, 146 Beaver Creek Road, Unit 8, Richmond Hill, Ontario L4B 1C2.

Quest Nature Tours ((416) 221-3000 FAX (416) 221-5730, 36 Finch Avenue West, Toronto, Ontario M2N 2G9.

Regent Holidays ((905) 673-3343 FAX (905) 673-1717 or (905) 300-6205 Airport Road, Building A, Mississauga, Ontario L4V 1E1.

Sunquest Holidays ((416) 482-3333 FAX (416) 485-2089, 130 Merton Street, Toronto, Ontario M4S 1A4.

IN MEXICO

Cubamar ((52-5) 601-1302 FAX (52-5) 604-6215, Eje Lázaro Cárdenas No. 623, Colonia Portales, 03300 Mexico DF.

Havanatur/Taíno Tours ((52-5) 559-3907, Avenida Coyoacán No. 1035, Colonia del Valle CP, 03100 Mexico DF.

Hotel Colony sunset on Isla de la Juventud.

AS Tours ((52-5) 575-9814 FAX (52-5) 559-5097, Insurgentes Sur 1188-602, 03200 Mexico DF.

IN THE UNITED KINGDOM

Cubanacán UK Ltd. ((44-171) 537-7909 FAX (44-171) 537-7747, Skylines, Unit 49, Lime Harbour, Docklands, London E14 9TS.
Havanatur UK ((44-181) 681-3613 FAX (44-181) 760-0031, Interchange House, 27 Stafford Road, Croydon, Surrey CRO 4NG.
Journey Latin America ((44-181) 747-3108 FAX (44-181) 742-1312, 14-16 Devonshire Road, Chiswick, London W4 2HD.
Special Places (01892 661157 FAX 01892 665670 E-MAIL specialplaces@cricketer.com, Brock Travel Ltd., 4 The White House, Beacon Road, Crowborough, East Sussex TN6 1AB.
Progressive Tours ((44-171) 262-1676 FAX (44-171) 724-6941, 12 Porchester Place, Marble Arch, London W2 2BS.
Regent Holidays ((44-117) 921-1711 FAX (44-117) 925-4866, 15 John Street, Bristol BS1 2HR.
South American Experience ((44-171) 976-5511 FAX 944-171) 976-6908, 47 Causton Street, Pimlico, London SW1P 4AT.

IN EUROPE

Havanatour Paris ((33-1) 44-51-50-85 FAX (33-1) 42-65-18-01, 24 Rue Quatre Septembre, 75002 Paris. (This is the same Havanatur network, having simply adopted a more French-like spelling.)
Guamá SA ((34-1) 411-2048 FAX (34-1) 564-3918, Paseo de La Habana 28, 28036, Madrid, Spain.
Havanatur Italia ((39-11) 669-0632 FAX (39-11) 650-4608, Via San Anselmo 40, 10125, Torino, Italy.
Havanatur Beneux ((31-10) 411-2444 FAX (31-10) 411-4749, Hofplein 19, 3032 AC Rotterdam, The Netherlands.
Fietsvakantiewinkel ((31-0348) 421844 FAX (31-0348) 423839, Spoorlaan 19, 3445 AE Woerden, The Netherlands.
Tropicana Touristik ((49-30) 853-7041 FAX (49-30) 853-4070, Berliner Strasse 161, D-10715 Berlin, Germany.

IN AUSTRALIA AND NEW ZEALAND

Cubatours ((61-3) 9428-0385, 235 Swan Street, Richmond, Victoria 3121, Australia.
STA Travel ((64-9) 309-0458, 10 High Street, Auckland, New Zealand.

TOURISM AGENCIES IN CUBA

Tourism agencies and operators in Cuba are government run, which does not mean they necessarily offer the same services and prices. We recommend you take the time to compare, ask many questions and try to get precise information. Remember that the people you will be dealing with have probably never traveled around Cuba, so you cannot always expect accurate advice concerning your destinations. Many operators offer discounts on hotel rates (up to 30%), at least for the more expensive venues.
Cubanacán SA ((53-7) 21-9457 or 20-0569 or 24-6006, Calle 68 and Avenida 5, Miramar, Postal 16046, Zona 16, Havana.
Cubatur ((53-7) 33-4121 or 33-3388 FAX (53-7) 33-3104, Calle F, No.157, between Calles 9 and Calzada, Vedado, Havana. Be forewarned, many travelers have complained about their services.
Havanatur ((53-7) 24-2273, 24-2161 or 24-2121 FAX (53-7) 24-2877, Calle 2, No. 17, between Avenidas 1 and 3, Miramar, Havana. This pioneer in Cuban tourism, with agencies throughout the world, comes recommended.
San Cristóbal ((53-7) 33-9585 FAX (53-7) 33-9586, Calle Oficios No. 110, between Calles Lamparilla and Amargura, La Habana Vieja.
Rumbos ((53-7) 66-2113 to 66-2218 FAX (53-7) 33-4194, Línea No. 60 at the corner of Calle M, Vedado, Havana.
Easy Travel ((53-7) 24-5263, 24-5265 or 24-4679 FAX (53-7) 24-4598, Bungalow 687, Hotel Comodoro, Havana.

MONEY

As a tourist in Cuba, you will be expected to pay for everything in United States dollars — few hotels, restaurants, shops, businesses and taxis accept anything else. It may seem rather ironic that the same United

States dollars were illegal until 1993. In fact, Cuba has a triple-currency system: the official Cuban peso or *moneda nacional*, made up of 100 centavos and ostensibly linked to the United States dollar at the rate of one to one (although, for all practical purposes, one United States dollar is worth about 26 pesos); the United States dollar; and the *peso convertible*, which is interchangeable in value with the dollar. You will probably receive this tourist currency in exchange for United States dollars during your stay in Cuba, but try to dispense with them before you leave: in the-

You can get cash advances on these major credit cards at the Hotel Nacional and Hotel Habana Libre as well as at various banks in Havana. It is worth mentioning that Visa and MasterCard are the most widely accepted cards in Cuba. Your passport is generally required whenever you pay by credit card in Cuba. Generally, between two to five percent commission is charged.

Cuba's banking system has diversified in keeping with the gradual decentralization of the island's economy, and a host of foreign banks have opened in Havana. Most Euro-

ory they can be exchanged for United States dollars, but in fact, you may find it difficult to do so. In the unlikely event that you receive any Cuban pesos, you are not allowed to bring them home as souvenirs.

When bringing United States dollars in cash into the country, make sure you have plenty of small denominations. United States travelers checks and credit cards issued outside the United States such as Visa, Banamex, Access, Carnet, Diners Club, Bancomer, and MasterCard, as well as MasterCard, Visa, and Diners Club travelers checks are accepted in Cuba. Neither personal checks nor travelers checks drawn on United States banks are accepted in Cuba (and obviously American Express is not valid).

pean currencies are accepted for exchange at tourist centers and banks. You will probably find the Banco Financiero Internacional most useful. The Casas de Cambio SA (CADECA) in Havana and Varadero are frequently patronized by locals to change United States dollars and pesos back at the free-market rate. ATM machines are just beginning to make an appearance in Havana, especially in tourist-orientated La Habana Vieja.

Banco Financiero Internacional ((53-7) 33-3423 or 33-3424 is located at Calle Línea No. 1, Vedado, Havana and ((53-5) 33-7002, at Avenida Playa and Calle 32, Varadero.

The *peso convertible* is interchangeable with the dollar.

TAX

Departure tax is generally included in your ticket price, however, you may find that you have to pay US$15 when you depart.

TIPPING

Service charges are not included in restaurant bills, and tipping at your discretion is greatly appreciated. Tipping is hoped for, rather than officially acknowledged, for most services. If you hire a driver, guide, or translator, for example, they will be crushed if they perform well and you do not give them a decent tip at the end of your stay, although they will never ask you directly. Bear in mind, when you are trying to work out how much to tip in United States dollars, that this does not represent a conversion into Cuban pesos; in effect, dollars have the same buying power for Cubans as they do for you. However, don't make the mistake of tipping in pesos: it will not be well received.

You may soon start to notice that tipping is unofficially courted everywhere, most notably by determined chambermaids, who construct elaborate swans and roses (and sometimes, even Santería *orishas*) from your bath towels to adorn your bed, and leave little flower-festooned notes in their attempts — quite touching — to communicate with you in whatever your language might be. You can leave a tip in an envelope on your bed when you leave.

You should tip (not over-tip) museum guides, hotel guards who watch your belongings or rental car, or anyone within the service industry who has been helpful. However, don't make the mistake of offering money to Cuban government officials: anything smacking of bribery could be taken the wrong way and cause you considerable embarrassment.

On the other hand, the Cuban government is also concerned about tourists inadvertently encouraging young children to beg for pens, soap, sweets and money. Many Cuban parents and school teachers would prefer that tourists give donations of pens, crayons or other items for children to schools (see WHAT TO TAKE, below).

TRAVEL INSURANCE

Order medical insurance to cover any vacation accidents or illnesses. Cuba is generally a safe country, but it's wise to insure personal belongings. Ask your insurance company or travel agent for more information and make sure your travel insurance covers Cuba.

EMBASSIES AND CONSULATES IN CUBA

Austrian Embassy ((53-7) 24-2394, Calle 4, No. 101 at Avenida 1, Miramar.
Belgian Embassy ((53-7) 24-2410, Avenida 5, No. 7408 at Calle 76, Miramar Playa.
British Embassy ((53-7) 24-1717 or 33-1286 FAX (53-7) 24-8104, Calle 34, No. 708 at Avenida 7, Miramar.
Canadian Embassy ((53-7) 24-2516, Calle 30 No. 518 at Avenida 7, Miramar.
French Embassy ((53-7) 24-2132, Calle 14 No. 312, between Avenidas 3 and 5, Miramar.
Italian Embassy ((53-7) 33-3334. Paseo No. 606, between Calle 25 and 27, Vedado.
Japanese Embassy ((53-7) 33-3454, Calle N No. 62 at Calle 15, Vedado.
Mexican Embassy ((53-7) 24-2383, Calle 12 No. 518 at Avenida 7, Miramar.
Netherlands Embassy ((53-7) 24-2512, Calle 8 No. 307 between Avenidas 3 and 5, Miramar.
Spanish Embassy ((53-7) 33-8029, Capdevila No. 51 at Calle Agramonte, Centro Havana.
Swedish Embassy ((53-7) 24-2563, Avenida 31 No. 1411, between Calles 14 and 18, Miramar.
Swiss Embassy ((53-7) 24-2611 Avenida 5 No. 2005, between Calles 20 and 22, Miramar.
United States Interests Section ((53-7) 33-4401 to 33-4403, Calzada between Calles L and M, Vedado.

GETTING AROUND

You don't have to spend much time in Cuba to notice how the nation's transportation system is suffering under the Special Period. Makeshift vehicles of many ingenious kinds spluttering thick plumes of diesel are a common sight along the island's highways, including large trucks converted into buses, while horse-drawn carts or *calesas* are frequently used in the provincial towns. Meanwhile, Cubans everywhere have a difficult and often frustrating time getting around: long lines form at city bus stops, at the exit of towns and at crossroads along highways. Yellow-clad officials known locally as *amarillos* have the task of organizing those waiting for a ride. (Most government vehicles are legally required to pick up hitchhikers if they have the room.)

What this means is that if you intend to travel by public transportation in Cuba, be prepared to cope with all the vicissitudes that come your way, with the spirit of stamina and enterprise that Cubans themselves have spent years perfecting. This is precisely why many visitors who would otherwise travel independently opt to join tours when they travel around Cuba. But that doesn't necessarily mean you.

BY AIR

Cubana de Aviación, the national airline, has an extensive domestic air network. There are daily flights from Havana between Santiago de Cuba and Varadero and regular flights to Baracoa, Bayamo, Camagüey, Ciego de Ávila, Guantánamo, Holguín, Las Tunas, Manzanillo, Moa, and Nueva Gerona (on the Isla de la Juventud) between two and three times a week. Flights within the country are not very expensive, however they are 25 percent cheaper if you book them in conjunction with your international ticket from abroad. Check with your travel agent about this. All payment must be made in United States dollars and tickets must be purchased at least a week in advance. Most domestic flights are on small veteran propeller aircraft — usually Russian Yaks and Antonovs, although Cubana recently acquired four Fokker F-27s. Cuba has two other airlines — Aerocaribbean and Aerogaviota, which fly some of these routes, although Aerogaviota is the only local airline which flies to Cayo Largo.

In Havana, all three airlines leave from Jose Marti International Airport. Any domestic flight requires you to check in 60 minutes before flight time, and the baggage limit is 20 kg (44 lb). It can be difficult to figure out which airport terminal to go to — there are no directions. Aerocaribbean's terminal is at the western end of the airport — not always easy to find. Always get directions about which terminal to go to from your local travel agent or, as a last resort, if you are getting there by taxi have your driver wait while you check you have the right terminal.

RENTAL CARS

Traveling around Cuba in a rental car or jeep is probably the most satisfying way to see the country, although setting off on the road may not be for the timid. Cuba has the most extensive road system in the Caribbean, and has developed a fairly comprehensive network of dollar-friendly Servi-Cupet Cimex gas stations and Rumbos-operated roadside cafeterias and restaurants across the country. The Carretera Centrale (Central Highway) is not an expressway, but it does run from one end of the country to the other. The Vía Blanca is an expressway and runs from Havana to Varadero. The National South Expressway is an eight-lane highway (still under construction) that links Havana to Sancti Spíritus, Las Tunas to Bayamo and Havana to Pinar del Río.

There are many car rental companies in Cuba, and many different makes of rental cars and jeeps to choose from, some air-conditioned and with a car radio and tapedeck. You need to be at least 21 years old and have a valid driving license (either an international license or a license from your home country) and at least a year's driving experience. The rental fee must be paid in advance and a refundable US$200 to US$250 deposit is required, although a credit card imprint may suffice. Two optional insurance plans are available, and you should probably pick one. Advanced reservations for car rental are recommended.

Horizontes Hoteles offers a Flexi-Fly and Drive program, designed to appeal to independent travelers. The rental car and accommodation packages range from six to thirteen days and are available from Havana, Varadero, Holguín, and Santiago de Cuba, and they include vouchers that allow travelers to use all Horizontes hotels island-wide (only the first night's accommodation is pre-arranged; after that travelers can design their itinerary on a flexible day-to-day basis). A standard rental car is provided with unlimited mileage, as well as insurance. No drop-off charges apply for ending your journey somewhere else than your starting point. You will be given a complete list of Servi-Cupet stations and a suggested driving itinerary. You can contact Horizontes Hotels or Cubanacán (the parent company) for further information.

slightly into the direction of the skid — the last thing you should do is brake suddenly, which can cause you to spin dangerously out of control.)

Your rental agency will give you a list of places to call for breakdown service. They will either come and repair your car, or the agency will arrange for you to pick up another car and will reimburse you for the time lost or add extra days to your schedule.

Servi Cupet-Cimex is the main gasoline distributor; many stations also sell diesel fuel. If you get a diesel car, the fuel

In general, expect the unexpected on Cuban roads. There are a few things to remember, however. In Cuba, traffic moves on the right. Make sure your horn works — you'll need it. Avoid driving at night at all costs: few roads or towns have streetlights and potential dangers include cattle, potholes, and tractors or bicycles without lights; very often when you set out in the morning you will see the wrecks of cars that crashed the night before. Cuban drivers often don't indicate before stopping, turning, or passing, so be alert. When you pass, blow your horn as you do so, especially if nearing a left-hand turn. Flat tires are unfortunately not an uncommon phenomenon in Cuba. (If it happens, accelerate ever so

costs are generally half the rate of gas although, of course, it is less environmentally friendly.

Make sure you have a good road map: for example, the Cuban-produced *Automapa Nacional*, available at hotel shops or car rental agencies, which has up-to-date highway information and Cuban road rules. You'll find that road markings and signs are virtually nonexistent. Remember that dirt roads — often marked as secondary roads — sometimes become impassable during the rainy season. Try to see Tomás Gutiérrez Alea's film *Guantánamera* for a sense of life on Cuban roads.

It is useful to discern the meaning of car plate colors: yellow plates mean private use or a foreigner's car; blue and red mean government-owned (and so can be asked to take people on board); green means military-owned; dark red belongs to a rental car agency; black belongs to foreign embassies; white license plates with red letters are owned by farmers cooperatives; and white license plates with blue letters indicate high-ranking provincial or central government officials.

In the unfortunate event of an accident, Roberto Gonzalez Sehweret ((53-7) 32-6813 FAX (53-7) 33-3786, at the corner of Calles J and 23, Vedado, Havana, is an attorney who

the Flexi-Fly and Drive program call **Horizontes Hotels** in Havana ((53-7) 33-4238 or 33-4361 FAX (53-7) 33-3166.

Rex ((53-7) 33-9160 FAX (53-7) 33-9159, Avenida de Ranchos Boyeros and Calzada de Bejucal, Boyeros. Havana. This is the most exclusive rental car and limousine company in Havana. Rex offers modern Volvo cars and luxury limousines with professional bilingual drivers. Prices are high, but the company prides itself on offering an exclusive service. Unlike other rental companies, Rex requires renters to be over 25 years old.

specializes in car accidents involving foreigners.

Car Rental Agencies

Transautos Reservations ((53-7) 33-5532 FAX (53-7) 33-4057. Agencies: José Martí International Airport ((53-7) 33-5763; Havana ((53-7) 33-4038; Varadero ((53-5) 33-7336; Trinidad ((53-419) 41-4011; Camagüey ((53-32) 27-2428; Santiago de Cuba ((53-226) 33-5015 extension 3207 have a variety of cars, including Peugeots.

Havanautos ((53-7) 24-2369 or 24-2891, Calle 36 No. 505, Avenida 5, Miramar, Havana.

Cubanacán SA Reservations ((53-7) 20-2188 or 20-2189; Hotel Comodoro office ((53-7) 22-5551 or 22-7761. For details about

BY TAXI

If you wish to travel around Cuba by car, but don't want to drive yourself, you may want to consider the option of a **long-distance taxi**. As with most things in Cuba, there are two versions: a *colectivo*, a service taxi (often a veteran American car or a battered Lada) whose driver negotiates a gaggle of peso-paying passengers along routes of varying length; and a privately hired version, involving the customer (you) hiring a driver and car and paying a daily fee as well as all fuel costs. Other add-on costs can include the

OPPOSITE: Embarking on the road from Camagüey to Santa Lucía. ABOVE: Taxis for tourists in Havana.

driver's accommodation and food. **Panataxi** ((53-7) 81-3311, 81-3008 or 81-3065 are probably the most reliable and cost effective, but **Turistaxi** ((53-7) 33-5539, 33-5540 or 33-5541 is a good, slightly more up-market and expensive option. Contact them about their various prices for destinations, both one-way and round trip. The *colectivos* don't generally take tourists.

Aside from these options, you can't fail to notice or to lust after a ride in one of Cuba's *taxi particulares*: the old Chevrolets, Buicks, De Sotos and Kaisers that trundle

Panataxi; both operate 24-hour services. In Santiago de Cuba, contact Turistaxi ((53-226) 4-2474 or Taxis Cubalse ((53-226) 4-2361 or 4-1165. In general, taxis arrive promptly after being called. Negotiate fares beforehand if the taxi has no meter.

BY TRAIN

It is an interesting piece of trivia that Cuba is now the last Caribbean country with a functioning railway, now that the Jamaican rail system has been phased out. Trains

along on balding tires in various states of repair. If you opt for a ride in one of these unlicensed taxis, you could find yourself in a debate with the Cuban police, but usually you are more at risk of breaking down, due to a flat tire or an empty tank. Still, it can be worth the experience. Remember, for your own safety, that it's better to tell the driver that you don't want his friend (or friends) to drive along with you, and always negotiate the rate beforehand. Some tourists come to a private arrangement when it comes to hiring a car and driver for longer trips, but this type of free-enterprise initiative is officially illegal in Cuba.

For short distances in Havana you can get about by the taxi services, Turistaxi and

somewhat erratically service all the regional capitals, and although not an easy ride all the way, are in general much more reliable and hassle-free than Cuban buses. Tickets are relatively easy to get, and leaping on a train can be a colorful way to see the country.

Cuba's railway system extends across the country from Havana, via Matanzas, Santa Clara, Ciego de Ávila, Camagüey and Las Tunas, from which provincial lines service Cienfuegos, Bayamo and Guantánamo. In addition, there is a very slow train that chugs between Havana and Pinar del Río; as well as the "direct" overnight train from Havana to Santiago de Cuba, which takes 15 hours to cover the 900-km (560-mile) distance. This can be a good alternative to flying or driving. A relatively short trip that allows you to experience train travel in Cuba is the Hershey Line from Casablanca, an electrified train that plies the old route past sugar plantations once owned by the American Hershey chocolate company.

When riding the rails, prepare for the constant billows of smoke from your fellow passengers in what are frequently sealed compartments.

To purchase tickets, you will have to go through the Ferrotur agency in Havana,

which allows tourists to buy tickets up to an hour before departure, although of course, prices are in United States dollars. Contact Asistur (see TOURIST INFORMATION, above).

BY BUS

Since 1991, all bus services for Cubans have been badly hit by the Special Period. You'll see reconstituted buses made from converted trucks, often with two buses hitched together by all manner of spare parts (and in some cases, almost anything with wheels). Referred to by all as *guaguas* or *camelos* (camels), it would be hard to recommend these to you as a way of getting around. Cubans will roll their eyes at you and pro-

nounce you *"loco"* if you express an interest in riding one. Since waiting for public transportation in Cuba is like waiting for Godot, most Cubans give up waiting at interminable lines and try to hitchhike (known as *hacer botella*, or making a bottle with the hand).

With so many Cubans having to stand in line for what services actually exist, you may wonder whether it is really considerate to take away someone else's seat. If you do want to investigate getting about the country by bus, you will have to contact the state agency Empresa Omnibus Nacionales ((53-7) 70-6155, Avenida Independencia No. 101, Havana, which operates all inter-provincial services. You should try to book as much in advance as possible.

A new bus company in Havana, **Viazul** ((53-7) 81-1413 or 81-5652, is said to offer comfortable air-conditioned buses; advanced reservations are recommended.

BY BOAT

Until recently, the only way to see Cuba by boat was to take a yacht cruise or charter (see SPORTING SPREE, page 30 in YOUR CHOICE). Now, new cruise terminals are being planned for Cuba, with the general mood in tourist officialdom being that some time in the future, the island will become a major cruise destination within the Caribbean. At present, there are two main cruises around the island, which also visit other points within the Caribbean.

The *Costa Playa*, based in Havana, plies between the Isla de la Juventud, Santiago de Cuba, Montego Bay, Gran Cayman and Cancún.

The *Melía San Juan*, based in Cienfuegos, has various options: you can combine itineraries of three, five or eight days, always leaving from Cienfuegos, traveling to Cayo Largo, Santiago de Cuba, Montego Bay, or Cayman Brac. Operated by the Spanish Sol Melía chain, this four-star cruise ship (130 m or 425 ft long and 19 m or 63 ft wide) has 203 cabins and an additional nine suites and royal state-rooms.

Contact Asistur (see TOURIST INFORMATION, above, for reservation details).

Train service can be erratic, but the experience colorful.

ACCOMMODATION

When you arrive in Cuba, a certain suspension of judgment seems to set in when it comes to appreciating (or not) the hotel you are staying in. After all, this is a country where things are not as they are elsewhere, a society with an economic siege mentality due to the United States embargo. When your chambermaid is a trained lawyer, your waiter earns more than a university professor, and when Cubans themselves are not of-

ficially allowed to stay in the nation's tourist hotels (but ladies of the evening seem to be a rather visible exception to that rule) it can interfere with your reasoning (see THE TOURISM BOOM, above).

You might experience the embargo for yourself: an elevator breakdown due to power-shedding or the lack of a spare part might mean you have to walk up to your hotel floor; the hotel doctor dispenses medicines donated by other tourists on their departure.

If you are staying at a large foreign-managed or joint-venture hotel complexes you can expect it to be of an international standard. They offer the best food on the island, although the food is often not especially

Cuban. Although the prices of these hotels are usually higher, they are nonetheless recommended for the superior quality of their service.

The pricing category in this book has been divided as follows: **Expensive** is US$120 and above; **Moderate** is US$65 to US$120; and **Inexpensive** is US$65 and below. Sometimes, considerable reductions can be had (for fixed dates with advanced reservations), notably through Havanatur.

The star system is not an internationally recognized rating, but is awarded by the Cuban government and included as a useful reference. It does not, however, necessarily indicate a standardized level of taste or comfort.

For more information about other accommodation options, such as staying with Cubans, see BACKPACKING, page 47 in YOUR CHOICE.

Below are the Central offices of the major Cuban accommodations providers.

Habaguanex SA ((53-7) 33-8693 or 33-8694 FAX (53-7) 33-8697, Calle Oficios No. 110, between Calles Lamparilla and Amargura, La Habana Vieja.

Gran Caribe ((53-7) 33-0575 to 33-0582 FAX (53-7) 33-0565, 33-0238, Avenida 7 No. 4210, between Calles 42 and 44, Miramar, Havana.

Horizontes Hoteles ((53-7) 33-4042, 33-4238, or 33-4361 FAX (53-7) 33-3161 or 33-3166, Calle 23 No. 156, between Calles N and O, Vedado, Havana.

Cubanacán Hotels SA ((53-7) 33-6427, Avenida 9 and Calle 146, Miramar, Playa, Havana.

Cubamar ((53-7) 30-5536 or 66-2523 FAX (53-7) 33-3111, Paseo No. 752 at the corner of Calle 15, Vedado, Havana.

Gaviota SA ((53-7) 22-7670 or 29-1059 FAX (53-7) 33-2780 or 33-1879, Calle 16 No. 504, between Avenidas 5 and 7, Miramar, Havana.

Grupo Sol Melía ((53-5) 66-7013 FAX (53-5) 30-7012, Hotel Melía Varadero, Carretera Sur, Varadero. The group also has toll-free numbers in the following countries: Belgium (0800 188 66; France (05 41 31 65; Germany (01 30 23 01; Italy (16 70 11 692; Spain (900 14 44 44; England (0800 282 720; United States TOLL-FREE (800) 33-MELIA.

Guitart Hotels ((53-7) 33-3202 FAX (53-7) 33-3292, Hotel Habana Libre, Fourth Floor, Vedado, Havana.

EATING OUT

The price categories given in this guide refer to the price of a meal per person, and are as follows: **Expensive**: US$30 and above; **Moderate**: US$15 to US$30 and **Inexpensive**: US$15 or under.

BASICS

TIME

Cuban time is five hours earlier than Greenwich Mean Time, making it the same time as United States Eastern Standard Time (the same time as New York), and six hours earlier than Central European Time. Daylight savings applies from April to September, during which clocks are turned forward an hour, then turned back at the beginning of October.

ELECTRICITY

The common electrical voltage in Cuba is 110 volts, 60 cycles, exactly the same as in North America. However some joint-venture hotels have installed outlets providing 220 volts. Flat parallel plugs are the norm, so bring an adapter if your appliance differs. Confusingly some of the newer hotels have European-style outlets with two round plugs. For sensitive electrical equipment, keep in mind that brownouts and spikes are frequent.

WEIGHTS, MEASURES AND TEMPERATURE

Cuba uses the metric system, and measures temperature in centigrade.

BUSINESS HOURS

Shops are generally open from 8 AM to 8 PM, although never be surprised at mysterious "Cerrado" signs at any hour. That being said, most of the time, and throughout the country, there is not a great deal to buy. Despite high summer temperatures, Cubans do not take a siesta. Banks and government offices are generally open from Monday to Friday from 8:30 AM to 12:30 PM and then in the afternoon from 1:30 PM to 5:30 PM.

COMMUNICATION AND MEDIA

You should be able to make international phone calls and send a fax from your hotel anywhere in Cuba. The top hotels have direct-dial satellite communications from you room; otherwise you need to go through the operator, which is generally fairly quick. You can call the United States, although you will always have to request this call through the operator. Naturally, surcharges are added to any telephone or fax service from your hotel.

Portable phones are available in Varadero, Havana and Santiago de Cuba: the concierge at the top hotels will be able to tell you who to contact.

Cuba has a national post system that is fairly reliable, although don't be too sure that any gifts you may try to send back to Cuba later will actually reach your friends.

DHL has offices in Havana ((53-7) 33-1876 FAX (53-7) 24-0999 at Avenida 1, at the corner of Calle 42, Miramar; and in Varadero ((53-5) 66-7330, Calle 10 No. 319, Iberostar, Barlovento.

NEWSPAPERS AND TELEVISION

You can't go to Cuba and not read *Granma*, the nation's official Communist Party newspaper, named for the boat that carried Fidel Castro's band of revolutionaries back to Cuba from Mexico in 1956. (As the writer Martha Gellhorn noted with some amusement as she heard street vendors shouting out the name of the nation's newspaper, *Granma* means "Grandma.") *Granma International*, the weekly version, is published in English, Spanish, French, and Portuguese. It usually carries long transcripts of Fidel Castro's speeches (often reminiscing about the old days in the Sierra Maestra with Che and Raul); reports on the latest progress in Cuban medical science, on labor students in Pinar del Río, or new economic accords with

Electrification for tourism near Rancho Hatuey, Sancti Spíritus.

Norway or Canada, for example; or carries articles like "Who Are They Afraid Of" about the recent United States missile installations in Florida. You can buy Granma International at the Centro de la Prensa (Press Center) on Avenida 23 in Vedado, Havana.

There are several publications that visitors may find useful or interesting. The *Business Tips on Cuba*, *Prisma*, and *Cuba Internacional* are all bilingual English-Spanish publications aimed at either tourists or business travelers, sold at the main hotels or the airport shop.

Other Cuban publications include *Trabajadores de Cuba* (the Worker's Party newspaper), the *Juventud Rebelde*, the *Tribuna de La Habana* and the *Habanero*. There are many provincial and regional newspapers across Cuba.

Outside Cuba, one of the best publications for information about Cuba is the *CUBA Update*, published monthly by the Center for Cuban Studies in New York, and available on a reasonably priced subscription (see the listing for the Center for Cuba Studies in TAKING A TOUR, page 59 in YOUR CHOICE). Another useful publication to help you keep up to date is *The Cuba Report*. For subscriptions, contact ((305) 372-1089, 501 Brichell Avenue, Suite 200, Miami, FL 33131, USA.

Cuban television has two national channels: CubaVision and Tele Rebelde, as well as provincial channels. Radio Rebelde, Radio Progreso, Radio Reloj and Radio Enciclopedia Popular (music-only) are the main radio stations. Cuba has one international radio channel, Radio Havana Club which operates 24 hours a day in several languages and Radio Taíno, which broadcasts in Spanish and English.

Satellite and cable television, including the CNN and Discovery channels, is usually provided in Cuba's top hotels, while Canal del Sol is a tourist-orientated channel that broadcasts a mixture of advertising, sports and movies.

ETIQUETTE

In general, Cubans are very conscious of good manners, and take great pains themselves to be hospitable, presentable, and well-mannered to their foreign guests or business partners. Dressing in a dignified manner is *de rigueur* in formal or business situations, as is listening carefully and politely even if you are not conversant in Spanish. Humor and personal warmth are the qualities most likely to endear you to people on all levels of society in Cuba, and never underestimate Cuban pride.

If you want to take photographs of people, always ask beforehand (although this can change the nature of the photograph) by asking "*Puedo tomar una foto?*" (Can I take a photograph?).

Other important things to remember involve not inadvertently meddling with Cuban superstitions. When in Cuba, do as the Cubans do, and always pour a glass for the *orishas* when you open a bottle of rum. Never absent-mindedly set an empty rocking chair in motion when you are in a Cuban person's home: this is viewed as calling death into the house. If you ever have cause to discuss another person's illness, never gesture to the same part of your own body as you describe the symptoms — Cubans believe this can result in you getting the same illness. Cubans will tell you not to look in a mirror during a thunderstorm and to smoke a cigar on Mondays to ensure good luck for the week. Finally, if you are a woman, never put your handbag on the floor, for Cubans believe that this invites bad luck with financial matters. Put it on a chair or table instead.

On the street, you may be taken aback by people making hissing sounds: this is not meant to be interpreted as a hostile gesture, merely a way of getting attention. Cubans also frequently hiss this way to attract attention in restaurants, but this may not be a habit that it is politic for you to adopt.

HEALTH

The risk of picking up any serious illness in Cuba is low; you are far more likely to come home with diarrhea — nicknamed *la turista* — than anything else. Vaccinations are not required to enter Cuba, however you would be wise to be inoculated against Hepatitis A. Other standard inoculations include typhoid, tetanus, and polio. If you are going to spend an extended period of time in Cuba, you might consider getting a rabies inoculation.

The eastern region of Santiago de Cuba in particular reported a crop of cases of dengue fever ("breakbone fever"), a severe and painful flu spread by mosquitoes. For dengue fever (as for HIV and AIDS) there are no jabs, and there is no vaccine against food poisoning either. The government's response to the dengue fever threat has been regular insecticide sprays, sometimes by air and sometimes from moving trucks. Try not to breathe in the fumes, and make sure you bring and use a strong brand of mosquito repellant.

painkillers; which can be very hard to come by due to the United States embargo. Tales of dirty syringes, adhesive tape used in the absence of bandages, and surgery without anaesthetic are not uncommon.

On the other side of the coin, the Cuban government has set up a range of clinics offering treatment to foreigners as part of its so-called Health Tourism program, run by **Servimed** ((53-7) 24-2658 or 24-2023 FAX (53-7) 24-1630, Turismo de Salud, Calle 18 No. 4304, between 43 and 47, Miramar, Playa, Havana, which is a branch of Cubana-

Hotels generally have a doctor on call, and the larger hotels have medical centers, but bring any medicines you require (plus a copy of your prescription, which may have to be inspected at customs). Also bring your own contraceptives, vitamins, and sunscreen. You may need to watch out for that intense Cuban sun. If you are traveling with children, make sure they get enough (bottled) water and not too much sun, and bring with you any medication they may need.

Although Cuba has an enviable reputation within Latin America as well as other developing countries for its medical expertise and public health, at present Cuban hospitals and clinics frequently lack basic supplies, such as antibiotics, bandages and

cán. More than 5,000 people visit Cuba each year seeking specialized treatment, including heart and eye surgery, organ transplants, pediatric surgery, vitilago, psoriasis, alopecia, and laser treatment, mostly from Latin America, but some as far away as Australia. Cuba has engineered several unique treatments, such as PPG, which brings down high cholesterol (and reputedly has a stimulating effect on the male libido), and is also reported to be making progress on an AIDS vaccine.

In Havana, the Cira García Central Clinic for Foreign Patients caters exclusively to foreigners, while the capital's leading hos-

Reading a newspaper in Old Havana.

pital, Hermanos Almeijeiras, has two floors reserved for foreigners. Should you fall ill or need emergency treatment, you would be well advised to take advantage of these clinics, and not the hospitals reserved for Cubans.

Most hotels boil or filter their water, and thus it is potable, but you may wish to be on the safe side and drink only bottled or boiled water. Otherwise, an unwelcome stomach upset or possibly even infection with Hepatitis A may result. Bottled water is plentiful at neighborhood supermarkets and street stalls, but always check when you buy it that the seal is unbroken. Drink a lot of water and wear a hat and light loose clothing to prevent dehydration and heatstroke.

Finally, there is one ailment that can strike visitors, especially during the Cuban winter: the *catarro Cubano* ("Cuban cold"). The best way to deal with it is to take a lot of liquid, rest, hot weak tea (no milk), with plenty of honey and lemon, and perhaps the odd splash of rum. Aspirin should help to bring the fever down.

TOILETS

There's not much to say about toilets in Cuba except that they are of an "international standard" in most hotels. In La Habana Vieja, water shortages can be a slight problem from time to time. However, while on the road, be prepared for pretty appalling loos, which you can usually expect to find at Servi Cupet-Cimex gas stations. Have a supply of packaged tissues and soap with you if you will be discommoded by the absence of these essentials.

SECURITY

Cuba is, generally speaking, quite a benign and safe country, especially compared to some other islands in the Caribbean. Still, the convergence of the rise of tourism and widespread economic desperation (born of the United States-imposed fetters on the Cuban economy, many say) has lead to a rise in some petty crimes, such as pickpocketing, bag-snatching and theft of personal belongings from hotel rooms or even private houses. Be aware that, especially in

La Habana Vieja, thieves often work as a pair, swooping past on bicycles for a swift getaway with your handbag. Crime is rarely violent however, and rarely directed at foreign tourists.

When you stray off the beaten path, in the semi-darkness of backstreet Old Havana for example, you should have your wits about you. Although Havana is truly a great city for the wanderer, if you have even a remotely cautious disposition it is better not to be completely alone wandering the city in the middle of the night.

There is rarely a sense of menace — people usually either ignore you as you pass or offer a crooked grin or even a welcoming wave. People may approach you from their doorways, offering various things, ranging

from their house to rent, their car to "borrow" and even in some cases, themselves (or someone they know). While many friendships may be made on the street in Cuba, beware of outright hustlers of either sex, and be careful about invitations to be taken to another part of the city by someone you have just met.

That takes us to the next segment of this advice column. Prostitution is an ever-present reality in Cuba. After dark, along Havana's Avenida 5, the Malecón and in La Habana Vieja, and increasingly in Santiago de Cuba as well as other provincial cities such as Camagüey, it can sometimes seem that there is a veritable forest of women clad in tight Lycra or whatever finery they can muster, who are definitively on the prowl.

Cuban taxi drivers often wryly joke that they only have one dangerous animal in their country — their *jineteras*, figuratively speaking, "female jockeys," or "women who go along for the ride."

Visitors should be aware that since April 1997, a series of small bombs were detonated in Havana hotels and nightspots popular with foreign tourists. The explosive devices were small but potentially dangerous, and in one case caused the death of one person. Be alert and wary of unattended packages or bags in public areas.

In Havana, the drug trade is a small but burgeoning fact of life. Penalties are high and crackdowns are sporadic. You may no-

Various means of transportation in Baracoa.

tice that La Habana Vieja is now full of police in blue uniforms, who frequently stop people on bicycles or on the street to inspect their identity papers as part of the crackdown on petty crimes.

You should also be aware that as a foreign visitor you are not allowed to photograph military or police installations, or harbor, rail, or airport facilities.

You can contact the **Tourist Police** at ((53-7) 30-1621 or 30-3119.

WOMEN ALONE

Cuba is not an intimidating destination for women traveling alone. Indeed, especially if you are a business traveler or journalist, you will notice that male chivalry rather than Latin machismo generally comes to the fore. Foreign women on their own, although much less frequently than their male counterparts, may find themselves approached by Cuban men, but this is very rarely threatening.

WHEN TO GO

With its tropical climate, Cuba is best visited during late-December, January, February and March, when the weather should be charming: generally, the sky is clear, the sun warm and the evenings delightful. This is, in fact, the Cuban winter, which begins in early December, with average temperatures around 21°C (75°F). (It pays to remind yourself that it truly is winter if a cold front hits, creating unsettled or uncomfortably cold and wet weather.)

From April to December, when it is *very* hot, with average temperatures from 30°C (86°F), you may take comfort in the remark that it is never as hot in Havana as in New York during summer. This may be a fallacy: it certainly *feels* hotter in Havana. In some parts of Cuba, the mercury climbs even higher, such as the island's hottest province, Oriente.

May to November is the wettest time of year (June being the wettest month); November is also hurricane season, with storms hitting the Cuban coasts from August to October as well. During summer, there are frequent thunderstorms with intense lightning, often preceded by formations of towering cumulus clouds, oppressive heat, then what the Cubans call the *aire de agua*, a fresh humid breath of air. When hurricanes hit, they can be ferocious and deadly, such as Hurricane Flora in 1963 that killed 4,000 people and Hurricane Lili which devastated swathes of Matanzas Province in 1996.

There are two seasons in Cuba for tourism: the high season between December 15 and April 14, and the low season from April 15 to December 14. Hotel rates can decrease by as much as 15 percent in the low season.

WHAT TO TAKE

It's always (or almost always) warm in Cuba. Bring light summer cotton or linen clothes and a light jacket for cooler evenings; also, air-conditioning in hotels and restaurants can be freezing. Remember good walking shoes and sandals. Sunglasses are very necessary, as is a hat. Also take a warm sweater and woollen socks if you plan to visit mountain areas of Cuba, where temperatures become quite cool at night. Although casual dress is the norm throughout Cuba, looking sloppy is not considered chic and may offend your Cuban hosts. If you are working, then wear a semi-formal tropical version of your "work outfit." Only important business meetings require men to wear a jacket and tie: while you can always take your cue from Cuban men who often wear the long-sleeved *guayabera* to official functions or the best restaurants. On the beach, of course, skimpy bathing suits are fine, but remember that topless bathing is confined to tourist areas.

When it comes to medication, very little is easily available in Cuba, and you should bring with you everything you think you might need, such as aspirin, or strong painkillers, first aid equipment, condoms (nicknamed "*el quitasensaciones*" or "killjoys" in Cuba), tampons and sanitary napkins, eye drops, and treatment for diarrhea, indigestion, as well as vitamin supplements. Strong mosquito repellant is essential, as is sunscreen. Any left-over medicine will be gratefully received by the hotel doctor, or given to Cuban friends.

If you stay in Cuba for several weeks, you may find that there are quite a few things

you regret not bringing with you. They could include an electric kettle for making your own tea (tea-drinking is not an institution in Cuba); supplies of muesli and biscuits; adapter plugs for your appliances (very hard to get hold of once you are in Cuba); a plastic line and pegs to hang washing to dry; a cassette deck or walkman; and gifts for your new Cuban friends.

Gifts are personal things. However, if you experience warmth and hospitality extended to you by Cubans you meet, you may well wish you had something to give back to them. Gifts could include perfume, makeup, underwear, fashionable clothes and Lycra garments for women (Cuban ladies are often fond of Lycra); while men often appreciate grooming essentials, such as aftershave, deodorant, and razors, as well as T-shirts, baseball caps, and cigarettes. Fashion magazines and novels are gratefully received. Soap, coffee, and basic toiletries are severely rationed in Cuba, so these can make small gifts too. Also, music cassettes of popular music abroad make excellent presents. If you plan to rent a car and driver for a stretch of time, he (drivers are almost always male) will definitely appreciate car accessories and good car wax.

You can also pick up many gifts in the dollar-only stores.

An example of a recently authorized private enterprise: watch-battery installation.

LANGUAGE BASICS

From wafts of songs on street corners to snatches of overheard conversation, it doesn't take long to understand why Cubans call their idiomatic version of Spanish "the loving tongue." You will quickly familiarize yourself with Cuban-Spanish if you already have a working knowledge of Spanish, although most Cubans will go out of their way to communicate with you and to make you feel welcome, and many speak

in "hat" and "ll" is pronounced as "i" as in "machine."

VOWELS

Vowels are pronounced as follows:
"A" — as in "father"
"E" — as in "bet"
"I" — as in "machine"
"O" — as in "note"
"U" — as in the "oo" in "food"
"Y" — is considered a vowel when it stands alone or appears at the end of a word. When

English. Cubans appreciate your attempts to speak their language. Take a short course in Latin American Spanish or bring along a phrase book and try at least a few basic phrases. At the very least, always say *por favor* ("please") and *gracias* ("thank-you"). *Buenos días* ("good morning") and *buenas tardes* ("good afternoon") should always be used as a greeting, while you should preface your address to someone with either *señor*, *señora* or *señorita*.

With regard to pronunciation, Cuban Spanish has most in common with Puerto Rican or Dominican Republic Spanish, as well as Latin American Spanish. It does not have the Spaniard's characteristic "th" lisp. The letter "j" is pronounced "h" as

alone, it means "and" and is pronounced as the Spanish "i."

CONSONANTS

Consonants are pronounced as follows:
"B" — is pronounced as in English, and often replaces what in English would be "v," as in "Habana."
"C" — is pronounced like the "s" in "sea." If it is before "e" or "k," then "c" is pronounced like "k" in English.
"CH" — as in "church"
"D" — resembles "h" as in "feather"
"G" — is like a "h" in "hat" when placed before "h" and "i"; otherwise it is a hard "g" as in "go."

"H" — is always silent
"Ñ" — as in "ny" of "canyon"
"Q" — is pronounced like the English "k"
"RR" — is rolled
"Z" — like "s" as in "lass"

COMMON EXPRESSIONS

hello *hola*
yes *sí*
no *no*
good morning *buenos días*
good afternoon *buenos tardes*

good evening *buenos noches*
good-bye *adiós*
see you later *hasta luego*
thank you *gracias*
please *por favor*
My name is… *Mi nombre es/Me llamo*
What is your name? *Come se llama?*
How are you? *Como esta usted?/Que tal?*
Fine, and you? *Bien, y usted?*
Pleased to meet you *Mucho gusto, encantado/encantada*
Friend or companion *amigo/amiga* or *campañero/campañera*
I don't understand *No entiendo*
Do you speak English? *Habla usted inglés?*
I don't speak Spanish *No hablo español*
Pardon me *Perdóneme*

Travelers' Tips

Excuse me *Con permiso*
Don't mention it *de nada*
Where is…? *Dónde está…?*
What is…? *Que es…?*
I want… *Quiero…*
How much is…? *Cuanto cuesta…?*
Is there…? *Hay…?*
Do you have any…? *Tiene…?*
The check please *La cuenta, por favor*
I am lost *Estoy perdido*
I do not feel well *No me siento bien*
Help! *Socorro!*

DAYS

Monday *Lunes*
Tuesday *Martes*
Wednesday *Miercoles*
Thursday *Jueves*
Friday *Viernes*
Saturday *Sábado*
Sunday *Domingo*

TIME

What time is it? *Que hora es?*
morning *mañana*
today *hoy*
yesterday *ayer*
tomorrow *mañana*
week *semana*
month *mes*
early *temprano*
late *tarde*
later *después*

NUMBERS

one *uno/una*
two *dos*
three *tres*
four *quatro*
five *cinco*
six *seis*
seven *siete*
eight *ocho*
nine *neuve*
ten *diez*
eleven *once*
twelve *doce*

OPPOSITE: A café in Isla de la Juventud.
ABOVE: The famous La Bodeguita del Medio.

323

thirteen *trece*
fourteen *catorce*
fifteen *quince*
sixteen *dieciséis*
seventeen *diecisiéte*
eighteen *dieciocho*
nineteen *diecinueve*
twenty *veinte*
twenty-one *veintiuno*
thirty *treinta*
thirty-one *treinta y uno*
fourty *cuarenta*
fifty *cincuenta*
sixty *sesanta*
seventy *setenta*
eighty *ochenta*
ninety *noventa*
one hundred *cien*
one hundred and one *ciento uno*
five hundred *quinientos*
one thousand *mil*
one million *millon*

DIRECTIONS

here *aquí*
there *allí/allá*
near *cerca*
far *lejo*
left/right *izquiereda/derecha*
straight *derecho*
at the corner *a la esquina*
at the back of *al fondo*
before *antes*
behind *atrás*
city block *cuadra*
next *proximo/proxima*
soon *pronto*
entry *entrada*
exit *salida*
open *abierto*
closed *cerrado*
pull *jale*
push *empuje*

LOCATIONS

money exchange *casa de cambio*
airport *aeropuerto*
bus station *terminal de omnibus*
bus *guagua*
train station *estacion de ferrocarriles*
ticket office *taquilla*

post office *correo*
gas station *gasolinera*
hospital *hospital*
bathroom *baño, lavabo*

AT THE HOTEL

hotel *hotel/villa*
room *cuarto*
bed *cama*
key *llave*
front desk *carpeta*
soap *jabón*
towel *toalla*
purified water *aqua purificada*
hot *caliente*
cold *frio*
blanket *manta*
bill *cuenta*
credit card *tarjeta de crédito*
What does it cost? *Cuánto cuesta*
per night? *per noche?*

IN THE RESTAURANT

waiter *camarero*
waitress *camarera*
breakfast *desayuno*
lunch *comida*
dinner *cena*
table *mesa*
fork *tenedor*
knife *cuchillo*
spoon *cuchilla*
wineglass *copa*
glass *vaso*
plate *plato*
bowl *tazón*
bread *pan*
butter *mantequilla*
sugar *azúcar*
milk *leche*
eggs *huevos*
coffee *café*
tea *té*
ice *hielo*
without ice *sin hielo*
a little, please *un poco, per favor*
beer *cerveza*
soda water *refresco*
mineral water *aqua mineral*
bill *cuenta*
change *cambio*

SLANG

When it comes to Cuban slang, you are bound to pick up some along the way. Cubans will smirk if you ask for some papaya: in Cuba this word is slang for the female sex organ. Other slang vocabulary include *yuma* ("foreigner"), *bisbe da buisness* ("a dirty deal"), *dolores* ("dollars"), *puro* ("cigar"), *chisme* ("gossip") and *apagone* ("power outage").

RECOMMENDED READING

Don't expect to find many of the books recommended here during your stay in Cuba, except those printed by the Australian publisher Ocean Press.

History And Politics

ANDERSON, JON LEE. *Che Guevara: A Revolutionary Life*. Grove Atlantic Press, Bantam, 1997.

BETHELL, LESLIE, editor. *Cuba: A Short History*. Cambridge: Cambridge University Press, 1993.

BORGE, TOMÁS. *Face to Face with Fidel Castro*. Melbourne: Ocean Press, 1993.

BOURNE, PETER. *Castro: A Biography of Fidel Castro*. New York: Dodd, Mead & Company Inc., 1986.

Case 1, 1989, the translation of the *Vindication de Cuba*, the official account of the case against General Arnaldo Ochoa.

CASTANEDA, JORGE. *Companero: The Life and Death of Che Guevara*. New York: Alfred A. Knopf, 1997.

CASTRO, FIDEL. *Che: A Memoir, by Fidel Castro*. Melbourne: Ocean Press, 1994. Here, Fidel Castro describes his relationship with Guevara.

DEUTSCHMANN, DAVID, editor. *Che Guevara and the Cuban Revolution: Writings and Speeches of Ernesto Che Guevara*. Sydney: Pathfinder, 1987. This is an excellent collection of Che's thoughts and pronouncements. Deutschmann is also the editor of *Che: A Memoir* by Fidel Castro.

FRANKLIN, JANE. *The Cuban Revolution and the United States: A Chronological History*. Available from the Center for Cuban Studies, New York.

GEYER, GEORGIE ANNE. *Guerilla Prince: The Untold Story of Fidel Castro*. New York: Little, Brown and Company, 1991.

GRIMBEL, WENDY. *Havana Dreams: A Story of Cuba*. New York: Knopf, 1998.

GUEVARA, CHE. Che Guevara's own important works include *Guerilla Warfare* (1960), *Reminiscences of the Cuban Revolutionary War* (1963) and *Man and Socialism in Cuba* (1965).

HIGGENS, TRUMBEL. *The Perfect Failure: Kennedy, Eisenhower and the CIA at the Bay of Pigs*. New York: W.W. Norton, 1992.

HINCKLE, WARREN. *Deadly Secrets: The CIA-Mafia War Against Castro and the Assassination of J.F.K.* New York: Thunder's Mouth, 1992.

LOCKWOOD, LEE. *Castro's Cuba, Cuba's Castro*. New York: Vintage Books, 1969. An American journalist's first-hand account of Fidel Castro and the history behind the Revolution, including the transcript of a seven-day interview with Castro.

MATTHEWS, HERBERT L. *Revolution in Cuba*. New York: Charles Scriber's Sons, 1975. Herbert L. Matthews is the *New York Times* editorial writer who interviewed Castro in the Sierra Maestra in 1957. His book is a sympathetic exploration of the personalities, motivations and achievements of the Castro revolution.

SZULC, TAD. *Fidel: A Critical Portrait*. New York: Morrow, 1986. A shrewd and riveting profile of Fidel Castro's extraordinary life, filled with interesting facts and details.

THOMAS, HUGH. *Cuba, or the Pursuit of Freedom*. London: Eyre & Spottiswoode, 1971. This 1,700-page epic is by one of the leading scholars of Latin America, covering Cuban history between 1762 and 1962. Thomas is not a fan of Castro or his revolution, yet this book is both an excellent resource and good historical reference.

QUIRK, ROBERT E. *Fidel Castro*. New York: W.W. Norton & Company, 1993.

Travel Literature And Commentary

MICHENER, JAMES A. and JOHN KING. *Six Days in Cuba*. Austin, Texas: University of Texas Press, 1989.

MILLER, TOM. *Trading With the Enemy: A Yankee Travels Through Castro's Cuba*. Athenaeum, Maxwell Macmillan International, 1992.

SMITH, STEPHAN. *Land of Miracles — A Journey through Modern Cuba*. New York: Little, Brown and Company, 1997.

TIMERMAN, JACOB. *Cuba — A Journey*. London: Picador, 1994.

GÉBLER, CARLO. *Driving Through Cuba*. London: Simon & Schuster and Hamish Hamilton, 1988.

Anthologies

Both of these books are excellent anthologies, with compelling writing by a number of famous writers.

MILLER, JOHN and SUSANNAH CLARK, eds. *Chronicles Abroad — Havana*. Chronicle Books, 1996.

RYAN, ALAN, ed. *The Reader's Companion to Cuba*. A Harvest Original, Harcourt Brace and Company, 1997.

Literature

CARPENTIER, ALEJO. *Reasons of State*, London: Writers and Readers, 1977; *The Chase*, New York: Farrar, Straus and Giroux, 1989; *Explosion in a Cathedral*, New York: Harper & Row, 1989. The late Alejo Carpentier spent most of his life in Paris, but is regarded as one of Cuba's most famous writers this century.

FUENTES, ROBERTO. *Hemingway in Cuba*. Secaucus, New Jersey: Lyle Stuart, 1984.

GARCIA, CRISTINA. *Dreaming in Cuban*. New York: Ballantine Books, 1992. An interesting and moving novel about real and imaginary worlds, Afro-Cuban religion and their impact on a Cuban family.

GREENE, GRAHAM. *Our Man In Havana*. London: William Heinemann Ltd., 1958.

GUILLÉN, NICHOLÁS. *Patria o Muerte! The Great Zoo and Other Poems*. New York: Monthly Review Press, 1972.

HEMINGWAY, ERNEST. *The Old Man and the Sea*. New York: Scribner's, 1952; *Islands in the Stream*, New York: Scriber's, 1952.

INFANTE, GUILLERMO CABRERA. *Mea Cuba*. Translated by Kenneth Hall with the author. The Noonday Press, Farrar, Strauss and Giroux, 1994. This humorous, political autobiography by one of Cuba's greatest writers-in-exile explores the nature of the Cuban revolution and the lives of those it has involved or affected, from political figures and writers to everyday people.

Guillermo Cabrera Infante has also written: *Infante's Inferno* (New York: Harper & Row, 1984); *Three Trapped Tigers* (New York: Harper & Row, 1971); *View of Dawn in the Tropics* (New York: Farrar, Straus and Giroux, 1978).

IYER, PICO. *Cuba and the Night*. New York: Knopf, 1995. A haunting, voluptuous atmospheric novel of passion and regret. Iyer's chapter on Cuba in *Falling Off The Map: Some Lonely Places of the World*, is pertinent travel writing also.

KRICH, JOHN. *A Totally Free Man. An Unauthorized Autobiography of Fidel Castro*. Berkeley, California: Creative Arts Book Company, 1981. Although it is out-of-print, this extraordinary work — a fictional confessional that dares to enter the mind of Fidel Castro — is well worth trying to get hold of.

MARTÍ, JOSÉ. *Major Poems*. New York: Holmes & Meir, 1982.

Society and Culture

GONZALEZ-WIPPLER, MIGENE. *The Santería Experience*. Englewood, New Jersey: Prentice-Hall, 1982.

HATCHWELL, EMILY and SIMON CALDER. *in Focus — Cuba, A Guide to the People, Politics and Culture*. New York: Latin American Bureau, 1995.

INFANTE, G. CABRERA. *Holy Smoke*. London: Faber & Faber, London, 1985.

JIMENEZ, ANTONIO NUÑEZ. *The Journey of the Cuban Cigar*. Havana: Cubatabaco, Havana, 1988.

MURPHY, JOSEPH. *Santería: African Spirits in America*. Boston: Beacon Press, 1988.

ORTÍZ, FERNANDO. *Los Negros Curros*, Havana: Editorial de Ciencias Sociales, 1986. Also by Ortíz: *Tobacco and Sugar* (New York: Alfred A. Knopf, 1947) and *Black Witches* first published in 1906. The late Fernando Ortíz was the first Cuban to write seriously and authoritatively about Cuba's African heritage and history.

OSPINA, HERNANDO CALVO. *Salsa — Havana, Heat, Bronx Beat*. London: Latin American Bureau, 1995. A work that investigates the origins and development of Cuba's famous music.

SARDUY, PEDRO and JEAN STUBBS. *Afrocuba*. London: Latin American Bureau, 1993. An

anthology of Cuban writing, including poetry and non-fiction.

Photographic Books

Cuba: Image and Imagination. New York: Aperture Foundation, Number 141, Fall 1995.

GORGONI, GIANFRANCO. *Cuba Mi Amor.* Verona: Parise Press, 1990. Includes a prologue by Gabriel Garcia Márquez. Text by Fidel Castro.

KUFELD, ADAM. *Cuba.* New York: W.W. Norton & Company, 1994. With an Introduction by Tom Miller.

LEWIS, BARRY and PETER MARSHALL. *Into Cuba.* Alfred van der Marck Editions, 1985.

SMITH, WAYNE and MICHEAL REAGAN. *Portrait of Cuba.* Atlanta: Turner Publishing Inc., 1991.

The Outdoors

AZTARAIN, ROLANDO DIAZ. *Yachtsman's Guide Cuba.* Havana: Marina Puertosol, Marina Gaviota and Marina Marlin, 1997.

CHARLES, SIMON. *A Cruising Guide to Cuba.* Cruising Guide Publications, 1994.

WILLIAMS, D. *Diving and Swimming Guide to Cuba.* Provides specific information on depths, currents, and required diving expertise as well as helpful advice on accommodations, transportation and dive operators.

Two girls reading in Trinidad.

Quick Reference A–Z Guide to Places and Topics of Interest with Listed Accommodation, Restaurants and Useful Telephone Numbers

Photography Credits

All photographs by Mireille Vautier, except for those on the following pages, by Nik Wheeler: Cover, page 3, 4, 5 *both*, 7 *left*, 50 *bottom*, 53, 58, 61, 62–63, 89, 106–107, 108, 120 *right*, 121, 131, 135, 284–285, 285, 288, 289, 290–291, 292–293, 293, 305, 322, 323.